THE ECONOMIC PROBLEMS OF HOUSING

THE
ECONOMIC PROBLEMS
OF HOUSING

Proceedings of a Conference held by
the International Economic Association

EDITED BY

ADELA ADAM NEVITT

WITH AN INTRODUCTION
BY
SHERMAN J. MAISEL

MACMILLAN
LONDON · MELBOURNE · TORONTO
ST MARTIN'S PRESS
NEW YORK
1967

MACMILLAN AND COMPANY LIMITED
Little Essex Street London WC2
also Bombay Calcutta Madras Melbourne

THE MACMILLAN COMPANY OF CANADA LIMITED
70 Bond Street Toronto 2

ST MARTIN'S PRESS INC
175 Fifth Avenue New York NY 10010

Library of Congress catalog card no. 67–13167

PRINTED IN GREAT BRITAIN

CONTENTS

REPORT ON THE PROCEEDINGS

ACKNOWLEDGEMENTS

THE International Economic Association wishes to thank all those who contributed to the success of the Conference recorded in this volume. The Association is supported by grants from UNESCO and from the Ford Foundation and without these it would not have been able to undertake this work.

This Conference was held in the delightful environment of Ditchley Park near Oxford. All the participants will long remember with gratitude the beauties of the house and of its conference room, the glories of its gardens, and the indefatigable kindness of Mr. H. V. Hodson, the Warden, Mrs. Hodson, Captain Grant and all the staff.

The success of such a Conference depends on the quality of the papers and of the discussion. To all those who contributed in that way, the Association wishes to record its gratitude.

LIST OF PARTICIPANTS

Mr. K. D. Arndt, Deutsches Institut für Wirtschaftsforschung, Berlin, Germany.

Mr. J. Azcarate, Centre de Recherches et de Documentation sur la Consommation, Paris, France.

Mr. J. B. Cullingworth, Department of Social and Economic Research, University of Glasgow, Glasgow, U.K.

Professor D. Donnison, London School of Economics & Political Science, London, U.K.

Professor L. Fauvel, Paris, France.

Professor Jørgen Gelting, Institute of Economics, University of Aarhus, Aarhus, Denmark.

Professor James Gillies, Graduate School of Business Administration, University of California, Los Angeles, U.S.A.

Professor William G. Grigsby, Institute for Urban Studies, University of Pennsylvania, Philadelphia, U.S.A.

Dr. N. Halevi, The Hebrew University of Jerusalem, Israel.

Professor Erik Hoffmeyer, Danmarks Nationalbank, Copenhagen, Denmark.

Dr. Per Holm, Ekonomisk Planering, Stockholm, Sweden.

Dr. Edward Kuminek, Warsaw, Poland.

Professor Assar Lindbeck, The Stockholm School of Economics, Stockholm, Sweden.

Professor Sherman J. Maisel, Center for Research in Real Estate and Urban Economics, University of California, Berkeley, California, U.S.A.

Dr. Jiri Musil, Research Institute for Building and Architecture, Prague, Czechoslovakia.

Professor Richard F. Muth, Institute for Defense Analyses, Virginia, U.S.A.

Dr. Nazarevsky, c/o Association of Soviet Economic Scientific Institutions, Moscow, U.S.S.R.

Professor Richard Netzer, Graduate School of Public Administration, New York, U.S.A.

Miss Adela A. Nevitt, London School of Economics and Political Science, London, U.K.

Professor J. Parry Lewis, Department of Economics, University of Exeter, Exeter, U.K.

Dr. Tadeusz Przeciszewski, Instytut Budownictwa Mieszkaniowego, Warsaw, Poland.

The Economic Problems of Housing

Professor E. A. G. Robinson, The Marshall Library, Cambridge, U.K.

Mlle Élisabeth Salembien, Centre de Recherches et de Documentation sur la Consommation, Paris, France.

Mr. Ingemar Ståhl, Forsvarets Forskningsanstalt, Stockholm, Sweden.

Dr. P. A. Stone, The National Institute of Economic and Social Research, London, U.K.

Dr. Duccio Turin, U.N. Economic Commission for Africa, Addis Ababa, Ethiopia.

INTRODUCTION

BY

SHERMAN J. MAISEL

I

THE Conference on the Economic Problems of Housing of the International Economic Association was held at Ditchley Park, Oxfordshire, England, April 6–12, 1965. The Conference was intellectually stimulated by its surroundings which furnished a grand example of good housing created as a result of excellent initial design and creative renovation.

The Conference was aided tremendously through the fine work of the staffs of the International Economic Association and the Ditchley Foundation. It was particularly fortunate to have Miss Adela Adam Nevitt of the London School of Economics to compile the record of the proceedings. Her summary of the discussion in this volume is the result of a truly herculean task of interpretation and presentation which enables the reader to obtain an excellent picture of the true flow of ideas.

Several considerations led to the decision of the IEA to hold a conference on housing. Housing remains a critical personal and governmental problem in virtually every country of the world. Housing is expensive of resources. A vast number of people live in dwellings considered inadequate by most if not all observers.

A general belief exists that despite the importance of housing both the tools for and the application of economic analyses in this sphere have lagged. Most countries have large, complex, and expensive housing programmes and policies. A tremendous need exists for a better understanding of what these programmes are accomplishing or failing to accomplish. There is also a critical shortage of knowledge as to how to improve them.

Most housing policies have been built up on an *ad hoc* basis from decisions accumulated over a vast number of years. In some areas, rent controls adopted to meet the emergency conditions of World War I are still in use. Other countries have piled one type of policy upon another in an attempt to shore up programmes which are recognized as having major shortcomings, but which appear to be either economic, social, or political necessities.

Housing programmes have been forged by a combination of politicians, reformers, social workers, engineers, planners, architects, and occasionally economists. In many countries the policies in use have severe internal contradictions. They are frequently not responsive to their expressed goals.

The International Economic Association felt that sufficient attention was now being given to housing by economists throughout the world to make an interchange of ideas and concepts profitable to all participants. It also was deemed likely that the record of a Conference on this subject could make a useful addition to the general knowledge and analytical concepts available in the housing field.

Delegates came from countries in which the housing market varied from ones where almost all units were publicly owned ; through others where supply was divided among publicly owned units, plus many under rent control, with still others in a free market ; to countries where almost all units are rented or traded with only a minimum of public action.

The Conference was highlighted by an increased recognition of the fact that even though strong institutional differences existed among the countries represented in the manner in which housing was supplied and distributed, the similarities of the problems faced by each were great. As a result, economic analysis even though developed under totally dissimilar conditions had many useful concepts to offer. These could aid in solving problems no matter which type of market existed.

II

The similarities in problems of housing supply and demand and the reasons for these similarities rapidly became evident to the participants. Certain basic physical and demographic conditions constrain the manner in which shelter whether from the elements or for privacy can be made available to individual families. These exogenous forces in turn shape similar economic responses.

Critical is the fact that houses are large, complicated, durable, and consequently expensive. No simple cheap method has been found to house people in our complex developed societies. As a result the amount of capital or resources embodied in a house is very large compared with its daily output of shelter.

The papers of Donnison, Muth, and Cullingworth covered some

aspects of these general problems. From them and their related discussion, we are able to see some of the major reasons for the existence of world-wide housing problems.

The large capital investment needed for new dwellings creates major difficulties for both governments and individuals. At the overall level since the amount of resources expended on residential construction is high, there is direct competition with many other types of vital investment. At the family level, if in any period a household is required to pay currently any large share of the total capital cost of the building in order to obtain shelter, it may have very little income left over for the necessary consumption of other goods. To make room in its budget for other goods considered more necessary or desirable, a household may choose housing which is substandard. As a result such families run the risk of both physical and mental ill-health.

Houses tend to be extremely durable. Unless considerable care is taken with their planning, future generations will live with the results of current mistakes.

Durability also means that the ratio of current production to the total existing stock is small. Speed-ups or lags in the start of production will cause major fluctuations in the amount of income earned from the construction industry, but they will have barely noticeable impacts on the rate at which current shelter services are furnished. The ability to fluctuate as well as the fact of actual fluctuations have created major issues for many economies.

Since we are living in a stock of houses built over many past periods, riddles abound for current maintenance decisions. There should be some level at which to embody features in a house which will give an optimum relationship between the cost of construction and future maintenance expenses. The costs of current maintenance expenditures are also related to future benefits. Houses may be highly renovated to improve their future services. Finally, at some time it may become economic to remove a house from the stock rather than to renew it by a massive addition of capital.

High costs put a critical premium on the ability to improve housing productivity. Since most areas experience a shortage of both national resources and individual incomes, any resources saved can be put to excellent use. The methods of housing production have developed over thousands of years. In recent years some countries have experienced a rapid shift in production methods while in others change has evolved more slowly.

Most countries face problems in attempting to evaluate their own progress as well as that which appears to be taking place elsewhere. Much of the Conference discussion was aimed at learning and attempting to evaluate changes which were reported from other areas.

The difficulty of creating sufficient individual units is compounded by growing urbanization in almost every country. In many cases of developing nations, this means a major shift in the type of unit required. In place of the native or indigenous hut, they must build the far more complex units required by town or city living. In other areas, the shift is from one type of urban unit to larger more dense structures. In all countries there is a need for major investments in the urban infrastructure.

The conferees found that just as universal as are the problems caused by housing are the needs for related decisions. These decisions fall into similar patterns because they follow directly from the underlying problems.

In the majority of countries, the most important determination is that of the amount of resources to be made available for house-building. This decision determines the number of new and used units in the stock as well as their level of maintenance.

Closely related are judgments as to what quality and type of housing may be inhabited. Because of high cost, individual families may attempt to inhabit units which the particular social value system considers substandard. Decisions must be made as to whether, and if so how, to enforce particular minimum standards at any given time.

If the normal financial charges based upon the capital contained in a house exceed a socially desirable share of a family's income, a decision must be reached as to what level of payments is proper. If market costs are larger than a family can afford, methods must be devised to lower the amount the family is required to pay. The difference between the private and social costs must be shifted either to other groups or to the nation.

Provisions must also be made as to how to allocate and re-allocate the stock of housing. In the course of the Conference, many interesting questions were raised as to the efficiency of the allocation systems used in each of the participating countries.

It was brought out that planning decisions were required both with respect to the physical use and the development of land. Again the degree and the manner in which such determinations are made varies greatly.

Various speakers discussed the techniques utilized in particular countries in an attempt to deal with the problem of fluctuations. Even in planned or semi-planned economies such decisions turned out not to be as highly centralized as one might expect given the degree of overall governmental control of the housing markets.

Requirements also exist in the general area of mangement of the current stock. Repair and maintenance are necessary. Allocations of houses to tenants are not automatic no matter what the system. Furthermore, someone must collect whatever rents or charges are levied.

Finally, many difficult production decisions must be made. Countries attempting to further the number of innovations may aid in research and development. Others have put considerable stress on the organization of the market to insure a more steady rate of production and with more standardized units. In still others whole new systems of production have been tried.

III

The Conference considered some of the goals of housing policy. The numerous decisions required by public bodies have led to their implicitly or explicitly adopting particular goals. These they hope may be achieved either through the market mechanism or through official actions.

Usually the policies aim at assuring some minimum or optimum standard of housing. Goals are measured in such terms as space per person, sanitation, repair, or environment. In each case a desire exists to raise the average level of housing or to insure that the number of families who fall below a given minimum is as small as possible.

Closely related to the goal of fewer substandard units are attempts to insure some desired distribution of housing. When rents fall below the market level, how houses are divided becomes a critical problem. The papers of Holm, Lindbeck, Ståhl, Gelting, Przeciszewski, and Musil all contribute knowledge concerning the goals of distribution policy as well as the problems of achieving them.

In many cases governments have found that contrary to their initial desires and expressed goals much of their housing action has been to enforce limitations and controls over the resources made available. In place of raising standards, countries find that their housing programmes deal mainly with the methods and the amounts of cuts to be made in the total resources used for shelter.

Since resources are limited, another goal stresses the use of those available in the most efficient manner. Emphasis is placed on achieving improvements in productivity and on a rapid rate of innovation.

Tied closely to the goal of efficiency in the use of resources is that of stability in the rate of housing production. Stability holds out hopes for important gains in productivity. In addition its impact may be still wider. It may help to reduce the fluctuations of the total economy. In some cases, however, countries have picked an opposite goal : that of destabilizing residential construction. This seemingly perverse goal has been selected with the hope that counter-cyclical movements of building would increase the stability of the entire economy.

One of the fascinating debates which cropped up in many sessions of the Conference considered whether desired goals were more likely to be achieved if countries adopted specific housing policies or whether current results could be improved by allowing the free market to make the decisions in a *laissez-faire* manner.

In the course of the discussion, it became clear that it was necessary to differentiate between the existing situation in many countries where policies were adopted with but slight logic and the possible results from a set of rational policies. A few felt that only the present types of situation could be analysed since adoptions of more rational programmes were extremely unlikely.

In contrast, many delegates simply assumed that a national housing policy was a necessity. Such assumptions arose either because of the political basis of their governments or because of a strong political demand for action in this sphere. Still others were willing but had to be convinced that a national housing policy could lead to improved economic and social conditions.

The economic reasons listed for the belief that an adopted policy might improve on *laissez-faire* were numerous.

It was pointed out that government action at the present affects housing in many ways. Included among the typical government policies which influence housing are (1) taxation of property, of income, and of capital gains ; (2) interest rates ; (3) land development ; (4) efforts to increase or curtail investments ; and (5) programmes having to do with the availability of labour, wages, and prices.

Even if housing were not considered separately and no specific determinations were made taking housing effects into account, it would still be a fact that some policy would be adopted. They would, however, result from numerous independent acts rather than from a unified approach. Since governmental actions are necessary and frequent, it appears sensible that they be analysed in terms of their housing as well as other impacts.

A public policy may be required in order to align differing private and social value judgments. In contrast to the general public *mores*, some families may be willing to live in substandard units. The rate at which the private market makes natural resources available for construction may differ greatly from the public view of the optimum infusion of resources. Housing may also be a social good whose consumption should be subsidized. It is also a collective good whose impact extends far beyond the family circle.

Very significant external economies probably exist in the housing market. These arise from such factors as the need to co-ordinate locations, cost advantages which arise if fluctuations in the rate of construction can be decreased and if demand can be simplified, as well as through possible downward movements of cost curves as a result of public or other external expenditures on planning and research. Public action can aid in insuring that these economies are achieved.

Periods of war and sharply higher demand in booms have made it difficult to adjust supply to demand. As a result government intervention in order to smooth erratic movements may be economic. Similarly, the government may hope to improve forecasts and market behaviour since the free market as a rule lacks adequate knowledge. The government may also improve the difficult adjustments which occur because of the long lags between the time when the first signs of demand appear and the time when the final supply has been constructed to fill these needs.

It was also pointed out that in many areas the government desires to use housing policy in order to redistribute income directly. Some countries have also tried to change the preference functions of families with respect to their housing. Neither of these are actions which can be performed by a *laissez-faire* market.

The form of government intervention and the policies adopted have varied widely. A tremendous number of techniques based upon controls, direction, persuasion, subsidies, and similar policies are evident.

Very common in many countries is the use of rent controls. Ownership may remain in private or co-operative hands, but the amount of rent and frequently the right of occupancy is determined by the government. Another typical policy is for the government to intervene in the financing process. This may occur through making credit available or perhaps as frequently through making part of the cost a charge against the fisc. The power to tax also appears as a powerful shaper of housing paths.

In many countries the public enters as the chief builder of units and in still others as the owner of the dwelling stock. Even when the public does not build or own, it frequently has a say in what is produced through control over land development and through furnishing the majority of community facilities.

A final set of policies attempts to create methods to improve productivity. These may be direct through the use of new builidng techniques or governmental jobs. They may be less direct through design and standardization. In many countries research projects attempt to lower costs. In still other major efforts have been made to increase the scale of builders.

IV

Several sessions were concerned with attempts to shape the tools of economic analysis to the requirements of the housing market. Many speakers felt that political and social relationships in the housing field were so paramount that purely economic analysis was nearly impossible. They emphasized the need for examination of the historical and institutional forces which had produced and constrained present situations.

Questions were raised as to whether basic economic principles could possibly be universal. Many policies were based primarily on value judgments derived from each country's unique desires. Were not the institutional and cultural divergences so wide that international generalizations would be nearly impossible?

Many answered strongly that this need not be the case. The economist analyses the effect of different policies aimed at reaching particular goals. He need not be concerned with how these goals or other constraints are arrived at.

As a major example economists from all types of countries explored some of the implications of the use of the price system to achieve certain goals in both planned and less-planned economies. The question raised was whether or not a market could serve as an efficient computer to best allocate resources.

Every market contains particular supply and demand variables. These could be very different from those which would exist under *laissez-faire*. Governments can intervene in order to shift either supply or demand better to meet their goals. Given the fact of government intervention what type of market mechanism will give the most efficient results? Can countries more readily achieve their goals if they attempt to use free prices to allocate resources instead of depending on direct allocations, queuing, or individual bargains with side conditions?

Rent control was picked by several as a major type of policy which appeared to them to be inefficient in achieving its goals. It was claimed that rent controls might have many and often conflicting aims. In some systems rent control was adopted as a policy to achieve higher levels of housing consumption. In others emphasis was placed on its importance in bringing about security of tenure and freedom of choice. In some it was expected to increase the consumption of low income groups and perhaps to shape the form of consumption.

In still other countries rent controls were thought of primarily as stabilization devices. They aimed at controlling the construction market or perhaps at dampening inflation by holding down prices. They also were thought of as means of improving the shape of the income distribution — increasing the available shelter of some at the expense of others.

Even when these goals were not contradictory, some participants felt their achievement was being hindered by current rent control policies. The point was made that if redistribution and stabilization were attempted through more direct policies, the price system could be freed and used to furnish valuable information which was now being lost. More direct policies could be devised which would better utilize the market's strength and which would improve the level of housing and the allocation of resources.

An example discussed of how the price system could improve market functioning was the growth of co-operative housing in both the socialist and non-socialist economies. Co-operatives were spreading rapidly because they made more individual savings or resources available to the housing market and also improved the level of maintenance.

When housing was treated as a free good and allocated on some social or political grounds, people could not express their individual choices as to where housing rated in their preference scales. Even if they wanted to, they had no way of increasing the percentage of income they spent on housing. Co-operatives gave an opportunity for those who wished to consume more housing at the expense of other goods. At the same time by making maintenance a direct charge against the individual's family income instead of the income of the State or the landlord better care was taken of property. More minor maintenance was performed without outside charges and assistance.

In the discussion of related analytical topics, it was evident that the problem of establishing a description of the market mechanism that could be used for analysis was far from simple. Significant difficulties arise in conceptualizing a market whose components differ widely in size, location, and quality of unit. Demographic and geographic variables keep intruding.

It appeared, however, to be the general opinion that while these problems were troublesome the type of models discussed did give promise of good results. Indeed, in some cases such as problems of demographic variation, many observers felt that major progress was made in clarifying the type of analysis necessary in this sphere.

V

Many of the discussions were concerned with the evolution of specific types of governmental policy or with some of the general problems met with in attempts to forge policies in particular countries. Thus the papers of Grigsby, Hoffmeyer, and Gillies dealt primarily with financial variables, Netzer considered tax policies. Messrs. Andrejewski, Przeciszewski, and Musil and Madame Pjanic discussed some of the policies in socialist economies while Messrs. Halevi and Turin dealt with policies among developing nations.

Financing is critical in the housing market because large amounts of capital must be furnished for the individual dwelling. In many areas the saving of this capital is performed primarily by the State. In other cases it is a function of financial intermediaries, while in some countries most of the burden falls on the individual.

When a dwelling has been constructed, it furnishes a stream of shelter services. The costs of these services are a function of the current interest on the capital contained in the house as well as of the rate of depreciation or use of the capital. These costs can be related to the family's payments. In certain cases, families pay only a small part of these current costs. The State subsidizes the difference. In other cases, families pay more than the current real costs.

If the family's payments exceed the true costs of capital and depreciation, the household is saving. The larger the amount of saving in its shelter payments, added to its real costs, the more difficult it is for the family to occupy an adequate unit.

Several of the papers and considerable discussion examined various aspects of this problem. It differs greatly in its impact and importance in the various countries depending on the institutional structure of both dwelling ownership and the initial form of financing.

Where houses are started primarily in a private market, the terms of financing are shown to be a significant determinant of the rate of construction. Governor Hoffmeyer's paper indicates that both interest and vacancies have important effects on housing starts. This paper makes a significant addition to previous studies conducted along similar lines in the United States and Great Britain.

Professor Netzer's paper considers the tremendous variation in the types and impact of housing taxation among different countries. In some nations only slight amounts of revenue are raised from real property while in others the level of taxation on housing is so high as to be a major influence on consumption levels.

The significance of taxation as a housing variable seems to have been sadly neglected. There are several indications of perverse relationships. Some countries whose stated goals have been to use government aid in improving housing standards have at the same time reduced the willingness to occupy shelter by placing very high burdens through the real property tax on the occupiers of good housing.

In the discussion of individual countries, participants called attention to vast differences in their problems, in their institutions, and in the way they have attempted to meet their needs. Many countries suffered severe shortages as a result of war damage or the stoppage of construction in that period. In others the rate of growth and of urbanization have caused heavy strains. Frequently extreme housing needs are accompanied by large requirements for other types of capital and a shortage of available resources.

The Conference pointed out differences in the organization of production, of ownership, of accumulating resources, and of allocating existing dwellings. In many cases, major difficulties have arisen in past procedures. The methods of determining needs by type and area, the manner in which resources can be obtained, the procedures for allocation of dwellings, and the maintenance of the existing stock have all created serious problems in particular countries.

The same type of difficulties appear to have cropped up again and again no matter what type of government or how its housing goals and objectives were stated. At the Conference there was a continual questioning as to whether economic analysis was being used to furnish the best available guide to an efficient use of resources. The use of the price mechanism versus other forms of control and allocation was debated vehemently.

In developing economies further questions of the relation of housing policy to general foreign trade policy arose. In addition to consuming large amounts of scarce capital, it was found that in a majority of cases a high percentage of the materials going into houses has to be imported. A severe shortage of skilled construction labour was also common. As a result the costs of housing compared with typical wage rates of the population were even higher than in developed economies.

VI

Throughout the Conference one major hope expressed was for some solution of the housing problem through a reduction in production costs. The papers of Kuminek and Nazarevsky are concerned with such possible improvements in the method of production. Even though cost reduction has been a major objective of housing programmes throughout the world, success has been far less than hoped for. It did appear possible, however, that among certain countries such as those reported on in the Conference significant breakthroughs were occurring.

In general prerequisites for lowered housing costs include a better control of the process and a stabilized demand. The first steps towards rationalization, therefore, have frequently been the introduction of such a continuity in demand. In some areas, with the aid of a steady demand, the building industry has been able by itself to reduce its costs.

In other countries a second approach has been through the growth of scientific management. Major advances have been made with respect to prefabrication. In these cases, prefabrication is usually thought of as a system whereby major components are produced and then installed as units in the dwelling.

Finally, significant attempts are now being made to industrialize construction through the use of large panel construction and through the introduction of the precast volume unit house. The objective of these systems is to remove a very high percentage of work from the site to a factory.

In Russia, conditions appear excellent for factory fabrication. The sites are very large. Whole new communities are planned and built as units. The number of different types of layouts for individual dwellings has been reduced so that only 16 or so occur. Major shortages of certain types of labour exist which would hamper conventional construction. In contrast the methodology of the factory makes it possible to employ less skilled labour. This makes greater production feasible. Furthermore, in many sections of the country, building is faced with severe weather problems. Factory fabrication can be expected to reduce the problems caused by climatic conditions.

It is not evident, however, whether this experience is transferable to other areas. The basis of the success of the system for the Soviet Union could be due to causes which would not apply elsewhere. It is not known whether the transference of more production to the factory saves resources or simply uses the particular ones available in a more efficient manner.

The problem faced by many countries is that usually industrialized building (or factory fabrication) requires more expensive materials and high transportation costs. Offsets occur between the higher factory costs and the hoped-for saving in on-site labour. In areas where on-site labour is not a high proportion of the total, either because the process has been well rationalized as in the United States or because labour may be less expensive as in some of the developing countries, it has not been shown that the higher costs of the industrialized process create sufficient savings in on-site cost to make the more complex procedures worth-while.

The conferees agreed that traditional building has been altering in most countries. A gradual evolution has occurred which includes a day-by-day or year-by-year response to a changing situation with respect to technology, labour, and materials. The possibility always exists that a sudden breakthrough could move the industry to a new and much lower cost curve. Some drastic change could make production far cheaper. If such a possibility exists, then to obtain it there must be some new way of reaching this lower cost curve. The examples of Russia and Poland indicate that major shifts in the methods of production are possible. The interesting questions discussed at length are whether on this totally different cost curve the expenses are actually far less and if so whether these economies would hold in all countries or only in some. The Conference gave no clear answer to these questions. They remain interesting areas for further international co-operation and research.

The discussion dealt with other forms of rationalization also. Most significant were those economies which developed when nations used their housing policy to guarantee a firmer and less diverse market. Such cost savings had occurred in many of the Western European countries. With a large enough market and a reduction of variety, sizeable forms of rationalization emerged. Frequently, these programmes which guaranteed larger markets and more preliminary planning also brought about a better relationship between the purchaser, the designer or architect, and the builder.

Certain observers seemed to feel that these governmental programmes introduced the conditions necessary for industrialization and the use of factory construction. When they did, however, they also caused major reductions in the costs of traditional construction. The increases in the productivity of the traditional methods were so great that they may well have surpassed any savings possible from an introduction of factory methods.

Other important problems on the cost side were also considered. It was pointed out that in many countries the constraint on construction was frequently that of one or a few particular resources. As a result a programme which made the best possible use of these scarce resources might give a far larger amount of potential construction even though its actual costs in the typical accounting sense seemed far out of line. Traditional accounting frequently fails to consider total social costs. In comparison to what might be a better social technique, it might show additional charges for labour and other goods. If, however, these would be unused and wasted with the original technique, then these are not valid costs for public policy purposes.

As an example three cases were cited : one where the constraint was that of investment in capital-producing equipment ; another where the constraint was that of skilled labour ; and a third where the constraint was that of imported materials. It is clear that in each of these cases, the method of production required would differ greatly. By using large amounts of easily available resources, one might obtain a type of construction which, while it would not give the lowest possible cost, would result in the highest level of construction. Plans were needed which made the best possible use of the particular resource in short supply.

Another interesting difference among countries which became evident was related to the supply of construction labour. Most European observers constantly made the point that the construction industry, because it was in the open and had many extremely hard physical tasks, had a most difficult time retaining labour. Unskilled labour tended to come into the construction industry from agriculture, but as other jobs opened up in industry they moved out as rapidly as possible. As a result one of the major constraints to more housing was the shortage of labour and the task of maintaining a requisite labour supply.

In contrast in the United States, where construction wage rates are among the highest of any industry, exactly the opposite problem exists. Observers believe that a large labour backlog exists willing to enter the construction labour market. It is only because of problems of restricted entry that they do not come in. As a result, in the United States the wage rate rather than the amount of labour is one of the critical restraints on production.

Some discussion took place of the problem of establishing standards of construction and particularly those for the adoption of codes and regulations. These are all questions closely related to the amount and need for building and housing research. Most countries have attempted to improve productivity by some action along these various lines. There was little indication that success in these areas has been great. The technical knowledge required for codes and regulations is frequently missing. Research can help to improve standards and codes, but it is expensive and painfully slow.

It is also difficult to reach agreement upon what level of standards should be required. In most cases a concern exists as to the possible trade-offs between current and future expenditures. Since houses are so durable, any changes in construction have results which last far into the future. We have traditional concepts of how durable houses should be. Even if it could be proved that savings in capital would pay off, it is hard to get people to change their ideas as to what is necessary in a house.

A closely related question deals with the type of construction and probable future maintenance needs. There were many comments that in some countries the need for current production was so great that the sacrifice of current quality had become too large. As a result future maintenance costs would be raised. There was some feeling that this was a critical problem. Some countries had reached the point where they would be better off by shifting their current programmes. It was possible that a larger volume of good standard housing could be obtained through putting more resources into the maintenance and renewal field rather than into new construction.

The Conference served as an introduction to the complex field of housing. There was agreement that while much had been learned there was still far more to learn in the future. The need for better analysis is urgent. Economics can aid in clarifying many of the problems and in estimating some of the more difficult inter-relationships. The task is not easy since so many national programmes have been developed primarily from a political or institutional point of view. No revolution in thought or in action is likely. Even a small speed-up in evolution, however, can save badly needed resources and improve existing allocations. Most of the conferees considered the speed-up in the development of the field to be a goal whose achievement would be well worth while.

Chapter 1

THE POLITICAL ECONOMY[1] OF HOUSING

BY

D. V. DONNISON

Professor of Social Administration,
London School of Economics and Political Science

I. INTRODUCTION

IN a paper to be discussed at a conference to which experts in many fields and from many countries will contribute, it may be helpful to survey the context — the social, economic, and political environment — within which a government's housing policies develop, with the aim of identifying and relating to each other the principal features of this environment and the principal academic disciplines capable of throwing light upon it. My purpose is not primarily to advance economic theory — still less to advocate any specific housing policy — but to explore the extent and character of the impact which governments can make upon the housing conditoins of their countries, and the factors which determine the scope and limits of government activity in this field.

I shall proceed as follows. (*a*) First the general character of a country's 'housing problems' must be examined. This analysis calls for a consideration of current housing conditions, and future developments likely to affect those conditions. A preliminary note should be taken of the factors determining the way in which this situation is perceived and interpreted by government: any analysis of 'demands', 'needs', or 'requirements' that is to have practical application expresses 'subjective' or 'ideological' commitments of some kind, but such commitments can nevertheless be analysed in a reasonably 'objective' or scholarly fashion. (*b*) Next we should consider the volume, productivity, and deployment of the resources available to government and to the country at large for meeting the needs so far identified. (*c*) We can then examine the structure of political authority, the general character of the rôle assigned to government, and the administrative, legal, and technical means available to government

---

[1] 'Political economy: the art of managing the resources of a people and of its government.' *Shorter Oxford English Dictionary.*

I

in the special field of housing. (*d*) Finally it should be possible to reassemble these aspects of our subject, and attempt some classification and clarification of the housing responsibilities and objectives assumed by governments under various circumstances.

This analysis will be applied mainly to the 'market economies' of Western Europe, but comparisons will occasionally be made with the 'command economies' of Eastern Europe. Most of the evidence used is derived from United Nations' sources and much of the argument will be presented and documented at greater length in the study of 'Major Long-Term Problems of Government Housing and Related Policies'[1] carried out by staff of the UN Economic Commission for Europe with the assistance of Professor Adam Andrzejewski and myself. The attempt to cover so vast a field within the space of this short paper will inevitably result in the omission of many important topics and superficial treatment of the remainder, but the analysis may nevertheless have some value, not so much for its specific findings as in the opportunity it provides for the integration and confrontation of disciplines and discussions too often conducted in isolation from each other.

II. HOUSING REQUIREMENTS

To be of much interest, any analysis of housing requirements must deal with a considerable period of time, for the stock of dwellings changes so slowly — in European countries typically increasing at about 2 per cent and being replaced at less than $\frac{1}{2}$ per cent per annum — that little change can be achieved in the short run. An analysis of requirements, or of the likely components of effective demand, over the next ten or twenty years can be made in four steps. There will be : (*a*) changes in the population to be housed (due to natural increase and international migration) ; (*b*) changes in the number of households a given population will produce (due to changes in demographic structure, and changes in living standards and cultural patterns reflected in altered 'headship rates') ; and (*c*) changes in the number of dwellings required by a given number of households (due to changes in the numbers of shared or 'secondary' dwellings). To proceed to an estimate of the investment required year by year in order to attain the standards indicated by the foregoing steps, certain

[1] *Major Long-Term Problems of Government Housing and Related Policies.* Vol. I and II, United Nations, 1966. Reference ST/ECE/HOU/ 20.

assumptions must be made about (*d*) the standards of housing to be achieved, followed by estimates — partly derived from these assumptions — of (*e*) the rate of replacement (whether through planned clearance schemes or spontaneous redevelopment), other gains or losses (due to the abandonment of dwellings, net conversions to and from non-housing uses, and the net effects of amalgamation and subdivision of hitherto separate dwellings) and the volume of maintenance, repairs, and modernization to be expected.

This approach provides a means of distinguishing different types of housing situation and the patterns of requirements likely to arise from each. Three of these situations may be briefly illustrated.

(*a*) In the early stages of industrialization populations often grow rapidly as death rates fall and birth rates remain high. The increase in population is heavily concentrated in the developing industrial centres, but there is still no reduction in the population of rural areas. At this stage the demographic 'climate' is so rigorous that priority tends to be given (by the market and by government policies alike) to sheltering the rapid growth of households in the expanding cities. There is unlikely to be a great deal of replacement, secondary dwellings will be rare, and sharing may increase. Turkey today, the U.S.S.R. between 1917 and 1952, and the U.K. 100–150 years ago illustrate this pattern in different ways.

(*b*) At a later stage of economic development the rate of growth of the population is often checked ; family size falls, living standards rise, major changes in demographic structure occur, cities continue to grow in size, and rural areas tend to lose population at an increasing rate. Changes in demographic structure (more old people, earlier marriages, etc.) and the reduction of sharing may then sustain as rapid a growth in the demand for separate dwellings as before, despite the slower pace of natural increase. Meanwhile losses from the dwelling stock may also proceed at a rapid rate, owing to the abandonment of rural housing, spontaneous conversions and replacements, and large-scale changes of land use brought about by the growth of 'tertiary' industries in city centres. Various features of this pattern are to be seen in France, Sweden, and possibly Hungary.

(*c*) At a third stage, natural increase may fall still further, and changes in demographic structure proceed more slowly ; internal migration may continue, but most of the movement is now from one town or suburb to another ; virtually the whole population has an urban pattern of living. The demographic climate has now become extremely 'mild', and a growing share of any further additions to

3

the housing stock must be devoted to raising headship rates — particularly among the youngest and oldest households, the single and the previously married. There may also be a considerable increase in secondary dwellings. Large-scale replacement programmes are generally needed at this stage, but the bulk of replacement must now take place in long-established towns and in places where people will continue to live in future years ; it no longer proceeds automatically as a by-product of migration and rural depopulation. The U.K., Belgium, and Czechoslovakia all show features of this pattern.

Many countries cannot be fitted into this simple typology. Economic and demographic evolution do not always march hand in hand : Holland and Poland, for example, combine a reasonably advanced stage of industrialization with many of the demographic characteristics of an earlier phase of economic development. Portugal, though still at an early stage of economic development, has a comparatively modest rate of demographic growth. In Western Europe, international migration has skimmed off the high rates of natural increase often found at earlier stages of development (32 per cent of Italy's, and 150 per cent of Ireland's, 1952–61, for example) and has deposited the increment in countries at a later stage of development (doubling West Germany's and Switzerland's rates of natural increase, for example).

Moreover, the identification of these patterns of requirements does not of itself imply that needs will be met or demands rendered effective. The institutions of government and of the market may be oriented to meet certain requirements while others are neglected. In the U.K., for example, new houses built for sale through the market have for many years catered mainly for young married couples with incomes somewhat above the average manual worker's earnings ; house designs, and lending and repayment procedures, income and property tax procedures — all the institutions involved, whether public or private — have been shaped to render this type of demand effective. For many years, too, most of the housing provided by government was designed for equally well-defined groups (until recently, for demographically similar households drawn from lower income groups). There is likely, therefore, to be a considerable lag before the U.K.'s transition to a new housing situation (type (c) above) compels government or the market to cater effectively for the new pattern of requirements arising from this situation. Paradoxically, the shortages and hardships created by failure to adapt to new requirements may distract the attention of government from the

4

realities underlying these requirements and render it harder to bring about appropriate changes in policy; for in areas of shortage it is families supporting several children on one low income that suffer most and attract most political attention, yet their hardships may be largely due to the scarcity of housing appropriate for single and childless households — households who are compelled as a result of this scarcity to take over dwellings better suited for family occupation.

The discussion of 'housing requirements' in the foregoing paragraphs may suggest that the provision of housing is a market and political response to patterns of requirements which arise from autonomous economic and social changes. But this causal sequence is frequently reversed. Just as public health policies fundamentally alter the patterns of demographic growth, and educational policies may encourage or inhibit certain economic developments, so the provision of housing is increasingly seen by governments as a means of shaping the social and economic evolution of their countries.

III. HOUSING RESOURCES

Within the space of a few paragraphs, we can do no more than identify the main groups of factors to be considered in any analysis of the resources available to governments for the solution of their housing problems : the existing stock of dwellings, the volume of productive resources available for investment in housing, and the factors determining the productivity of these resources — these three aspects of the problem will be briefly examined for the light they throw on the rôle of government.

We have already shown that a country's current stock of housing is a product of a long history. Hence countries with a well-developed and long-established industrial and urban framework and slow rates of demographic growth and movement (*e.g.* U.K., Belgium) have the most plentiful *quantity* of housing, though the *quality* of this stock may compare less favourably with that of countries which have for the previous generation had both a high living standard and a rapid rate of urban growth (*e.g.* Sweden) or replacement (*e.g.* West Germany). Countries without these advantages have poorer housing standards, both quantitatively and qualitatively.

Since the stock of housing grows so slowly, the redistribution of the existing stock provides the only means of eliminating bad conditions rapidly and on a considerable scale. Such redistributions require a systematic policy of building and conversion designed to match the stock more closely (in size distribution, etc.) to the population of households to be sheltered. Redistribution can then be brought about by administrative means, and by a deployment of subsidies, personal housing allowances, rent regulation, and other measures designed to foster the flows of movement required. Few countries have devoted much attention to these problems, but those which have taken the problem seriously (*e.g.* Holland and Czechoslovakia) have achieved considerable success — an incidence of overcrowding, for instance, which compares favourably with that to be seen in other countries having a higher average of dwellings and rooms per head.

Turning to the construction of new houses, it is clear that the poorer countries are at a serious disadvantage. The demographic pressures they confront would present no overwhelming housing problems if it was only necessary to provide additional dwellings of the standard typical of the current stock. But for compelling reasons of politics and public health new houses must be built at a standard not far removed from that of new building in much richer countries. Meanwhile there are many other demands for investment which are regarded as being more urgent than the building of houses; and government resources are severely restricted — the poorer the country, the smaller the proportion of its national income devoted to current government expenditure.

Improvements in the productivity of the building industry, which provide a potential escape from these difficulties, are exceedingly difficult to bring about until the industrial base on which they must rest has been firmly founded, and until severe scarcities of labour prevail and are expected to continue. (A comparison between the experience of Czechoslovakia and Poland suggests that the scope for industrialization in the building industry depends as heavily upon these factors in the centrally planned economies as in the market economies.)

Confronted with severe scarcities of dwellings, rapidly growing needs and painfully slow increases in building productivity, and pressure to build housing of a relatively high standard, governments in the rapidly developing but poorer countries have been compelled to adopt one or both of two policies : they have had to spread their building resources thin by imposing severe restrictions on maximum standards of construction; and they have turned a blind eye to considerable areas of housing (in the centrally planned economies, generally in rural areas; in market economies, generally in the shanty-town fringes of growing cities) which develop, uncontrolled, at very poor standards.

IV. ADMINISTRATIVE STRUCTURE

The institutional system sustaining and shaping the state's contribution to housing reflects the geographical, political, and other necessities that determine the general character of government in the country concerned, and is marked, too, by the pressures which first compelled government intervention in the housing field — a story that generally has several origins with potential conflicts continuing between them. These origins may be found in the protection of public health, agricultural reform, the provision of employment, the prevention of inflation, the prosecution of total war, or elsewhere : from the start, the government interventions which together constitute the field of 'housing policy' have a variety of divergent objectives.

On closer examination, however, the structure and procedures of government do not appear to be the dominant factors determining the character of the state's contribution to this field or the character of the householders' rights and obligations. Just as in the provision of collective forms of medical care, where every country has devised its own way of deploying, organizing, and paying doctors, so also in the housing field a fascinating diversity of administrative systems can be employed for similar purposes.

The main 'functions' to be performed in connection with the provision of housing are : (*a*) the determination of patterns of investment and economic development, and the growth and location of employment associated with them ; (*b*) the physical planning of land uses ; (*c*) the selection, preparation, and development of sites for housing ; (*d*) the construction or reconstruction of houses and associated social capital ; (*e*) the 'management' of housing, including the selection of occupiers and the arrangement of subsequent transfers and exchanges, the repair and maintenance of the property, the collection of rents and mortgage repayments, etc. These five functions — which may be left entirely in private hands — pose distinctive but closely related questions at national, regional, and local levels.

Both in the centrally planned and in the market economies, governments have intervened to perform, support, or regulate these processes to widely varying degrees. Some have intervened extensively at all three levels — national, regional, and local — while others have concentrated their efforts at one or two levels only. A meaningful classification or typology of governments' contributions to the housing field calls for an analysis of the extent to which they have succeeded in relating these different functions to each other, and in evolving an appropriately linked hierarchy of policies at local, regional, and national levels.

V. THE RÔLE OF GOVERNMENT

In the space remaining it is only possible to illustrate very briefly and dogmatically the typology that may emerge from the discussion presented in the preceding sections of this paper : three types of rôle assumed by governments of the market economies of Europe will be outlined.

(a) Where a high rate of natural increase and rapid growth of cities produce a rigorous demographic 'climate', where tax revenues and savings are small, and administrators and professional staff of experience, skill, and integrity are scarce, where government has not — or has only recently — attempted to devise procedures for economic planning, then the total effect of government interventions in the housing field is bound to be limited, and these interventions are liable to be as diverse and ill-co-ordinated as their origins. Housing subsidies of various kinds tend to be directed to the rising urban middle class, while public health authorities endeavour to control unplanned developments of poor quality on the fringes of the growing industrial centres ; different (and potentially rival) agencies may build or finance housing for different regions, and different classes of the population — for key industrial workers, farmers, middle-class housing associations, civil servants, and so on. One public agency may foster labour-saving technical development in the construction industry while another fosters house-building as a means of reducing unemployment. At this stage housing may be subject to the impact of many government interventions, but these interventions do not constitute a 'housing policy' and were never intended to do so. Features of this pattern are to be seen in Portugal, Turkey, and Italy, and until some years ago in Spain.

(b) In highly industrialized countries with a higher standard of living and slower rates of demographic growth and change, where there are long-established systems of local government with a tradition of public health and poor law administration, and where the building industry and the supply of credit from the private market have been adequate to meet a large proportion of housing needs, then government may have intervened on a considerable scale to perform or control many of the functions listed in the previous section, but these interventions will often have been regarded as 'temporary', and designed to meet the needs of specific groups not adequately catered for by the free market — large families, the poor, those living in houses due for demolition, etc. Many countries in north-west Europe have passed through this phase of 'social' housing policies, in which government has a fundamentally residual rôle ; it is a rôle still to be seen in Switzerland and (until very recently at least) in the U.K.

(*c*) Many countries which attained a standard and stage of economic, social and administrative evolution broadly similar to those of the countries mentioned in the previous paragraph found, during or after the Second World War, that the normal technical and financial instruments required for the building of houses had been crippled or eliminated ; at the same time the experience of wartime destruction and shared hardship, followed in some cases by political revolution or something like it, gave a new urgency and impetus to housebuilding. Appropriate marginal adjustments could not be made — or would involve intolerable lags. Structural changes were required which led governments to embark on a 'housing drive' that soon created severe shortages of building land, materials, labour, and credit. Although the 'housing problem' was initially perceived as finite and temporary in these countries too, the attempt to resolve one bottleneck after another led government into an increasingly comprehensive involvement in all the functions of housing policy. Calculations and projections of housing needs dealt with the whole country and with increasingly long periods of time ; government retained building licences and controls of various kinds over rents, prices, land uses, and the distribution of housing amongst households ; subsidies, loans, tax reliefs, and other forms of assistance were not concentrated upon one sector of the market but spread in ways that gave government more pervasive methods for the regulation of the whole housing programme ; and growing efforts were made to improve the performance of the building industry. Subtle shifts of power occurred : regional units of administration gained strength at the expense of local units, economic planners at the expense of auditors and accountants, ministries of construction at the expense of welfare and local government ministries. Most important of all, government secured effective control over a large and continuing flow of small savings, much of which was directed into investment in housing — though the methods employed for this purpose were enormously varied (including severe tax and generous credit policies in Norway, the imaginative use of tax reliefs in West Germany, public control of small savings banks and an earmarked percentage tax on employers' wage bills in France, growing reliance on pension funds in Sweden, and so on). In these countries (and also in Holland, and more recently in Spain) a new form of 'comprehensive' housing policy began to take shape.

The comprehensive character of the aims adopted by these governments, and the attempts they have made to relate and integrate the different functions to be performed in the housing field and to do this at national, regional, and local levels, together amount to a new and distinctive type of rôle. It remains to be seen how much further this development will go : in some countries it is regarded as part of a permanent commitment of government to a more active rôle in all spheres of economic and domestic policy ; elsewhere it is still considered to be no more than a local and temporary aftermath of the Second World War.

VI. CONCLUSION

It must be stressed again that this analysis has not been designed to identify 'good' or 'bad' housing policies — nor those producing the biggest output of dwellings. (High and low building rates are to be found in each of the three categories distinguished.) Its purpose has been to explore and illustrate some of the principal factors to be considered by those interested in the scope and limits of governments' contributions to this field, and to relate economics to other disciplines that must play a part in the analysis of these problems. Doubtless more satisfactory analyses and comparisons can be devised, but this one already poses a number of interesting questions.

It shows, for example, that the simple contrasts often employed in international comparisons of housing policy (contrasts between the extent of rent controls or the proportions of new building commissioned by public investors, for instance) deal only with particular instruments of housing policy and tell little about the rôle of government. The extent and character of this rôle is a much more complex affair, which depends on economic and social circumstances, and on political decision. Developments taking place in Western Europe, coupled with others in Eastern Europe which we have not had space to discuss, are producing a very interesting convergence between the functions and problems of government under apparently different régimes. Government planning and direction may be most urgently 'needed' in rapidly developing but poor countries where the balance between needs and resources is most unfavourable, but their potentialities for bringing about any real change in the housing situation are greatest in richer countries. As these potentialities are recognized, government regulation may become increasingly pervasive in many spheres. If such systems are to remain economically efficient and to afford the citizen opportunities for choice and responsible participation, fuller information about their operation must be made more freely available to a better informed public.

Chapter 2

SLUMS AND POVERTY

RICHARD F. MUTH[1]

Institute for Defense Analyses, Virginia, U.S.A.

I. THE REASONS FOR THE EXISTENCE OF SLUMS

MOST discussions of the slum problem emphasize factors which increase the relative supply of poor-quality housing. In some, the increase in the supply of slums results from a decline in the demand for good-quality housing in the older, central parts of cities. Age and obsolesence, the fall in transport costs brought about by the automobile, and encroachment of hostile land uses are reasons often given for the decline in demand. In other discussions of slum formation, the increase in poor-quality housing supply is said to result from external diseconomies, market imperfections, or faulty taxation. By limiting the amount of investment in residential real estate, such factors would result in a poorer average quality of the housing stock than is socially desirable.

While the reasons given for the existence of slums are varied, the effects of slums which are explicitly noted are usually quite similar. As a result of quality deterioration the older residents of affected areas move to newer neighbourhoods where the available housing is more suited to their tastes and circumstances. Their places are taken by lower income households who have less of an aversion to living in areas of poor-quality housing. The association of slums with poverty is thus attributed to the effects of dwelling unit condition on the location of households by income. Indeed, by inhabiting slum dwellings, lower income households are frequently said to intensify their poverty.

While objections can be raised on *a priori* grounds to many of the reasons commonly given for slums, some may have a limited empirical relevance. They share a common deficiency, however, in that none

[1] I wish to thank Martin J. Bailey for his helpful comments on an earlier version of this paper and for discussions with him at various stages of the research summarized here. He, of course, is not responsible for any of my mistakes.

can account for, and many are inconsistent with, three simple empirical facts about slums. Since all stress factors which increase the supply of poor-quality housing, all imply that slum housing should be especially cheap. But, if anything, it would seem that slum housing is expensive in relation to its quality. Closely related is the fact that urban renewal programmes almost universally require government subsidy. Acquisition costs alone typically exceed the resale value of the cleared site by a large margin.

Finally, contrary to widespread belief, it would appear that in recent years the quality of the housing stock in U.S. cities has improved markedly. Estimates made by Beverly Duncan and Philip M. Hauser[1] indicate that, of the six Standard Metropolitan Areas studied, only in New York, where rent controls are still in existence, did the number of substandard dwellings[2] increase from 1950 to 1956. In the five other SMA's and in the cities of Chicago and Philadelphia the number of substandard dwellings declined on the order of one-third in six years' time. About 90 per cent of this decline was due to the improvement of quality of given units and only about 10 per cent to demolitions, mergers, and other changes.

II. THE DEMAND FOR POOR-QUALITY HOUSING

The facts I have just discussed can be much more easily explained on the basis of factors influencing the relative demand for poor-quality housing. I would expect the relative demand for poor-quality housing to vary inversely with the per household consumption of housing. An increase in housing consumption can take many forms : more rooms per dwelling, larger rooms, better-quality materials, larger lot sizes, etc. Indeed, casual observation would suggest that increases in housing consumption typically take place in all these ways. The strong association between slums and crowding may merely reflect the fact that these are closely related aspects of a low per household consumption of housing. Recent research suggests that income is the principal determinant of the per household consumption of housing and that the latter increases at least in

---

[1] *Housing a Metropolis — Chicago* (Glencoe, Ill. ; The Free Press, 1960), pp. 56-58. The data used were from the 1950 Census of Housing and the 1956 National Housing Inventory, which employed identical definitions of housing condition.

[2] A substandard dwelling is one reported by the census to be dilapidated and/or without private bath and hot running water.

proportion to income.[1] I would therefore expect the demand for poor-quality housing to vary inversely with income per household.

The relative price of slum housing and the proportion of dwelling units which are poor-quality also depend upon conditions of supply. There is good reason to expect that the relative supply of slum housing is less than perfectly elastic. Slum housing in U.S. cities today is rarely newly constructed as such ; rather, it is produced primarily through the conversion of existing dwellings to smaller ones and, by deferring maintenance and repair, allowing them to deteriorate in quality. Certain dwellings are probably more costly to convert to poor-quality ones, particularly single-family dwellings and any dwellings built on large lots. With an increase in the demand for poor-quality housing, then, the relative price of slum housing and the returns to the owners of existing slum dwellings would tend to rise as dwellings are converted.

It is not difficult to account for a strong and rising demand for poor-quality housing in U.S. cities during the first half of this century. During this time the *per capita* stock of non-farm housing showed relatively little increase in the U.S. I would attribute this primarily to the fact that the relative price of housing rose greatly during the period.[2] Low income migrants to the U.S. have tended to congregate in cities. While the flow of migration from abroad was greatly reduced following 1920, large-scale migration of lower income persons from the rural South has taken place ; this migration was especially heavy during the 1940's. During the same time higher income households have tended to move to the outer parts of metropolitan areas in the U.S. It is quite likely, then, that the per household consumption of housing in the central cities actually declined prior to 1950. If so, the relative price of slum housing would tend to rise with the increase in the demand for it. Urban renewal projects which replace poor-quality housing with other land uses would lose money because, in effect, they would be shifting sites from high-priced to low-priced uses.

If the above analysis is correct, how can one account for the marked improvement in housing quality that took place during the early fifties? Unlike the first half of this century, a substantial increase in

---

[1] Margaret G. Reid, *Housing and Income* (Chicago : University of Chicago Press, 1962) and Richard F. Muth, 'The Demand for Non-Farm Housing', Arnold C. Harberger (ed.), *The Demand for Durable Goods* (Chicago : University of Chicago Press, 1960), pp. 29-96.

[2] Muth, *op. cit.*, pp. 73-74.

housing consumption appears to have taken place during this period. Data from the 1956 National Housing inventory indicate that the number of occupied dwellings in the U.S. increased by 16·5 per cent from 1950 to 1956 while population increased by only about 12 per cent.[1] More importantly, the increase in average value per unit was striking. The median value of one unit, owner-occupied dwellings increased by 54 per cent and the median contract rent of tenant-occupied dwellings by 47 per cent, as compared with an increase in construction costs of only 27 per cent.[2] Goldsmith's estimate of the stock of private non-farm housekeeping units (including land) in 1947–49 prices increased by 23 per cent from the end of 1949 to the end of 1955.[3] In addition, migration from the rural South slowed noticeably during the 1950's, and the incomes of lower income groups rose rapidly during the forties and early fifties. Thus, I would expect the demand for poor-quality housing to have declined.

III. AN ANALYSIS OF THE DETERMINANTS OF HOUSING QUALITY

This section discusses the results of a detailed regression analysis I have made of the determinants of housing quality among census tracts on the South side of Chicago both in 1950 and 1960 and among various central cities of the U.S. in 1950. In my study I have tried to include variables reflecting as many of the supply and demand factors for poor-quality housing as possible. I have also studied the determinants of the location of households by income level within cities, partly because of its obvious bearing on the theories of slums discussed in Section I. Because of space limitations I cannot discuss my analysis here in great detail. Rather, I will merely summarize my findings. I have included in the appendix some of my major regression equations together with a brief description of the data used and reasons for the comparisons I made.

The one variable to which the proportion of dwelling units substandard was most consistently and strongly related was the income of

[1] Data on number of units, median value and median contract rent cited here are from the U.S. Bureau of the Census, *1956 National Housing Inventory*, Vol. III, Pt. 1 (Washington : Government Printing Office, 1959).

[2] As measured by Boeckh index or residential construction costs for brick structures. Because of the removal of rent controls prior to 1950, the above increase may overestimate the quality improvement of tenant-occupied dwellings.

[3] Raymond W. Goldsmith, *The National Wealth of the United States in the Postwar Period* (Princeton, N.J. : Princeton University Press, 1962), Table B–12, p. 235.

their inhabitants. The only exception I found was in conventional least-squares regressions for South Chicago in 1960, but two-stage least-squares regressions using the same data suggest that this apparent lack of effect of income on housing quality resulted from least-squares bias attributable to inclusion of a measure of crowding in the regression equation. Furthermore, the association between income and dwelling unit condition found in the conventional least-squares regressions with the latter variable treated as dependent cannot be attributed to the effect of housing quality on income. The latter effect could conceivably be important within any given city, but there is little reason to believe that the average income in, say, Chicago exceeds that in Atlanta because Chicago's better housing quality attracts higher income families to that city. If the association found using data for census tracts in South Chicago really reflected the effect of housing quality upon the location of households by income, it should vanish when condition and income are treated as jointly dependent in a two-stage least-squares analysis. Yet, if anything, the coefficient of income was numerically larger in the two-stage than in comparable conventional least-squares regressions.

Not only do slums appear to be mainly the result of poverty, but my analysis indicates that housing quality improves dramatically with income. While the income elasticities of the proportion of dwelling units substandard vary somewhat according to the method of estimation and data used in the comparisons, all are numerically quite large. For the South Chicago comparisons in 1950 the implied income elasticity varied from $-2 \cdot 5$ to $-3 \cdot 2$, while for 1960 it was as large as $-4 \cdot 6$. The inter-city comparisons for 1950 yielded elasticity estimates of from $-2 \cdot 0$ to $-3 \cdot 2$. Much of the difference for the different sets of data results from differences in the mean values of income at which the elasticities are evaluated. The form of the comparison used, with proportion substandard in logs and income in natural units, is such that the elasticities increase numerically as income increases. Clearly, though, such elasticities are large enough to account for the quality improvement from 1950 to 1956 found by Duncan and Hauser, assuming that the per household consumption of housing in real terms grew at the plausible rate of about 2 per cent per year.

I have also examined the location of households by income level on the South side of Chicago for both 1950 and 1960. My results suggest that the effect of dwelling unit condition upon income is quantitatively quite small. I estimated the elasticity of income level with respect to dwelling unit condition to be -0.07 and -0.04 respectively for 1950 and 1960. In addition, when income in 1950 is included among the determinants of income level in 1960, the coefficient showing the effect of the proportion of dwellings substandard on income became negligible. I found, however, that there was a strong negative association between crowding and income level in 1960, even when both were treated as jointly determined in a two-stage least-squares regression analysis. Thus, it may be the character of the occupants of surrounding dwellings rather than poor housing quality as such which higher income households seek to avoid. It makes little practical difference, however, since crowding and poor condition are so highly correlated and both are primarily the results of low incomes.

While I find that housing quality is most strongly and consistently related to income, I did find a few other variables which appear to affect the condition of the housing stock. Housing tends to be of better quality rather than the reverse in areas of rapid population growth, especially so among cities, whose population growth rates tended to vary more than among census tracts on Chicago's South side. This finding casts doubt on the hypothesis that slums result from diseconomies associated with rapid population growth. It is best explained, I believe, by the fact that housing demand and the profitability of maintaining existing structures vary directly with the rate of population growth.

Dwelling unit condition was also found to be very sensitive to housing prices in the inter-city comparisons I made. The elasticity of the proportion of dwellings substandard with respect to construction costs was estimated at from 1.5 to 3.6. The similarity of the latter with my estimated income elasticity bears out my contention that housing quality is mainly an indicator of housing demand, for in my earlier study I found that price and income elasticities of housing demand are about equal numerically.[1] In addition I found a strong positive association between proportion substandard and urbanized area size, and the latter's coefficient is about what one would expect if it reflected the effects of higher land values on housing prices. Other explanations for this last association are not consistent with the variation of the per household expenditures on housing with city size, which I also examined. Despite the above evidence for the large response of dwelling unit condition to housing prices, none

[1] *Op. cit.*, pp. 72-73.

of the comparisons I made indicate that a higher proportion of Negroes than whites inhabit substandard dwellings when income is held constant. For this reason I doubt that residential segregation of Negroes results in higher housing prices for them or restricts them to areas of the worst housing quality.

My empirical results provide little or no support for the various supply-side hypotheses of slum formation which I was able to subject to empirical test. There was a strong positive association between the proportion of dwellings built prior to 1920 and the proportion substandard in South Chicago in 1950. The age variable's coefficient was insignificant in the other comparisons, however, and actually negative in some comparisons for South Chicago in 1960. There appears to be little truth in the common assertion that crowding breeds slums. No partial association between crowding, as measured by the proportion of dwellings with more than one person per room, and condition was found for South Chicago in 1950. Significantly positive coefficients were found for the other two comparisons, but these appear to be largely the result of least-squares bias. When estimated by two-stage least-squares treating crowding and condition as jointly determined, the coefficients of the crowding variable became much smaller and statistically insignificant. In addition, none of the three comparisons made indicate that housing is of poorer quality in the more densely populated areas of the city once the effects of other variables have been removed.

To test the hypothesis that housing is of poorer quality in areas of rapid population turnover, I included a measure of migration in the condition comparisons. The migration variable had negative and significant coefficients of roughly the same magnitude in the two comparisons for 1950 but was negligible in South Chicago for 1960. The difference is due, I suspect, to the lingering effects of rent controls in 1950. In the South Chicago comparisons there was no tendency for the proportion of dwellings which are substandard to decrease with distance from the city centre once income is held constant. Such a decrease would be expected if poor housing quality were the result of a decline in demand for housing in the central parts of cities because of the introduction of automobile transportation. Nor do I generally find a higher proportion of dwellings substandard in areas adjacent to manufacturing or retail centres as would be expected if slums were caused by the external diseconomies imposed by mixtures of land uses or hostile surrounding uses of land.

IV. CONCLUSIONS

The results of my analysis clearly imply that slums are mainly the result of poverty. In the data I analysed, housing quality is consistently and strongly responsive to the incomes of its inhabitants. Quality, however, appears to be of little importance in affecting the location of households by income. In addition, I find virtually no evidence for supply-side theories of slums. A clear policy implication of my analysis is that urban renewal programmes will do little or nothing to alleviate the slum problem in the long-run since they do nothing to alleviate poverty. The widespread popular and scholarly support for urban renewal programmes results, I believe, from theories of the causes of slums which have little empirical validity.

APPENDIX

This appendix gives a few more details of the regression analysis summarized in Section III and presents some of my major regression equations.

I first examined 1950 data for the South side of Chicago, defined as the area within the city limits south of 22nd Street and the Sanitary and Ship Canal. In the larger study of the determinants of the spatial pattern of residential land use of which the material reported on here is a part, I paid particular attention to Chicago's South side because I am most familiar with it and because the Negro and low income residents of the city tend to be concentrated on the South side. Particular attention was also given to Chicago because, having long been studied by social scientists, much data is available on various characteristics of interest that is not readily obtainable for other cities.

The data I used were for a stratified random sample of 69 census tracts or combinations of tracts. Tracts were divided into six strata defined by variables closely associated with dwelling unit condition, namely age of dwellings and the income and race of their inhabitants, in an attempt to increase the extent to which these closely associated characteristics would vary independently of each other. Tracts were combined for comparability between 1950 and 1960, and any tracts with fewer than 100 persons or in which I knew of public housing projects were omitted from the list of tracts from which my sample was drawn.

I first computed several least-squares regression equations with dwelling unit condition and then with income as the dependent variable. The larger study of which the analysis discussed here is a part was especially concerned with spatial characteristics of urban residential land use. For this reason several location variables were included, namely the distance of the census tract from the Loop, variables allowing for differences in the intercept and in the coefficient of distance for tracts located within one mile of rapid transit or express-type highway routes, and four dummy variables describing proximity of a tract to manufacturing and retail centres. Measures of age of dwellings, crowding, gross population density, population growth, owner-occupancy, and number of dwellings per structure were among the dwelling and neighbourhood characteristics included in each of the regressions. Besides income and race, population characteristics such as persons per household, proportion of adults over 65 years old, occupation, education, and place of earlier residence were included as well. Those variables whose coefficients were roughly as large as their standard errors and of the correct sign as well as certain others in which I am especially interested were then included in a two-stage least-squares regression analysis which treated dwelling unit condition and income as jointly determined variables. The resulting estimated regression coefficients are shown in the body of Table 1 in the column and row defined by the variables to which they refer, while the standard errors are shown in parentheses directly below the coefficients to which they refer.

For South Chicago in 1950, conventional and two-stage least-squares estimates using a given set of variables were practically identical. One other point about the South Chicago findings for 1950 should be noted explicitly. If, as is sometimes argued, residential segregation restricts Negroes to areas of worst, oldest, or most central housing, one would expect positive coefficients for the Negro area dummy variables in the income equation. Strongly negative coefficients were observed, which initially suggested to me that Negroes on the whole lived in newer housing than one would expect on the basis of their incomes. When other variables, mainly crowding and income a decade earlier, were included in the income equation in 1960, though, the Negro dummy variable coefficients became negligible. I suspect, then, that the Negro area coefficients for 1950 really reflect the effects of these omitted variables.

I next made a similar analysis of 1950 data for central cities of urbanized areas for which the Boeckh index of residential construction costs was available. This was done to check on my initial results obtained from data for census tracts within a single city. There is little reason to believe that income is affected by dwelling unit condition as among the various cities. Furthermore, there is little reason to expect that housing demand as among various cities is much influenced by the age of their dwellings. Construction costs, which are the principal determinants of housing prices, vary rather substantially among cities but are probably almost uniform within any given city, and population growth rates vary much more among cities than among census tracts in South Chicago. The major reason for examining inter-city data, however, was to check for possibly omitted variables. Since the pattern of inter-correlation of variables is likely to be quite different among cities than within them, one would expect to find different coefficients in the inter-city comparisons if important variables have been omitted.

Most of the dwelling unit and population characteristics included in the South Chicago comparisons were included in the inter-city comparisons. The intra-city location variables were omitted, of course. Some additional characteristics which are more or less uniform for a single city but vary among cities such as construction costs and urbanized area size were also included. The major difference between the South Chicago and inter-city estimates for 1950 was that the coefficient of the crowding variable, measured by the proportion of dwellings with one or more persons per room, was strongly positive in the latter. As noted in the text, this effect largely disappeared in the two-stage least-squares regressions which treated condition and crowding as jointly dependent (see Table 2). The age of dwellings variable was not significant as among cities, though its coefficient in the conventional least-squares regression was roughly comparable to that observed for South Chicago. Rather surprising was the fact that the age of city variable had a strongly negative coefficient in the condition regressions, just the opposite to what one would expect on the basis of many arguments given for the existence of slums. Because the coefficient of this variable was so highly significant, being about three times as large as its standard error, I retained it in the two-stage least-squares condition regression shown in Table 2, but I have no good explanation for it.

Finally, as a further check on my initial results, I examined 1960 data for the same South Chicago tracts used in the 1950 comparisons. The only further experimenting done was to test alternative measures of dwelling condition and crowding made possible by the more detailed tabulations of the 1960 census, neither of which proved to be decidedly superior to the 1950 measures, and to include income a decade earlier to test for lags of adjustment. The conventional least-squares regression with housing quality the dependent variable gave quite different results in 1960. The coefficient of the crowding variable was strongly positive and the income coefficient was negligible. In addition, in some regressions there appeared to be a higher proportion of dwellings substandard in the more densely populated census tracts. Therefore, I treated crowding and population density as jointly determined along with condition and income in the two-stage least-squares regressions for 1960. Because crowding or space per person is largely determined by income and density by the location variables, especially distance from the Loop, their effects in the conventional least-squares regressions may have been the result of least-squares bias. It would indeed appear that this is the case from the coefficients estimated by two-stage least-squares shown in Table 3. The coefficient of PEROOM is small as compared with its standard error and that of

GRODEN has the wrong sign. The coefficient of INCOME, however, is about one and a half times its standard error and comparable in magnitude to those shown in Tables 1 and 2.

TABLE 1

THE DETERMINANTS OF DWELLING UNIT CONDITION AND INCOME BY
CENSUS TRACT, SOUTH CHICAGO, 1950

Explanatory Variable *	Dependent Variable	
	SUBSTD	INCOME × 10⁻³
INCOME × 10⁻³†	−·91‡	—
	(·15)	
SUBSTD†	—	−·20‡
		(·11)
DISCBD	·055	·024
	(·039)	(·020)
RAPSLO	−·023	·0097
	(·022)	(·013)
AGEDUS	1·1‡	−·51‡
	(·43)	(·31)
RETMAJ	·55§	—
	(·17)	
SAMHOU	−2·6‡	—
	(1·2)	
GROPOP	−·30§	—
	(·16)	
MANMAJ	—	−·10
		(·14)
NEGMAJ	—	−1·3§
		(·20)
NEGMIN	—	−·78§
		(·15)

* For glossary, see p. 25 below.
† Treated as jointly dependent.
‡ Significant as anticipated at the 1-tail 0·10 level.
§ Significant as anticipated at the 2-tail 0·10 level.

TABLE 2

THE DETERMINANTS OF DWELLING
UNIT CONDITION BY CITY, 1950

Explanatory Variable	Dependent Variable SUBSTD
INCOME × 10⁻³	− ·67†
	(·21)
CONCST × 10²	·72
	(·67)
AGESMA	− ·11
	(·036)
PEROOM*	·15
	(·24)
SAMHOU	− 2·9†
	(1·4)
GROPOP	− ·56‡
	(·16)
URBPOP	·15†
	(·093)

* Treated as jointly dependent.
† Significant as anticipated at the 1-tail 0·10 level.
‡ Significant as anticipated at the 2-tail 0·10 level.

TABLE 3

THE DETERMINANTS OF DWELLING UNIT CONDITION AND INCOME BY CENSUS TRACT, SOUTH CHICAGO, 1960

Explanatory Variable	Dependent Variable	
	SUBSTD	INCOME $\times 10^{-3}$
INCOME $\times 10^{-3}$	$-\cdot71$	—
	$(\cdot66)$	
SUBSTD*	—	$-\cdot050$
		$(\cdot18)$
DISCBD	$-\cdot030$	$-\cdot020$
	$(\cdot097)$	$(\cdot060)$
RAPSLO	$-\cdot060$	$-\cdot028$
	$(\cdot047)$	$(\cdot028)$
AGEDUS	$-\cdot30$	$-1\cdot4\dagger$
	$(1\cdot6)$	$(\cdot49)$
PEROOM*	$2\cdot3$	$-7\cdot3\dagger$
	$(7\cdot8)$	$(1\cdot9)$
GRODEN*	$-\cdot69$	$-\cdot16$
	$(\cdot31)$	$(\cdot23)$
INCM50 $\times 10^{-3}$	$-\cdot16$	$\cdot46\dagger$
	$(\cdot49)$	$(\cdot25)$
RETMAJ	$\cdot51\ddagger$	—
	$(\cdot31)$	
SAMHOU	$-\cdot34$	—
	$(1\cdot7)$	
GROPOP	$-\cdot21$	—
	$(\cdot33)$	
PERHOU	$1\cdot5\ddagger$	—
	$(\cdot59)$	
MANMAJ	—	$\cdot32$
		$(\cdot29)$
NEGMAJ	—	$-\cdot026$
		$(\cdot41)$
NEGMIN	—	$-\cdot024$
		$(\cdot29)$
RETMIN	—	$\cdot32$
		$(\cdot25)$

* Treated as jointly dependent.
† Significant as anticipated at the 1-tail 0·10 level.
‡ Significant as anticipated at the 2-tail 0·10 level.

DEFINITION AND SOURCES OF VARIABLES USED

Variables used in all comparisons

SUBSTD—Natural log of the proportion of dwellings dilapidated and/or without private bath. Unless otherwise noted, all data for South Chicago are from U.S. Bureau of the Census, *1950 Census of Population*, Vol. III (Washington, D.C. : U.S. Government Printing Office, 1952) and *U.S. Census of Population and Housing: 1960*, Final Report PHC (1) (Washington, D.C. : U.S. Government Printing Office, 1962). For cities in 1950 the condition data are from *1950 Census of Population*, Vol. III, *op. cit.*

INCOME—The median income of families and unrelated individuals (families) in 1949 (1959) for 1950 (1960). For cities in 1950 the data are from U.S. Bureau of the Census, *1950 Census of Population*, Vol. II (Washington, D.C. : U.S. Government Printing Office, 1952), Pt. 1, Table 93. The 1950 income measure is designated INCM50 in Table 3 to distinguish it from 1960 income.

AGEDUS—Proportion of dwellings built prior to 1920 (1940) in 1950 (1960). The data for cities in 1950 are from U.S. Bureau of the Census, *Census of Housing* : *1950*, Vol. I (Washington, D.C. : U.S. Government Printing Office, 1953), Pt. 1, Table 30.

PEROOM—Natural log of the proportion of dwellings with more than one person per room for cities in 1950 ; the data are from *ibid.*, Pt. 1, Table 29. The square root form was used for South Chicago in 1960.

GRODEN—Population divided by total land area in natural logs. For South Chicago, land area measurements were obtained from Chicago Community Inventory, 'Gross Land Area and Gross Population Density of Census Tracts and Community Areas for the City of Chicago, 1950' (unpublished, November 1952). For cities in 1950 the density data are from U.S. Bureau of the Census, *1950 Census of Population*, Vol. I (Washington, D.C., U.S. Government Printing Office, 1952), Pt. 1, Table 17.

SAMHOU—Proportion of persons 1 (5) or over who lived in the same house in 1949 (1955) as in 1950 (1960). For cities in 1950 the data are from *1950 Census of Population*, Vol. II, *op. cit.*, Pt. 1, Table 86.

GROPOP—Natural log of the ratio of 1950 (1960) population to :

    For South Chicago, 1930 population by census tract from Ernest W. Burgess and Charles W. Newcomb (eds.), *Census Data of the City of Chicago, 1930* (Chicago : University of Chicago Press, 1933), Table 1. The year 1930 is the earliest for which comparable census tract data are readily available.

    For cities in 1950, 1900 population by SMA from Donald J. Bogue, *Metropolitan Growth and the Conversion of Land to Nonagricultural*

Uses (Oxford, Ohio : Scripps Foundation, 1956), Appendix Table II, pp. 28-32.

Variables used for South Chicago comparisons only

DISCBD—Distance of census tract to the Loop in miles.

RAPSLO—DISCBD if within one mile of rapid transit route or express highway and 0 otherwise. The coefficient of this variable measures the difference in the rate of change per mile between tracts within one mile of these facilities and all other tracts.

RETMAJ—1, if within one mile of the largest class of non-CBD retail centres, and 0 otherwise, as identified in Brian J. L. Berry, *Commercial Structure and Commercial Blight* (Chicago : Department of Geography, 1963), Table 5.

PERHOU—Persons per household.

MANMAJ—1 if within a square mile section of the city containing 8 or more manufacturing establishments employing 50 or more workers. Data on establishments by square mile section are from Department of City Planning, City of Chicago, *Location Patterns of Major Industries in the City of Chicago* (Chicago : City of Chicago, 1960), Map 3, p. 10.

NEGMAJ—1 if Negro population 80 per cent or more, and 0 otherwise.

NEGMIN—1 if Negro population 5 to 83 per cent, and 0 otherwise.

RETMIN—1 if within 1 mile of the second largest class of non-CBD retail centres, and 0 otherwise, as identified in Berry, *op. cit.*

Variables used for Inter-City comparisons only

CONCST—Boeckh index of residential construction costs for brick structures supplied by its compiler, Mr. E. H. Boeckh of Washington, D.C.

AGESMA—Number of decades since the SMA first attained a population of 50,000, from Donald J. Bogue and Dorothy L. Harris, *Comparative Population and Urban Research via Multiple Regression and Covariance Analysis* (Oxford, Ohio : Scripps Foundation, 1954), Appendix Table 1, p. 73.

URBPOP—Natural log of urbanized area population from *1950 Census of Population*, Vol. 1, *op. cit.*, Pt. 1, Table 17.

Chapter 3

HOUSING AND THE STATE: THE RESPONSIBILITIES OF GOVERNMENT

BY

J. B. CULLINGWORTH
Senior Lecturer in Urban Studies, University of Glasgow

I. INTRODUCTION

THE object of this short paper is to discuss the rôle of the State in the field of housing, to show how complex are the ramifications of 'the housing problem', and to analyse a few of the significant economic issues related to housing policy. Obviously in a short paper the discussion must be highly selective and illustrative rather than comprehensive. This would be the case even if attention were restricted to one country : it must be very much more so when one ranges over a large number of countries at different levels of economic development and with different political and economic systems.

The main issues raised stem from two important characteristics of housing : its high capital cost and its extreme durability. As a consequence, government action is commonly required to ensure an adequate supply of housing, to maintain socially acceptable standards, and to provide financial assistance to families unable to pay market prices. At the same time, the importance of housing in relation to national investment and national and regional economic development programmes is such that 'housing policy' cannot be regarded merely as a social policy having little impact on, or connection with, economic growth. Furthermore, the interest of governments in both social and economic objectives of housing policy involves concern for a wide range of related issues, for example, the building industry and the supply and price of land.

II. THE HIGH CAPITAL COST OF HOUSING

Housing is different from other economic goods in many ways. A house is (compared with other household purchases) extremely costly. The capital cost of a new social dwelling in many European countries is about four times the annual earnings of an adult male

27

industrial worker. In the least industrialized countries of Europe the relative cost of a dwelling is even greater, rising in some cases to over ten times the annual average earnings.[1] Furthermore, though there is no uniform pattern of building costs in the more economically advanced countries, it seems that the cost of a dwelling in terms of wages is higher now than at the beginning of the century. These higher (real) costs are partly due to higher standards imposed by the State. Both the high capital cost and the pressure for higher standards are related to another peculiarity of housing—its extreme durability. Though the life of houses may differ according to standards of construction, design, maintenance, the tempo of social and economic change, and a host of other factors,[2] they are generally regarded, in Europe at least, as items of capital investment destined to last for several generations. Attempts to design short-life houses at a low cost have not yet proved successful. The situation in the United States, however, is significantly different : the average one-family house in that country is typically of light construction designed to last for a considerably shorter period than is usual in Europe. At the same time the American social attitude towards housing (as illustrated, for example, by the very high rate of residential mobility)[3] is markedly different from that in Europe : rather than being regarded as a long-term capital asset, a house is commonly viewed more as a consumption article of limited life. This attitude, which is but one aspect of the highly mobile character of the American way of life,[4] is facilitated by the high real incomes of American families. Despite the fact that American houses are typically of a much higher standard than European houses,[5] and that building costs in the United States are higher than in Europe,[6] the cost of an American dwelling s less than three times the average annual income of its purchasers.[5]

[1] Economic Commission for Europe, *Financing of Housing in Europe*, United Nations, Geneva, 1958.
[2] See Economic Commission for Europe, *Cost Repetition and Maintenance: Related Aspects of Building Prices*, United Nations, Geneva, 1963.
[3] See, *e.g.*, P. H. Rossi, *Why Families Move*, Free Press, Glencoe, and U.S. Bureau of the Census, Current Population Reports, 'Mobility of the Population of the United States, April 1961 to April 1962', *Population Characteristics*, Series P–20, No. 127, 1964.
[4] There is, of course, a large amount of literature on this. For a recent sociological comparison of Britain and the United States see H. E. Bracey, *Neighbours on New Estates and Subdivisions in England and the U.S.A.*, Routledge & Kegan Paul, London, 1964, particularly chapter 2. A more general comparison of British and American housing is given in D. D. Newman, 'Housing in Britain and America', *Monthly Labor Review*, U.S. Department of Labor, May and June 1960.
[5] *Financing of Housing in Europe, op. cit.*, Table 37, p. 40.
[6] Milton Gilbert *et al.*: *Comparative National Products and Price Levels*, OEEC, Paris, 1958.

Nevertheless, even at this favourable average cost-wages ratio, annual charges (including maintenance) must not be higher than 7 per cent of the capital cost if the proportion of income to be devoted to rent is not to exceed 20 per cent. In countries where the cost-wages ratio is 4, the annual charges have to be 5 per cent or less of the capital cost if housing is to account for no more than a fifth of income. In most European countries, for this requirement to be met, interest rates would have to be about 2 to 3 per cent. In fact, interest rates are generally very much higher than this. Alternative calculations based on different assumptions do not significantly affect the general proposition that the high capital cost of new housing in terms of average wages, necessitating long-term credit, involves annual costs that may be regarded as being undesirably high for those on average incomes and *a fortiori* insuperably high for those with low incomes. This is a major field within which governments have operated a housing policy.

III. HOUSING STANDARDS

The long life of housing has another aspect which is inter-related with these financial issues. Since houses last for such long periods of time it follows that the standard of new housing (and the standard of upkeep of old housing) is of concern to future generations as well as the one for whom the houses are initially provided. What is regarded currently as a socially acceptable housing standard may well be considered inadequate for future needs. This line of thought should not be pressed too far : the future can be under — as well as over — discounted. But it is here that one peculiar feature of housing assumes particular importance : the fact that houses are located in a (generally) fixed position on land. In other words a house cannot be considered in the same way as most economic goods since it is (generally) immobile in itself and (until it is demolished) determines the physical use of the land on which it is situated. Thus when assessing future needs the question is not merely whether new houses are of an adequate construction (which can be decided on the basis of a broad estimate of life), but also whether they provide sufficient space both within and outside for needs which can be expected to become effective demands in the foreseeable future. Future space needs within a house are difficult to predict in spite of the common assumption that houses will need to be bigger to accommodate the increasing number of possessions future households may be expected to have. (Relevant factors here are the future size distribution of households, the rate at which very young and elderly people form separate households, the amount of residential mobility, the growth of secondary dwellings, and so forth.) Future space needs outside a house can (on current indications) be expected to increase as private car ownership increases. Thus a significant aspect of policy (even if termed 'planning' rather than 'housing policy') which can affect the supply and cost of housing, the insistence on a level of density or a type of layout which will accommodate an expected future increase in the ownership and use of cars. Some British local planning authorities are currently insisting that all new dwellings shall have at least one car space : since these authorities are generally situated in the more affluent areas of the country, where car-ownership is comparatively high but where land costs are likewise high, the effect is to increase the cost of new housing.

This question of future needs and standards is complex, but clearly it is one which, *given the long life of houses*, falls within the scope of government responsibility. Politically it may be difficult to impose standards based on future needs if these are very markedly different from the standard of existing housing. Added point is given to this when the new standards involve financial costs which have the effect of further increasing the proportion of households who are unable to meet the full economic cost of housing. Basically, however, the issue is the same as that which was raised when minimum standards of sanitation were introduced in the nineteenth century. If the State imposes standards which involve costs greater than can be borne by lower-income groups it forces upon itself the further responsibility for ensuring that these costs are met in some other way.[1]

Similar issues arise where, for 'non-housing' reasons, a particular costly type of housing development is required, for example in national parks, in remote areas, or on sites of high land cost. Again a

---

[1] An official committee of inquiry calculated that increases in housing standards in England and Wales between 1938/39 and 1947 had raised the cost of a post-war house by 26 per cent (in 1947 prices). The committee commented that in view of the fact that these higher standards were 'the largest single item in the increased cost which is subject to Government influence . . . the policy regarding the standards of accommodation and equipment of new houses should be reviewed afresh in the light of present-day conditions'. Ministry of Health, *The Cost of House-Building* : *First Report of the Committee of Inquiry*, HMSO 1948.
More recently, however, a committee set up to consider standards (rather than costs) have made recommendations which would involve an increase in the cost of a 1961 house of around 10 per cent. Central Housing Advisory Committee, *Homes for Today and Tomorrow*, HMSO, 1961.

policy of restraining the growth of large cities will, in the absence of an equally effective policy restraining demand, have the effect of increasing housing costs possibly to the level where lower income groups are forced to occupy — and over-occupy — houses at a standard well below that which is socially acceptable, or even be driven into institutional accommodation for the homeless.[1]

As these illustrations show, government policies aimed at particular problems can create further problems thus involving an extension of the area over which State responsibility is necessary. State responsibility does not necessarily involve direct State provision. Indeed, even a cursory study of policies in Western Europe and the United States is sufficient to demonstrate that the techniques of direction, control, persuasion, and encouragement are multitudinous. It lies beyond the scope of this paper to analyse these techniques, though reference to a few of them will be made later.

IV. THE SUPPLY OF CAPITAL FOR HOUSING

So far attention has been concentrated on questions of housing costs and standards. These are crucial, but there are many other issues which are inter-related and which warrant discussion. The increased real cost of housing, due to State-imposed minimum standards, does not necessarily involve State intervention in the supply, capital financing, or subsidizing of housing, but in most countries other factors have combined to make some action essential. In particular, the high capital cost of housing and the necessity for long-term credit has meant that capital for housebuilding has had to be obtained in competition with other investments. These other avenues have increased markedly during this century. There are now many demands for short-term credit which provide better returns for the investor.[2] Indeed, with the exception of Switzerland, where special conditions apply, State intervention in the capital market for housing has been necessary in all West European

---

[1] Cf. C. Cockburn, 'Rented Housing in Central London', *The Guardian*, February 21, 1963, reprinted in D. V. Donnison, C. Cockburn, J. B. Cullingworth, and D. A. Nevitt, *Essays on Housing*, Occasional Papers on Social Administration No. 9, Codicote Press, Welwyn, 1964; and J. Greve, *London's Homeless*, Occasional Papers on Social Administration, No. 10, Codicote Press, Welwyn, 1964.

[2] Furthermore, 'over much of western Europe the propensity to save has been reduced by many factors, including policies of social security and full employment, redistribution of incomes and inflation'. *Financing of Housing in Europe, op. cit.*, p. 4.

countries. The character of this intervention, however, has ranged widely from direct public provision of housing, to tax concessions for lenders and special taxes on employers.

The rôle of governments in supplying or influencing the capital market for housing in the post-war period has coincided with an increased concern with national investment programmes. Indeed, in practice, this aspect of housing policy cannot be divorced from general economic policies. Even where, as in East Europe, the State *directs* the national economy, the scale of the housing programme must be determined in the light not only of housing considerations, but also of the availability of resources and other claims on them. Furthermore, since a major objective of government policy throughout Europe has been a rapid rate of economic growth, this has involved a large-scale programme of industrial development, movement of workers (particularly from agriculture to manufacturing industries)[1] and a parallel growth in towns. Quite apart from other factors such as population growth, household formation and rising standards of living, economic policy has involved a commitment to major house-building programmes.[2] (This is another aspect of the immobility of housing — migrant workers cannot take their houses with them.[3]) Planning policies to restrain urban growth and regional migration, to develop new and expanded towns and to promote regional development have likewise committed governments to economic planning and related housing programmes.

V. THE BUILDING INDUSTRY

Even when national economic considerations have forced governments to restrain investment programmes, housing has often received special consideration, either nationally or regionally. In this con-

---

[1] The proportion of the labour force in agriculture has declined in most European countries, *e.g.* in Belgium from 17 to 8 per cent (1930–60); in France from 37 to 23 per cent (1931–60); in Hungary from 53 to 38 per cent (1930–60); in Sweden from 36 to 16 per cent (1930–58); in Great Britain from 6 to 4 per cent (1931–60); in Western Germany from 27 to 14 per cent (1939–60). This trend is continuing; and will involve large housing commitments in many countries. The percentage of the labour force in agriculture ranges from 4 per cent in the United Kingdom to 70 per cent in Rumania. See F. Dewhurst, J. Coppock, and P. L. Yates, *Europe's Needs and Resources*, Twentieth Century Fund, New York, 1961; International Labour Office, *Year Book of Labour Statistics* (Annual); and G. McCrone, Agricultural Integration in Western Europe, *Planning* (P.E.P.), Vol. XXIX, No. 470, April 8, 1963.

[2] See *Major Problems of Government Housing Policy, op. cit.*

[3] Indeed, migration tends to increase the total number of houses required since it breaks up larger households.

nection it is interesting to note that restraints imposed on housing programmes in order to combat problems of inflation and the balance of payments have led to increasing concern about the impact on the development of the building industry. Furthermore, the commitment of governments to long-term housing and other programmes has necessitated an appraisal of the overall demand on the building industry and its capacity to meet this demand. In Britain the indications are that the demand cannot be met without 'drastic changes'. The National Economic Development Council has stressed that 'steps already taken by Government, by public authorities, and by the industry to introduce new techniques must be pressed forward. What is clear is that there is no certainty, in present conditions, that the industry will be able to meet the demands upon it. And the possibility cannot be ruled out that by falling short it may hold back the expansion of the economy as a whole.'[1]

Government has thus become deeply concerned with the promotion of efficiency in the building industry, the expansion of the supply of skilled manpower, the forward planning of construction programmes, and the promotion of industrialized building.

Industrialized building methods can achieve significant increases in construction output only if the number of systems is kept low, since their effectiveness is dependent upon large-scale demand for a limited number of components. With a large number of competing systems the danger is that no one system can attract sufficient orders to maximize the benefits of large-scale production. In countries where there is direct control over (or public ownership of) the construction industry this problem does not arise, but where the construction industry is privately organized there may be a particularly difficult organizational and political problem. This is so at the present time in Britain where there is a very large number of different industrialized building systems. State encouraged oligopoly is not easy to achieve in political terms, particularly since it does not seem clear which system should be selected. The solution which appears to have found acceptance is the establishment of a National Building Agency[2] responsible for research, evaluation, and co-ordination of local and private building programmes.[3]

---

[1] National Economic Development Council, *The Construction Industry*, HMSO, 1964, p. 22. (At present about a half of the demand on the building industry in Britain comes from the public sector. Almost a half of this is for new housing.)

[2] The British tend to be perverse in nomenclature. As with 'Building Societies' the National Building Agency is not itself responsible for building operations.

[3] See White Paper, *A National Building Agency*, Cmnd. 2228, 1963.

The Economic Problems of Housing

A review of problems such as these underlines the importance of political factors. Public control of the building industry or the capital market may seem a logical theoretical answer to particular problems, but where this is not politically acceptable some other *modus operandi* has to be sought. In West European countries planning is of a pragmatic and predictive character, and though such terms as 'national plan' are used, the meaning is different from that in East European countries. The relevant techniques are designed to *influence* rather than to direct. Indeed, it is a declared long-term aim in some countries to re-create a 'free market' in housing. More generally, policy is directed towards supplementing or influencing the market in order to achieve socially desirable objectives.

The distinction between short-term and long-term aims, however, is often an elusive one. Thus rent control though commonly devised as a short-term measure 'pending the return to normal conditions', has, in some countries, a history of forty years. Debates on rent control have been — and still are — heated, not only because of differing views on the character and timing of decontrol proposals but also because of basic disagreement on the adequacy of a free market in privately rented housing. Though one school of thought regards rent control as a necessary temporary expedient in conditions of acute shortage, others look upon it as a desirable permanent technique for maintaining rents at a socially desirable level.

Within the compass of a short paper it is not possible to analyse all the relevant issues, but it is worth noting that rent control is frequently blamed for problems which have much deeper causes — under-occupation, and the decline of private investment in rented housing for example.[1] In several countries where rent control has taken the form of frozen rents the argument that this has led to inadequate maintenance seems to be well justified,[2] though the extreme old age of many of the houses in this sector makes it debatable whether free-market rents would result in a wholesale improvement. This is a field in which evidence is often scanty and arguments are put for-

[1] For research evidence on these questions see J. B. Cullingworth, *Housing in Transition*, Heinemann, 1963, and *Trends in English Housing*, 1965; A. A. Nevitt, *Housing, Taxation and Subsidies* (Nelson, 1966); City of New York City Rent and Rehabilitation Administration, *People, Housing and Rent Control in New York City*, 1964; D. V. Donnison, C. Cockburn, and T. Corlett, *Housing Since The Rent Act*, Occasional Papers in Social Administration, No. 3, Codicote Press, Welwyn, 1961; P. G. Gray and E. Parr, *Rent Act 1957: Report of Inquiry*, Her Majesty's Stationery Office, London (Cmnd. 1246), 1960.

[2] As in Britain, for example. By contrast rent control in New York has been much more flexible and landlords have been allowed to increase rents in order to meet increased maintenance costs.

ward with an intensity in inverse ratio to the amount of evidence. It is clear, however, that governments have been more concerned to accept responsibilities for the supply of new houses than they have for the fate of existing houses. Furthermore, measures designed to encourage the improvement of privately rented old houses may take insufficient account of the changes which have taken place in the pattern of property ownership, in the relative attraction of other investments, in the comparative cost of improving old and building new houses, and so forth.

It is these changed circumstances which have considerably enlarged the rôle of governments in housing. As an early ECE report noted (in relation to the frequent assertion that rent control had had the effect of limiting the total output of housing) : 'In some countries, the true explanation of the low level of new building appears to be in the failure of the state to recognize its responsibilities in conditions quite different from those which ruled in the heyday of the speculative builder, rather than in its failure to create conditions for successful enterprise in building.'[1]

The changed circumstances are such that unaided private providers of *new* housing can meet the needs of only the higher income groups. Nevertheless in some countries it has been argued that by a process of 'filtering' the needs of successively lower income groups are automatically met. This seems an eminently reasonable proposition until it is examined in detail. It then appears that the concept of filtering is by no means a clear one,[2] and that even when it is precisely defined the process is limited in operation by several factors. Among these is the size distribution of the different income groups. The higher income groups constitute a relatively small group, whereas the houses they vacate in preference to new buildings will (at a lower price) be demanded by the much larger groups in the next income tier. The resultant reduction in price will therefore tend to be small. The lower in the price scale at which it is possible to inject new houses, the greater will be the benefit to lower income families. But to the extent that the filtering process is successful the result may tend to be 'self-corrective'. Lower rents and lower purchase prices for

[1] Economic Commission for Europe, *European Rent Policies* (E/ECE/170), 1953, p. 30.
[2] Cf. R. U. Ratcliffe, *Urban Land Economics*, McGraw-Hill, New York, 1949, pp. 321-2 ; E. M. Fisher and L. B. Winnick, 'A Reformation of the Filtering Concept', *Journal of Social Issues*, Vol. VII, 1951, pp. 47-85 ; I. S. Lowry, 'Filtering and Housing Standards', *Land Economics*, Vol. XXXVI, 1960, pp. 362-70 ; W. G. Grigsby, *Housing Markets and Public Policy*, University of Pennsylvania Press, 1963, chapter 3.

owner-buyers will reduce the profitability of the provision and tend to dry up the new supply. Institutional arrangements for lending, and tax reliefs for borrowing may increase the effective demand and thus benefit further groups. Yet, unless there is direct aid to the lowest income groups the supply will cease before prices fall to the level which they can afford.

The dynamics of the situation are, of course, much more complex than this highly capsulated summary may suggest. But it is clear that so far as the lower income groups are concerned direct aid is likely to be more effective in improving housing conditions than reliance on processes of filtering.[1] This is now generally accepted and public policies in many countries are increasingly directed to providing housing assistance to defined needy groups. The improvement in the general housing supply, the desire to reappraise policies in the light of this, and the need to devote more resources to improving the quality of older housing and to redevelop obsolete areas, have all contributed to this. Rehabilitation and redevelopment in particular bring to the fore the problems of the lowest income groups which are not so obvious when attention is concentrated on increasing the total stock of housing. The necessity for government assistance with redevelopment is further underlined by the difficulties of site assembly, and by the high cost of clearance and redevelopment. Without government aid, policies designed to achieve physical urban renewal may actually exacerbate the housing conditions of the poor, since the effect will be a reduction in the availability of low-cost dwellings.

VI. CONCLUSION

Several fields of government responsibility for housing have been briefly analysed or mentioned in this paper. The relevance of these and the practical scope for action varies between countries with different political and economic systems and with different standards of living. Many issues relevant to 'the housing problem' have not been raised — land availability and prices for instance. Nevertheless some indication of the breadth and complexity of the responsibilities of government for 'housing' has been given.

[1] Cf. W. G. Grigsby, *op. cit.*, and A. L. Schorr, *Slums and Social Insecurity*, U.S. Department of Health, Education and Welfare, Social Security Division, Research Report No. 1, 1963.

Chapter 4

A DISAGGREGATED HOUSING MARKET MODEL

BY

PER HOLM

Ekonomisk Planering, Stockholm

I. INTRODUCTION

THE housing market has certain characteristic features, which distinguish it from the majority of other commodity markets. These special features are due to the supply side. A house or flat is a capital good of unusually long life. It is geographically fixed. The production costs per unit are high.

On the majority of local markets, the continuous new production of housing comprises only a negligible proportion of the total supply. The old 'stock' of housing — *i.e.* its size, structure, and standard — is of variable, but usually very great importance in satisfying current demand. The influence of new building on total supply will be of a marginal nature. Moreover, the pattern of residential production as regards different sizes and standards of dwelling units will also be decided essentially by the structure of the old housing stock.

This leads to certain simple hypotheses :

(1) The size and direction of the demand for housing is determined to some extent by the structure of the old housing stock, in that today's preferences are influenced by earlier consumption habits and the current supply. The structure of the housing stock has been determined in its turn by economic development during a past period.

(2) The importance of price as a regulator of the scope and structure of demand and production will be different and more complicated on the housing market than in traditional, aggregated market models.

II. A SIMPLE MODEL OF THE HOUSING MARKET

2.1. Definitions

The supply of housing is measured in dwelling-units, rooms (surfaces), and standard. Dwelling-units and rooms are defined in the

37

traditional manner.[1] The standard of dwelling-units is measured by each unit being classified according to its technical fittings and equipment and its date of construction. Dwelling-units are then grouped according to a combination of these properties in 'standard classes' on a scale where 1 indicates the lowest and (*e.g.*) 8 the highest standard to be found on the market.[2]

On the *consumption side*, the number of *households* and the number of *persons* resident are counted as consumption units. A household consists of all persons living in a unit.[3]

The number of dwelling-units demanded is *ex post* equivalent to the number of households. The housing demand can also be measured in rooms. When the demand for rooms of different standards is added together and weighted with their standard, we get the total housing demand. As a rule, this can only be expressed in monetary units.

The rent (housing cost) is the expense incurred by a household which has full legal possession of a dwelling-unit. In a free market in equilibrium, total housing expenditure is a measure of the total housing demand.

2.2. *Structure of Supply*

Let us assume that we are studying a local housing market and have at a certain time divided the existing dwelling-units into size

---

[1] See, *e.g.*, *U.S. Census of Housing 1960*, Vol. II, Washington, 1963. The room is obviously no exact measure of surface. If the surface of a dwelling-unit is measured in sq. m. we get an exact measure, but surface is from several points of view a less adequate unit for the calculation of, *e.g.*, 'living space standards' than the room. 'After all, the typical family does not seek to buy or rent an abstract quantity of space. The space that it acquires must have certain attributes : the envelope must be distinct and separate from others, all internal space must be interconnected, it must be equipped to take care of the nutritional needs of the family. In short, the adoption of such a unit of account takes cognizance of most (but by no means all) of the realities of the housing market.' L. Winnick, *American Housing and Its Use*, New York, 1957, p. 12.

[2] An ordinal standard scale created in this way will naturally be inexact in many respects. In Sweden, however, differences in the equipment, the technical standard — and also the planning — of different units are due to the buildings having been erected at different times. The combination of data on facilities and year of building therefore gives a useful scale of standard that can be set against the evaluations of the consumers. Obviously, however, the consumer's assessment is not based entirely on the unit's 'technical' standard. Other less tangible properties, above all those connected with the residential environment, such as type of house, town plans and location, have an important influence on the consumer's choice between units. The latter type of differences in standard has been disregarded in the following analysis.

[3] The demand for units is determined by the propensity of different demographic groups to form households. This propensity is measured by household quotients. These quotients can be in their turn assumed to be determined by — in addition to the demographic factors — incomes, prices, and preferences.

classes — as reckoned by rooms — and 'standard' classes — as reckoned by facilities and year of building. The supply of units on the market can then be shown as illustrated by the diagram in Fig. 1. Each square can be taken to correspond to a 'commodity' (= 'dwelling-unit type' D_{11} D_{21} D_{31}), belonging to the commodity group 'dwelling-unit'.

If we calculate the mean rent for each type of unit (square), we can assume that the 'balanced market rent' will increase within each size group with rising standards and within each standard group by increasing size (no. of rooms). This means that average rents on the market for different types of unit could be illustrated as in Fig. 2. We call this shape the 'rent surface' for the rent structure of the market.

Fig. 3 shows an example of the structure of supply in 1960, taken from a medium-sized Swedish town. The example shows that supply is characteristically concentrated in certain sizes and standard classes. This skewness in the supply is of decisive importance for the adjustment of the market to changes in demand.[1]

2.3. *The Structure of Demand*

If at a given time we record on a local housing market the number of households and the housing market is in equilibrium, we can obviously describe how the total demand from the households breaks down into units of different sizes and standards by using the same simple matrix as for supply, Fig. 3. The only difference is that it will now be the number of households (=the total number of dwelling-units minus the number of empty units) that is reported in the different squares of the diagram.

According to the traditional view, the housing demand is supposed to be determined by demographic factors — the size and structure of the population — the incomes and preferences of households, and the prices of dwellings and all other commodities.

A number of studies have shown that housing preferences differ significantly between persons (owners/tenants) of different age and marital status and between different sizes of household. For a given type of household, however, housing preferences are influenced also by different environmental factors, including above all the structure of the housing supply on the market to which demand is directed.

---

[1] Obviously, the uneven distribution shown can be traced at least partly to the class division used, particularly as regards the standard of facilities and the year of building.

With the help of the analysis schedule, we can describe very simply how different groups of households are distributed on the market and measure the correlation between consumption in standard of housing and consumption in housing space (cf. Fig. 4). The schedule has thus been used to study how housing consumption varies with the essential factors of size of household, age, and income. (See also Fig. 6.) Under certain assumptions the differences obtained can be interpreted as determined by differences in demand.

In statistical studies on how the consumption of housing varies with income, it is possible to calculate the income elasticity of both space-demand and standard-demand.

As long as the analysis relates to a given market at a certain point in time, the supply is given and the differences in consumption between various groups can — with optimum adjustment — be regarded as determined by demand.[1] For an economically and demographically uniform group it is possible to measure the spread of units of different sizes and standard, and we can here speak perhaps of 'individual specific preferences'.

Regardless of what factors are measured, however, the 'choice' of households and thus the housing consumption are largely determined by the supply of units at any given time. The structure of supply, in its turn, is more the result of economic development during the preceding half-century than the current situation. Nor is this all. It is possible that the structure of supply has an independent influence on the preferences of households and thus on the size of demand.

III. ANALYSIS OF THE INTERPLAY BETWEEN SUPPLY AND DEMAND ON THE HOUSING MARKET

3.1. *Changed Income — unchanged Structure of Household*

Let us now use our analysis schedule to study how the housing market reacts to changes in income. The following assumptions are made as regards the initial situation :

On a local housing market, the supply of dwelling-units has been recorded in a size/standard matrix of the type presented in Section 2. The market is 'homogeneous' in the sense that there are equal numbers of units in each size/standard square. There are as many households as there are units and the housing market is in a state of balance,

---

[1] When the analysis schedule is used to compare two different local markets, it should be possible to select demographically and economically equivalent groups and study how the supply, the structure of the housing stock influences demand.

totally and on each sub-market. The relative steps on the standard scale and the size scale as measured by the housing cost (rent) are in the initial position of equal size. The number of households is assumed to remain unchanged throughout the period of analysis. The income elasticity of the housing demand is positive and identical for all households.

Let us now suppose that an increase in income occurs among the households and that this increase is relatively of equal size for all households.

The result of an income increase is naturally that the households seek larger units and units of a higher standard. They are concerned to move upwards and to the right in our standard model (cf. Figs. 5 and 6). It is probable that demand has a relatively slow 'rate of reaction' to the income increase. Certain households 'on the margin' immediately seek a new dwelling-unit, while others follow after a certain time — depending partly on the size of the income increase.

It is now conceivable that the move upwards occurs in different directions. The households can seek first a better standard or more space or a combination of these. A simple numerical example can illustrate the pattern of reaction.

The number of units and households in each square is 100. After the increase in income, 30 of these households desire new and better housing. Ten of these want only to raise their standard, 10 only want more space, while 10 want to take both these steps. The result is shown in Fig. 7.

According to our premises, the number of households desiring to move from a standard square to a higher square is the same over the whole market.[1] It is assumed for the present that rents are not influenced. After the move, the number of units demanded will be the same for all types of unit except in standard and size-classes 1 and 6. A surplus of units will arise in squares $D_{11}-D_{51}$ along the x-axis and $D_{11}-D_{15}$ along the y-axis. The reserve of units is concentrated on the smallest and worst types. The surplus is greater in square D_{11} than in other squares, as no move upwards from 'worse' types of unit is here conceivable. In a similar way, the surplus demand for the 'corner units' will only be half the demand for other marginal units.

A necessary condition for the switch taking place and the balance of the market being retained, with unchanged rents in the old stock,

[1] This presupposes a certain relationship between the income elasticity of housing demand and the difference in rent between different types of unit.

is naturally that new residential production should be of such a volume and distribution over the different types of dwellings, and made available at such prices, as to permit a move upwards from the units in the border zone to a sufficient extent, but not to hinder the total upwards adjustment.

This latter condition is unlikely to be fulfilled in one important respect : opportunities for increasing the supply of large units of low standard are limited, and in fact can only exist in the fusion of small units.[1] To the extent that the supply of units is changed by new production, the new units belong predominantly to the highest standard class.

If the supply of large units of lower standard cannot be adapted to the increased demand, the demand in the upper part of the matrix (cf. Fig. 5) must be transferred to other parts of the stock, *e.g.* further upwards or to the left. The demand pressure on large units of low standard will probably be transferred to units of higher standard and smaller units.

In spite of an unchanged number of households, we now have a much greater demand for housing as reckoned in rooms and standard. It is possible under given conditions quantitatively to calculate how additional housing should be distributed over sizes of unit for the adjustment process to proceed at unchanged rents — and theoretically also to what extent the standard of fittings, etc. can be increased. The value of the total increase in housing demand will be equal to the difference between the rent value of the increment and the value of the units made vacant.

We can take a step in the direction of a more realistic analysis by assuming that the income increased supply of cheap, small units caused by the move upwards will lead to an 'explosion' of households, *i.e.* the formation of new households.[2] If we drop the assumption of unchanged rents, then a change of rents in the units liberated can be expected to stimulate such an 'explosion'. Only in the special

---

[1] Changes in the supply by means of conversion seem to be common in the United States. 'In the last two decades a significant proportion of the increase in the housing stock came from conversions of existing structures.' L. Grebler, D. Blank, and L. Winnick, *Capital Formation in Residential Real Estate*, Princeton, 1956, pp. 87–88. Conversions in Sweden do not seem as yet to have attained as great an importance as in the United States during the period 1940–50, but they have had an important influence on housing production during the post-war years.

[2] We can refer in this context to the income elasticity of household formation or of the household quotients. Measurements made in Sweden since the war have shown that the formation of households by, particularly, unmarried persons has a relatively high 'income elasticity'. Household formation can also be influenced by increased incomes leading to an increased marriage rate. See P. Holm, *Bostadsmarknaden i ett extanderande samhälle*, Stockholm, 1964.

case when the newly formed households demand liberated or newly built units will a balance be created at unchanged rents.[1]

By our original assumptions, the rent structure of the market has not altered with the changes in supply and demand so far discussed, other than that the rent for the newly built units corresponds to the increased willingness to pay rent in the border stratum resulting from the income increase.

The argument can be summed up as follows : an income increase for the households leads to an increased demand for larger and better fitted units, which leads in its turn to an increased demand for newly built units, stimulating also the formation of new households. At the same time, it provides an impulse for the clearance of substandard housing and the conversion of small units.[2]

3.2. *Changes in Demand by an Increase in the Number of Households*

Our analysis so far has been based on special premisses. We have therefore been able to assume that the rent structure of the market remained unchanged during the process of adjustment. Let us now consider certain cases in which it is necessary explicitly to take into consideration the formation of rents.

Let us suppose that the number of households on a given market increases, *e.g.* by immigration. The price elasticity of the number-demand is assumed to be low and the supply of newly built units sufficient to correspond to the increased demand. The newly built units are assumed to belong to the highest standard-class. The structure of the immigrants — their distribution by age and marital status — and their incomes are assumed to be the same as in the base population. This will mean that their propensity to form households and their housing preferences will agree with those of the base population.

The result will be competition for the existing units. This will provoke tendencies to price increases in the old housing stock. Owing to price-rigidity, prohibitive rents, or the inertia of the existing households, the demand which cannot be satisfied in the old stock will now be directed towards newly built but on the average more expensive and therefore smaller units than the average size in the older stock.[3]

Tendencies to changes in price structure — in the relation between

---

[1] In reality, there arises the further complication that the 'explosion' of households changes their structure and thus the scale of preferences for the 'exploded' households.

[2] This, of course, says nothing as to the relative importance of income changes for the total housing demand, as compared with other demand factors.

[3] Implicit here is an assumption that the newly built units of a given standard cannot be erected or offered at lower prices than units in the existing stock.

prices for units in different sizes and standard classes — will naturally become more marked if the assumption of an increase in the number of households is combined with an assumption of an increased demand for space and standard due to an income increase among the households occupying the existing stock.

In the latter case, the additional demand for newly built units stemming from the immigrants will be directed towards smaller and thus cheaper units than the demand from the part of the base population that desires to increase its housing consumption following an increase in income. The households in the latter group whose demand is directed at newly produced units can as a rule be assumed to have on the average higher incomes and/or preferences for standard and space than the average household. It follows that with a given rate of income growth and given prices for the newly built units, the distribution of new production over sizes of dwelling-unit will vary with the volume of immigration. The greater the immigration, the fewer rooms per unit in the new production.

If the structure of supply is like that in Sweden and to an even greater extent in Eastern Europe, *i.e.* if there is an almost complete lack of large units of medium standard, the increased demand for higher standards and larger units that arises with an income increase among the households living in small units of poor standard (bottom left corner of matrix) can be satisfactorily met only by the demand-move in the matrix taking place upwards. The realized demand is displaced in the system, and the final effect is to reinforce the tendency to a displacement of demand in the direction of smaller units in the new production as described above for the homogeneous market.

The course of the adjustment process is obviously decided in these more complicated cases by how fast the supply of new units can be adapted to the change in demand, by the degree of price mobility (or price rigidity) in the stock of old housing and by the price elasticity of demand for different groups of household. Our knowledge of these factors is so incomplete that it is hardly meaningful in such cases to use our diagram as the basis for a more precise model. I will add here only certain general reflections as to how different factors can be thought to influence the 'rent structure' of the market.

3.3. *The Rent Structure*

On a market of the type under consideration, there is a strong correlation between the size and structure of supply and the 'rent structure' of the market. The rent structure can then be defined as the shape of the surface drawn in on Fig. 2. If we select a diagonal in the size-standard matrix and for each type of unit (square) calculate the rent per unit, then this variation in rent can be reproduced in an ordinary diagram. The line that joins together the rent for these units of different sizes and standard can be termed a 'rent standard line'.

Fig. 8 gives examples of such a 'rent standard line' from two Swedish towns.

If the housing market is 'homogeneous' in the sense previously assumed, the shape of the rent surface and the size of the 'steps' along the standard-scale and the size-scale should not be influenced by movements arising from income increases of the type assumed in Figs. 4 and 5. This applies on the supposition that the units liberated are regarded as obsolete.

If, however, we discard our assumption of a homogeneous supply, *i.e.* the supply of units in the different squares varies, then income increases should lead to changes in the number-demand for different types of unit which will produce changes in the 'steps' on the size-standard scale of rent. There arises a tendency for rent increases to occur in the types of unit where the supply is small. If a balance is to be reached for these types of unit, there must be a certain increase in rents. With the types of unit in ample supply, on the other hand, rents tend to fall as a result of the move, the departures exceed the new occupants, etc.

Let us now assume, on the other hand, that we are comparing two markets with an identical supply but with different distributions of income among the household. This leads to different rent structures. In community A, where the distribution of income is assumed to be very uneven, with a low rent payment capacity in the lowest income brackets and a high rent payment capacity in the highest brackets, the slope of the rent surface (rent standard line) will be steeper than in community B, where the total income of households is the same as in A, but the distribution of income is more even. The slope of the rent standard line can with a given structure of household and income be assumed to be dependent upon the structure of the stock and elasticity of the supply. A small supply of high-standard units or inertia in the supply of new housing will lead to a steep rent standard line. This makes more difficult the process of upward adjustment with rising incomes. A different structure of supply can lead to a flatter rent standard line, increasing the chances of a rapid rise in housing standard following income increases.

45

If we disregard such differences in income distribution, it is clear, however, that the number and price of the new units will influence decisively the formation of prices throughout the chain. The supply of new units in sufficient numbers and at relatively low prices will stimulate the move upwards and tend to reduce the price of older housing.

Special problems arise on the market when the demand for units increases rapidly above the previous level and new building on a large scale is required to meet the greater demand. The supply of housing is in the short run relatively inelastic and can usually be best increased by new production. If the increase in demand is largely a result of the income increase, there will arise a demand pressure which — in agreement with our previous analysis — will be greatest for the units having the highest standard. This tends to change the rent structure so that the rent standard line slopes more steeply. To create a balance, the tendency of households to increase their space and standard must be held back. This demands a higher rent increase on units of higher standard than on others.[1]

IV. AN EXAMPLE OF THE USE OF THE ANALYSIS SCHEDULE

4.1. *To Calculate the Importance of Different Factors influencing a Household's Choice between Units of Different Size and Standard on a Given Market*

Let us now use our analysis schedule to study empirically how households of different kinds move on the housing market following changes in income. This analysis can make use of 'indifference maps', in which the standard and size of the dwelling-unit are regarded as two different commodities. The consumer (household) can buy different combinations of space and standard, depending on his income, his preferences, and the price of the unit. We are seeking the combination of size and standard that is optimal for a given household.

In Fig. 9 we have taken a size-standard diagram for a total housing market and joined together the squares (types of unit) with the same rents into 'iso-rental lines'.[2] Upwards and to the right in the diagram

[1] An analysis along these lines can lead also to certain conclusions as to the demand pressure created by rent control.

[2] The rent cost curves have been drawn in the diagram as straight lines. Their shape may of course differ from a straight line, but if they were non-linear the following conclusions would not be altered.

means higher rent. We have then drawn in the indifference curves.[1] These indicate that a certain type of household is indifferent to the different squares — *i.e.* regard as of equal value the types of dwelling-unit — that are cut by the same indifference line. A household prepared to expend a given sum on housing, *i.e.* which is on a given iso-rental line, will try to attain the highest indifference curve, *i.e.* the tangential point between the iso-rental line and an indifference curve. With a higher income and greater willingness to pay rent it is possible to reach a higher iso-rental line and a higher indifference curve.

We know that with a given expenditure a household of four persons will have a greater preference for space than one of two persons. The 'consumption curves' of households following income increases can therefore be assumed to differ in appearance. Price changes between size and standard will change the slopes of the iso-rental lines and therefore the 'consumption curves' of households following income increases will also differ in appearance.

In Fig. 10 A–C there are given the results of a survey in which the lines drawn in can be said to correspond to the 'income-consumption curves' of different groups of households. The material for these examples is taken from the Swedish town whose housing market was illustrated in Fig. 3.

The material was processed as follows. The standard classes registered were assigned the values 1–8. The size of the units has been measured, as in the diagram, by the number of rooms. The households were then distributed after the following variables: number of occupants, age of the head of household, and income of household (husband and wife) before taxation.

For each group of households there were then calculated the mean standard change in standard points and the mean space standard in rooms. The three diagrams in Fig. 10 sum up these results, which should be regarded primarily as a suggestion for deeper analysis.

In Fig. 10A there has been selected for analysis the group 'married couples aged 35–49'. Households have been distributed by size (number of occupants) and by income. (The diagram shows only the mean values for seven income groups.) For each household group the space points have been plotted in along the x-axis and the standard points along the y-axis. The points for each household group have been joined together to make an 'income-consumption' curve.

[1] The convexity of the indifference curves is invariant for all monotonic increasing transformations of the utility functions.

The results are clear enough. Large households have higher preferences for space than small households, this is obvious. But if we compare a certain type of household, we find that with low incomes an increased income means primarily a consumption of more standard. Up to an income level which lies between the lower quartile and the median the lines run almost perpendicular, the increased income means only a higher standard and not more space. With incomes around and over the median, space increases markedly and the curves bend off to the right.

The convex shape of the curves can naturally be explained by the structure of supply; if a family wants to raise its standard at a 'reasonable' cost, it has no real choice.[1] But the structure of the supply of dwelling-units between which households with low incomes have to choose is a product of the housing market of the 'Twenties and Thirties'. What factors at that time prevented a more differentiated supply on the Swedish housing market?

A current situation survey of the type reported here can naturally be supplemented by a study of how households have shifted between units of differing size and standard over a period of time.

Such studies have been made and confirm the picture given here of the pattern of movement. It can be added that movements seem in the majority of cases to involve households shifting one or at the most two steps up on the size-standard scale. It should be added also that it is often difficult to interpret the results of an analysis of this type on a market as imperfect as the housing market. Such problems of interpretation are particularly difficult if there is an excess demand. One household group or income group may be further away from its optimum than another.

---

[1] As mentioned before, the shape of the curves is partly dependent on the chosen scale of the 'standard' scale.

Holm — A Disaggregated Housing Market Model

ANALYSIS SCHEDULE

RENT STRUCTURE OF A LOCAL HOUSING MARKET

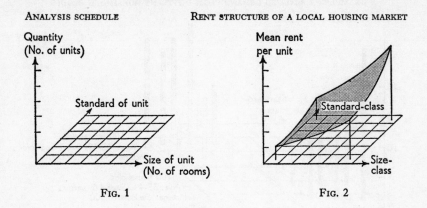

FIG. 1

FIG. 2

VÄXJÖ 1958. NO. OF UNITS IN DIFFERENT SIZE- AND STANDARD-CLASSES

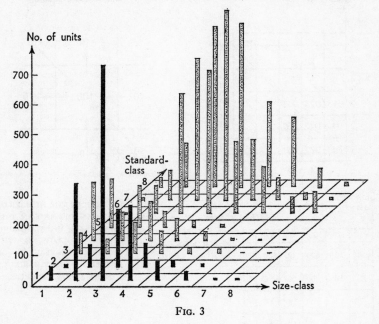

FIG. 3

49

EXAMPLE OF REALIZED DEMAND FROM DIFFERENT HOUSEHOLD GROUPS

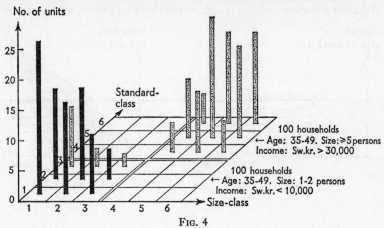

FIG. 4

SCHEMATIC DIAGRAM OVER MOVEMENTS OF HOUSEHOLDS ON A HOUSING
MARKET AS THE RESULT OF AN INCOME INCREASE

A. On total housing market

B. To and from one size
and standard square

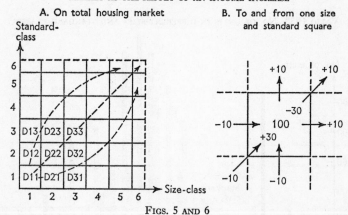

FIGS. 5 AND 6

A. Net change - 30 households
(30%) move from each
size- and standard-class

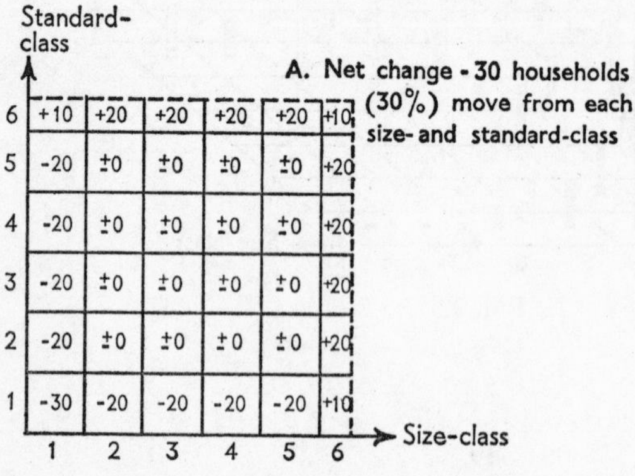

CHANGE IN THE NUMBER OF
UNITS IN DEMAND IN DIF-
FERENT SIZE- AND STANDARD-
CLASSES FOLLOWING THE
UPWARDS MOVEMENT OF
HOUSEHOLDS AS THE RESULT
OF AN INCOME INCREASE

FIG. 7

EXAMPLES OF RENT STANDARD LINES

A. ACTUAL RENT STANDARD LINES IN 1960: TWO MEDIUM SIZED TOWNS, VÄSTERÅS AND SKELLEFTEÅ

B. RENT STANDARD LINES FOR TWO COMMUNITIES WITH THE SAME SUPPLY BUT DIFFERING STRUCTURES OF INCOME

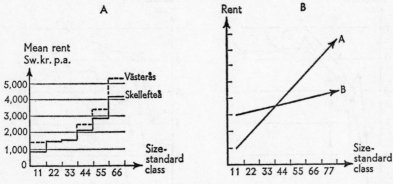

FIG. 8

THEORETICAL EXPLANATION OF HOW HOUSEHOLDS CHANGE THEIR DEMAND FOR SIZE OF UNIT FOLLOWING CHANGES IN RENT COSTS AND INCOME

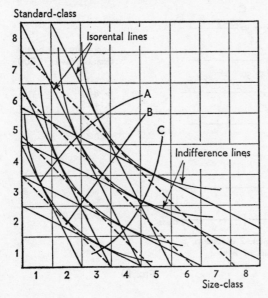

FIG. 9

51

VÄXJÖ 1958. EXPANSION PATH FOR SIZE AND STANDARD IN DIFFERENT AGE AND INCOME GROUPS

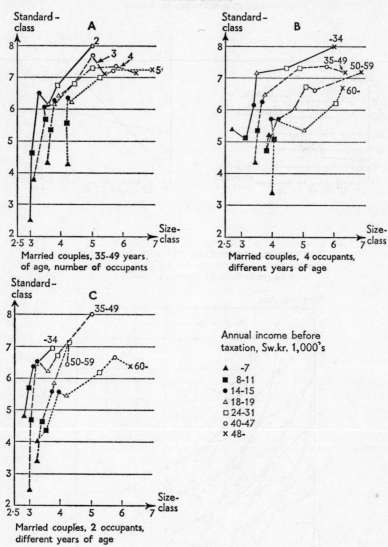

Married couples, 35-49 years. of age, number of occupants

Married couples, 4 occupants, different years of age

Married couples, 2 occupants, different years of age

Annual income before taxation, Sw.kr. 1,000's

▲ -7
■ 8-11
● 14-15
△ 18-19
□ 24-31
○ 40-47
× 48-

FIG. 10

Chapter 5

RENT CONTROL AS AN INSTRUMENT OF HOUSING POLICY

BY

ASSAR LINDBECK

The Stockholm School of Economics

I. INTRODUCTION

Two main problems are discussed in the present paper : (1) the usefulness of rent control as an instrument of housing policy, and hence the effects of such control, and (2) the possibilities of realizing the goals of housing policy by other methods, without rent control.

Whereas price control in most markets of the economy has usually been confined to periods of war, or immediately after wars, government control of rents tends in some countries to become a more or less permanent phenomenon. To some extent this may be explained by well-known, rather specific properties of the market for housing. Thus, reference is often made to the limited elasticity of supply of housing in the short run due to the smallness of annual production of new dwellings as compared to the existing stock of dwellings (partly because of the long durability of houses), the geographical immobility of dwellings and the high capital-output ratio of housing. It is also often believed that demand for housing is characterized by a combination of a rather high income elasticity and a low or moderate price elasticity (particularly with respect to the *number* of dwellings demanded).

All these factors, to the extent they are present, tend to make short-run equilibrium rents rather high (compared to the long-run equilibrium level) during periods of rapid economic growth and substantial shifts in the inter-regional distribution of population, with considerable income and capital gains by house-owners as a result. Undoubtedly, these circumstances are often regarded as arguments for rent control. Moreover, due to the limited availability of land with good location, prices tend to rise for such property when cities are expanding, with resultant continuous capital gains for the owners. However, in some countries, another reason for the reliance on rent control is no doubt the limited consideration given in the design and implementation of housing policy to the importance of the price system for the functioning of the housing market.

II. A SIMPLE MARSHALLIAN MODEL

A simple Marshallian equilibrium model may, in spite of the drastic simplifications implied, serve as a frame of reference for the subsequent discussion. In diagram I below, the stock-supply of dwellings at a given moment is denoted by the vertical SS-line. (The problem of aggregation is neglected here.) DD is the (stock-) demand curve ; this is less elastic if the volume demanded is measured by the number of dwellings than if size and equipment-standard of dwellings are also included in the volume component. Let us further assume that rent happens to be r^1, and an equilibrium (at point a) therefore exists in the *housing market*.

The flow-supply curve for dwellings during a given period is assumed to be UU (measured from the SS-line). Thus, it is assumed that house-building is stimulated by higher rents.[1] Below r_1 incentives are created for disinvestment in housing. As UU passes through point a, equilibrium is assumed to prevail even in the *house-building* market, in the sense that no incentives exist to increase or reduce the stock of dwellings ; thus long-run, or stationary, equilibrium is assumed to prevail.

Suppose now that demand for housing increases, whether because of population increase, expansion in *per capita* income or changes in preferences of households, and that the new demand curve is $D'D'$ Momentary equilibrium is then at point b at rent r_2, whereas *short-run* (one-period) *equilibrium* is at point c at rent r_3. The position of the *long-run* (stationary) *equilibrium* depends on whether the housing market is a constant-cost industry or not. The presumption seems to be that it is an increasing-cost industry. The reason is that increased demand for housing raises rents, and hence land values, for the existing stock of houses with better location than new houses. (As house-building in long-run equilibrium equals reinvestment, it does not seem to be very important for the position of the long-run equilibrium position whether the house-*building* industry is a constant-cost or not.

---

[1] This assumption about a rising flow-supply curve for dwellings is consistent with several different market forms — not only pure competition but also, for instance, monopolistic competition if r is defined as the average rent in the market (or in a given submarket).

Cost conditions in the house-building industry, reflected in level and slope of the flow-supply curve, greatly influences the *speed* by which the long-run equilibrium is approached, however.) Hence, the long-run equilibrium position will presumably not be at point *d*, with the housing stock S^nS^n, but at a point along the $D'D'$-curve to the north-west of point *d*.

Let us, to begin with, assume that the dynamic properties of the market are such that rents start rising due to excess demand for housing, created by the assumed shift in the demand curve, and that a new short-term equilibrium in the housing market at the end of the period attained at point *c*, rent being r_3. At the beginning of the next period stock-supply is given by the $S'S'$-curve. The new flow-supply curve is U' (the part of the curve to the left of $S'S'$ is not shown in the diagram). The short-run equilibrium at the end of this period is at point *e* at rent r_4. The stock-supply and flow-supply curves in the next period are $S''S''$ and U'', respectively, and the process repeats itself until a new long-run equilibrium is attained.

The diagram illustrates *inter alia* the idea that momentary and

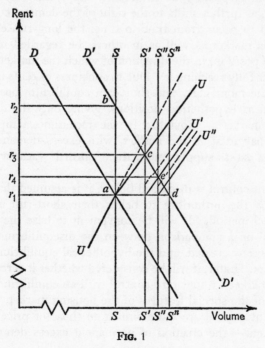

FIG. 1

short-run equilibrium rents can be rather high (compared to the long-run equilibrium rent) in a market of this type, and that the achievement of a new long-run equilibrium, *i.e.* equilibrium in both the housing market and the house-building market, may take rather a long time (each period may be thought of as, say, a year). During the approach to long-run equilibrium, 'excess profits' will be earned in house investment, and income and capital gains will accrue to owners of houses produced earlier, particularly houses with good location.

If prices of production factors are driven up by the increased building activity, the flow-supply curve in the first period might look something like the broken curve starting from point a instead of the curve UU, which means, of course, that the short-run equilibrium rent would be higher than r_3. Particularly if prices of production factors are sticky downwards, the flow-supply curves in later periods would also be higher than indicated by the curves U' and U''; this is indicated by the broken curves in the diagram. This would prolong the process of reaching a long-run equilibrium position. (Of course, productivity increases in house-building works in the opposite direction, by pushing down the flow-supply curves.)

However, as further shifts to the right of the demand curve would be expected to occur from time to time, the long-run equilibrium may, in this market as well as in others, be regarded mainly as a *hypothetical* position, in the direction of which the market is moving without ever fully reaching it. Due to stickiness of rents in the short run, even the momentary and short-run equilibrium positions may be regarded as hypothetical positions, giving only the direction in which the market is moving. In the meantime, temporary disequilibria may exist in the market, with excess demand (housing shortage) or excess supply (more than 'normal' vacancy rates) for housing.

When rent control is discussed below, it is assumed that rents are regulated by the authorities to below their short-run equilibrium levels in each period. It will be convenient to base the analysis of rent control on a comparison between the disequilibrium situation which is thereby created, and the hypothetical equilibrium situation in the market. Later, it will be considered whether it is reasonable to identify a market without rent control with an equilibrium market.

In spite of the special features of the housing market, the experiences of rent control are quite similar to those of price control in other markets — the creation of permanent excess demand (short-

56

ages), queues, limitations to consumer sovereignty, black and grey markets, limitations to incentives for producer efficiency, difficulties in finding criteria for distributing goods among consumers, etc. Actually, due to some special properties of the housing market, particularly the long life of dwellings, these problems are in some respects, as pointed out below, more severe than in many other markets.

III. THE OBJECTIVES OF RENT CONTROL

The effects of rent control depend, of course, on the control system. Instead of analysing a number of different systems, the present paper deals with the type of control used for two decades in Sweden, according to which rents cannot be raised without the approval of the authorities. However, it is hoped that the subsequent discussion will be relevant in the main for most control systems where rents are regulated below their equilibrium levels, so that excess demand for housing (housing shortage) prevails. The exposition will be illustrated with empirical data from the Swedish housing market during the period of rent control, mainly in footnotes.[1]

To evaluate the usefulness of rent control it is necessary to specify the motives for (retaining) such control under peace-time conditions. Even though the motives vary somewhat, the following seem to be of importance in several countries. It is obvious, however, that many of these arguments played very little, if any, rôle when rent control was originally introduced. Thus, many of them have been invented during the course of rent control, mainly as arguments for not *removing* rent control.

(1) To stimulate general housing demand in order to achieve a

---

[1] In the Swedish system, rents in houses built before the introduction of the control system are regulated on the basis of rents at the time when the control system was introduced (*i.e.* in 1942). In houses built later, rents are based on actual production costs, including schematically calculated costs on equity capital, and running costs.

Approval to increase rents is given by the authorities only as compensation for schematically calculated increases in running costs and interest rates on borrowed funds. Between 1939 and 1963 rents (excl. fuel and light) in the cost of living index have risen by 80 per cent while prices of consumer goods in general have risen by 170 per cent (including rents). At the same time average wage rates (per hour) for industrial workers, as well as *per capita* disposable income of the household sector, have risen by about 450 per cent.

Thus, real income in terms of housing has risen by 205 per cent while real income in terms of other commodities has risen by 105 per cent. All figures in the paper are, if not otherwise pointed out, from official Swedish Statistics.

high and rapidly increasing housing consumption of the population as a whole. (The general housing consumption goal.)

(2) To keep down rents of *new* houses in order to stabilize costs and volume of house construction. (The construction market stabilization goal.)

(3) To prevent a (considerable) redistribution of income and wealth from tenants to house-owners (the general income-distribution goal) and also to achieve a more equitable distribution of real income among tenants (the inter-tenant income distribution goal).

(4) To help low-income families, particularly such families with children, to compete in the housing market with other household categories. Thus, the authorities want to guarantee these families a larger fraction of total housing consumption than they would get in a market without rent control. (The housing consumption distribution goal.)

(5) To direct total demand for housing consumption in favour of large well-equipped dwellings. (The housing-demand composition goal.)

(6) To dampen tendencies to cost inflation. (The general anti-inflation goal.)

IV. THE GENERAL HOUSING CONSUMPTION GOAL

The idea that rent control could contribute to a higher general housing standard, often implied in defence of rent control, is paradoxical. As at a given point of time a country's general (average) level of housing consumption depends on the stock of existing dwellings, the level and structure of rents have no immediate effect on the general housing standard.[1] Hence, when the removal of rent control is often criticized, by the adherents of rent control, on the ground that this would reduce general housing consumption, a confusion is probably made between quantity of housing *demanded* (which undoubtedly would be reduced) and housing *consumption* (which for the population as a whole, approximately speaking, would not be immediately affected). *Or* it is not the immediate effects that are considered.

However, rent control results in an expansion of tenants' consump-

---

[1] Neglecting short-run variations in the vacancy rate and also neglecting rapid changes in the rate of conversions of apartments to other uses, such as offices.

tion of other commodities, for which supply more or less automatically adjusts to changes in demand. This phenomenon is due both to a conventional income effect and to a 'spill over' of unsatisfied demand in the housing market to other markets (assuming that not *all* unsatisfied demand for housing results in increased 'involuntary' saving). Thus, it is not the tenants' housing consumption which is stimulated by rent control but rather their consumption of other commodities.

On the macro level, the increased demand by tenants for consumer goods other than housing, due to rent control, is to some extent counteracted by reduced demand by house-owners. However, this reduction can be expected to be smaller than the expansion of demand by tenants, as a considerable fraction of changes in income of house-owners automatically goes to tax payments (in Sweden the marginal tax rate can be expected to be at least 50 per cent for private house-owners), and the marginal propensity to consume can hardly be expected to be higher for house-owners than for tenants (possibly the opposite).[1]

Thus, when rent control is said to be an appropriate means of increasing a country's general (average) housing consumption, it must be the effects after some time, hence via house-building, that are considered. However, the argument is still difficult to follow. If rent control keeps down rents below their 'free market' level not only in existing houses but also in new ones, rent control would, of course, have negative effects on house-building, assuming that this is positively related to the profitability of new houses.

As existing dwellings in a system with rent control, and hence with excess demand for housing, can be let out (at regulated rents) practically regardless of quality, the incentives, as well as the availability of liquid funds, for maintenance will, as is often pointed out, presumably be rather low. Hence the stock of dwellings can be expected to deteriorate (unless the control system is constructed so as to stimulate maintenance expenditures). Even via these effects rent control tends, in the long run, to have a negative influence on general housing standards.

The negative effects of rent control on general housing standards are, at least in principle, accentuated by the incentives created by rent control to demolish houses and use the land for something else, such as office buildings (if office rents are not efficiently controlled too) or possibly new apartment houses (if the rent control system keeps

[1] Wealth effects on consumption are neglected.

profitability lower in older houses than in new ones).¹ At the same time, it is probable that rents in some low-quality houses will be kept *up* (*i.e.* above their 'free market' levels) by the general excess demand for housing created by rent control. There will thus be less incentive to renew such houses. Thus, rent control could lead to renewals in the 'wrong' part of the housing market.

In some countries, where private investment in housing has fallen considerably during the period of rent control, house investment by non-profit organizations, such as public authorities and co-operatives, has instead expanded considerably.² Such shifts in the ownership of the stock of houses have important implications for the performance of housing policy. For instance, we cannot be so sure any longer that the volume of house-building is positively related to the profitability of new houses, as we have no generally accepted theory for the behaviour of co-operative and public enterprises in the housing market, particularly not for how they would behave in a market without rent control. Moreover, there are no guarantees that non-profit enterprises will adjust rents, particularly not in old houses, to the equilibrium rent structure.

To know how house investment by non-profit enterprises would be influenced by the removal of rent control, we have to know both their price and their investment behaviour. If they behave as private enterprises in both respects, they will of course expand housing investment if rent control is removed, provided this removal leads

---

¹ In Sweden the number of demolitions have (in 1965) induced the authorities to introduce regulations which prevent house-owners from pulling down old houses, if these, in the view of the authorities, include dwellings appropriate for housing purposes. After some time this will probably result in the houses deteriorating.

² In Sweden, which is an extreme example in this respect, the ratio between private, public, and co-operative housing investment, and in the long run also the distribution of the *stock* of dwellings between different kinds of owners, have changed drastically during the post-war, rent control period. While in 1939 88 per cent of all new dwellings in apartment houses (with more than two apartments) were private, and the private share in 1945 was still as high as 65 per cent, the figure in 1964 was only about 20 per cent. Of the 80 per cent of new dwellings which are now (1965) non-private about 43 per cent are co-operative and 57 per cent are owned by municipalities or other non-profit organizations. This drastic change has affected the structure of ownership of the stock of dwellings in Sweden. Since 1945 the private share of dwellings in apartment houses has fallen from 80 to about 50 per cent, which means that about 25 per cent of all dwellings (including residential houses) are now public or co-operative. (It can be pointed out that the rent control system is not the only factor behind these altered proportions. It has, since World War II, been a conscious policy of the government, as well as of many municipalities, to promote public and co-operative housing in Sweden. Some of the means have been more favourable credits for public and co-operative housing than for private housing, and favouring non-profit enterprises in town and city planning, for instance when municipalities decide who is allowed ready-planned land for building purposes.)

to higher rents not only in older houses but also in new ones. If, on the other hand, they keep rents unchanged even after the removal of rent control we can feel confident that they expand housing investment only if they are stimulated in their investment behaviour by the size of excess demand for dwellings rather than by profitability. (If rents in private dwellings are raised, but rents are unchanged in non-profit enterprises, we would expect excess demand for dwellings in non-profit houses to rise at the same time as total excess demand would fall.) If non-profit enterprises keep rents unchanged but have an investment behaviour of the same type as private investors, one would expect their investment to be unaffected by the removal of rent control (at least for the time being). Only if they behave as private firms in their price policy, and thus raise rents, but react on excess demand rather than on profitability in their investment behaviour, would a decline in their investment be expected as a result of the removal of rent control.

The notion that rent control contributes to increased housing consumption is sometimes developed along rather different lines. Instead of arguing that rent control via high demand for housing automatically (hence via the market) creates high housing investment, it is asserted that the excess demand situation in the housing market ('housing shortage') creates political pressure on the authorities to stimulate house production (presumably at the expense of investment in other sectors of the economy). The idea is somewhat similar to the notion of unbalanced growth for underdeveloped countries, as formulated for instance by Hirschman, according to which the creation of bottlenecks by excess demand in particular sectors is an efficient way of persuading the authorities to expand investment in these sectors.

This argument is rather difficult to evaluate. One problem with the argument, as applied to rent control in highly developed countries, is that it is presumably the same authorities who decide, at top level, whether rent control is to be retained and how much to stimulate house construction. Thus, it is somewhat unclear *who* is supposed to put pressure on *whom*. And if the authorities really want to stimulate investment in housing, this can be done directly (for instance by subsidizing house production or consumption, or by easy credit).

Actually it is rather easy to turn the argument upside down : as demand for other types of consumer goods are stimulated by rent control, the authorities may, to prevent inflation, find it necessary to restrict rather than expand house-building, because this is a rather simple administrative method of reducing total demand in the economy. Thus, it is not completely unlikely that the stimulus created by rent control to consumption in other markets, has actually induced the authorities to dampen rather than stimulate house-building. However, we are now in rather deep water, as it is difficult to construct a theory which explains the behaviour of governments.[1]

V. THE CONSTRUCTION-MARKET STABILIZATION GOAL

Another argument developed in favour of rent control is that the removal of such control, by raising rents in new houses, would disturb the stability of the market for house-building — via higher demand for production factors, possibly due to 'unrealistic' expectations among house-investors concerning the long-run equilibrium position of rents — with increases in production costs as a result.[2] Thus, it is often argued that it is 'desirable', from the point of view of market stability, to prevent a temporary excess demand situation from resulting in higher rents. In terms of our diagram, it is argued that the stability of the market can be improved by using rent control to prevent a shift in demand (or supply) from raising rents to r_2 or r_3. If for instance r_4 is expected by the authorities to be the long-run equilibrium level, it might be argued that it is 'desirable' not to accept a much higher rent increase than to r_4.

However, even if the basic assumptions behind this argument are accepted, it does not necessarily follow that (retaining) rent control is the only conceivable, or even the most efficient, method for achieving stability. An alternative method might be to combine the removal of rent control with restrictive measures of economic policy, such as higher interest rates on loans (in general or to housing).

The worries for the stability of the market, which imply that the removal of rent control would stimulate house-building, looks as an apparent contradiction to the earlier discussed argument that rent control is an appropriate means of stimulating higher general housing consumption. A possible reconciliation might be to argue that,

---

[1] If the argument that rent control is a powerful stimulus to high house-building is correct, we might expect that the fraction of resources devoted to this would be large during periods of rent control, as compared to other periods. It is therefore of some interest to note that total housing construction as a fraction of GNP, as well as of total gross investment, in Sweden has fallen since the end of the thirties and the first post-war years. (Rent control was introduced in 1942.) Whereas the relation of house investment to GNP was 7·4 per cent in 1938/39 and 8·8 per cent in 1946, it had fallen to 6·7 per cent in 1963. Housing construction as a percentage of total gross investment was 30·3, 30·9, and 21·4 per cent respectively in the same periods.

[2] By a disturbance of stability is here simply meant that the amplitude of fluctuations in house-building is increased.

because of downward stickiness of prices and wages, cost increases immediately after the removal of rent control would tend to be permanent. As a result, it may be argued, future house-building would be lower than if increases in production costs had been prevented by rent control. Thus, the argument would basically be an attempt to show that rent control promotes more house-building *in the future*. The argument suggests in fact that greater incentives for house-building today would be unfavourable to house-building tomorrow. (In terms of diagram I, it is thus assumed that rent control can prevent the flow-supply curves U, U', U'' from shifting upwards to the broken curves.) It remains to be explained, however, how house-investment can be stimulated when rents are controlled. In theory, it is quite conceivable, of course, that a rent policy which accepts some rent increases, though smaller than to r_3, could prevent the flow-supply curves from shifting upwards without holding back incentives to house-building very much. However, this would mean creating a more or less permanent excess demand for new dwellings.

It is important to note, however, that even if the assumptions behind the argument were granted, rent control may not be the most efficient remedy. Reductions in the profitability of housing investment by other economic policies, such as measures of monetary or fiscal policy, are alternatives.

Moreover, the 'once-and-for-all' increase in costs of production which in the absence of restrictive measures of economic policy might follow the removal of rent control, has to be compared with the *permanent* tendency for production costs to rise in a market with a permanent excess demand, due to the lack of market-resistance in such a situation against shiftings of cost increases on to prices.[1] This does not mean, of course, that (short-term or long-term) equilibrium in the market for dwellings is a *sufficient* condition for efficiency in the house-building industry. It might very well be that the market, due to the great number of small firms with small research expenditures, often is rather slow in increasing efficiency even when no permanent excess demand for housing exists.

---

[1] This would mean that the gains from technological development in a market with a permanent excess demand would tend to wind up in the hands of the owners of the production factors, such as landowners, construction workers, house builders and sellers of intermediary products to house construction.

It is possible, though difficult to prove, that the fairly rapid increase in building costs in Sweden during the post-war period, in spite of the availability of considerable technological improvements in house-building, to some extent ascribe to this tendency to a permanent excess demand for dwellings, and hence to the lack of market-resistance to cost increases.

VI. THE INCOME DISTRIBUTION GOAL

In the political debate about rent control, at least in Sweden, the reluctance to accept a redistribution of income and wealth from tenants to house-owners has been a major argument against the removal of rent control.[1] As low-income groups tend to devote a larger proportion of disposable income to housing than do higher-income groups, the gain in real income due to rent control is proportionately greater for the former than the latter. However, influencing the distribution of income by rent control is a rather clumsy procedure, as the gains in income will be rather stochastically distributed on people in various income brackets, particularly if rents vary considerably between houses built in different years, so that for instance tenants in older houses are favoured regardless of whether they are rich or poor. As in the Swedish system young families (often with small children) tend to be concentrated in rather new houses (as people are reluctant to leave their inexpensive apartments in older houses, due to the low rents in these), families with small children are generally at a disadvantage as compared to other tenants ; this seems to be against established goals in housing policy. Clearly, a more elegant method of favouring low income groups, and people with children, is to subsidize these particular groups (without using rent control), rather than keeping down rents for everybody living in houses built in certain years.[2]

VII. THE HOUSING CONSUMPTION DISTRIBUTION GOAL

To the extent that rent control affects the distribution of income in favour of low-income groups, housing demand also probably tends

[1] It would be interesting to know, of course, how large the income redistribution would be. As we know neither the size of excess demand nor the price elasticity of demand (in Sweden) it is however impossible to give a realistic forecast at present.

According to a rough estimate, an increase in rents by 25 per cent in private apartment houses in Sweden would lead to a redistribution of income from tenants to house-owners of about the same magnitude (about 400 million Swedish crowns) as a redistribution by one-half of a per cent of national income from employers to employees. See R. Bentzel, A. Lindbeck, I. Ståhl, *Bostadsbristen* (The housing shortage), Stockholm, 1963, pp. 86-87. As pointed out, however, at least 50 per cent of the income increase for house-owners would automatically go to the public sector in the form of taxes.

[2] Another important factor in considering the distributional effects of rent control is the effects on prices of residential houses. Even if prices on residential houses are free, rent control on apartments can have considerable effects. As excess demand for dwellings in rent-controlled apartment houses 'spills over' into the market for residential houses, prices for these tend to be pulled up. (A counteracting tendency may arise if tenants presently living in rent-controlled apartment houses have higher preferences for residential houses than do people presently living in residential houses.)

to be redistributed in favour of these groups. Whether this redistribution of housing *demand* between households in different income brackets also results in a corresponding redistribution of housing *consumption* will depend on how housing consumption is actually distributed in the rent-controlled market. It is therefore of interest to analyse the principles by which housing consumption is distributed in the regulated market.

The prevention of equilibrium in the housing market violates the sovereignty of the consumer in disposing of his income as he pleases. The marginal rate of substitution between housing and other commodities cannot be equated to the price ratios ; and the structure of rents of different apartments does not reflect the evaluations of these apartments by households.

These problems are particularly acute, of course, during a period of rapid inflation, as in this case a rent control system based on historical building costs results not only in low rents as compared to prices of other commodities but also in lower rents in older houses than in new (even after allowing for differences in quality). To some extent, these 'non-planned' distortions of the structure of rents may be removed by a more flexible system of rent control than has been implemented in most countries, such as by special price-index clauses on rents and possibly also by index-loans to house-building.

Whereas in a commodity market with equilibrium the distribution of the commodity between different households is determined by a general market mechanism — *i.e.* mainly by the distribution of income and wealth and by individual preferences — the commodity distribution in a market with price control and excess demand must take place according to some other principles. In Sweden the following principles seem to predominate.

As the bulk of the dwellings available during a year consists of the existing stock, rather than of houses produced during the year, the main problem in the distribution of housing consumption concerns the stock of existing dwellings. In a system characterized by rent control and protection against eviction, the leading principle for the distribution of housing consumption during a given year is that those who already have contracts are in a preferential position compared to those with no apartment of their own, even though some people in the latter group may have a higher 'need' for the apartments in question in the sense that they are willing to pay a higher rent than some people in the former group (possibly without having a higher income).

It is not fully known how people without an apartment of their own can get one. One possibility is to join the queues organized by municipalities or co-operative organizations. The allotment principles in these queues are rather complicated and difficult to grasp. The dominating principle seems to be waiting time, presumably not because waiting time is regarded as a good measure of the 'need' for a dwelling but because of the difficulty of finding less arbitrary principles.[1] The most usual way of obtaining apartments in Sweden, however, seems to be via personal contacts, mainly contacts with relatives, friends, or the employer.[2] As in other markets where price control is exercised, grey and black markets have arisen, of course. In these markets wealth and borrowing capacity are important factors for the distribution of house consumption. A contract for an apartment becomes in the rent-controlled society an asset, which can be transformed into money or some other asset. A further way of obtaining an apartment is via the 'free', legal sectors of the housing market, *i.e.* primarily the market for residential houses.

Thus even if it is believed that the queue system, administered by municipalities, is the ideal (or least unfair) method of distributing housing consumption, it is quite clear that only a limited part of housing consumption in Sweden during a given year is distributed via this mechanism. This is mainly because the authorities do not ration the *stock* of dwellings, which would require rules for how many rooms or square feet every person is allowed to occupy. Obviously price control and rationing are much more complicated matters in a durable goods market than for perishable goods. In the latter case, commodities can in each period be distributed according to some

---

[1] Somewhat shorter waiting time is required for families with children, and in some places certain occupations, such as civil servants, physicians, nurses, construction workers, etc., have priorities. In many places, a quota is simply given to a firm which can then distribute the apartments mainly as it wishes.

The waiting time in the official queues in the city of Stockholm in January 1965 was about 8–10 years. In municipalities immediately outside the city of Stockholm the waiting time was about half of that in the city of Stockholm.

[2] According to an unpublished study for three Swedish towns, the most usual ways by which tenants had obtained their apartments was : via their employer (20–24 per cent), via exchange for some other apartment (2–18 per cent), via official or co-operative queues (14–29 per cent) or 'some other way' — mainly relatives, friends, advertisement, black markets, etc. (30–57 per cent). *Bostadsbyggnadsutredningen.*

A study for Stockholm among people just taking out marriage licences has given rather similar results : via the employer (17 per cent), via official or other queues (29 per cent), via relatives or friends (31 per cent), via advertisement or other ways (19 per cent). W. William-Olsson, *1000 brudpars hem*, Stockholm, 1965, p. 39. Some deficiencies in the sample make the figures in the latter study uncertain.

Both studies indicate that only a minority of the households obtain their apartments via the official queues.

socially accepted (or enforced) principle, and everybody can — neglecting the black market — be forced to pay the same price. In the case of durable goods, however, prices and consumption during a given period are mainly determined by how the commodities have been distributed in the past. Thus, unless the authorities also enforce rationing of commodities obtained earlier, it is quite impossible to achieve a distribution of consumption according to some socially determined principle. Whereas the general (average) housing standard is successively rising, a minority of the population is unable to get apartments of their own, even though the preferences for housing for many people in this group may be relatively high.[1] This is probably one of the most severe problems connected with rent control, particularly as a permanent phenomenon. Whereas the effects of rent control on house-building might be largely eliminated, the problems created on the consumption side, such as the problem of the distribution of housing consumption, are very difficult to solve.

In this complicated pattern for the distribution of housing consumption in the Swedish rent-controlled housing market, who gains and who loses, as compared to a market with equilibrium rents? Low income groups are favoured in the sense that their real income, and hence presumably their housing *demand*, is kept up relative to the demand by higher-income groups. However, this does not necessarily mean that their housing *consumption* is favoured. It is quite

---

[1] The following figures for people per 100 rooms, number of vacancies, and number of people in the official queues in Stockholm are instructive in this respect.

Year	Number of People per 100 Rooms	Number of Vacancies	Number of People in the Queue
1921	—	66	
1926	126	620	
1930	120	1,323	
1935	111	3,547	
1940	105	3,068	
1945	99	68	
1950	95	0	51,162
1955	89	0	94,130
1960	85	0	106,910
1963	—	0	122,600

Assuming that the average size of the family in the queue is 2·5 persons, the queue would represent about 315,000 people, *i.e.* about 40 per cent of the total population in the city of Stockholm. About 45 per cent of these are people living in Stockholm without an apartment of their own, about 8 per cent are living outside Stockholm and the rest (about 47 per cent) have an apartment of their own in Stockholm but want another (usually larger) one. In the first group about 37 per cent are households consisting of two or more people.

possible that low-income groups as a rule have less contacts with people who can help them get apartments — employers and 'influential' relatives and friends. Low-income groups are also in a rather weak position in the black and grey markets, as well as in the free market for villas, where wealth, liquidity, and borrowing capacity become important factors. Disfavoured in terms of housing cost are also lodgers in furnished rooms, where rents are in practice not controlled.

Favoured are undoubtedly older people with apartments from earlier on, whereas young people and people who have just moved geographically from one place to another are disfavoured. Taking all these factors together, it is very doubtful whether the present system of distributing housing consumption in a country such as Sweden — where only a fraction of housing consumption during a given year is distributed according to the principles of the public queues — can be said to favour low-income groups, and families with children, as compared with a system with equilibrium rents.

VIII. THE HOUSING-DEMAND COMPOSITION GOAL

Another problem with rent control is that there are no guarantees that the composition of production on different kinds of dwellings follows consumer preferences; practically any type of dwelling can be let out, which means that there is very little market testing of new dwellings. For instance, we do not know if the heavy reliance on large apartment houses in Sweden after World War II — only about 20 per cent of production is in the form of residential houses — really corresponds to the preferences of households. (The picture is further complicated by the fact that home-owners are favoured, as compared to tenants in apartment houses, by the taxation system.)

However, the advocates of rent control have pointed out that the control system directs housing demand towards larger and better equipped apartments than would be the case if rents were higher. The question remains, however, as to what is gained by raising demand for higher and better dwellings in a market with excess demand (housing shortage). One conceivable argument for such a policy is that it is 'desirable' to direct the composition of housing demand in this way in order to obtain a composition of house-building which reflects the preferences of consumers in the future rather than today. Thus, it seems to be assumed that house investors in a free market are short-sighted in the sense that they consider mainly the demand structure at present but forget to plan for the future composition of housing demand. The realism of this hypothesis concerning the behaviour of private investors is naturally very difficult to evaluate. Let us, however, for the sake of the discussion, *assume* that private investors behave in this way.

A change in demand in favour of larger and better equipped dwellings will presumably not arise suddenly but rather by a continuous process, whereby (in a market without rent control) profitability would tend to rise for large and better equipped apartments, so that production factors would be attracted over to the construction of such dwellings. Thus, it does not seem self-evident that, in a market without rent control, the market mechanism would be unable to adjust the stock of dwellings to slow changes in the structure of demand.

Let us assume, however, that it is 'desirable' to have another composition of housing production than automatically tends to arise in the market. Then a change in the composition of production today could be achieved by subsidizing production of, for instance, large and well-equipped apartments; obviously the creation of excess demand for such apartments by rent control is not necessary.

IX. THE GENERAL ANTI-INFLATIONARY GOAL

When rent control was introduced during the war one main motive was to fight inflation. It can still be argued, of course, that a removal of rent control would create an impulse to cost inflation. Even if this impulse may not be greater than other such impulses that appear from time to time, it cannot be denied that a removal of rent control would have such effects.[1]

On the other hand, a removal of rent control would increase the saving ratio in the economy, as a large part of the income increase for house-owners would go to the public sector in the form of taxes. Thus, the removal of rent control would be rather similar to an increase in sales taxation (though restricted to one commodity: housing) and hence increase the economic scope for investment in

[1] As housing expenditure constitutes about 10 per cent of total consumer expenditures (excl. fuel and light) in Sweden, and as about half the stock of dwellings is in apartment houses, the immediate effect on costs of living of a 20 per cent increase in rents (excl. fuel and light) would be about 1 per cent.

the economy without running into demand inflation.[1] Thus, the disadvantages of impulses for cost inflation of a removal of rent control has to be balanced against the smaller risks for demand inflation. The increased room for investment might be used, for instance, to boost house-building.

X. CAN HOUSING POLICY DO WITHOUT RENT CONTROL?

Several effects of rent control have been discussed in the previous sections. There are, of course, others, such as restrictive effects on labour mobility (due to the housing shortage), with related losses in efficiency for the economy as a whole. However, a major problem in this paper is whether the main objectives of rent control, as defined on page 57, can be reached with other policy measures (hence without rent control). Some alternative policy measures have already been mentioned in the exposition above. A more systematic account of such policy alternatives will be summarized below.

(1) The first goal was to try to achieve a more rapid increase in the general (average) level of housing consumption than 'automatically' tends to arise in the market. As this goal can be accomplished only by stimulating house-building, appropriate measures are subsidies and/or easy credit for house-building, or possibly for housing demand (at least in new houses), whereas rent control is obviously of doubtful value in this case.

(2) The second goal, to stabilize the house-building market, can in principle be achieved by stabilization policy of the same kind as in other sectors of the economy, even though the problem might be more delicate for this market than for some others. However, there is no reason to believe that stabilization of the market for house-building nowadays would fail as it did before World War II, *i.e.* before the start of modern stabilization policy. By general monetary policy, specific credit actions for the housing market, investment taxation (or investment subsidies), possibly also physical controls, it should be possible to stabilize this market in the same way as other investment sectors in the economy, where stabilization policy in several European countries has been rather successful in recent decades.

[1] If there are sales taxes (or other indirect taxes) on other consumer goods, there will be a fall in consumer good tax revenues due to the fall in consumption of goods other than housing. This tends to dampen the contractive effect on the economy of the rent increase.

(3) If the authorities want to prevent redistributions of income and wealth from tenants to house-owners (to a larger extent than is automatically achieved via existing marginal tax rates), higher property taxation, specific taxes on property in the form of houses, and sales taxes on housing expenditures are examples of adequate policy measures. In a market with equilibrium rents, a sales tax on housing expenditure cannot be immediately shifted to tenants, as the supply curve momentarily is completely inelastic. (Only by changes in the supplied volume can a tax be shifted forward.) Even over a few years, the possibilities of shifting the tax on to tenants is rather limited, as flow-supply is small when compared with the existing stock of dwellings.

If the authorities are anxious to protect real income of some specific group among tenants, such as low-income families with children or elderly people, more progressive tax rates in income taxation, higher children's allowances, and higher old-age pensions are examples of adequate policy measures ; these are more direct ways than rent control of supporting exactly the groups which the authorities wish to help.

Non-profit enterprises may not raise rents on their own initiative in a market without rent control, which would prevent equilibrium in the housing market. This phenomenon is an important one in a housing market such as the Swedish one, where about a quarter of all dwellings are public or co-operative. Here the price policy of these enterprises becomes of the same importance as the rent control by the government. If it is regarded as unfair that housing costs are raised only for people living in private apartment houses, a sales tax on housing consumption has obvious advantages, as thereby housing costs would be raised also for people living in public and co-operative houses, as well as in villas. Due to price rigidities even in the private housing market, temporary shortages can be expected also for such dwellings even in the absence of rent control. This phenomenon might be particularly relevant after a long period of rent control. If so, a housing tax could help to move rents towards equilibrium even in private houses.

(4) If the authorities do not accept the preferences of certain household groups, such as low-income families with children or elderly people, direct support of their housing demand, rather than general transfer payments, is an adequate measure. Subsidies for housing consumption for these particular groups seem to be a more effective measure for these goals than does rent control — which keeps

down housing expenditures for all tenants — particularly as it is doubtful if low-income groups can compete effectively on a market with a permanent excess demand, created by rent control.

(5) If the authorities want to direct the composition of housing investment in favour of larger and better equipped dwellings than automatically tend to be built in the market, specific subsidies for the production or consumption of such apartments is a possible measure.

(6) The sixth goal was to dampen tendencies to general inflation. In principle, it may be argued that general inflation can be fought with measures other than rent control. However, it is quite clear that the problem of how to fight cost inflation is not solved on the political level, even if in theory a number of appropriate techniques may be designed. Therefore, it seems realistic to assume that some increase in the general price level is unavoidable when rent control is removed. The authorities then have to evaluate this increase in the general price level against various disadvantages connected with rent control.

As in the case of practically all economic policy, the various measures have to be implemented interdependently rather than in isolation, as most measures have effects on several target variables at the same time.

Chapter 6

SOME ASPECTS OF A MIXED HOUSING MARKET

BY

INGEMAR STÅHL

Forsvarets Forskningsanstalt, Stockholm

I. INTRODUCTION [1]

DURING the last decades extensive price- and rent-regulating measures have been in operation on the Swedish housing market. Today the Rent Control Act of 1942 covers, broadly speaking, almost all rented flats in multi-family houses owned by private landlords and small housing co-operatives in the towns and other large urban areas. Privately financed one-family houses are exempt from rent control, irrespective of their geographical situation. Other categories exempt are flats in multi-family houses in rural and small urban districts, and all of the increasing number of dwelling-units in municipally owned, non-profit social housing corporations. The large co-operatives operating on a nation-wide scale are classified for the purposes of rent control with the non-profit corporations.

In a first approximation of a model of the present Swedish housing market, it is of primary interest to distinguish between, on one side, private companies or estate owners who can be described as 'profit-maximizing' and adopting ordinary market behaviour, and, on the other side, corporations or owners, whose rents are determined on the basis of historical building-costs and actual expenditures according to some administrative rules. The latter category primarily includes the rent-controlled units with administratively fixed prices. But it also includes the non-profit social housing corporations, although they are outside the legal rent control system. The non-profit corporations are conditioned not to show profits in the long run, and after negotiations with the tenants' associations they voluntarily use principles and rules for rent calculations that are very similar to those used in the rent-controlled units. The table below

[1] For a discussion of similar problems see also: R. Bentzel, A. Lindbeck, and I. Ståhl, *Bostadsbristen* (The Housing Shortage), Uppsala, 1963.

73

shows the distribution of the present stock of dwelling units between the two market categories at the time of the last census (1960).

TABLE 1

THE DISTRIBUTION OF DWELLING UNITS BETWEEN
DIFFERENT MARKET CATEGORIES 1960 *

Category	Number of Dwelling Units	%
I. Equilibrium-pricing or 'free' sector (F-sector) Rental units in private houses with 'free' rents and one-family houses	1,244,000	47
(Includes 'semi'-controlled one-family houses with State loans and maximized but index-linked selling prices)	(150,000)	(5)
II. Cost-pricing sector (C-sector)		
(a) Rental units in private houses under the Rent Control Act or rents fixed in connection with State loans	890,000	33
(b) Non-profit corporations	287,000	11
(c) Co-operatives	250,000	9
	2,671,000	100

* R. Bentzel *et al. op. cit.* p. 20.

The table and the distinction between the two main categories will need some supplementary remarks. The F-sector is dominant in rural areas and small urban districts where one-family houses constitute the main part of the stock of dwelling units. In cities and large towns and other urban districts the F-sector is restricted to one-family houses (of which a great part is 'semi-controlled', cf. the table). In comparison with other countries where the standard of living is the same one-family houses occupy a small part of the housing market in Sweden.

There is a tendency today to abolish rent control in small urban districts. Some older dwelling units in the cities are demolished or turned into offices while most of the new houses are formally outside the rent regulation but built and administered by non-profit corporations or co-operatives. These stated tendencies work in different directions and tend to cancel each other. We can therefore expect that the proportions between the sectors have not undergone any drastic changes since 1960. In the free sector another category of dwelling units may be included, *i.e.* sublet rental units. For sublet furnished flats rent control has been fairly ineffective. The existence of this grey market means that the border between the categories is somewhat vague.

For dwellings built before 1942 and still under rent control the rents of 1942 have been taken as base rents. The actual rent has been allowed to increase only after an increase in operating and/or loan expenditures. These increases are calculated on basis of insignificantly differentiated rules. In the old stock there still exists a relative rent structure reflecting the rent regulations during the period between the world wars. For dwellings built after 1942 the base rents are determined on specific rules for calculating operating costs and annuity based on present interest rates. Likewise for these new houses the rents are schematically changed on the basis of estimates of average changes in operating and capital costs. The principles adopted within the non-profit corporations and the co-operatives have practically the same effects regarding the rent structure.

The conclusion of this introductory remark is that in the Swedish housing market — independent of the pace in abolishing the rent control — there will be a large sector in the market with rents decided upon in an administrative framework and based on historical costs. Statements by the non-profit corporations indicate that they do not intend to abandon the principle of cost-determined rents and adopt regular market behaviour. A study of the housing market must therefore include questions such as the following :

(1) What methods and rules are used to determine the rents from historical construction costs and actual operating costs?

(2) How do these rules affect the income distribution and the allocation of the present stock?

(3) How is investment in housing affected?

  (*a*) What type of investment criteria can be used in non-profit corporations?

  (*b*) How can the policy of the *C*-sector affect the investment of the profit maximizing companies?

(4) If one accepts the existence of rent control and non-profit corporations as a political and hardly changeable fact is it then possible to find rules for rent calculations within the *C*-sector which minimize the distortions from pareto-optimal allocations?

In the following pages we will try to discuss some aspects of these questions.

II. SHORT-TERM EQUILIBRIUM IN A MIXED MARKET

To illustrate some structural features of a mixed market in an ordinary demand-supply diagram it will be necessary to make some drastic simplifications in the assumptions. We assume that housing can be treated as a homogeneous and an infinitely divisible commodity. This means that we neglect qualitative differences between the stocks in the two different sectors, constituting the 'mixed market'. In Fig. 1, the supply of the F-sector is indicated with S_F and the supply of the C-sector with S_C. The total supply in the market is $S = S_F + S_C$. In a short-term perspective we can assume that supply is totally inelastic regarding the rent level. The total demand curve is D. The fixed or controlled rent level — which presently can be assumed to be homogeneous for all dwelling units within the C-sector — is P_C. A hypothetical market equilibrium can exist at the rent level P_E, which is assumed to be above P_C.

Different additional assumptions can now be made about the behaviour in the C-sector with reference to the allocation and the distribution of the dwelling units. In the following we will discriminate between three different cases. They may be labelled as follows:

Case A. Queues but free individual optimization within the C-sector;

Case B. Queues and rationing;

Case C. Different kinds of arbitrary allocation.

Case A

The basic assumption underlying the first case is that the tenants are distributed *at random* in regard to their preferences and incomes in a queue and are successively allowed to optimize their consumption at the different rent levels. This means that a demand $D_C = S_C$ is satisfied in the C-sector and that the rest of the demand will be turned over to the F-sector. The demand in the F-sector, represented by D_F, will according to the assumption of random position in the queue or on the waiting-list be a fraction of the original demand for the whole market determined by

$$D_F = (1 - \frac{S_C}{D(P_C)})D$$

where $\dfrac{S_C}{D(P_C)}$ is the fraction of total demand that can be met in the C-sector. The equilibrium rent in the F-sector (P_F) will then be higher than the hypothetical equilibrium rent in the whole market.

The difference between P_F and P_E depends among other things on the price elasticity of demand and the size of stocks in the two different market categories.

The indifference-curve diagram in Fig. 2 describes the position of a household that has the opportunity to optimize at the fixed price level (budgetline L_1) and chooses the point C as an optimum position. A household with the same income and preference system but standing too far back in the queue has to optimize at the higher price level indicated by the budgetline L_3. Optimum is at the point A. The budgetline L_2 and the point B gives the position of a household optimizing at the hypothetical equilibrium rent level P_E. Each household will attain the regular conditions for an optimum position within the market-category to which it has been assigned. The value of the privilege of having been assigned to the C-sector can be determined by the difference in income between two parallel budgetlines, L_3 and L_4 where L_4 is tangent to the indifference curve in D. The point D is indifferent to the point C, the optimum position at the original income at the price level of the C-sector. This condition means that the household is indifferent between the possibility of

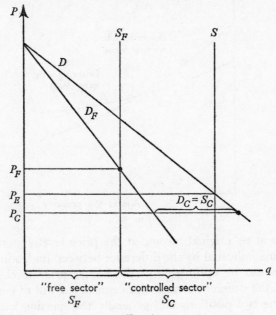

SUPPLY–DEMAND SCHEDULE FOR A MIXED MARKET

FIG. 1

77

INDIFFERENCE CURVES

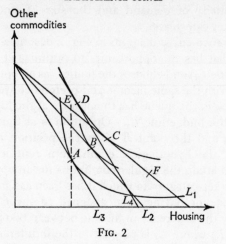

FIG. 2

THE DEVELOPMENT OF THE REAL RENT AMOUNTS
INVOLVED IN FINANCING WITH INDEX LOANS
AND NOMINAL LOANS

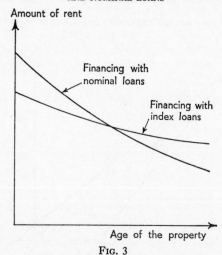

FIG. 3

optimizing at its original income at the price level P_C or to get an extra income indicated by the difference between budgetlines L_4 and L_3 and instead be optimizing at the higher price level P_F. The amount of the different commodities consumed will of course differ between the two positions and generally the housing consumption will be larger with the budgetline L_1 than with the budgetline L_4.

In comparison with a hypothetical total equilibrium situation at the price level P_E the mixed market will give the house-owners in the F-sector increased rents and higher estate values. Whether the total amount spent on housing by consumers is larger or not, is dependent upon the price elasticity of demand and the sizes of the respective stocks. On the other hand there is obviously an income redistribution in favour of the consumers assigned to the controlled market.

The assignment method can be further elaborated and may include correlation between, for example, income or preference structure and market assignment. In general the price level P_F will not be invariant for the introduction of such non-random elements into the queue system. But it is important to underline that even such non-random queue systems are compatible with free optimization for the household. It is also obvious that the households not assigned to the C-sector in general will prefer to go over to this sector. The method here outlined assumes that a redistribution of rental units will take place each year or period and that a household only gets an option for this year. In reality the options will be perpetual (see Case C).

Case B

Another method of allocating a given stock of housing between households is to combine queues with some method of rationing. This means that tenants who get the favour of an assignment into the C-sector can no longer optimize and as the normal conditions of optimum are not satisfied, the households have an excess demand or supply at the given income and the rent level in the C-sector. The situation is illustrated in Fig. 2. The point C on L_1 is still the optimum position for a household in the C-sector but an individual household will accept rationing which brings the household to, for example, the points E or F and will still be better off than at the F-sector price level. The 'rationing' may even work in the opposite direction, bringing the household to a point F, with more than optimal consumption of housing.

Generally queues combined with rationing will have a tendency to decrease the rent level in the F-sector. But it would even be possible to find rationing methods that could bring the rent level in the F-sector under the hypothetical equilibrium level P_E.

Case C

One of the most important features in the C-sector today in Sweden is the fact that a household which has been assigned to a rental unit has a perpetual option to rent the unit. In the indifference model this principle has the effect that regardless of the initial assignment method few households will remain in an optimum position because of changes in their income and preference structure. But, as was illustrated in Case B, there will be a vast set of consumption bundles that do not satisfy local optimum conditions but are preferred to a change into the *F*-sector and a resulting increase in rent level.

In comparison with the hypothetical equilibrium rent level P_E, indicated by L_2 in Fig. 2 housing consumption can be larger (*C* and *F*) or smaller (*D*). There is no guarantee that a depressed and controlled rent level will increase the housing consumption for all households in the *C*-sector.

III. NON-PROFIT RENT CALCULATIONS AND RENT DIFFERENTIALS [1]

A non-profit rent calculation generally means that the total present value of the rents of a house (after deduction for operating costs) will be identically equal to the initial production cost of the house. Consideration is taken of interest payments and the opportunity cost of the capital contributed by the owner (which generally is a very small part, especially for non-profit-making corporations). In such a system rent differentials may occur, due to the fact that construction costs for similar houses built simultaneously may vary for many different reasons.

But a more decisive factor behind the existence of rent differentials is probably the nominalistic feature in the elaboration of rent controls and similar systems. We will here make a short digression and point out some measures that may make the non-profit corporations calculate rents in a better agreement with the hypothetical price structure in an equilibrium market. The nominalistic feature means, that the part of the outgoing rent that is to cover the capital costs of the property is determined as an annuity fixed in *money*. But the *real* value of a *nominal* annuity diminishes when the monetary value falls. This means that the part of the rent covering the capital cost for a specific house is constant in money but falling in real value. A suitable division of the capital costs during the lifetime of the house

[1] For a more general discussion of the problems of index-loans see: *Index loans, an investigation published by the Swedish Ministry of Finance*, Stockholm, 1965.

should be linked to the development of the hypothetical market value of the rental units. But, if the rate of inflation more than corresponds to a normal yearly reduction in rent occasioned by wear and tear and decreasing relative moderness, the rent can be said to be too high at the beginning of the lifetime of the property and too low at the end.

Another formulation of the same problem is that the *rent structure*, through the nominalistic standard chosen for rent control or rent calculations, *will be dependent on the size of the inflation*. It is thus impossible to make a correct forecast of the size of the real rent for a house. One countermeasure against these partly destructive effects may be the introduction of index loans for the non-profit corporations. The primary effect of index loans is, that this type of loan facilitates or necessitates a rent calculation which automatically takes into account changes in the general price level. This rent calculation means, that compared with a calculation based on nominal loans with normal amortization terms, the capital cost part of the rent keeps pace with the monetary value. If the total real cost is the same for an index loan as for a nominal loan raised at the same time, the former allows for a better and more certain distribution of one and the same total rent sum during the period concerned.[1]

In many countries the rate of inflation is greater than the normal rate of depreciation. With index-loans and real rate of interest payments and amortizations fixed at a *real* annuity lower initial capital expenses are obtained than with money loans and an annuity fixed in money terms. Measured in terms of money, the cost-rent of a house financed on nominal loans will remain constant while the rent of a house financed by index loan will rise according to increases in the index used. The fundamental structure of rents with both types of loan is illustrated in Fig. 3.

Another factor determining the rent differentials is the fact that the rent calculations in rent control administration or in the non-profit corporations do not consider the changes in potential value due to, for example, the expansion of cities, to the construction of new thoroughfares or local centres. Such changes will in a market operating with a perfect price system be a cause of capital gains or capital losses. Unexpected changes in consumers' tastes will also result in

[1] If m is the money rate of interest (measured as an intensity), p the rate of change in price level and r real rate of interest on index-loans the following equation holds :

$$e^m = e^p . e^r = e^{p+r}$$

which gives

$$m = p + r$$

price changes in the equilibrium pricing market but not in the *C*-sector.

Beside the effects already mentioned we may also consider long-term changes in the relative marginal productivity between the construction sector and other sectors. In general, such changes will not effect the prices in the existing stock in the *C*-sector. These factors taken together cause a permanent situation with rent differentials and to a large extent unpredictable relative rents between different sub-markets of houses built in different years. In a market model this can be represented by a set of different rent levels within the *C*-sector. The demand-supply-schedule already given may be supplemented with a division of the *C*-sector into classes, each with a separate price level.

The concept of housing shortage or excess demand gets a rather specific interpretation in this kind of model. Unsatisfied households can exist in two different respects. Firstly, householders may wish that they could be assigned to a class with a lower rent level than their present one. Secondly, elements of rationing or involuntary changes from earlier optimal situations may give deviations from the local optimum conditions within a specific class or rent level. In the model we have also assumed that the *F*-sector is able to take care of all excess demand left over from the other sectors. Such a model is in many respects quite realistic. The markets for one-family houses or sublet furnished flats in combination with different kinds of grey and black markets guarantee that nobody will be without shelter, but perhaps at high prices and substantial trouble for specific groups. This discussion must finally be supplemented with an observation that flexibility is increased by the fact that the formation of households and families is affected by the allocation in the housing market.

IV. CONCLUSIONS ON INVESTMENT BEHAVIOUR IN A MIXED MARKET

A starting point for a discussion on investment in housing in a mixed market may be the investment-planning of a profit-maximizing enterprise in an equilibrium-pricing market. The theory of investment for this type of enterprise is often formulated in rather simple terms : the choice of investment-plan is made so that the expected present value of the net receipts of the investment is maximized. In the classic theory of investment the decisions are supposed to be made in small, decentralized units and it is therefore possible to assure that the environment is independent of the chosen decision. It is also possible to neglect repercussions on other enterprises' behaviour, since each unit is very small in comparison with the whole market. The needs of co-ordination, mutual communication, and control can be met by the information chains of the price system. The profit-maximization criterion in combination with a working price system is supposed to guarantee the attainment of a general pareto-optimal situation. There are many objections to the use of this type of investment-theory applied to the housing market. Broadly speaking the objections may be divided into the following two main groups :

(*a*) Investment in housing is heavily dependent upon predictions of future demand and production structures. Long-term planning and investment theory in a field in which economic theory is developing rapidly. For models of investment in housing it is sufficient to mention a few possible approaches for further studies : How are expectations of future demand and future prices formed and to what extent is it necessary to bring in information outside the price system for the predictions made? To what extent do different types of prediction methods contribute to the stability of the market? How can investment-plans be formulated to allow for 'flexible responses' towards uncertainty in the future?

(*b*) Town-planning and environment aspects result in different kinds of interdependencies in production and demand functions. This means that the price system is insufficient as an information instrument, even in the short run, to guarantee optimal investment behaviour.

To what extent is this description valid for a mixed market? Let us first comment on some new problems in the F-sector. Beside the already mentioned insufficiency of the price system for investment planning, the mixed market brings in a new kind of strategic uncertainty. This new uncertainty is connected with expectations of the future of rent regulations and the policies adopted by the non-profit making corporations. Partial abolition of rent control and a transition into regular market behaviour for parts of the formerly regulated sector affects the rents in the F-sector. Generally we may assume that a partial removal of the regulations will increase the rents in the F-sector, but as has been earlier demonstrated we cannot exclude the possibility that rent may decrease in sub-markets. The expectations of future rents in the *F*-sector will depend upon political decisions. The price system will no longer work as an effective co-ordination and information system and the uncertainty about future rent policy will very likely tend *ceteris paribus* to decrease the supply of new rental units.

When we turn to the *C*-sector and want to study investment behaviour of the non-profit corporations we are obliged to find other investment-criteria than profit maximization. The information about observed rental levels in different sub-markets is of little value. The same conclusions are valid for observations of excess demand in the market. There is no reason to believe that simple relations between the excess demand in different sub-markets and the investment-structure will give the same results as the operations of an equilibrium-pricing market. The argument behind this statement is simply that the existing rent structure depends too much upon irrelevant factors — *e.g.* the rate of inflation, the degree of state-financed loans, etc. — and may result in arbitrary excess demand structures.

We can also point to the fact that municipally owned non-profit corporations are operating on a scale where the effects on the environment may be significant for the individual corporation. This results in a need for much more integrated investment planning. In this paper it is not possible to investigate further the problems connected with the criteria for investment selection in large non-profit corporations. We can only point to the fact that the lack of an operating price system, the size of the corporations and the potential possibilities of co-ordinating housing investments and other municipally directed investments, make great demands on the planning methods used.

Chapter 7

ON THE ECONOMIC EFFECTS OF RENT CONTROL IN DENMARK

BY

JORGEN H. GELTING

Institute of Economics, University of Aarhus

I. THE SHORTAGE OF HOUSING

FROM the point of view of economics the most important feature of houses is their exceptional durability in consequence of which the annual addition of new apartments or houses amounts to only a few per cent of the total stock. In most countries at most times the annual growth amounted to only some one to three per cent of the physical stock. Though these figures underestimate the economically relevant rate of growth by ignoring changes in quality, it is obvious that in periods of rapidly rising aggregate real income a housing shortage in the sense of increasing relative scarcity of house room is apt to arise.

It is worth while recalling this because it goes to show that the post-war housing shortage in most Western European countries is a consequence not merely of war and post-war rent control policies. Even if rents had not been controlled but had been allowed to rise in response to market forces, a housing shortage would probably have made its appearance in the sense that the number of vacancies would have declined strongly. Experience shows that rents are rather sticky to the extent that relatively large and persistent changes in the vacancy rate are required to set the rent level moving.

However, looking at the post-war position in the Danish housing market like that of most other Western European countries, it is evident that rent control has been a major factor intensifying the housing shortage.

Some impression of the distortion of the rent level may be gathered from a comparison of rent levels of rented apartments according to age in 1960 and in 1940, when the housing market was substantially free and a fairly comfortable margin of vacant apartments existed.

Table 1 suggests that the rent problem is by no means merely a question of pre-war versus post-war rents. Rather there is a continuum of disequilibrium rent levels.

85

The Economic Problems of Housing

TABLE 1
INDICES OF RENT LEVELS IN DANISH TOWNS
ACCORDING TO AGE OF APARTMENT 1940 AND 1960

	0–5 Years Old	6–10 Years Old	11–25 Years Old	More than 25 Years
1940	100	95	85	80
1960	100	80	65	55

Source : Danish official housing statistics 1940 and 1960. Apartments with central heating only. Indices, rent of apartments 0–5 years old = 100, cover apartments of all size groups weighted by number of apartments.

In the Danish discussion of the early post-war period it was frequently pointed out that though at the ruling rent level a housing shortage existed in the sense of excess demand for housing space, manifest in the almost complete disappearance of the margin of vacant apartments, the housing standard had improved insofar as the number of occupants per room or apartment had fallen. Measured in this way, the housing standard has, indeed, continued to improve during the post-war period. The changes have not in general been large. However, the summary figures of number of occupants per apartment (by size classes) cover up a tendency within each size class of apartments towards a division in two groups with an increasing and a decreasing number of occupants. Table 2 shows this tendency for 3 size classes of apartments in Copenhagen, and in the largest provincial town, Aarhus.

TABLE 2
DWELLINGS BY NUMBER OF OCCUPANTS
(Percentages)
COPENHAGEN

Number of Occupants	2 Rooms		3 Rooms		4 Rooms	
	1940	1960	1940	1960	1940	1960
0	2·6	0·6	2·2	0·5	1·9	0·4
1	18·4	25·2	7·3	14·2	5·6	12·0
2	36·8	35·1	30·3	32·7	25·2	30·4
3	24·8	21·1	29·1	22·9	29·8	23·7
4	11·6	13·5	18·2	18·9	21·3	19·8
5	3·9	3·4	7·9	7·6	9·8	8·6
6	1·3	0·9	3·1	2·3	3·8	3·2
7	0·6	0·2	1·1	0·7	1·5	1·1
8	0·3	0·1	0·8	0·2	1·1	0·9

AARHUS

Number of Occupants	2 Rooms		3 Rooms		4 Rooms	
	1940	1960	1940	1960	1940	1960
0	2·3	—*	3·4	—*	3·6	—*
1	15·0	25·3	5·6	10·7	3·4	5·9
2	33·0	36·9	24·9	28·4	18·5	21·0
3	26·8	20·5	27·7	23·8	26·4	22·3
4	14·6	12·7	19·7	23·5	22·9	26·3
5	5·4	3·6	10·4	9·6	13·1	13·9
6	1·8	0·9	4·8	3·0	6·6	6·4
7	0·7	0·2	1·9	0·6	3·1	2·6
8	0·3	—	1·5	0·4	2·5	1·6

* Vacant apartments not covered in 1960 sample.
Source : Danish official housing statistics 1940 and 1960.

This development reflects both the tendency towards a fall in the number of occupants in old apartments where the same tenant has been in possession for a long period of years and the efforts of the public housing boards to raise the number of occupants in apartments becoming vacant.

II. THE CHANGES IN HOUSING STANDARDS

It is clear that since *per capita* real income has risen by about half from 1940 to 1960 it cannot be validly argued from a slight fall in the number of occupants per apartment or room that the housing standard has not deteriorated relatively. Furthermore it is evidently unsatisfactory to measure the housing stock simply by the physical quantity of houses or rooms without any adjustment for differences of quality between housing accommodation of different types and ages. For the Copenhagen area a quite crude attempt has been made to measure the increase in the housing stock 1940 to 1960 taking quality improvements into account. From the rent statistics of 1940 when rent levels presumably roughly reflected consumer preferences in a free market we have an interrelationship (see Table 1 above) between rent level and the age of apartments. It has been assumed that in a free market the corresponding relationship would have held in 1960 and that the annual output of housing services from the part of the 1940 stock still existing in 1960 did not decline between 1940 and 1960. Corrected figures are thus derived for the increase in the housing stock. It is found that whereas the number of rooms rose by 38 per cent, against a population increase of 29 per cent, the quality adjusted increase in housing supply amounted to about 60 per cent.

With adjustment for quality changes housing standards would therefore appear to have improved greatly. However, as *per capita* real income has increased by about 50 per cent, housing standards have not improved in step with the general rise in living standards. Assuming an income elasticity of demand for housing close to one, the implication is that in a free market rents would have risen relative to other prices.

It is, of course, possible to make only a very rough estimate of the rise in rents required in 1960 to re-establish a free market. Due to rent control there has, in fact, occurred a decline in rents relative to other prices of almost 40 per cent with, however, a very large spread around this rough average. Correspondingly, the rise in rents required to re-establish a free market would vary greatly as between apartments of different types and ages. It is generally assumed that the total rise in annual rents required would at the present time amount to about one billion Danish kroner or some two to three per cent of total private consumption.[1]

III. THE CONSEQUENCES OF REMOVING RENT CONTROL

Several of the economic effects of rent control are, presumably, best elucidated by a discussion of the consequences of the removal of these controls — together with the discontinuance of the control by housing boards of new leases of apartments becoming vacant. The subsequent rise in the rent level would affect the vacancy rate, the intensity of utilization of the housing stock, the volume of new building, the distribution of income, and total effective demand.

Ignoring a relatively small group of very old apartments of extremely poor quality, the rise in rents would in general be largest for pre-war apartments. The tendency towards an equalization of rent levels (adjusted for differences of quality, etc.) between old and new apartments would over a period of years result in a more intensive use especially of that part of the older, previously cheap apartments which have not through a change of tenant in recent years come within the purview of the housing boards. To that extent the rise in

[1] Relative to the consumption expenditure of the households affected as tenants the rise would, of course, be much larger, probably some 5 to 6 per cent.

rents by inducing more intensive utilization will act similarly to an increase in the stock of houses and tend to call forth a margin of vacant apartments of the various types and ages. On the other hand, with the termination of rationing by the housing boards of apartments becoming vacant, a latent demand — particularly from persons living singly — will become effective. It is therefore not obvious what the net change will be in the demand for additions to housing space through new building. Probably demand would abate somewhat with an effect also on prices of one-family houses.

It is often stated that under present conditions where old apartments are disproportionately lower in rent than apartments newly built, emerging vacancies will tend to be concentrated on the new apartments and that, consequently, there is an increasing risk of greater instability in building activity compared to conditions in a free housing market where a rising vacancy rate would affect apartments of all age groups. At the same time it is mostly assumed that rent control — by inducing a less intensive use of the old housing stock — keeps up the demand for new building. Thus, rent control should both delay the appearance of vacancies and concentrate them, when appearing, on the newly built apartments.

As already indicated, the correctness of the former conclusion is somewhat in doubt. It may further be questioned whether under present economic conditions the removal of controls will suffice to spread emerging vacancies over the entire housing stock. Inflation may well proceed at such a rate and the rate of productivity advance in the building industry prove so low that the equilibrium rent level consistent with a free housing market will be steadily rising even for most old apartments. But because of stickiness actual rents may fail to rise at the rate required so that vacancy levels will tend to be systematically lower for old than for new apartments. This points to an important shortcoming of at least the Danish discussion of the housing market problem which has been dealt with largely as that of finding a suitable once-for-all remedy.

IV. EFFECTS ON OTHER ACTIVITIES OF REMOVING RENT CONTROL

Apart from any change in new building the removal of rent control may affect activity levels by changing total spending on other goods than housing services.

When rents rise money and real income is transferred from tenants to owners. At unchanged tax rates total tax revenues will rise because the taxable income of owners has increased, whereas the increased expenditure on rent of tenants is not deductible from taxable income. This effect may, of course, be neutralized through a reduction of tax rates or an increase in public expenditure. Apart from this, will the rise in rents call forth any change in total effective demand?

If tax rates or public expenditures are adjusted so that the balance of government revenues and expenditures remain constant, total disposable incomes will have risen by exactly the amount of the increase in the value of the current supply of goods and services including housing services. The disposable income of tenants is unchanged, but their expenditure for rent has risen. To throw light on the reaction of tenants data have been analysed from an income and consumption survey carried out in 1963 by the Danish Statistical Department of blue- and white-collar workers' households. The linear regression of savings on disposable income and annual rent was computed for two samples of close to 400 households each, all living in rented apartments. The samples were not classified according to number of persons per household or other possibly relevant characteristics.

Blue-collar workers : $S = 769 \quad + 0{\cdot}18 \, (Y - 20986) - 0{\cdot}21 \, (R - 1337)$
$$\pm 0{\cdot}024 \qquad\qquad \pm 0{\cdot}21$$
White-collar workers : $S = 2360 + 0{\cdot}23 \, (Y - 26424) - 0{\cdot}36 \, (R - 1895)$
$$\pm 0{\cdot}027 \qquad\qquad \pm 0{\cdot}29$$

For what they are worth — which is not much — these results are consistent with the plausible hypothesis that approximately the same change in savings and thus in spending is caused by a higher level of rent as by an equally lower level of disposable income. The above results do not allow any conclusion to be drawn concerning the further hypothesis that the response of savings would be somewhat stronger and the response of spending (on other goods than housing) would be somewhat weaker to the largely accidental and from the point of view of the consumer arbitrary differences in rent under rent control than to differences in expenditure for rent due to a widespread movement in rent levels. Tentatively we may conclude that a rise in rents by one billion Dkr. would reduce tenants' spending on other things by some 750–800 mill. Dkr.

Mostly it is taken for granted that total savings would rise because of a higher propensity to save of owners than of tenants due to higher average incomes. Firstly, however, we have little evidence that — at least beyond a quite low level of income — the marginal, as distinguished from the average, propensity to save is a rising function of income. Secondly, we have only scanty information on the distribution of ownership of apartment houses. We know, however, that the major part of pre-war apartments (by number of apartments) are owned by private individuals, and for the largest provincial town, Aarhus, we have a fairly detailed distribution of apartment houses (based on number of apartments and also on taxable value of houses) by occupation of owners. This information gives no support to the idea of a heavy concentration of ownership on persons with high incomes. It may be suggested, therefore, that the removal of rent control to a smaller extent than generally assumed will lead to a change both in the vertical distribution of income and in the total flow of savings.

V. EFFECT ON RATE OF INTEREST

Concern has finally been voiced that if rent control is removed and if this step is not accompanied by heavily increased taxation of owners (which it almost certainly would be), the rate of interest will rise in consequence of new borrowing by owners on the basis of increased capital values. Since the real income loss of tenants is not capitalized, huge private capital net gains will certainly arise. From this may arise both a wealth effect and an income effect. In so far as owners merely wish to hold their additional capital in more liquid form it is hard to see why their desire should not be accommodated, if need be by appropriate operations by the central bank. If on the other hand the capital gains secured induce owners to increase their spending (in contrast with the usually assumed increase in net savings) maintenance of overall economic balance may require the institution of deflationary economic policies. But there is, of course, no necessity why these should take the form of a rise in interest rates.

Chapter 8

DETERMINANTS OF FLUCTUATIONS IN HOUSE-BUILDING IN DENMARK 1880-1940[1]

BY

E. HOFFMEYER

and

K. MORDHORST

Danmarks Nationalbank, Copenhagen

I. INTRODUCTION

DURING the inter-war period it became gradually accepted by most Danish economists and politicians that house-building is very sensitive to short-run variations in the long-term interest rate. The introduction of this view was probably mainly due to two circumstances : one was the heavy building crisis in 1907–8 accompanied by bank failures and shortage of money ; another was the impact of Wicksell's theories on Danish economists. Since then it has been accepted almost as a matter of fact that house-building must be influenced strongly by short-term fluctuations in the long-term interest rate. Reference is mostly made to theoretical considerations — investment calculations in durable equipment — and rarely to thorough empirical investigations.

By way of introduction it must further be mentioned that financing of housing in Denmark is traditionally provided by long-term loans — 40–60 years — through credit mortgage institutions. These are debtor organizations, that issue long-term bonds which are sold by the individual debtor on the capital market. This means that bonds are sold in a constant flow by a large number of persons. Price fixing of these bonds is free and they are ordinarily sold below par, depending of course on the nominal rate of interest (the coupon rate). Everybody, who has real assets, may join a credit mortgage association and issue bonds whether his asset is an old or new one-family

[1] We are indebted to Mr. N. Thygesen of the University of Copenhagen for helpful remarks and assistance with the planning of the statistical work. The computations have been run by Mr. Vestergaard, Regnecentralen.

house, an apartment building, a factory, or an office building. The market for these bonds is therefore very broad and price fixing is not — as regards commercial and savings banks — influenced by institutional customs, and in particular not by rationing behaviour when availability of funds is scarce.

According to the view mentioned changes in the long-term rate of interest are thought to have an immediate and heavy impact on house-building, whereas other relations are less observed, *e.g.* the acceleration principle. The main purpose of this investigation is to test the empirical validity of this generally accepted theory regarding the interrelationship between the long-term interest rate and house-building. Investigations in other countries[1] do not offer conclusive evidence ; the long-term rate of interest plays a rather insignificant rôle in Derksen's and Maisel's relations,[2] but has a somewhat more prominent place in Muth's results.

The following sections contain : in Section II, a discussion of theoretical problems concerning the assumed model; in Section III, an explanation of the methods used in constructing the time series, which are included in the analysis; and, in Section IV, the results of the regression analysis.

II. THE STRUCTURE OF THE MODEL

From an operational point of view the simplest method is just to establish some sort of relationship between the long-term interest rate and house-building — or disprove it. It is, however, necessary first to clarify the nature of the model we have in mind. There are at least two rather different ways to attack the problem.

The first is to analyse the relationship between final demand for housing and the price of housing. The rate of interest has a great impact on rent, and the relationship between final demand and the rate of interest is therefore implicit in the price and income elasticities obtained from the analysis.

One major problem here is the tricky question of the quality of housing. It is sometimes stated that it is not reasonable to assume that household formation should be dependent on the rate of interest,

---

[1] J. B. D. Derksen, 'Long Cycles in Residential Building : An Explanation', *Econometrica*, April 1940. S. J. Maisel, 'A Theory of Fluctuations in Residential Construction Starts', *American Economic Review*, June 1963. R. F. Muth, 'The Demand for Non-Farm Housing', in *The Demand for Durable Goods*, ed. A. C. Harberger, Chicago, 1960.

[2] Derksen, *op. cit.* p. 106, and Maisel, *op. cit.* p. 376.

but it does not follow from this statement, that there is no connection between house-building and the rate of interest, because the variable may be the quality of housing, which means that the quality of house-building is negatively correlated with the long-term rate of interest.

There are several indications that quality is a variable, but it has not been possible to construct quantitative estimates for this factor. This is really a serious drawback for the statistical analysis, which applies also to other analyses.

The second method is to accept that housing is provided at some (variable) quality according to family formation, but to concentrate on the substantial fluctuations in housing starts. The basic market forces are not analysed, but the major problem is here the fluctuations, which can be analysed in an inventory model as suggested by Maisel.

In this connection the crucial variable is 'the incentive to build' in the perspective that it is necessary to build some day, but the decision is whether you should start this year or next, *i.e.* should you as a builder fill your inventory now or let it run down!

From a theoretical point of view it seems much less obvious that the long-term rate of interest should play an important rôle in this model concentrating on short-run supply. It must be necessary to assume first that long-term financing is the only available possibility (re-contracting or forward markets being ruled out) and second that builders have definite expectations regarding the rate of interest, as it normally takes about one to two years between starting to plan the house and the final financial arrangement.

According to these lines of thinking expectations become important and these are also very difficult to measure — the structure of expectations are ordinarily assumed, not tested, in the models.

These rather negative assertions have not prevented the undertaking of the statistical analysis, but restricted it to the primitive and modest question of the operational significance of a relationship between the long-term rate of interest and house-building, as it must be expected that conclusive evidence regarding the structure of the relationships cannot be obtained by the present analysis.

III. CONSTRUCTION OF THE TIME SERIES

As factors exerting major influence on house-building it was decided in addition to the long-term interest rate to take explicit account of changes in demographic factors and of real income and vacancies.

However, house-building has in this country been highly influenced by a variety of governmental policies ever since the beginning of the nineteen-twenties. As it is very difficult to attach quantitative values to this policy factor, it was desirable to include also a number of years not characterized by varying degrees of governmental interference.

No data are available for house-building all over the country until after World War II. Even for the larger towns outside Copenhagen data are only available from about 1917, whereas data for house-building in Copenhagen go back to 1876.

It was, therefore, decided to cover the period 1880–1940 and consequently confine the geographical scope of the study to Greater Copenhagen meaning the growing area which is commonly characterized as belonging to the capital.

(1) *Measurement of House-Building*

The difficulty in obtaining a good measure of house-building is not fundamentally different from the ordinary index number problem. But the weighting problem is thought to be rather important in this connection, because some of the factors determining house-building may be supposed primarily to influence house-building as measured by the number of dwellings, while other factors may be supposed mainly to influence house-building as measured by the size and/or quality of the unit.

Figures for the value of house-building at constant prices might have accounted for both quantitative and qualitative changes in house-building. However, investment figures are not available, in any case not figures with a satisfactory degree of reliability.

The data used are number of dwellings completed each year, distributed by number of rooms, and rent figures, also distributed by number of rooms.

The composition of house-building on the various sizes of apartments has been changing during the period. This might have been easily overcome by weighting the number of apartments by rent figures for the various sizes of apartments. But as a matter of fact the relative prices of apartments of the various sizes have changed substantially during the period. At the beginning of the period rent per room is lower in a small than in a large apartment, while the opposite is the case at the end of the period. This trend in relative rents may well be accounted for by changes in the relative qualities of small and large apartments. The two-room apartments built at the beginning of the period were intended for workers and can generally be supposed to be of much lower quality than larger apartments built at the same time. Such marked differences in quality related to the size of the apartment do not seem to matter very much later on. With growing demand for conveniences outside the living rooms, *e.g.* bathroom and kitchen installations, this tends to make a room more expensive in a small than in a large apartment since only living-rooms are counted as rooms.

The substantial change in relative rents necessitated a special investigation, as it was found desirable to take account of the changing composition of house-building as regards apartments of the various sizes. It was, therefore, decided to carry out the investigation with house-building measured in alternative ways. The series computed are :

(1) number of dwellings completed each year ;
(2) number of dwellings completed each year multiplied by average number of rooms =total number of rooms ;
(3) number of dwellings completed each year weighted together by relative rents at the beginning of the period ;
(4) number of dwellings completed each year weighted together by relative rents at the end of the period ;
(5) number of dwellings completed each year weighted together by relative rents at the time of construction.

It should be noted that the rent figures for apartments of the various sizes are average figures with rather large dispersions. Attention should also be drawn to the fact that until World War I the rent figures available are not broken down according to age of construction. This is not thought to cause much trouble as there does not seem to be large differences in the price (and quality) of new and old apartments in this part of the period. After World War I the rent figures used are based on rents in new buildings.

(2) *Measurement of Demographic Factors*

While demographic factors are measurable there is no straightforward way of measuring the demographic need for housing, except by reference to some arbitrary standard.

Such a standard might be thought of as a housing figure per inhabitant or per household (presupposing that a household is defined not as one or more people occupying together a unit of housing, but without reference to the housing circumstances of the household). The composition of the population by age and marital status could be taken into account, but still the weights attached to each group would be arbitrary.

As a matter of fact, the data showed over the entire period a nearly constant relation between effective demand for housing (as measured by (unweighted) number of occupied dwellings) and the number of married couples, which can be considered an exogeneous variable in this connection. This implies a nearly constant relation between the effective demand of married couples and the effective demand of unmarried people.[1]

This empirical knowledge is used as a means of obtaining a measure of the influence of demographic factors on house-building by assuming that net changes in the number of married couples indicate the same relative changes in the influence of demographic factors on house-building.

Since data on the number of married couples are only available in census years, *i.e.* normally every fifth year, it was necessary to estimate annual figures. The estimates are based on annual figures for marriages contracted, divorces and deaths by marital status in Greater Copenhagen and immigration to Greater Copenhagen. No information was available with respect to the number of marriages dissolved by death (which regarding a 5-year period will be somewhat less than deaths of married people) and to the marital status of immigrants.

(3) *Measurement of Real Income, Long-term Interest Rate, and Vacancy Rate*

The time series on real income is not satisfactory, but no other statistics are available. The series used is the per person of labour force figure for net national product (at factor cost) in urban industries in 1929 prices.[2]

A time series regarding the long-term interest rate does not present special problems. The figures used are yearly averages.[3]

Regarding the vacancy rate there are yearly data on the number of dwellings vacant at the end of April and 5-yearly data on the housing

[1] While the ratio of occupied dwellings to married couples fluctuated about 1·5, the ratio of occupied dwellings to total population showed a rising trend starting with 0·23 in 1880 and ending with 0·35 in 1940.

[2] K. Bjerke and N. Ussing, *Studier over Danmarks Nationalprodukt 1870–1950*, Copenhagen, 1958, Tables I and II, pp. 142-5.

[3] E. Hoffmeyer, *Strukturændringer på penge- og kapitalmarkedet*, Copenhagen, 1960, supplement 3, p. 156.

stock. The data on the housing stock are not too reliable at the beginning of the period. However, yearly figures are estimated and the vacancy rate is calculated as the percentage of dwellings vacant.

A graphical representation of the time series used is shown on pages 99 and 100.

IV. THE REGRESSION ANALYSIS

The symbols used are :

B = House-bulding completed each year.
See page 96 for alternative definitions.

ΔH = Net growth in the number of married couples, average for the current year and the two preceding years.

i = Long-term interest rate, yearly average.

V = Percentage of dwellings vacant.

R = Net national product (at factor cost) in urban industries in 1929 prices, million kroner per 1,000 persons in the labour force.

The regression analysis was carried out on linear equations of the following types :

$$B = f(\Delta H, i, V, R)$$
$$\frac{B}{\Delta H} = f(i, V, R)$$

Altogether 18 formulations were tried with different timelags for the variables and each formulation was tested for three periods separately, namely 1880–1940 and the sub-periods, 1880–1914, and 1920–1940 excluding the war years. This amounts to 54 regressions.

The result must generally speaking be said to be disappointing. The coefficient of multiple determination was in many cases significant, but the Durbin-Watson statistic frequently indicated severe serial correlation, and except for ΔH the individual parameter estimates often did not differ significantly from zero on the ordinary t-test or came out with the wrong sign.

An attempt at refinement was to introduce a special lag term measured as the average deviation over a short span of years in the immediate past of the ratio of new house-building to net increase in the number of married couples from the overall average of this ratio, which was approx. 1·5 as mentioned in footnote 1, page 101.

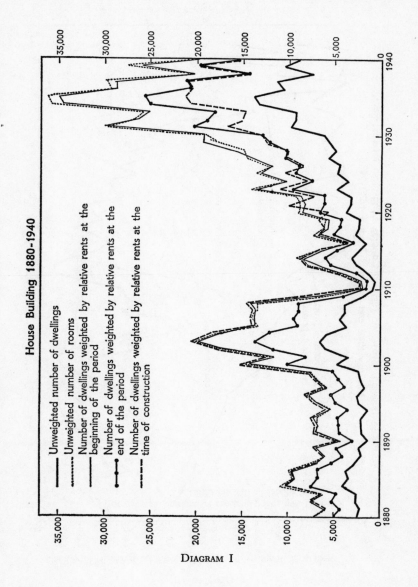

House Building 1880-1940

Unweighted number of dwellings
Unweighted number of rooms
Number of dwellings weighted by relative rents at the beginning of the period
Number of dwellings weighted by relative rents at the end of the period
Number of dwellings weighted by relative rents at the time of construction

DIAGRAM I

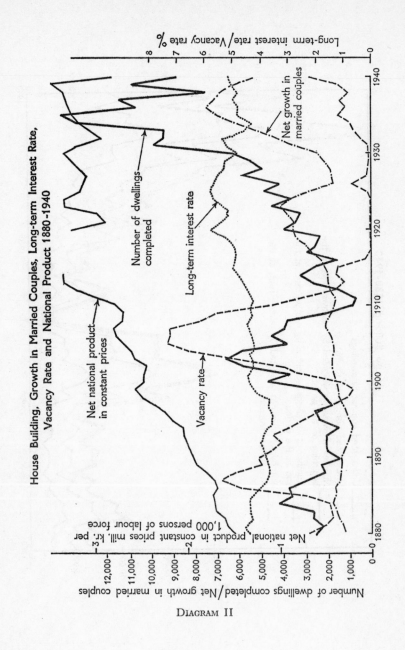

House Building, Growth in Married Couples, Long-term Interest Rate, Vacancy Rate and National Product 1880-1940

DIAGRAM II

$$1 \cdot 5 - \frac{\sum\limits_{t-1}^{t} B_\tau}{\sum\limits_{t-1}^{t} \Delta H_\tau}$$

This variable was thought to indicate whether house-building during some years had over-compensated or under-compensated the net increase in the number of married couples.

The inclusion of this variable improved the fit considerably — the coefficient of multiple determination rose to about 0·8 and the Durbin-Watson statistic to about 2, but the sign of the special variable came out wrong. A tendency to over-compensate would lead to further over-compensation and vice versa. This could hardly be acceptable for the entire period, and we shall therefore not report the empirical results with this formulation.[1]

A simple linear form of

$$B = f(\Delta H, i, V, R)$$

gave for the whole period of 1880–1940 a coefficient of multiple determination ranging from 0·60 to 0·76 for alternative definitions of B, while the Durbin-Watson statistic indicated severe serial correlation ($d < 1$).

However, the coefficients of i, V and R were not significantly different from zero. The coefficient of ΔH was highly significant (student's t ranging from 9 to 6).

The relatively best statistical fit for the entire period was obtained with B defined as the unweighted number of dwellings and with current values of the explanatory variables.

$$B_t = -1239 + 1 \cdot 5371 \Delta H_t + 392 i_t + 129 V_t - 72 R_t \qquad (1)$$
$$(2268)\ (0 \cdot 1655) \qquad (556)\ (131)\ (579)$$
$$R^2 = 0 \cdot 75 \ ; \qquad d = 0 \cdot 73$$

[1] The lag term variable may be taken to express a certain inertia which is no doubt a relevant factor in shaping the building cycle, *i.e.* the demand for housing may fluctuate rather substantially without giving rise to much response in the supply of new housing. Quite possibly a variable could be found which more directly represented this inertia than the variable here defined. It is, however, interesting to note one effect of the presence of this variable in the computations : Only when it is included in the regression do we get an estimate of the coefficient of V, the vacancy rate, which is significantly negative. Thus it might be useful to separate the inertia effect in two components : A tendency to continue house-building at the current level (or rate of growth) and a slowly working tendency to keep the vacancy rate at a normal level. That is to say the inertia effect is only slowly influenced by the vacancy rate.

The coefficient of the individual parameter R was positive and showed more tendency to be significant with B defined as the number of rooms or the weighted number of dwellings than with B defined as the unweighted number of dwellings.

These conclusions change, however, if the period is subdivided in the years 1880–1914 and 1920–40, disregarding the war years.

The model does not fit the data 1880–1914. None of the coefficients are significant.

For the period 1920–40 current values of the explanatory variables gave a coefficient of multiple determination ranging from 0·63 to 0·74 for alternative definitions of B. The Durbin-Watson statistic was close to 2 when B was defined as number of dwellings weighted by relative rents at the time of construction. For other definitions of B d ranged from about 1·3 to about 1·5.

However, regarding the partial coefficients only that of i was significant by the ordinary t-test. The negative coefficient of i was significant for all definitions of B with the highest t-value when B was defined as the number of rooms.

If for this period the explanatory variables are lagged one year the coefficient of i becomes more significant by the t-test, while the other partial coefficients remain insignificant. The introduction of a one-year lag instead of current values of the explanatory variables nearly doubles both the numerical value of the coefficient of i and the t-value of that coefficient. This holds good for all definitions of B. For instance we get with B defined as the number of dwellings weighted by relative rents at the time of construction :

$$B_t = 18335 + 0·7849\Delta H_t - 4469i_t + 2497V_t + 4380R_t \qquad (2)$$
$$(17005)\ (0·5473)\qquad (2015)\quad (1502)\quad (4040)$$
$$R^2 = 0·74 ; \qquad d = 2·06$$

and

$$B_t = 50583 - 0·0704\Delta H_{t-1} - 7398i_{t-1} + 4200V_{t-1} \qquad (3)$$
$$(11228)\ (0·5530)\qquad\quad (1921)\quad (2130)$$
$$R^2 = 0·75 ; \qquad d = 1·96$$

With B defined as unweighted number of dwellings we get still for the period 1920–40 :

$$B_t = 14299 + 0·4885\Delta H_t - 3076i_t + 1878V_t + 1891R_t \qquad (4)$$
$$(12393)\ (0·3989)\qquad (1468)\quad (1095)\quad (2944)$$
$$R^2 = 0·71 ; \qquad d = 1·54$$

and

$$B_t = 44716 - 0 \cdot 2081 \varDelta H_{t-1} - 6149 i_{t-1} + 2474 V_{t-1} - 1716 R_{t-1} \quad (5)$$
$$\text{(11044)} \; \text{(0·3606)} \qquad \text{(1247)} \quad \text{(1424)} \qquad \text{(2785)}$$
$$R^2 = 0 \cdot 80 ; \qquad d = 1 \cdot 26$$

Summarizing the results we may conclude that house-building appears to have varied with the long-term interest rate in the inter-war years, while it was not definitely sensitive to variations in the long-term interest rate prior to World War I.

The period 1880–1914 is characterized by two extreme building booms 1884–86 (in the peak year 1884 house-building was twice the 'normal' level) and 1900–8 (in peak years 1903–5 house-building was three times the 'normal' level).

These booms coincide with a more than normal growth in the number of married couples, but in no way with a growth which warranted the boom level of house-building.

The long-term interest rate was 15–20 per cent higher in the boom years than in the years between the two booms.

The most astonishing fact maybe is that in 1903–8 the boom level of house-building went on accompanied by an unprecedentedly high vacancy rate. Particularly during these years the attitude of the big private banks towards financing of house-building — resulting in the banking crisis of 1907–8 — contributes much to an explanation of the building boom. However, there must also have been a high degree of inertia in the reactions of building entrepreneurs, which inertia explains that a situation with 'too much' or 'too little' house-building could go on for years.

The high vacancy rates produced during the two building booms imply a weakening of the 'expected' relation between house-building and growth in the number of married couples.

This relation is maybe still more weakened by the fact that we have taken no account of demolitions. There are no data on demolitions, but there are 5-yearly data on the housing stock. As mentioned above, this data is not too reliable at the beginning of the period. However, compared with the figures for accumulated house-building they indicate a rate of demolition fluctuating from 3 to 35 per cent of yearly house-building.[1]

The inter-war years are characterized by housing shortage except for the last few years. Apart from the early thirties next to no demolitions occurred.

[1] The unusually high rate of 35 per cent applies to the years from 1906 to 1911.

The prolonged housing shortage which started during World War I implies that the 'expected' relation between house-building and growth in the number of married couples is not restored until the end of the period.

The 'over-production' during the building booms 1884–86 and 1900–8 combined with the housing shortage in most of the inter-war years explains why we find a statistically significant relationship between house-building and growth in the number of married couples when we regard the period 1880–1940 as a whole, but not when we regard the two sub-periods 1880–1914 and 1920–40 separately.

V. CONCLUSIONS

One reason for the unsatisfactory result of the statistical analysis is perhaps that we do not have sufficiently detailed time series for this long period.

It should not be forgotten, however, that the assumptions which we have to make in an inventory model like this are almost forbidding in their restrictiveness. As mentioned on page 93, we have to assume (1) that long-term financing is the only available possibility (recontracting and forward contracts being ruled out) and (2) that builders have definite expectations regarding the rate of interest. Furthermore, it must be assumed that the rent level does not change immediately and in the same direction as the interest rate.

The main conclusion is probably that the relationships are of a far more complicated nature than it is possible to discover by this analysis.

Chapter 9

HOME FINANCE AND HOUSING QUALITY IN AGEING NEIGHBOURHOODS[1]

BY

WILLIAM G. GRIGSBY

Institute of Urban Studies, University of Pennsylvania

I. INTRODUCTORY

THIS paper is directed to the problem of mortgage financing for old, inexpensive, one- and two-family homes that are not competitive with new construction, but are at or above minimum code standards ; and to the relationship of this problem to the level of expenditures for the maintenance and improvement of these homes. In American cities, it appears that such structures constitute as much as 15 per cent of the total occupied inventory.[2] Moreover, numerous additional dwellings, now in serious violation of local codes, were at some prior time no doubt in this category. The matter of adequate financing for ageing sectors of the stock is, therefore, a large component of the total residential finance problem. It is also a subject which American housing policy, in its emphasis on new construction and on rehabilitation programmes that operate largely outside normal market mechanisms, has almost completely ignored.

II. THE QUALITY-LIFE EXPECTANCY-FINANCING ISSUE

That a home financing problem in older neighbourhoods does indeed exist is commonly recognized. Yet it might be helpful to give it some dimension in order to focus the subsequent discussion.

In the City of Philadelphia, to cite a situation which is not atypical, mortgage payments required for an old $8,000 house are not appreciably less than those on a new $12,000 home. Thus, in the former

[1] I wish to thank Morton S. Baratz, Cushing Dolbeare, Christy Emerson, Frank Kristof, Grace Milgram, and Sue Moyerman for their many helpful criticisms and suggestions.
[2] According to rough calculations by the author, assuming values of one- and two-family rental units in this quality range to be approximately sixty times gross monthly rents.

case, the maximum loan which a buyer can obtain is about $7,000, at not less than 6 per cent, for not over fifteen years, necessitating a down payment of $1,000 and monthly level payments of $59.08. By comparison, on the $12,000 house, it would not be unusual for a mortgage institution to give a thirty-year 5½ per cent loan for $11,000, terms which would result in the same initial cash outlay and monthly charges of only $62.48 (Table 1). Assuming taxes on the more expensive structure were proportionately greater, though in Philadelphia this is uncertain, the tax differential would be $8.00. Outlays for maintenance and heat, however, might very well show a reverse relationship, assuming the older house was adequately maintained. Combining financing charges, taxes, and operating costs, therefore, it seems likely that the monthly outlays for the two houses would differ by less than 10 per cent, with virtually all of the difference being due to the tax component. Or looking at the matter somewhat differently, if the $8,000 house could be financed on the same terms as the $12,000 house, monthly mortgage payments would be only $39.76 and total costs correspondingly lower.

TABLE 1

COMPARISON OF TYPICAL MONTHLY OPERATING EXPENSES
OF NEW AND OLD SIX-ROOM SINGLE-FAMILY ROW HOMES
CITY OF PHILADELPHIA, 1964

Monthly Costs	Property A Value — $8,000 Age — 50 years	Property B Value — $12,000 Age — New
Financing	$59·08*	$62·48†
Taxes	16·00‡	24·00‡
Utilities	40·00§	40·00§
Maintenance	15·00‖	15·00‖
Insurance	1·00¶	1·50
Management	—**	—**
Vacancy loss	—††	—††
Interest foregone	—‡‡	—‡‡
Depreciation	—§§	—§§
Total	$131·08	$142·98

* $7,000, 15-year, 6 per cent, level payment loan.
† $11,000, 30-year, 5¼ per cent, level payment loan.
‡ $4/100 of assessed value. Assessed value assumed to equal 60 per cent of market

On the basis of evidence such as this, some analysts have concluded that the older sectors of the used stock and those who seek to buy homes in these sectors are being discriminated against by private lenders. Such apparently onerous terms are, in fact, said to lead to a shift to absentee ownership, conversions, lower maintenance, and decline in quality — the very consequences which lenders fear and seek to avoid. Their policies seem rational only because they help create the situation which has been prophesied.

Lenders contend on the other hand that : (*a*) Life expectancy of the older structures does not warrant a longer-term loan ; (*b*) the higher risk with respect to both buyer and property warrants a higher down payment ; (*c*) the family really is not being discriminated against, for if his home depreciates more slowly than the mortgagee has predicted, he simply accumulates equity faster ; (*d*) a lower down payment would mean higher monthly payments which the borrower quite possibly could not afford ; (*e*) the comparison in any case is not fair because most new-home buyers make down payments considerably above the minimum required ; (*f*) an older, cheaper house can be financed with loans exceeding fifteen years if in good condition and in a good neighbourhood ; and (*g*) after all, many families do buy old homes despite the more onerous mortgage terms.

Without more information, it is not possible to deal with all of these assertions. It does seem intuitively, however, that lenders may be over-compensating for the extra risks which their experience

value. There is some tendency in Philadelphia, however, for the AV/MV ratio to be higher on old, inexpensive homes than on new ones.

§ For structures of equal size and similar occupancy, water and electric bills should be about the same. Since newer structures are better insulated, however, and may have more efficient heating units, their fuel bill may be lower. Nevertheless, to avoid controversy, utility payments have been assumed to be equal.

‖ Annual maintenance assumed to be 1¼ per cent of market value of the new home and equal, in absolute terms, on the old structure. Assuming 'adequate' maintenance, somehow defined, this expenditure certainly will not be less on the old than on the new, but might very well be more. Again, to avoid argument, equality has been presumed.

¶ Assumed to be proportional to market value, though insurance rates are frequently higher in older areas.

** Structures assumed to be owner-occupied, so no management charge unless one is imputed.

†† Structures assumed to be owner-occupied.

‡‡ This is not an operating expense. The monthly interest loss for the first year on the $1,000 down payment at 4 per cent is $3·33. The interest loss in subsequent years depends on the amount of real equity accumulated, which in turn is a function of market trends and the rate at which the mortgage loan is repaid. If lenders have correctly assessed the remaining economic lives of the two buildings and if the mortgage terms accurately reflect these assessments, the amount of accumulated real equities should not differ greatly. One of the points at issue, however, is whether mortgagees do, in fact, forecast the future correctly.

§§ Unknown until property is transferred. The amount of actual depreciation is frequently obscured by the fact that owners take depreciation, as it were, in the form of alterations, additions, and even some forms of repairs, which actually improve the quality of the structure over what it was originally.

suggests do exist, and in any case it can be shown that, for one reason or another, payments on homes in the older, lower-quality neighbourhoods are excessive. The following section of the paper attempts to demonstrate this proposition and discusses a few of the immediately apparent implications.

TABLE 2

VALUE OF A HYPOTHETICAL RESIDENTIAL STRUCTURE OVER THE VARIOUS
STAGES OF ITS ECONOMIC LIFE, ASSUMING CONSTANT QUALITY,
FIXED AND PREDETERMINED LIFE EXPECTANCY, AND NO ACCUMU-
LATION OF EQUITY BY OWNER*

1	2	3	4	5	6
Age of Structure (Years)	Monthly Level Mortgage Payment ($) †	Term of Mortgage (Years)	Interest Rate on Mortgage Loan (%)	Monthly Level Payment $1,000 ($) ‡	Value of Structure Which Mortgage Payments can support ($) §
0	55	40	6	5·50	10,000
5	55	35	6	5·70	9,650
10	55	30	6	6·00	9,150
15	55	25	6	6·44	8,550
20	55	20	6	7·16	7,670
25	55	15	6	8·44	6,500
30	55	10	6	11·10	4,950
35	55	5	6	19·30	2,850
40	—	—	—	—	0

* See text for complete enumeration of assumptions.
† Remains constant because quality, as defined in text, remains constant.
‡ Rises over time, because, with change of ownership each five years as assumed in text, a new mortgage loan with shorter amortization period is created.
§ $\frac{\text{Column 2}}{\text{Column 5}} \times \$1,000$. Rounded to nearest $50.

III. MONTHLY MORTGAGE PAYMENTS AND HOUSING QUALITY

The widespread existence of similar down payments and monthly mortgage payments on structures having substantially different values does not, in theory, necessarily indicate different mortgage lending policies with respect to either the structures or the individuals acquiring them. In practice, however, it does suggest some problems with respect to the functioning of the housing market which demand attention. Both the theoretical and practical questions can perhaps best be illuminated by a series of illustrations which show how changes in quality and expected economic life of hypothetical residential structures affect monthly payments and market value. First, however, it is necessary to define our terms.

In ordinary usage, housing quality and expected economic life are not mutually exclusive. Higher quality implies longer economic life and vice versa. To simplify the analysis, housing quality is defined here in such a way as to eliminate this relationship. Specifically, it refers only to the *current flow of services* of a residential structure, not to the structure itself. As a consequence, it excludes durability, an attribute which is commonly regarded as one aspect of quality, but which, since it also has to do with the absolute level of services over time, is obviously an element of economic life as well.

To simplify things even further, quality is interpreted here to mean everything that would affect market value except space, expected length of flow of services, financing, real estate taxes, and perceived risks of ownership. Thus it includes not only condition of structure, but accessibility to work and community facilities, quality of surrounding neighbourhood, architectural style, modernity of household equipment, and services by the landlord. Because style is included as one of the factors, either a positive or negative shift in the quality of a dwelling could be occasioned by a simple change in tastes which render the unit more or less able to satisfy consumer preferences. Such an assumption would not always be acceptable. For some purposes, it is vital to regard quality and style as quite distinct characteristics. In the present instance, however, lumping the two together reduces the complexity of the discussion without altering the essential points.

Proceeding now to the analysis, imagine first a new $10,000 rental dwelling unit which has a firmly fixed life expectancy of forty years that is known in advance ; which does not change in quality either absolutely or relative to the rest of the inventory ;[1] and which has zero scrap value. Assume too that there are no real estate taxes, so that the only expense which may vary significantly over the life of the structure is monthly debt service. Assume further that the unit is transferred every five years to an investor who desires the same rate of return and perceives the same risks as the preceding investor ; whose credit rating is so high he is able to obtain 100 per cent financing for

---

[1] Thus it is very much like the one-horse shay. The illustration implies that the neighbourhood does not change in quality. The neighbourhood need not, however, have the same economic life as the house.

TABLE 3

VALUE OF A HYPOTHETICAL RESIDENTIAL STRUCTURE OVER THE VARIOUS STAGES OF ITS ECONOMIC LIFE, GIVEN CERTAIN ASSUMPTIONS REGARDING ORIGINAL VALUE, LIFE EXPECTANCY, CHANGES IN QUALITY, AND AVAILABLE FINANCING*

1 Age of Structure (Years)	2 Expected Remaining Life (Years)	3 Monthly Level Mtge Payment, Constant Quality ($)	4 Term of Mortgage (Years)	5 Interest Rate on Mortgage Loan (%)	6 Monthly Level Payment/$1,000 ($)	7 Value of Structure, Constant Quality ($)†	8 Value of Structure, Declining Quality ($)‡	9 Monthly Level Mtge Payment, Declining Quality ($)§
0	Indefinite	50	Unamortized	6	5·00	10,000	10,000	50·00
5	Indefinite	50	Unamortized	6	5·00	10,000	10,000	50·00
10	Indefinite	50	Unamortized	6	5·00	10,000	10,000	50·00
15	55	50	55	6	5·19	9,750	9,500	49·30
20	50	50	50	6	5·26	9,500	9,000	47·30
25	45	50	45	6	5·36	9,300	8,550	45·80
30	40	50	40	6	5·50	9,100	8,100	44·50
35	35	50	35	6	5·70	8,750	7,500	42·80
40	30	50	30	6	6·00	8,350	6,850	41·10
45	25	50	25	6	6·44	7,750	6,000	38·60
50	20	50	20	6	7·16	7,000	5,000	35·80
55	15	50	15	6	8·44	5,950	3,700	31·20
60	15	50	15	6	8·44	5,950	3,450	29·10
65	15	50	15	6	8·44	5,950	3,200	27·00
70	15	50	15	6	8·44	5,950	2,950	24·90

* See text for enumeration of assumptions. See footnotes * and ‡, Table 2, for explanation of columns 3 and 6.

† $\dfrac{\text{Column 3}}{\text{Column 6}} \times \$1,000$. Rounded to nearest $50.

‡ Column 7 minus $50 per year for each year of life of structure *after* year 10. Rounded to nearest $50.

§ $\dfrac{\text{Column 8} \times \text{Column 6}}{1,000}$. Rounded to nearest ten cents.

a period equal to the remaining life of the building ; and who chooses this financing because he does not desire to accumulate equity over his short period of ownership. Finally, postulate no booms or recessions, or changes in population, income or market knowledge that would affect rates of occupancy or sale prices.

Under these circumstances, where housing quality and investor motivation are constant and where economic life expectancy and all risks are known and invariant, what would be the shape of the depreciation (price) curve for the structure and how would financing terms and monthly payments shift in each succeeding five-year period?

This question is best answered indirectly. It is obvious on the face that monthly rentals[1] on structures providing services of equal quality must be equal, just as differences in quality of services must be reflected in differences in rent. Therefore, if, as assumed here, expenses and desired rate of return are also equal, so then will be monthly mortgage payments regardless of the age of the structure. Working backward, if monthly payments are equal and no real equity is accumulated, the value of the structure at the end of any five-year period will be the unpaid balance of the mortgage outstanding at that time. All of this is shown in Table 2 and Graph A where it may be seen that the depreciation curve is convex to the origin and describes a path precisely equal to that of a curve which would show the rate of accumulation of equity on a forty-year level payment mortgage. Or, in other words, as monthly payments per \$1,000 rise with successive decreases in term of mortgage, the amount of market value which can be supported by constant total mortgage payments declines at an increasing rate.[2]

It can be seen too that the assumption of a fixed life is not necessary to conclusions regarding monthly payments and quality. We can, in fact, generalize as follows : Regardless of age or expected remaining life, residential structures which provide services of equal quality should have equal monthly mortgage payments; and structures supplying services of different quality should have different payments ; if all other factors mentioned earlier are equal.[3] If the economic life

---

[1] Or monthly housing expenses for owner-occupiers.

[2] It might seem on the surface that the depreciation (price) curve should be linear ; that is, if quality is constant, the structure should be worth \$5,000 after 20 years, \$2,500 after 30 years, and so forth. It is necessary, however, to discount the value of future streams of services to arrive at present value. More precisely, value for any year X between zero and 40 would be the present value of an annuity for 40 minus X years.

[3] Particularly taxes, which, if *ad valorem*, do reflect quality differences, and thus in the real world would have to be included along with monthly mortgage payments in any comparisons.

of one dwelling is longer than that of another, this fact should be reflected in price, not monthly payments. No matter what combinations or changes in quality and life expectancy one assumes, these theoretical relationships hold.

The next question is : How much would monthly payments and prices be affected by *assumed* differences in quality? To illuminate

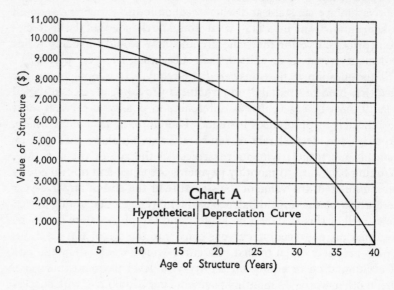

Chart A

Hypothetical Depreciation Curve

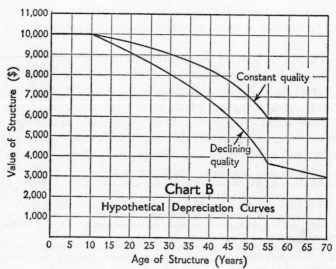

Chart B

Hypothetical Depreciation Curves

this matter, a second illustration is presented below, this time with a more realistic representation of economic life expectancy of the residential inventory.

Assume a structure which through the first ten years of its existence is expected to have an indefinitely long life; during the next forty-five years, a life expectancy of seventy years from date of construction; and for the remaining years of its existence, an economic life of fifteen more years, regardless of its age.[1] Further, assume somewhat unrealistically that mortgage lenders at any time will grant 100 per cent loans for the full length of the remaining anticipated life of the structure.[2] Finally, in order to provide a basis for comparison with situations of declining quality, which is our purpose here, assume initially that quality remains constant throughout the life of the structure.[3] The depreciation curve which results from these assumptions is presented in Graph B (line A) and Table 3 (column 7). Except for the first ten and the final fifteen years, the curve follows a path similar to that shown in Graph A, so needs no further explanation.

Now, to determine the effect of assumed declines in quality on the shape and level of the price curve and on monthly payments at successive points in time, let the level of maintenance, repair, and periodic modernization be such as to yield a rate of deterioration and obsolescence valued in the market at $50 (one-half of one per cent of the original value of the structure) per year, after the tenth year. Combined with the effect of decreasing life expectancy on value, this produces an over-all average depreciation rate after seventy years of one per cent per year (Graph B, line B, and Table 3, column 8) which is not out of line with several empirical studies.[4] The monthly

[1] The assumption of 15 years life expectancy would seem reasonably consistent with current mortgage practice of not granting loans of over 10 years on old, low-quality structures. At the other end, a presumption of an economic life expectancy of 70 years for new structures may not seem consistent with maximum mortgage loans of 30 years, but mortgage lenders limit the maximum term to 30 years for other reasons.

[2] This is simply to avoid the arithmetic problem of accumulated equity and does not affect the essence of any arguments to follow.

[3] In addition, of course, all the other assumptions presented in connection with the first model also apply.

[4] William Hoad, 'Real Estate Prices', unpublished doctoral dissertation, University of Michigan, 1942. Grebler, Blank, and Winnick, *Capital Formation in Residential Real Estate*, National Bureau of Economic Research, Princeton University Press, 1956. Robert W. Hartman, 'Demand for the Stock of Non-Farm Housing', unpublished doctoral dissertation, Harvard University, 1964. Hoad, closer to 1 per cent, is thought to be more accurate than Grebler *et al*. The loss in value due to deterioration and obsolescence must not be interpreted as equal to the amount of money required to restore the structure to its original quality, particularly when, as in this example, the definition of quality includes neighbourhood environment.

mortgage payments required to finance the purchase of the structure at its various value levels appear in Table 3, column 9.

Comparing columns 7, 8, and 9 in Table 3, it is apparent that the effect of assumed differences in quality on monthly payments and market value for our hypothetical structure do not approximate to reality. For example, in the fiftieth year, a quality difference of only 20 per cent $\left(\dfrac{(50)\ (40)}{10,000}\right)$ between old and new structures is associated with a price differential of 50 per cent $\left(\dfrac{10,000 - 5,000}{10,000}\right)$ and a monthly payment differential of almost 30 per cent $\left(\dfrac{50\cdot00 - 35\cdot80}{50\cdot00}\right)$. Similarly, at the end of seventy years, a quality differential of only 30 per cent results in a price that is fully 70 per cent lower and a spread in monthly payments of 50 per cent.

By comparison, it will be recalled that typical new $12,000 and old, obsolescing $8,000 structures in Philadelphia have virtually the same monthly mortgage payments (Table 1). The comparison is somewhat misleading, because for these dwellings the quality gap is reflected not only in the $3.40 difference in financing charges, but also, in part at least, in the $8.00 spread in tax payments.[1] That is, if the structures were either not taxed at all or taxed on the basis of current rents, the spread in capital values and hence in monthly financing charges might be greater. Even when the full tax load is included, however, the equivalent difference in monthly payments is a mere 15 per cent $\left(\dfrac{59\cdot08 + 16\cdot00}{62\cdot48 + 24\cdot00}\right)$, an amount which seems an inadequate reflection of quality differences.

IV. THEORY VERSUS REALITY

Although the model just presented fails to approximate the real world, it does describe a market which would probably be superior, from the stand-point of the consumer, to the one now existing. For this reason, it may be useful to inquire into its underlying assumptions and implications more thoroughly. Are the relationships revealed by the model a consequence of its simplifying constraints, or do they

[1] Again assuming maintenance expenditures are equal for the two structures, even though higher initial quality could imply less frequent replacement and repair of various parts of the structure.

correctly imply defects in the existing real estate market mechanism?

Perhaps the most critical assumption has to do with quality, for which there are no objective measures except those provided by the market itself. Since the functioning of the market is in essence the matter which is in question, we are left without any measure of quality at all, only value judgments. Nor is there any easy way out of this dilemma. Several of the seemingly obvious ways to identify and measure quality differences turn out on closer inspection to be unacceptable. For example, at first glance it might appear that the true difference between the quality of two structures is equal to the amount of money required to eliminate this difference. Some aspects of quality, however, are not reproducible in an existing structure except at great expense, if at all. Indeed this is a major barrier to unsubsidized rehabilitation efforts. A second possible method for determining differences in quality would be to have a sample of persons visit homes in various price categories and estimate what they, themselves, would be willing to pay for each structure. It seems probable, though, that persons who could afford products appreciably higher in quality than the ones which they were examining, whether these be houses or automobiles or food or clothing, would tend to undervalue the lower quality items. And conversely, that high quality items would tend to be undervalued by persons who could not afford them. Moreover, all observers would be influenced by the prevailing price structure.

There is, moreover, some evidence that differences in quality *are* reflected adequately in the market. Thus, in Philadelphia in 1960, at least 30 per cent of the households residing in single-family owner-occupied structures valued at less than $9,000 had reported value-income ratios of 1 : 1 or less, suggesting their ability to acquire much more expensive accommodations. In other words, no matter how the relationship of quality to value and monthly payments in the older, cheaper sections of the stock is viewed by 'impartial' observers, a substantial number of families who have actually made a market decision and who have a reasonably wide range of choice are evidently either not aware of any significant distortions or place such a low value on housing quality as to be unresponsive to them.[1]

The second major assumption which may be called into question is not part of the model itself, but is one of the reasons for its construction. This is the implicit suggestion that because quality

---

[1] Or are locked in as a consequence of price declines. This, however, would seem improbable for more than a small proportion of owners.

differences seem to be proportionally greater than monthly mortgage payments, the fault lies in financing practices. It might be argued, however, that unduly high prices, not conservative mortgage terms, explain the apparently excessive monthly payments for old units. Further, that if terms were liberalized, prices might simply rise correspondingly, leaving monthly payments the same.

This line of reasoning fails to consider that if demand is great enough relative to supply to consistently value houses at an excessively high figure, the economic life of these structures must be longer than lenders are ready to admit. Equally important, the argument is tantamount to a claim that financing terms are neutral in their effect on the market. Such is hardly the case. As increasingly conservative mortgage terms on older structures depress prices, they also prevent the accumulation of equities by existing owners, thus limiting potential demand by this group for more expensive units. Moreover, although liberalized mortgage terms would certainly stimulate additional demand from lower income families, this demand by definition would not inflate prices enough to leave monthly payments unchanged. Further, price inflation would certainly affect demand as purchasers with somewhat higher incomes observed a diminishing differential in prices between new and old structures without any change in either quality or economic life expectancy of the latter. Home buyers whose income and asset position is such that they are not dependent upon liberal financing for their acquisitions would be particularly responsive to such a change.[1] The shift of these families upward not only would stimulate new construction, but simultaneously would limit the extent of price inflation in the sectors of the existing stock from which these families came by an amount sufficient to yield some net reduction in monthly payments.

The key point, then, is much more than that financing is not a passive factor, an observation which all would accept. It is that liberalized financing of old, less expensive, used homes should, by providing support from below, stimulate the demand for new construction.

A third and final feature of the model which merits comment has to do with the relationship between financing and depreciation which, for purposes of simplicity, was defined in such a way that owners never accumulated any equity in their homes. In real life, variations

[1] Ramsay Wood, 'Credit Terms and Demand for Residential Construction', *Study of Mortgage Credit*. Committee on Banking and Currency, Subcommittee on Housing, United States Senate, 85th Congress, 2nd Session, United States Government Printing Office, 1958 pp. 87-121.

in down payments and amortization periods yield differences in real equities among owners which obscure comparisons of monthly payments and housing quality. Where payments appear to be excessive, for example, the owner may be amortizing his loan much faster relative to depreciation than are other owners with whose properties comparisons are being made.[1] To make the model a useful tool for evaluating actual situations, the original constraint with respect to financing must be relaxed to allow for normal differences in lending terms within sectors of the inventory which are of equal quality. With this modification, the conclusion of the model would be that, holding buyer risk constant, differences in quality among structures should be reflected in corresponding differences in monthly payments on the most liberal mortgage loans which can be readily obtained for these structures.

In conclusion, differences in quality among various parts of the residential inventory do not seem to be adequately reflected in prevailing prices and mortgage terms, though the extremely limited evidence that was examined is mixed. Perhaps, if lower quality housing had been included in the analysis, more firm judgments could have been reached. In any case, however, even if one cannot successfully argue that financing practices with respect to older sectors of the stock are discriminatory or irrational, or perverse, it does appear that more liberal mortgage lending policies in these sectors would not only benefit families who seek inexpensive residential accommodations in the existing stock, but would stimulate new construction as well.

V. CONSEQUENCES OF GENERAL RELAXATION OF LOAN CRITERIA

At the present time, use of liberal mortgage terms to provide better housing in older areas for lower-middle and low income families is

---

[1] Indeed, this is one argument which mortgage lenders make in defence of their policies with respect to older dwellings. Even when they err, so the argument goes, in assigning short economic lives to structures that continue in the inventory for many more years, the consequence is simply a more rapid than anticipated accumulation of equity by purchasers. Or in other words, mistakes on the side of caution simply benefit consumers and hence are no cause for concern. The problem with this argument is that it ignores the potential purchasers who are excluded from the market by undue caution. Consequently, to the extent that apparently excessive required monthly payments on old structures do have the effect of raising the rate of growth of real equities above the average for the total market, this is support for the contention that the payments are in fact too high. As already observed, though, the depressing effect of such policies on prices may tend to retard growth of real equities.

limited almost entirely to designated renewal areas and to structures that are rehabilitated to so-called 'long-term' standards.[1] This approach has proven to be slow, cumbersome, and quite inadequate to the task. Although there are a number of areas where striking improvements have been achieved, the rate at which rehabilitation is occurring is discouraging. And an unintended consequence in some instances is the displacement of resident families and the re-occupancy of the improved dwellings by higher income households.

The implications of this situation and of the preceding analysis are that more rapid gains could be achieved by making long-term, low-down-payment loans generally available in areas and for structures which are now denied such financing. Lower income families in large numbers could then move into better accommodations and part of the savings in monthly payments would in the normal course of events be applied to better maintenance and limited rehabilitation. The visual results would not be so striking as in the case where all the savings which result from refinancing are applied to renovation, but the improvements would be more widespread. This at least would seem to be the argument.

In order to check this reasoning in a preliminary way, a comparison was made of the position of mortgagors under existing versus liberal financing, assuming a general change in mortgage lending policies in old areas (Table 4). Given the assumptions in Table 4, not all of the hoped-for consequences appear to be likely, because about one-half of the reduction in monthly payments due to a longer amortization period is offset by a larger mortgage and by premiums for insurance that would be necessary to attract debt capital. Part of the insurance is an extra benefit as well as an extra cost to the borrower, but it still increases his total cash outlay, if only slightly. Monthly payments on debt, and also taxes, are affected additionally by the rise in prices (in this case assumed to be 5 per cent) which more favourable credit terms would engender.[2] The net result is only a modest decline in monthly payments, not enough to have a material effect on maintenance, repairs, and rehabilitation. Indeed, since the

---

[1] An exception may be New Haven, Connecticut, where the Federal Housing Administration now interprets code and long-term standards as one and the same.
[2] Thus for buyers who can afford the higher down payments and monthly charges, the liberalized credit has undesirable consequences. See Ramsay Wood, *op. cit.* By the same token, however, it brings benefits to sellers, but since most sellers, particularly the absentee owners, probably have higher incomes than the buyers, the price rise is not neutral in its welfare effects. Against this argument, though, must be weighed the possibility that increased construction occasioned by the change in credit will ultimately reduce prices and rents in the lower-quality stock. This aspect of the question has already been discussed.

principal consequence of the change in credit terms would be a shift in occupancy to families with both lower earnings and fewer liquid assets, unless various carrots and sticks were used to generate higher levels of maintenance and rehabilitation, no increase in this activity would occur except that which owner-occupancy itself would precipitate.[1] And to the extent that improvements did occur, monthly housing costs would rise, because for the lower income immigrants, the leverage of liberal financing would already have been exhausted at the time of purchase.

The principal benefits, then, would accrue not in the areas in which liberalized credit were extended, but to the families who received it.[2] Admittedly, they would probably have to pay higher prices than formerly existed and their mortgage payments would continue over a much longer period of time, but they would also have better housing

TABLE 4

COMPARISON OF MONTHLY OPERATING EXPENSES FOR AN OLD, SIX-ROOM
SINGLE-FAMILY ROW HOUSE, UNDER TWO DIFFERENT ASSUMPTION
AS TO FINANCING, CITY OF PHILADELPHIA, 1964

Monthly Costs	I Value — $8,000 15-Year, Level Payment Mortgage, $7,000, 6%	II Value — $8,400* 30-Year, Level Payment Mortgage, $8,000, 5½%
Financing	$59·08	$44·94
Taxes	16·00†	16·80†
Utilities	40·00‡	40·00‡
Maintenance	15·00§	15·00§
Property insurance	1·00‖	1·00‖
Mortgage insurance	—	3·33¶
Mortgagor insurance	—	1·88**
Total	$131·08	$122·95

* Value of $8,400 assumes that liberal credit increases prices by 5 per cent.
† See footnote   ‡, Table 1. ‡ See footnote §, Table 1.
§ See footnote ‖, Table 1.   ‖ See footnote ¶, Table 1.
¶ Assumed to be one-half of 1 per cent of outstanding value of mortgage.
** Assumed to be 3 per cent of monthly payments on mortgage, taxes, and propert insurance.

[1] A possible exception would be existing owners who had already paid off most of their mortgage loans and chose to rehabilitate with funds obtained by refinancing. Without encouragement of such activity, however, there is no reason to expect it to occur at any greater scale than is the case today.
[2] And to the home-building industry, but this point has already been discussed

than before. The difference should be particularly pronounced for families moving into owner-occupancy from marginal rental units where a large portion of their total payment represents a return for entrepreneurial risk and management expense.

In brief, although the lower monthly payments would create a potential for rehabilitation (in Table 4, about $1,000 of improvements could be financed without increasing total payments), upward filtering of families would substantially reduce it. The consequences of extending liberalized mortgage terms widely throughout the older sectors of the housing stock would, therefore, not only be quantitatively different from the effects of credit extension that is tied to rehabilitation, but qualitatively different as well.

VI. REVERSING PRESENT LENDING POLICIES

Although, as stated earlier, it cannot be demonstrated that individual mortgagees are unduly cautious with respect to the risks of making loans in lower-quality areas, it does seem possible that for the group as a whole steps could be taken which would lessen the likelihood of severe loss by any single institution and thus provide the basis for a change in lending policies. The federal government has already done much to overcome mortgage finance problems associated with creating new inventory. It now needs comparable procedures to effect a more orderly market for old structures as well.

The most obvious first step would be for lending institutions and the Federal Housing Administration to either abandon or rationalize the concept of economic life as a basis for determining mortgage terms, since its use obscures the nature of the problem to be solved. Each residential structure does indeed have an economic life which is not simply the period of years over which it provides a flow of services, but its value in each of these years. There is, however, virtually no knowledge on which to base estimates of the future economic life of various types of structures or to justify present FHA practices in arriving at estimates of remaining economic life. This fact is reflected in the abysmal predictive record which lenders have amassed. Actually, while they talk generally about economic lives of twenty, thirty, forty, and fifty years for various structures, their policies constitute a statement that they really have no idea as to how to make specific predictions, and, therefore, quite understandably, grant terms that minimize risk of loss either through or in case of foreclosure. Thus, short-term mortgages are granted not where economic life has been shown to be brief, but where risks and uncertainties are greater than average.

This would suggest that a solution to the problem lies in the direction of identifying these uncertainties, protection against which demands a high fee, and converting them to socialized risks which could be handled actuarily for a lesser charge. Among the greater than average uncertainties which mortgage investors in older areas face are the possibility of loss of income by borrowers, diminution in over-all demand, lower quality occupancy, neighbourhood decline, and ultimate complete and permanent rejection of mortgaged structures by the market.

Extension of mortgage insurance programmes to older dwellings would seem to be one obvious approach. It seems apparent, though, that much more is needed to change lending practices, especially since insurance and liberal terms probably would not extend to the lowest levels of the inventory where stabilization is also needed. The problem here is particularly acute, because the increment to new construction which would be supported by better financing in older areas would lead to increased abandonment in some of these areas. Thus, unless care were taken as to where credit terms were liberalized, the prophecy of longer economic life, as implied in these terms, would not, in contrast to the pessimistic prophecies that underlie present lending policies, be even partly self-fulfilling. Rather, it would be self-defeating.

How to identify structures actually nearing the point of retirement and how to treat them are, then, crucial questions. At the moment, government programmes, in so far as their effect on these structures is concerned, are almost perverse. For as private new construction and residential renewal are accelerated to expand the supply of housing, there is a corresponding acceleration of abandonments at the bottom, a condition which intensifies investor uncertainty, perpetuates high rates of return and guarantees low levels of maintenance. The potentially favourable effects of faster filtering are in this manner at least partially unrealized. The situation is made worse by the fact that public housing takes primarily 'good' families, leaving private enterprise to cope with the maintenance and other difficulties created by problem tenants.

Two proposals which have been offered to improve both mortgage financing practices and housing quality in the lowest sectors of the inventory are, first, a guaranteed retirement price for residential structures, and, second, the assurance that all families can afford to pay enough rent to acquire standard accommodation. Analysis of these possibilities is beyond the scope of this paper, but, to end on a note of hope, their examination by others suggest that perhaps they are less utopian than might initially seem to be the case.[1]

[1] Background papers prepared for the Existing Housing Committee and the Finance Committee of the Philadelphia Housing Association by the staff of the Association, 1964.

Chapter 10

HOUSING TAXATION AND HOUSING POLICY[1]

BY

RICHARD NETZER

Graduate School of Public Administration, New York University

I. INTRODUCTORY

IN much of the world, the supply of housing is largely determined by private investment decisions; in some other countries, housing investment decisions are public ones in large part, but housing is offered at close to economic prices, and consumer decisions as to the disposition of consumption expenditures have a bearing on the level and composition of the housing stock. In either situation — wherever private investment and/or consumption decisions heavily influence the resolution of a country's housing 'problem' — governmental housing policy measures include not only the familiar positive financial inducements in the form of subsidies and favourable credit terms but also the negative instrument of taxes on housing.

In some Western countries, there is awareness that existing fiscal systems tax housing consumption at high rates and therefore offer a policy variable with much leverage. This is indicated by the use of tax abatement and tax exemption schemes to foster particular kinds of housing construction. However, systematic analysis of overall tax effects on housing decisions for an entire economy is infrequent. The purpose of this paper is to classify the types of tax impacts on private housing decisions to be found in developed Western countries; to present some quantification for a few cases, notably for the United States; and to make some non-quantitative judgments as to the overall effect of tax systems in various countries.

[1] A considerable portion of the research underlying this paper was done in connection with a study of the economics of the property tax in the United States, sponsored by the Brookings Institution Programme of Studies in Government Finance.

II. NEUTRALITY AND UNNEUTRALITY OF TAXATION

Private housing decisions are, of course, affected, as are all private consumption and investment decisions, by aggregate fiscal policies. For example, under the 'balanced-budget multiplier' hypothesis, total private expenditure, including that for housing, might very well be greater if the budget is balanced at a high rather than at a low level of public expenditure. In this analysis, however, the concern is with *differential* tax effects on housing as such. The overall tax level may be high or low, and taxes on income, expenditure and/or wealth may be high or low without necessarily having differentially favourable or adverse effects on housing decisions.

What we seek, therefore, is evidence of lack of tax neutrality with respect to forms of private consumption and types of private investment. Since tax systems are complex and have evolved over many years, typically without real effort to secure this kind of neutrality, we should expect to find numerous unneutralities, some favouring housing and some discouraging it. The question for housing policy is the net effect of these offsetting unneutralities in taxation (other policies affecting housing provide a variety of unneutralities, but are beyond the scope of this paper).

(i) *Income Tax Provisions* [1]

Among the major theoretical advantages of income taxation is its neutrality among specific types of investment and consumption decisions. Income taxes do, of course, affect the choice between income and leisure and perhaps have a bearing on willingness to accept risks, especially with graduated rates and inadequate income-averaging provisions ; with graduated rates, they are likely to have some overall impact on the consumption function (consumption relative to before-tax income) as well. But in concept the income tax might be expected to be neutral with regard to housing decisions.

However, there are at least three aspects of income taxation which may produce significant unneutralities with respect to housing : the treatment of capital gains ; provisions for depreciation and investment allowances ; and the treatment of income and expenses connected with owner-occupied housing.

The tax treatment of capital gains is relevant here because the nature of real estate markets and the real estate investment process is

---

[1] A major source for the information on tax provisions in Western Europe which underlies this and subsequent sections of this paper is Federation of British Industries, *Taxation in Western Europe, 1964* (London, 1964).

such that a significant share of the returns from private investment in real estate are realized in the form of capital gains. For example, property developers frequently do not retain ownership for very long periods, but instead sell out their interests to long-term investors. If capital gains are favourably treated in general under the tax laws, and if property developers can secure this favourable treatment, this kind of investment is likely to be encouraged.

The questions here, then, are :

Do a country's personal and company income-tax systems treat capital gains in general relatively favourably?

Does this favourable treatment apply equally to real estate and to other types of investment?

If so, is housing investment treated like other real estate investment?

Most countries tax capital gains realized in the ordinary course of business as ordinary income, but the definition of this varies. The major variable relates to the treatment of all other capital gains. In some places, such as Ireland, they are not taxed at all. In most places, they are fully taxable if not held for specified periods, which range widely from as little as six months to as much as ten years ; a few countries tax gains realized within the statutory holding period at preferentially low rates (*e.g.* for individuals in Austria). In most cases, gains realized beyond the holding period are free of tax entirely, but in some places, like the United States, even these long-term gains are taxed, although at preferential rates.

It appears that capital gains on residential real estate are usually given equal treatment with those on other real property.[1] However, very frequently capital gains on real property are treated substantially less favourably than those of other types, by providing for a longer statutory holding period. The following are some examples of this kind of distinction :

| | Holding Period for — | |
	Real Property	Securities
Austria	5 years	1 year
Finland	10 years	5 years
Germany	2 years	6 months
Norway	10 years	none
Sweden	10 years	5 years
United Kingdom	3 years	6 months

[1] One exception to this is Italy, where apparently capital gains on residential property are not taxed at all, whereas most other types of gains are subject to ordinary taxation.

It is likely that investment in housing is more discouraged by generally favourable treatment of capital gains combined with an exceptionally long holding period for real property, as in Austria and Britain, than by the less favourable, but across-the-board treatment prevailing in countries like Greece and the United States.

Nearly all Western countries make provision for tax-free recovery of investment in long-lived assets before their useful lives have expired, through large initial allowances or other types of accelerated depreciation. Some provide for actual tax reductions to encourage investment, through investment allowances or credits or tax-free investment reserves. If such provisions exist, and if they are not available on equal terms for investments in housing, then housing investment is likely to suffer more than it would in the absence of these provisions altogether.

This form of unneutrality does seem to be the prevailing practice in Europe. For example, the investment allowances and investment reserves provisions in Greece, the Netherlands, and Norway do not apply to housing at all, and apply only partly in Belgium. Initial allowances in Austria, Denmark, Ireland, Norway, Sweden, and Britain do not apply to housing. Only in a few places is housing equally treated in connection with these types of investment incentives, Switzerland for example, while in Germany housing is on balance given specially favoured treatment in this regard.

Under the American income tax, housing and all other investment had been treated equally in this respect, as in connection with capital gains, up to quite recently ; there is some opinion that this combination was a positive encouragement to multi-family housing investment in the largest cities beginning in the late 1950's. However, in the past two years, liberalized depreciation rules and an investment credit have been put into effect, neither of which affect housing.

Perhaps the most nearly universal income-tax unneutrality, and this time one tending to *encourage* housing investment and consumption, is in connection with the treatment of owner-occupied housing. Over the years, economists have generally agreed that the imputed rental value of a house constitutes income to owner-occupiers, income that could be realized by renting the house to others or by investing the same amount in capital assets which produce actual money income. Therefore, as Richard Goode has put it :

The omission from taxable income of the imputed rental value owner-occupied dwellings frees from income tax the return on a particular kind of investment and thus improves the net-of-tax returns on it, compared with that on other investments.[1]

Since this return can be realized only in the form of current consumption, this tax advantage can be viewed alternatively as a reduction in the price of owner-occupied housing to income tax payers, a reduction which encourages consumption of this service in preference to non-housing goods and services in general and in preference to rented housing in particular. In the developed countries, the evidence suggests that owner-occupiers generally consume more housing than renters with similar incomes, in which case any tax measure which encourages owner-occupancy may be said to markedly encourage housing consumption overall.

The views of economists have had indifferent success in persuading governments to tax the rental value of owner-occupied housing on an equal footing with other forms of income. This imputed income is nominally subject to tax in a number of countries, but under terms which are highly favourable in nearly all cases. For example, in Ireland, Italy, and Belgium, this imputed income is taxable, but the rental values used are very low ones, based on price levels prevailing many years ago. In recent years, before its abolition in 1963, Britain's Schedule A tax also did not reflect current market rental values. In Greece, the large exemptions provided probably limit the application of this tax to few householders. In France and Belgium, special deductions and abatements similarly minimize the impact of the tax.

Most other countries simply ignore this form of income in their income tax laws. The United States is perhaps the extreme case, for although imputed income is free from tax, house-owners are permitted to deduct certain expenses involved in generating this income — mortgage interest and local property tax payments — in computing taxable income. The result is a potent inducement to consumption of owner-occupied housing. Goode has estimated that, in 1958, the tax saving from this package of features amounted to $3·2 billion, more than 12 per cent of the gross rental value of owner-occupied housing and nearly 9 per cent of the gross rents of all housing.[2] If it is assumed that the price elasticity of demand for housing in the United States is near unity, then total housing consumption has been significantly increased by this tax treatment.

[1] Richard Goode, 'Imputed Rent of Owner-Occupied Dwellings Under the Income Tax', *The Journal of Finance*, Vol. 15 (December 1960), p. 512.
[2] *Ibid.*, p. 513. The estimates for 1960 in Table 2 in this paper amount to slightly higher proportions, for non-farm housing only.

(ii) *Indirect Taxes*

Indirect taxes, unlike income taxes, are of course quite frequently particular rather than general in application, applying only to specified factor inputs or types of output. Indeed, indirect taxes are often designed to be markedly unneutral ; for example, consider the virtually universal practice of taxing motor fuel, alcoholic beverages, and tobacco products at rates far above those applying to almost any other types of goods or services. However, it does not appear that systems of indirect taxes are explicitly designed to favour or discourage housing consumption *vis-à-vis* other consumption (aside from those goods singled out for extra-heavy taxation, such as cigarettes and liquor) ; rather, it appears that such unneutralities as do exist with respect to housing are more or less accidental consequences of the nature of the indirect tax devices employed.

There are three major indirect tax features frequently producing such unneutralities. First, in a number of countries, there is fairly heavy reliance on taxes levied on the value of real property as such, a reliance which tends to result in a substantial tax deterrent to housing consumption. Second, exceptionally high transfer taxes on conveyances of real property are frequently the case. Third, and to some extent offsetting the two preceding conditions, indirect taxes of more general application, notably general turnover taxes, often do not fully apply to housing expenditures and the services generated in connection with housing.

Taxes levied on the value of land and buildings as such are fairly widely used, typically for the fiscal support of local rather than central governments. Some data on the use of these real property taxes in a number of countries in recent years appear in Table 1. As the table shows, these taxes are rather important in the United States, Britain, Canada, and Ireland, where they provide between 11 and 16 per cent of total tax revenue of all governments, central as well as local. They are of somewhat less importance, but still significant, in the other countries with tax systems which reflect British experience in Denmark, and — to a lesser extent — in Japan and Belgium. Elsewhere, real property taxes are of rather small consequence.

In all the countries in which real property taxes are relatively important, housing comprises an important share of the tax base. For example, it is estimated that slightly over half the revenue from American taxes on real property is derived from non-farm residential

TABLE 1

REAL PROPERTY TAXES AS PERCENTAGES OF TOTAL TAXES AND
NATIONAL INCOME IN SELECTED COUNTRIES IN RECENT YEARS*

	Per cent of	
Country and Year	Total Tax Revenue	National Income
United States, 1962	12·6	3·5
Australia, 1961–62	6·6	2·0
Canada, 1960–61	15·8	5·1
Ireland, 1962–63	13·5	3·8
New Zealand, 1962–63	7·6	2·3
South Africa, 1961–62	7·5	1·4
United Kingdom, 1963	11·2	4·2
Austria, 1962	1·6	0·7
Belgium, 1962	4·4	1·2
Denmark, 1961–62	7·9	2·3
France, 1961–62	2·2	0·6
Germany, 1963	2·2	0·6
Iceland, 1961	1·5	0·4
Luxembourg, 1962	2·5	0·8
Netherlands, 1962	2·2	0·6
Norway, 1962	0·6	0·3
Japan, 1963	4·6	0·8

* Adapted from Table 1.3 of the author's forthcoming volume on *The Economics of the Property Tax in the United States,* to be published by the Brookings Institution in 1965. Estimated personal property tax revenues have been excluded for Japan, the United States, and Canada.

property.[1]   As of April 1, 1963, residential property accounted for 48 per cent of rateable values in England and Wales.[2]   For Denmark as of 1960, it appears that housing was approximately 40 per cent of the total value of real property.[3]   Fragmentary data suggest similar figures for Canada and South Africa.[4]

In these countries, real property taxes on housing comprise a rather large percentage of housing expenditure as recorded in national income and product accounts.   That is, considered as expenditure taxes, they have rates which are generally well above those applying

[1] Estimated by the author in chapter ii of his Brookings Institution study. American property taxes typically apply to personal as well as real property; housing is therefore a somewhat smaller share of the total tax base.
[2] *Report of the Commissioners of Her Majesty's Inland Revenue for the Year Ended 31st March 1963* (Cmnd. 2283, March 1964), Tables 163-5.
[3] Estimated from various tables in Denmark Statistical Department, *Statistical Yearbook, 1963–64,* Vol. 68 (April 1964).
[4] For example, in 1962/63 in Durban, the housing proportion was 45 per cent. From O. D. Gorven, *Local Government Taxation in Durban* (1963).

to other forms of consumer expenditure. For example, in the United States in 1963, housing property taxes, estimated at $9·2 billion, equalled 20 per cent of the rental value of non-farm dwellings in the national income accounts.[1] In the metropolitan areas in the north-eastern part of the United States, where property tax rates are highest, housing property taxes frequently exceed one-fourth of housing expenditures.[2]

In Britain in 1963, local rates on residential property amounted to £483 million, nearly 25 per cent of total housing expenditure of £1,945 million.[3] Danish central and local government housing property taxes appear to have been approximately 15 per cent of housing expenditures in the national accounts in recent years ; in Canada a comparable estimate for 1963 is 18 per cent.

In some of the countries in which real property taxes are of importance, land values are generally or commonly taxed at rates which are higher than those applying to buildings. For example, this is the case in western Canada, South Africa, Denmark, Australia, and New Zealand. To the extent that real property taxes consist of land value taxes, which are likely to be capitalized into the value of the land, they do not represent any great disincentive to housing consumption or investment ; the purchaser of housing sites will offset higher annual taxes with a lower purchase price. Indeed, high land value taxes are likely on balance to encourage housing construction : by increasing the annual costs of holding land suitable for housing off the market, these taxes should make for a more smoothly functioning market in development sites.

But land value taxation aside, unless one assumes a significantly different degree of price elasticity of demand for housing than for other types of consumption, these exceptionally high rates of housing taxes are surely significant deterrents to housing consumption.

Transfers of title to capital assets have always attracted the attention of tax-hungry governments, and, since real property conveyances involve official recordings or registration, they have been particularly popular objects of taxation. Where asset transfer taxes are used, more often than not, real property transfers are taxed at rates far in excess of those applying to transfers of securities and similar assets. More-

[1] National income accounts data from *Survey of Current Business*, July 1964. Housing property taxes estimated to be 46 per cent of total property tax revenues of $20 billion.
[2] Based on *1960 Census of Housing* data analysed in the Brookings Institution study previously cited.
[3] U.K. Central Statistical Office, *National Income and Expenditure, 1964* (August 1964), Tables 18 and 20.

over, these rates are often high ones in an absolute sense. For example, they are in the 5 to 7 per cent range for Germany, Italy, Luxembourg, the Netherlands, and Spain, and some of these countries apply mortgage taxes in addition. Rates can exceed 10 per cent in Belgium, Finland, and Greece.

It is noteworthy that real property transfer taxes are neither high nor discriminatory in any of the countries in which annual real property taxes are relatively high. For example, there are no important transfer taxes in Ireland or Denmark, and transfer taxes are low and non-discriminatory in Britain and the United States. Thus, to some extent, these two forms of indirect taxes affecting housing may be considered partial offsets to one another although the capitalized cost of a high annual property tax of the Anglo-American variety is likely to far exceed even the highest transfer tax known elsewhere. And a few developed Western countries combine low or non-existent annual property taxes with neutral or non-existent transfer taxes, such as Norway, Sweden, and France.[1]

In most countries today, the system of indirect taxes includes a broad-based tax or set of taxes applying to the receipts from sale of a wide range of goods and services. In some countries, this is a tax imposed at one stage in the production-distribution process, on retailers or manufacturers or wholesalers, but not all three. In others, the tax is imposed at more than one stage, in some cases only on the value added in that stage but in others on gross turnover. Usually, these are central government taxes ; in the United States, the general turnover tax system is that of the state governments, but applies in areas which include more than 85 per cent of the country's population.

Typically, housing expenditures in considerable part escape the general turnover tax net. This is for two reasons. First, turnover taxes apply only to money transactions, and a significant proportion of real housing expenditure is in kind rather than in money, that is, the imputed rental value of owner-occupied dwellings. But even this in-kind expenditure can be reached indirectly and partially by turnover taxes on money transactions, provided the taxes apply to the factor inputs used to produce housing services at *some* stage in the life-cycle of owner-occupied dwellings, that is, if they apply to construction costs, purchased maintenance services, interest receipts on mortgage loans and the like.

[1] Prior to 1963, French real property transfer taxes were decidedly high, but a reduced rate applied to housing.

However, here the second factor enters : turnover taxes seldom apply to *all* goods and services involving an exchange of money. Usually, they are more limited in their coverage of services than of tangible goods. If they are single-stage taxes, they are almost sure to miss a large share of the inputs that produce housing services, especially if they apply only to sales at retail. For example, the single-stage turnover taxes in Denmark and Britain (purchase tax) apply explicitly only to goods, not including buildings. Most state retail sales taxes in the United States cover some services, but rarely do these include services connected with construction, housing maintenance, or housing finance. A similar situation applies with regard to the general turnover taxes in Finland, Greece, Ireland, Norway, and Sweden, for the most part.

However, in a few other countries in Western Europe, the turnover tax system does reach a significant proportion, although not necessarily all, of housing expenditures. The French value added tax system appears to be more nearly neutral with respect to housing than any other country's. In Austria and the Low Countries, turnover taxation applies to a good deal of housing expenditure, too. It is noteworthy that turnover taxation is most likely to reach housing expenditure when real property taxes on housing are low or non-existent.

III. A QUANTITATIVE APPRAISAL FOR THE UNITED STATES

Since so many of the tax effects on housing discussed up to this point are offsetting ones, it would be desirable to present some quantitative appraisal of the net outcome in individual countries. Time and data limitations preclude doing this adequately except for the United States.

The United States is a special and perhaps extreme case. Very little housing is publicly provided, and thus the housing market outcome relies very much on private decisions. Housing consumption expenditure is a rather high proportion of total consumption expenditure (13 per cent in 1963), which is related to the high degree of owner-occupancy of houses. Because of this last fact, the more important tax consideration is the neutrality of the tax system with respect to the disposition of personal income, rather than with respect to investment decisions.

Table 2 presents some estimates of the offsetting effects of three types of tax unneutrality in the United States, as of 1960 : high local property taxes ; favourable Federal income tax treatment of owner-occupiers ; and the almost total exclusion of housing expenditure from general consumption taxes. Essentially, the table examines the neutrality question from the standpoint of consumer expenditure decisions.

TABLE 2

OFFSETTING TAX EFFECTS ON NON-FARM HOUSING IN
THE UNITED STATES, 1960

(Estimated amounts in millions of dollars)

Item	Owner-Occupied Housing	Tenant-Occupied Housing
Gross rental value*	25,430	11,797
State and local property taxes†	4,845	2,260
Federal income tax advantages‡—		
Exclusion of imputed net rent	1,425	—
Deductibility of mortgage interest	1,075	—
Deductibility of property taxes	945	—
Total	3,445	—
Equivalent of other taxes on consumer expenditure at—		
5 per cent of rental value	1,272	590
10 per cent of rental value	2,543	1,180

* From National Income accounts in *Survey of Current Business*, July 1964, Table 14. Non-farm owner-occupied housing estimated at 95 per cent of farm and non-farm combined.

† Estimate based on 1960 Census of Housing data ; derivation described in chapter ii of the author's forthcoming volume on *The Economics of the Property Tax in the United States*, to be published by the Brookings Institution in 1965.

‡ Estimated at equal to 19·5 per cent of the relevant expenditure item, following a procedure similar to that used by Richard Goode in 'Imputed Rent of Owner-Occupied Dwellings under the Income Tax', *Journal of Finance*, Vol. 15 (December 1960), pp. 504-30.

It is clear that from the standpoint of taxes on expenditure as such, the American tax system is powerfully unneutral *against* housing in general. Real property taxes on housing far outweigh the advantage stemming from housing's freedom from other consumption taxes. In the United States, the highest rate used for a general retail sales tax at present is 5 per cent, and this is unusually high. Housing property taxes are nearly four times this level. Excluding taxes on and consumption of gasoline, alcoholic beverages, and tobacco, indirect taxes on non-housing consumption in the United

States aggregate 9–10 per cent.[1] Housing property taxes are nearly twice this level.

For owner-occupiers as a class, however, the Federal income tax advantages plus the consumption tax exclusion produce the overall result of a mild degree of unneutrality *in favour of* housing consumption. This is very uneven among income groups. The expenditure tax penalty on housing is probably distributed roughly proportionally among income groups, except for a distinctly high penalty for those with very low current incomes. The income tax advantage, however, increases as income rises, because of the graduated rate structure.

The system as a whole is also massively unneutral *against* rental housing. Since tenants, in the United States, tend to have lower incomes, we conclude that the American tax system provides a real inducement for better-off families to increase expenditure for owner-occupied housing, but tends to restrict net-of-tax demand for housing on the part of families lower in the income scale, or for whom owner-occupancy is unsuitable.

Moreover, as noted earlier, recent changes in the Federal income tax provisions connected with depreciation allowances and the investment credit have made investment in assets other than apartment buildings relatively more attractive. Capital gains in general are relatively less favourably treated now, as well. As a result, it appears that the entire range of U.S. tax law substantially discourages investment in and consumption of rented housing.

In Britain, as noted earlier, the local rates on housing amount to an even larger proportion of housing expenditure than do real estate taxes in the United States, and other indirect taxes do not reach housing expenditure at all. Table 3 indicates the net result of this situation, as of 1963, that is, its impact on consumer choice. Even when offsetting subsidies are considered, housing expenditure is more heavily taxed than other expenditure, including in other expenditure heavily taxed outlays for drink, tobacco, and the running costs of motor vehicles. When the latter are excluded, it appears that expenditure taxes on housing less subsidies are nearly three times as great as those on the general run of non-housing expenditure — 18 per cent versus 7 per cent.

The now favourable tax treatment of income from owner-occupied dwellings in Britain almost certainly does not offset this net dis-

---

[1] Estimated for 1963 from *Survey of Current Business* July 1964, on the assumption that 85 per cent of all indirect business taxes (other than on liquor, tobacco, gasoline, and housing) apply to consumer expenditure.

TABLE 3

CONSUMER EXPENDITURE AND EXPENDITURE TAXATION
IN THE UNITED KINGDOM, 1963*

(Amounts in £ million)

	Type of Consumer Expenditure			
	Total	Housing	Non-housing	Non-housing excluding Drink, Tobacco, and Running Costs of Motor Vehicles
Consumer expenditure	19,663	1,945	17,718	14,617
Taxes on this expenditure	3,446	485	2,961	1,368
Subsidies	516	137	379	379
Taxes less subsidies	2,930	348	2,582	989
Taxes as per cent of expenditure	17·5	24·9	16·7	9·4
Taxes less subsidies as per cent of expenditure	14·9	17·9	14·6	6·8

* From U.K. Central Statistical Office, *National Income and Expenditure, 1964*, Tables 18 and 20.

advantage, in the aggregate. This imputed income is estimated at £391 million for 1963. Unless owner-occupiers of housing on the average were subject to a marginal income and surtax rate of 55 per cent, which seems unlikely, the British fiscal system contains a pronounced disincentive to housing consumption in the aggregate. It surely is a disincentive to consumption of rental housing.

The Danish tax system has a similar effect. We have previously estimated that real property taxes on housing equal roughly 15 per cent of housing expenditure. In 1962, indirect taxes on non-housing consumption other than drink, tobacco, and owned transport equalled about 6 per cent of this consumption expenditure; in 1963, with the new purchase tax, the figure appears to be 8 per cent, still only about half the level of housing taxation.[1]

France and Germany provide striking contrasts to this treatment of housing. The French value added tax seems relatively neutral with regard to housing, but other indirect taxes (aside from those on drink, tobacco, and motor fuel) provide about one-half as much revenue as the value added tax,[2] and these largely exclude housing

[1] From Denmark *Statistical Yearbook, 1963–64, op. cit.* Also, see note (2) p. 136.   [2] *The Economist*, March 14, 1964, p. 1019.

expenditures. Since housing tends to be favoured under the income tax, the French fiscal system is on balance unneutral in favour of housing expenditure. In Germany, in 1962, indirect taxes (again excluding those on drink, tobacco, and motor fuel) totalled DM. 28·9 billion.[1] Real property taxes on housing probably amounted to less than 4 per cent of this amount, surely far less than housing expenditure as a proportion of total private expenditure, and the general turnover tax reaches little housing expenditure. Here, too, the tax structure provides an incentive for housing consumption.

IV. THE IMPACT OF TAXATION ON HOUSING

What then can we conclude in general about the impact of tax systems on housing? From the standpoint of consumer decisions as to the disposition of personal income, housing tends to be treated relatively unfavourably in much of the English-speaking world, in Denmark,[2] and to a lesser extent, in Belgium. In a few countries, such as Austria, the tax system is more or less neutral, but in most other places, housing consumption is less heavily taxed than consumption in general. In the Nordic countries other than Denmark, housing consumption is markedly favoured by the tax systems, which conforms with announced national policies of a non-tax nature favouring housing.

Few countries have tax systems which clearly encourage private *investment* in housing (aside from encouragement to owner-occupiers, considered here as consumers). In Germany, Ireland, and Italy, investment in housing is mildly favoured by the tax systems, but elsewhere such investment is either treated neutrally or moderately less favourably than non-housing investment. Where housing investment is treated somewhat less favourably, it is usually a consequence of not extending investment tax incentives to housing. It is, perhaps, permissible to cast a puzzled glance at national policies which purport to encourage housing as such and at the same time appear to regard private investment in housing as 'unproductive' (compared with, say, investment in industrial plant) and hence unworthy of investment tax incentives.

[1] *The Economist*, March 14, 1964, p. 1019.
[2] Professor Gelting has informed me that this unfavourable treatment, occasioned by real property taxation, will be eliminated under recent Danish legislation which provides for scheduled reductions in the building tax rate overtime and a fixed tax *base*.

Chapter 11

THE FUTURE OF FEDERAL HOUSING POLICIES IN THE UNITED STATES

BY

JAMES GILLIES

University of California, Los Angeles

I. INTRODUCTORY

THE first federal housing policies in the United States, as expressed in federal legislation, were developed in 1933. In the intervening 32 years an enormous amount of legislation dealing with a wide variety of housing and land use problems has been enacted with varying degrees of effectiveness.[1] On the explicit asumption that the factors which contributed to the success or failure of policies in the past will continue to influence the success or failure of policies in the future, it is the purpose of this paper to examine, albeit very briefly, certain segments of federal programmes in order to identify the most significant elements associated with their operation. Specifically, three general questions are examined :

(1) The connection between the urgency of problems legislation has been designed to solve and the success of the legislation.

(2) The relationship between legislation and its association with already existing institutions within the economy.

(3) The correlation between legislation and the operation of a price oriented market economy.

In the light of the answer to these questions the outlook for future housing policies in the United States is analysed, with specific reference to the suggested proposals in the Housing Act of 1964 for the construction of new towns.

[1] For a useful review of the legislation see Paul F. Wendt, *Housing Policy — The Search for Solutions* (Berkeley, California : University of California Press, 1962), pp. 142-273.

II. THE BACKGROUND TO FEDERAL
HOUSING POLICIES

Until recently, federal housing policies in the United States were developed in response to specific critical situations which may or may not have been directly related to housing. The earliest federal legislation directly associated with housing — The Home Owners' Loan Act of 1933 — was enacted to protect both mortgagors and mortgagees from losing their interest in real property because of the depression.[1] The National Housing Act of 1934,[2] while ostensibly designed to promote home-ownership through establishment of the Federal Housing Administration, in reality was developed because of the general collapse of economic activity in the 1930's and the assumption that stimulation of the residential construction industry would stimulate the entire economy.[3] The same reasons underlay the adoption of the United States Housing Act of 1937, although perhaps to a slightly lesser degree.

In short, while all the legislation of the 1930's bowed in the direction of improving housing conditions for low income groups, removing slums, and improving housing in general, without the depression none of the legislation would ever have been enacted. The motivation for the inauguration of housing programmes in the 1930's was not to evolve a cohesive housing policy for the nation but rather to use housing as a means of aiding in the elimination of the depression.

Nor was the situation radically different in the early 1940's. The Servicemen's Readjustment Act of 1944,[4] which provided eligible veterans with the opportunity of obtaining mortgage money below the normal market rate, was enacted not only on the grounds that veterans should be given preferential treatment in the post-World War II housing market but also, and perhaps more importantly, because economists predicted that there could be serious economic dislocation at the end of the war and that it was essential to have a post-war programme which would encourage construction and contribute to full employment.[5]

Even in the late 1940's, when it was evident that there was not going to be major unemployment of resources in the economy,

---

[1] C. Lowell Harriss, *History and Policies of the Home Owners' Loan Corporation* (New York : National Bureau of Economic Research, 1951).
[2] 48 *Stat. at L.*, 1246-65 (1934).
[3] R. U. Ratcliff, *Urban Land Economics* (New York : McGraw-Hill, Inc., 1949), pp. 263 *et seq.*   [4] 58 *Stat. at L.*, 284-301 (1944).
[5] For a discussion of some aspects of this point, see Hearings, *Housing Amendments of 1949*, p. 519 *et seq.*

housing programmes were developed in response to broad general objectives rather than in terms of meeting specific housing and land use needs. Title I of the Housing Act of 1949, whereby federal assistance was provided to local communities for the redevelopment of blighted areas,[1] was enacted with bipartisan support and after much debate as much in response to the declared need for protecting business activity and land values in central metropolitan areas as it was to the argument that new and better environments for central city dwellers should be created.[2]

By the early 1950's there was some shift in the general philosophy that housing legislation was important, not in and by itself, but rather in relation to what it might do to assist in solving other problems. A major characteristic of the 1950's was the apparent national shortage of housing, and legislation of the decade was specifically directed at solving this problem by increasing the flow of mortgage money into the housing market through improving the environment within which mortgage lending took place.[3]

In relation to the magnitude of the general problems they were designed to solve, which of these housing programmes were most successful? Analysis indicates that the legislation of the 1930's neither markedly influenced the course of general economic conditions in that period nor did it materially affect the housing conditions of the American people.[4] This does not mean that the legislation of the 1930's was never effective, for in fact it was, but not until the post-World War II period. In the 1950's, when the economy was once again prosperous, the demand for housing was great and the FHA-insured loan programme was used extensively.[5] Moreover, the impact of Federal Housing Administration methods on conventional lending was so great that mortgage lending procedures in the United States changed dramatically in the post-World War II period. Similarly, in the late 1940's and early 1950's the Servicemen's Readjustment Act of 1944 was used extensively and proved to be

[1] If a community establishes a local redevelopment agency, the federal government will, assuming certain basic conditions are met, pay two-thirds of the difference between the costs of assembling and clearing land and the amount for which it can be sold on the market.

[2] See Hearings, *Housing Act of 1949*.

[3] A complete assessment of the operations of various federal housing programmes can be found in the reports of the Commission on Money and Credit. All are available from Prentice-Hall, Inc., Englewood Cliffs, New Jersey.

[4] From 1934 until 1940 only 332,850 dwelling units were constructed under the FHA-insured programme.

[5] In the early 1950's over half of all the outstanding residential mortgage debt held on the security of one-to-four family structures was insured or guaranteed by the Federal Housing Administration or the Veterans Administration.

successful, not as a method of contributing to full employment in the face of a forecast economic decline (which never occurred) but rather as a method for assisting veterans in obtaining homes.

What has been the experience of the redevelopment legislation? After 15 years, it is still in a relatively unfulfilled stage. Of the 1,328 projects that have been approved, only 118 have been completed,[1] and the programme, rather than receiving increasing support, appears to be sustaining more and more attacks.[2] The task of the rehabilitation and redevelopment of older portions of cities has not declined but is increasing and indeed finding more effective ways to accomplish redevelopment may be classified as one of the most important domestic economic requirements in the nation.

The generalization apparent from this brief review of some, but by no means all, housing legislation is that there has been great variation in the extent to which and when legislation is translated into action. Most importantly, there is little correlation between urgency for solutions and the effect of the legislation. Clearly, the housing problems, to say nothing of the economic problems, of the depression were immense in scope, and yet housing legislation of that period was essentially ineffective both in terms of improving housing conditions and in assisting in the elimination of the depression. The current rebuilding of central sections of cities is essential, and yet the programme is at best only partially successful. On the other hand, the measures designed to assist in increasing home-ownership operated with enormous success in the post-World War II period — and contributed to the elimination of the apparent housing shortage of that period.

In short, past experience with housing policies in the United States indicates that urgency for a solution to serious problems is not a sufficient condition to assure effective operation of housing legislation. Other conditions than necessity or urgency are essential if legislation is to be effective.

III. MORE AND LESS SUCCESSFUL PROGRAMMES

The most successful housing programmes in the United States have been associated with the financing of home-ownership. It is

[1] 'Housing and Home Finance Agency', *Housing Statistics* (Washington, D.C., May 1964), p. 54.

[2] Martin Anderson, *The Federal Bulldozer: A Critical Analysis of Urban Renewal, 1949–62* (Cambridge, Massachusetts : The Massachusetts Institute of Technology Press, 1964).

agreed that the FHA-insured and VA-guaranteed loan programmes have been very important factors in increasing the proportion of families with their own homes from 30 per cent in 1930 to 60 per cent in 1960.[1] But other programmes, particularly those designed to provide housing for low income groups,[2] and to a lesser extent redevelopment activities, have allegedly been much less successful.[3] Why has this been the case?

There are many reasons for one type of programme developing rapidly and efficiently whereas another may not, but in the United States it appears that those programmes which basically have been (1) related to existing institutions within the economy and (2) have operated within the framework of the price system have been the most successful. These conditions are both met by the FHA-insured loan programme, which in effect insures the loans of existing lenders — life insurance companies, commercial banks, and savings and loan associations. In addition, it modifies but does not displace the market. It, in effect, operates to increase the demand for mortgage loans by bringing about lower interest rates, longer terms, and higher ratio of loans to lending values at the same time as it increases the supply of funds in the market by removing some of the risk of lending. Through the years the programme has been altered and changed, but its major objective has been the provision of a more effective market structure within which existing lenders operate. The net result has been that lenders — particularly the commercial banks, mutual savings banks, and mortgage lenders — have constantly supported the programme.[4]

The programme for providing housing for low income groups has had exactly the opposite experience. While an essential and important element of any housing policy is a programme for low cost housing, there has never been an effective low income housing programme in the nation.[5]

In the United States, the Federal Government, through the Public Housing Administration and local housing authorities, owns and operates housing which is provided on a subsidized basis to low income families. Unlike the situation with respect to mortgage

---

[1] *1964 Census of Housing*, Vol. I.
[2] See Robert M. Fisher, *Twenty Years of Public Housing* (New York : Harper, 1959).
[3] Anderson, *op. cit.*
[4] See statements of policy of the American Bankers Association, Association of Mutual Savings Banks, etc. The same conclusion may be drawn with respect to the operation of the Servicemen's Readjustment Act.
[5] Fisher, *op. cit.*

lending, there is no private enterprise group in the economy linked with the government in the programme. Moreover, the programme does not operate within the framework of a private price oriented market economy. As a result, the programme has not been able to grow and expand,[1] and organizations such as the National Association of Real Estate Boards have vigorously attacked public housing and continue to do so.[2]

Somewhere between these two dramatically opposite situations is urban redevelopment. The programme does not operate in direct association with any major type of institution within the economy. However, in its early stages urban redevelopment was given support of cities, who were concerned with the loss of sales to the outlying regions as population moved to the suburbs. Currently, most of these same business elements have elected to follow the population with their stores — witness the enormous development of shopping centres — and therefore support for urban redevelopment from this quarter of the business community has declined. However, there is still strong support for the programme from local governments through their national associations.[3]

The urban redevelopment programme has attempted to relate the redevelopment of blighted areas to private market forces, for the essence of the legislation is that after land is assembled and cleared it is sold to a private developer for rebuilding. However, the process of assembly with eminent domain is carried out through a public agency — and considerable attack has been levied on the propriety of using public powers to acquire land to be sold to private entrepreneurs for private profit. The marriage of public and private activities, in this case, has not been entirely successful.

Legislation in the United States to improve housing conditions — whether directly or through the improvement of the environment — in the past three decades has been successful primarily, therefore (1) when it has operated in conjunction with elements within society — *e.g.* commercial banks, life insurance companies, *et. al.* — and (2) when it has been designed to supplement the operations of the free market price system. All other legislation — public housing, urban

---

[1] It should be noted that the bonds of the Public Housing Authority are sold in the private capital market. But this tenuous link to major investors has not been sufficient to induce their strong support for the programme.

[2] See Hearings before a Subcommittee of the Committee on Banking and Currency, United States Senate, Eighty-eighth Congress, Second Session on *Housing Legislation of 1964*, p. 574.

[3] Subcommittee of the Committee on Banking and Currency, United States Senate, *op. cit.*, p. 789.

redevelopment, open space acquisition[1] — has not succeeded. Consequently, one can conclude that at this particular period in the development of the United States economy a necessary condition for success of housing policies is that they be designed so that they operate in conjunction with existing private institutions and are concerned with the allocation of resources through the price system.[2] If this conclusion is correct, it is helpful in evaluating the probable success of proposed future housing legislation in the United States.

IV. THE NEW TOWNS PROGRAMME

The United States, like most countries of the world, is undergoing enormous urbanization. Between 1950 and 1960 almost 90 per cent of the population increase in the nation occurred in urbanized areas, and in 1960 70 per cent of the population was classified by the Census as living in an urban area.[3] This increase in the urban population has led to a vast expansion in the suburban areas of the nation's cities — an expansion which has been characterized as disorderly, unattractive, and uneconomic.[4] It is not astonishing, therefore, that the most important new element[5] in the housing legislation presented by President Johnson to Congress in 1964 was provision for the creation of new towns on the periphery of existing cities.[6] In submitting the proposal, the President pointed out that 'the dramatic increase in (the) Nation's population projected for the coming decades

---

[1] At various times, legislation has been enacted whereby the federal government will assist local municipalities through loans and grants to acquire open space for specific purposes, making long-range plans, etc. By and large, these programmes have not been used effectively.

[2] The reasons for this particular situation are beyond the scope of this paper. Obviously, some of them are the general organization of the economy, the political structure of the nation, and the efficiency of governmental organizations. It is taken as given in the analysis of future policies that none of these underlying forces is going to change sufficiently in the foreseeable future to eliminate the necessity of structuring housing policies in forms that will operate within the framework of the economy as it now exists.

[3] *1960 Census of Population*, Vol. I, Part A, Table 3.

[4] See, for example, Lewis Mumford, 'The Future of the City', *Architectural Record*, October 1962, p. 132.

[5] Under the Emergency Relief Appropriation Act and the National Industrial Recovery Act of 1935, the Resettlement Administration was organized and one of the functions of the Administration was to construct complete new towns. However, activity under these programmes was very limited. See Clarence Stein, *Toward New Towns for America* (New York : Stein, 1956), pp. 119-87. In reality, therefore, the 1964 legislation marks a significant departure from the past.

[6] The proposal is quite different from those involved in the building of new towns in Great Britain and other European countries. See pp. 12-13.

— over 300 million by the year 2000 — and the increasing concentration of population around urban centres will create increased housing needs and intensified problems of community development which must be anticipated and acted upon immediately'.[1] In support of the legislation Dr. Robert Weaver, Administrator of the Housing and Home Finance Agency, argued that the nation 'cannot afford to build vast urban communities that will be obsolete and unmanageable within a decade'.[2]

The proposed legislation marked a major shift in housing policy in the United States in two important respects. For the first time an attempt was made to anticipate housing problems in advance and to establish methods of coping with them. Secondly, for the first time efforts were made to assure that when new housing was constructed it would be built in a planned environment with all the proper amenities. Interest was broadened from the house to the community.[3]

Given these objectives, it would be anticipated that such legislation would be given wide support. In fact, not only was it not supported but it was not enacted.[4] Consequently, although it may become law in 1965,[5] given its original reception it is a matter of concern as to how widely the legislation would be used once it is passed. This is a critical question, since there is little advantage in passing legislation which will never be operative.

How in fact did the legislation propose to cope with the great problems of city growth? Basically, it was a fivefold programme :

(1) Urban planning grants were to be made to regions and areas to pay for the planning of new towns.

(2) FHA mortgage insurance was authorized under a new title of the National Housing Act for insuring loans for acquisition and site development of land. Loans could be insured up to 75 per cent of the value of the developed land, and loans up to 90 per cent of development costs for major water and sewage facilities provided by the developer were also eligible for insurance. However, before insurance would be granted the

---

[1] Quoted in Hearings, *Housing Legislation of 1964*, p. 360.
[2] *Idem.*
[3] The only other legislation associated with improving the total environment — *i.e.* redevelopment legislation — has been concerned with revitalization of old, decayed areas.
[4] For an example of some public reaction, see the publication, *House and Home*, March 1964, pp. 6-10.
[5] President Johnson has more support since the election in November 1964 and may resubmit the measure.

specific plan for a new community had to be approved by the Administrator of the Housing and Home Finance Agency as to its soundness and as to the probability — as shown by the plan — that housing for families of all income levels would be provided.[1]

(3) The legislation required that site planning and public facilities systems be designed to assure economic and efficient utilization of the land in terms of open space, adequate public facilities, and the preservation of trees and scenic attributes.

(4) Public bodies with jurisdiction in the areas where new towns were built would be given financial assistance so they could provide public facilities, particularly water and sewage systems, needed for the new development. Basically, existing municipalities were encouraged to provide utilities to meet expected need, although this would mean excessive present development. The principal and interest on the portion of a loan granted to a community to provide for future development would be deferred until growth occurred.

(5) Finally, loans would be made available to local governing bodies for advance acquisition of land for future public requirements, such as water and sewage systems, roads, and schools. The law permitted deferment of payment of principal and interest on such loans until the land was put to use.[2] According to Dr. Weaver, 'these measures will help eliminate the costly cluster of blindfold growth and blunderbuss expansion . . . and . . . will make it possible for the metropolitan areas, our growing urban communities and our private developers to get there before the people do'.[3]

What are the prospects for the programme once it is finally enacted? In view of the experience of housing legislation in the past, they must be considered slight. The fact that there is an enormous need for the programme and considerable urgency is, as has been demonstrated, no guarantee that the legislation will be used. Indeed, urgency, logic, and need have never been sufficient conditions for the use of housing legislation in the United States in the past, and there is no indication that they will be in the future.

Most importantly, the legislation as proposed will not intimately

[1] Provisions are also made for insuring of land loans where smaller developments are contemplated. No attempt is made to cover the detail of the legislation in this paper.
[2] Hearings, *Housing Legislation of 1964*, pp. 368-70.
[3] *Ibid.* p. 361.

link any major private element of the economy with the programme. The logical support for the new town proposals should come from the building industry, but that industry, by and large, is not organized to use such an extensive programme.[1] In the United States, as in most of the world, the large majority of construction is still completed by relatively small firms. There are a few very large organizations which are capable of building complete new towns, but they are unlikely to be willing to operate under conditions where they must have approval for so many aspects of the operation from so many agencies of government.[2] The programme is not similar to the FHA-insured loan programme whereby the builder, by and large, operated within some very broad general legislative provisions. In the proposed programme, an enormous amount of the possible progress of an entire project lies in the hands of local governmental agencies, and yet in the past, local governments have been ineffective in using programmes currently offered through the federal government for protection of open space, improvement of design, *et. al.* Under such circumstances, it is predictable that private developers will be reluctant to use the legislation extensively.

Perhaps the most significant positive factor in the legislation is that it attempts to broaden the operations of the market. A central portion of the proposed legislation is the insurance of loans made by private lenders on land. This is an attempted extension of the Federal Housing Administration-insured loan programme which proved so successful in the past. However, the probabilities of wide use of this part of the programme are currently slight because, unlike the situation in the past when the FHA-insurance programme made it possible for lenders to continue with less risk something they had always done — that is, make loans on the security of residential real property — the proposed programme would require that private lenders become deeply involved in lending on unimproved land — something that they have done to only limited degree. Moreover, the proposed allowable rate of interest is too low to induce lenders to make such loans — even with a commitment from a government agency to buy the loans. The interest level, of course, could be changed, and if the rate of return is made competitive, it is possible

[1] Not only did the building industry, by and large, not support the legislation, they actively opposed it. The major concern was that it might further inflate land values. This position was also taken by some economists. For example, see Louis Winnick, *House and Home, op. cit.*, p. 10.

[2] There are a few large developers currently building new towns in the United States. Perhaps the best known is Columbia, Maryland.

that some major institutions will give serious consideration to such lending.

On balance, however, given the complications of the legislation and the normal operating procedures of average developers in the United States, it is highly unlikely that many 'new towns' will be constructed under the aegis of this legislation. This is not to say that no use will be made of the legislation, but in relation to the extent of the problems posed by suburban growth, its impact will be almost negligible.

The implications of this conclusion with respect to the 1964 new town programme are important for future housing policies in the United States. Housing problems in the United States have changed. The task is no longer one of assisting the great bulk of middle-income Americans to acquire a home or to provide an environment within which the mortgage market can operate effectively. The new needs are basically two. First, to control growth so that an attractive environment can be constructed — a general welfare problem rather than a narrow market problem.[1] Second, to provide housing for the tremendous number of low income groups that occupy the central sections of the major metropolitan cities — another broad general welfare problem rather than a market problem. Historically, what may be classified as the 'broad general welfare problems' have not been solved effectively through housing legislation in the United States — and there is nothing in current programmes to suggest that there is any more likelihood of them being solved in the future.

If the experience of the past is useful, it appears that solutions to future housing problems in the United States must be found through developing methods whereby existing private entrepreneurs within the economy will find it profitable to operate within these so-called general welfare areas. This would call for dramatic changes, since they have never been able to operate in such areas in the past. For example, it could involve the operation of low income housing projects by private entrepreneurs on contract to the federal government ; it might involve the development of complete new towns by private developers for a lump sum payment made by the federal government. It would remove the government from operating directly in the

---

[1] General welfare is used here in the broadest sense to denote problems that are of general as opposed to individual concern. In a sense, they are the macro rather than the micro problems of an economy and their essence is well described by John K. Galbraith in *The Affluent Society* (Boston, Massachusetts : Houghton Mifflin Company, 1958).

housing and urban development field in any way whatsoever. It has been through such private oriented programmes — and only such programmes — that housing policies have been effective in the United States in the past, and at this stage in the history of the nation it appears that only through similar programmes will solutions for future housing problems also be found.

Chapter 12

HOUSING POLICY AND HOUSING-SYSTEM MODELS IN SOME SOCIALIST COUNTRIES[1]

BY

ADAM ANDRZEJEWSKI

I. THE CONCEPT AND ELEMENTS OF A HOUSING MODEL

IN this paper I shall try to analyse a number of variants of the housing-system model prevalent in the socialist countries of Europe and to outline the tendencies of housing policy. When I speak of a 'model' here, I mean something rather different from what is generally meant by an economic model. In the paper which follows the word model will be used to signify the fundamental principles which characterize the organization and working of the housing system within a given economic system.[2] Just as one may speak, in this sense, of different models of the socialist economy, one may also speak of different models of the housing system. What is meant are not theoretical macro-economic models, but institutional models.[3]

A housing model so defined encompasses the economic and organizational aspects of the production, management, and distribution of dwellings as well as the system of meeting housing needs. I shall analyse some of the relevant problems, as follows :

(a) The property order, institutions, and executive agencies ;
(b) Sources of accumulation and the system of allocation of funds ;

---

[1] Translated from the French by Elizabeth Henderson.
[2] *Mały Słownik Ekonomiczny* [Short Economic Dictionary], Polskie Wydewnictwa Gospodarcze, Warsaw, 1958. Cz. Bobrowski uses the word model, in this sense, to describe a certain variant of the socialist economic system, that is, the whole set of management and planning methods applied in the economic policy either of a given country or during a given period. See 'Modèle gospodarki socjalistycznej' [Models of the Socialist Economy], in : *Zagadnienia ekonomii politycznej socjalizmu* [Problems in Socialist Economic Policy], Ksiazka i Wiedza, Warsaw, 1960.
[3] Western authors, too, use the term in this sense, with reference to Polish terminological sources; see, for instance, P. J. D. Wiles in *Political Economy of Communism*, Blackwell, Oxford, 1964.

(*c*) The system of housing distribution and consumer preferences ;
(*d*) Relationships between housing and the national economy.

While these are not all the elements that count, they are sufficient
to characterize the mechanism of the housing system as a whole.

When discussing economic models in general terms, I stressed
that they are part of a given social and economic system. For this
reason, we must make a distinction between essential and secondary
characteristics of the model. The former derive from the general
principles of the régime and have to do with such things as the
property order and the purposes, motives, and general forms of
economic activity.[1] The latter derive from the particular conditions
of the economy and social life in any given country, from the level
of economic development, the rate of growth, etc. ; they include the
methods and operational tools most commonly used for the implementation of economic and social policy and, in our case, of housing
policy.[2]

II. THE DEVELOPMENT OF THE HOUSING MODEL IN SELECTED SOCIALIST COUNTRIES

This report deals with housing problems in the Soviet Union,
Poland, and Yugoslavia.

It will be useful to recall briefly the general conditions in which
housing policy developed in these countries. Although at different
times, all three countries have taken the path of economic planning
and intensive industrialization, and have overcome their previous
economic backwardness by dynamic growth. All three, also, suffered
heavy losses and damage during the war. In the field of housing,
these circumstances found reflection in an initially great shortage, in
the need to do away with inherited social contrasts and in a rapid
expansion of new housing needs in the wake of urbanization and
population growth. In the early stages of urbanization housing
policy was faced with difficult problems, in so far as expanding

[1] In Marxist terminology, they result from the fundamental economic law of a
given social formation. This law is itself a result of the type of ownership in means
of production within the given social formation, and as such determines the purpose
which governs the use of the means of production and the whole of society's
productive forces. See O. Lange, *Ekonomia Polityczna* [Political Economy]. PWN,
Warsaw, 1959.

[2] The distinction between essential and secondary characteristics, so defined,
does not coincide with the classification (*a*) to (*d*) in the text above, but applies
within each separate item of this classification.

housing needs had to be met by very scarce investment funds ; but in the long run, town planning and economic development as a whole made room for more construction and a general improvement in the housing situation.[1] At the same time, the general rise in the standard of living altered the nature and the structure of housing demand. In these circumstances, the housing policy of socialist countries, which takes effect both through the State's direct action and through its indirect intervention, was closely linked to the objectives of economic development.

But in spite of these similarities, the housing problems of the three countries remain very different, as regards both the general situation and needs and the economic potential at the current level of economic development.   It follows that the objectives and resources of housing policy also differ considerably from one country to another.

These differences are most marked as between the Soviet Union and Yugoslavia ; Poland occupies an intermediate position, but its housing model, too, has its own peculiar characteristics which, apart from the forementioned reasons, are due to specific forms of urbanization, to the intensity of subjective housing needs, to certain traditions in the organization of public building, and so on.   Finally, the housing model reflects also the influence of the size of the country and the general forms of government organization.   The model of the national economy as a whole, and its differences in the countries under consideration, obviously exercised an appreciable influence on the housing model ; this applies especially to the part assigned to economic incentives in planning and guiding economic processes.

This somewhat lengthy introduction was, I feel, necessary in order to make it clear that the subsequent rather bare outline of housing models in actual fact covers a fairly rich and differentiated variety of economic and social content.   In any event, the models have to be considered in a dynamic context, in so far as many of their characteristics change with the progress of economic and social development.

[1] See A. Andrzejewski, *Polityka Mieszkaniowa* [Housing Policy], Arkady, Warsaw, 1959 ; D. L. Bronier, *Sovremienniye problemy jilichtschnovo hozaystva* [Contemporary Housing Problems], Vyjchaya Ckola, Moscow, 1961 ; Federal Institute for Town Planning, Communal Affairs and Housing, *Housing Development in Yugoslavia*, Belgrade, 1960 ; United Nations, *Report on the Seminar on Housing Surveys and Programmes with Particular Reference to Problems in the Developing Countries held at Zagreb, Yugoslavia, in October 1961*, Geneva, 1962, ET/ECE/HOU/5.

III. THE PROPERTY ORDER, INSTITUTIONS, AND EXECUTIVE AGENCIES

The housing models of socialist countries all have a common property order, which in its turn is reflected in the motives of economic activity. Private house ownership of the capitalist type has been suppressed along with private building based on the profit motive. But the problem was not solved in the same manner in the three countries under consideration. In the Soviet Union and in Yugoslavia urban land and tenement houses of any major size have been nationalized, since 1917–18 in the first case and since 1958 in the second. In Poland, land ownership passed fully into municipal hands only in Warsaw. Elsewhere, no formal change in ownership was made, although under current legislation the government is entitled to requisition land for building, and the system of official assignment of lodgings has in practice reduced the rôle of owners of rentable housing to one of administrators. In any event, the State has added greatly to its own landed and residential property by taking over 'abandoned' houses and estates in the newly incorporated western territories.

Apart from the vestiges of private ownership in old tenement houses in Poland, there are three main forms of housing ownership in the socialist countries under consideration : State, co-operative, and individual ownership (the latter meaning private ownership of and owner-occupied dwelling). The same threefold ownership pattern applies to new housing construction.

State housing construction is carried out either by local authorities (People's Councils) or by State firms and institutions on behalf of their own personnel. In the Soviet Union the forementioned bodies are directly responsible for housing construction. In Poland, the People's Councils use housing boards as intermediaries ; these are specialized organizations (*e.g.* the Housing Boards for Workers' Towns) which can also take on commissions from other public or non-public (co-operative) clients. In Yugoslavia, finally, there are Municipal Construction Funds, which are juridical persons and as such may directly engage in housing construction, alongside the forementioned agencies. In all three countries the firms which do the designing and actual building of houses and those in the building materials industry belong to the public sector.[1]

---

[1] In the case of individual ownership, the owner often does much of the building himself ; apart from that, there are also some small co-operative and artisan building firms in Poland and Yugoslavia, who work for individual owners if need be.

Housing co-operatives are most developed in Poland, where their traditions are as old as the century. There are two kinds of co-operatives, those with ownership reversion and those for renting only. The Union of Co-operatives represents their interest *vis-à-vis* government authorities. In the Soviet Union and in Yugoslavia housing co-operatives play a less important part and are expanding less fast. In all three countries co-operative building counts as a form of public building, alongside State construction.

Individual building takes place both in the towns, especially in small towns and suburbs, and in rural areas, where it involves almost the whole of the agricultural population. Only those who work for State farms and State forests benefit from State housing. Members of agricultural production co-operatives live in their own houses.[1]

IV. THE SYSTEM OF ACCUMULATION AND ALLOCATION OF FUNDS

As regards the sources of finance, State construction is financed by public funds, and co-operative and individual construction by the people's personal funds. Rents are kept low both for old and for new dwellings as a matter of policy ; this is a characteristic feature of the housing model in most socialist countries and applies, in the group of countries under consideration, to the Soviet Union and Poland. The rationale of this policy of low rents in socialist countries derives from their social conditions. It was thanks to this policy that the socialist countries were able, immediately after the war, to introduce radical changes in the housing conditions inherited from the capitalist economy and to even out inequalities through the distribution of dwellings newly constructed with public funds. No doubt, the low-rent policy at the time also answered the development needs of the economy. The direct allocation of budgetary funds for housing investment and maintenance enabled the amount and geographical distribution of housing funds to be adapted more flexibly to needs. But in the long run, a number of negative economic aspects of low rents have led the Polish authorities, at any rate, to

[1] In Soviet Russia all farming is organized either in State farms (Sovhoz) or co-operative farms (Kholkhoz). In Yugoslavia and Poland, the bulk of agricultural land is still farmed by individual owners, but sales co-operatives are highly developed. (Z. Struzek, *Rolnictwo europejskich krajow socjalistycznych* [Agriculture in the Socialist Countries of Europe], Warsaw, 1963.

let rents rise to a certain extent. In such cases the social interests of certain groups of tenants are usually safeguarded.[1]

Seeing that at present rates rents do not even cover the maintenance cost of existing housing, new construction and uncovered maintenance costs are financed by the State with funds accumulated outside the housing sector. In the Soviet Union, housing investment is financed by interest-free budgetary grants and, to a negligible extent, also by the capital funds of firms. (On these same principles, part of the earnings of firms may be spent directly on housing without entering the budget.) The amount of funds allocated to State housing investment and to grants for co-operative and individual construction is laid down in the economic plans. It follows that the allocation of the great bulk of housing resources depends upon the preferences of the central planners, which preferences are determined in the light of general considerations concerning the proportions and direction of economic development. The size of the funds which the population employs in self-financed housing, on the other hand, depends upon individual preferences and is susceptible to the influence of the classical methods of credit policy and to supply policy with respect to building materials ; a further powerful regulatory factor is the extent to which building land, much of which is owned by the State, is made available for non-State construction.

Yugoslavia has a somewhat different system of resource accumulation and finance for housing. Since 1955, resources accumulated in the housing sector are paid into special Housing Funds at the level of local government and federal republics : the Local and the Republican Housing Funds. These have juridical autonomy and were, at first, replenished by means of a special tax paid by employers on the basis of their wage bill. Since the rent increase of 1959, when an offsetting part of the housing tax was incorporated into wages, depreciation allowances out of the higher rents have become the chief source of money for the Housing Funds.

Construction costs are financed by interest-bearing credits, and in principle the conditions are the same whether it is the State, a co-operative or a private individual who is responsible for the construction. In this system, the bulk of public funds is accumulated in the housing sector at local level. At the level of the Federal Republics, the Housing Funds serve to make regional adjustments in the allocation of resources, in so far as such adjustments are necessary to

---

[1] The support given since 1957 in Poland to the development of co-operative building is a form of rent increase.

even out inequalities in economic development or local accumulation capacity, or for other economic and social reasons. The economic plan lays down the overall amount of construction in the light of accumulated resources.

Poland has an intermediary system of housing finance. State construction is almost entirely financed by the Housing Funds of People's Councils and firms. These Housing Funds were set up in 1957, but because rents are too low, most of the financial resources have to come from budgetary allocations as fixed in the economic plans. Co-operative and some individual building can take advantage of long-term credits at low or indeed zero interest rates ; these credits are granted by State banks outside the Housing Funds system. The Local Funds are also a source of supplementary credits for co-operative building, and thus can do much to make the use of budget allocations more flexible ; they can use these funds for State building, or transform part of them into additional credits to supplement bank credit for co-operative building, or use them for additional resource accumulation.[1]

The system of financing maintenance and working expenses for housing differs considerably in the three countries under review, especially as regards the nationalized public sector. In the Soviet Union and in Poland housing property is managed by the People's Councils, to some extent by other State institutions and firms, and, in places of fairly dense concentration, by special housing administration agencies. But since income from State housing is very low, part of the working and maintenance expenses have to be covered regularly by budgetary grants.[2] In these two countries, the system of financing housing investment and housing maintenance are thus entirely separate at local level.

In Yugoslavia, rentable housing property is nationalized and administered by the tenants ; current working expenses and repairs are financed by receipts from increased rents. Part of the rent is paid into the urban Housing Funds mentioned above and serves both for repairs and renewal of the housing stock.

[1] The main source of resource accumulation is part of the earnings of firms which remains at the disposal of the management for housing purposes.

[2] According to D. L. Bronier, *op. cit.*, income from the management of State house property covered in 1957 50·6 per cent, and rents only 32·4 per cent, of total expenses ; hence 49·4 per cent had to be covered by supplementary allocations.

In Poland the corresponding figures for 1962 were 47·6 per cent of expenses covered by income (17·9 per cent by rent), so that the excess to be covered was 52·4 per cent. Counting in also private house property, the excess of expenses over income to be covered by budgetary funds was still 44·7 per cent. (Warsaw Housing Institute, *Sprawy Mieszkaniowe*, 1963, No. 1.)

Maintenance and working expenses for co-operative and individual house property is in all the three countries entirely covered by the residents.

V. THE SYSTEM OF SATISFYING HOUSING NEEDS

From the point of view of the satisfaction of housing needs and the cost to the tenants, there are three distinct groups of housing, as follows :

(1) Public housing, that is, tenement houses either owned outright by the State or public institutions, or otherwise acquired by them for temporary use. In Poland, what remains of private rentable house property is subject to public control, as mentioned before. How much the tenants have to pay depends upon rent policy, upon the size of subsidies from public funds, and upon the level of services and amenities in each case.[1]

(2) Individual (or personal) housing, which is occupied by the owner and where utilization is of a permanent kind, in connection with ownership. Housing costs for the owners in principle include all cost elements ; State subsidies are negligible and are available only for newly constructed houses.

(3) Co-operative housing occupies an intermediate position between the two other groups. Although members are, in principle, supposed to cover all costs, government assistance often assumes considerable proportions.[2] Members of co-operatives are much freer than State-housing tenants in the choice and use of lodgings. Nationalized tenement houses administered by the tenants themselves may also be counted in the category of co-operative housing. This latter approach to the problem of socialized housing management is most developed in Yugoslavia.

In the Soviet Union, and in Poland, where the State subsidizes housing investment, the allocation of budgetary funds is a first step

[1] A. Andrzejewski, 'Le Prix du logement et certains problèmes de son règlement dans les pays capitalistes et socialistes d'Europe', *Zeszyty Naukowe Szkoły Głownej Planowania i Statystyki*, 1963, No. 38, Warsaw. In Poland, rents on the average do not exceed 1·1–1·2 per cent of the family budget ; in the Soviet Union the figure is 2 per cent and in Yugoslavia it was 4·9 per cent in 1961 (according to International Labour Office, *Yearbook of Labour Statistics*, 1962).

[2] In Poland, renting co-operatives receive 40-year interest-free investment credits up to 85 per cent of construction costs.

toward housing distribution, in so far as the choice of beneficiary agencies and geographical distribution predetermines the choice of the population groups to be served by new housing.

The second step is the assignment of lodgings to particular persons, and this is a matter of administrative decision on the part of local authorities, firms, etc. Since rents are so low, housing demand is to all intents and purposes not limited by economic considerations ; new State housing, which is not self-supporting, must, therefore, be subject to official control and distribution according to social and occupational criteria.[1]

Old tenement houses are subject to similar controls. But in new co-operative houses, where rents are higher (even though also partially subsidized), consumer preferences can and do find economic expression. This applies also to new individual construction, which is developing mainly in small towns and in rural areas.

In these cases we find a rather smaller disparity between the real cost and the use value of a lodging on the one hand, and, on the other hand, the rent, or the price paid by an individual for his lodging in the private sector ; we also find a complicated system of relative prices as between different forms of satisfaction of housing demand and different housing uses.

In Yugoslavia, the cost of housing to the consumer has gradually been aligned to construction and maintenance costs.

Administrative distribution procedures have been replaced by more economic methods, both in old and new housing. Given that prices fluctuate and construction costs have risen, rents now often differ in accordance with the date of construction.[2] Rent absorbs a far greater part of the family budget than in Poland and the Soviet Union, and this probably implies social assistance for certain groups of the population. However, the author of this report does not know what has been done in this respect.

From the point of view of consumer preferences, there are three main questions : (a) the choice of the manner of want satisfaction ; (b) the choice of the place and time of want satisfaction ; (c) the choice of the type and standard of the lodging. The greatest scope for the exercise of consumer preferences exists in the case of individual construction, or the purchase of an individual house. The

---

[1] Housing distribution is within the competence of public administration, although it normally takes place with the participation of social representatives and on the advice of professional and social organizations.

[2] Between 1959 and 1961 average rents rose by 260 per cent (Milojevic, 'Nejednake stanarine u starim i novim zgradam', *Komuna*, 1963, No. 1).

co-operative system allows for (*a*) and (*b*) — though on the question of time much depends, naturally, on the size of demand ; nevertheless, co-operative lodgings can generally be obtained more quickly. As regards (*c*), standards are, in principle, fixed in all countries, including Yugoslavia, by standard specifications both in co-operative and in State construction. Nevertheless, where rents are higher, amenities are generally better ; this applies particularly to co-operative housing.

VI. HOUSING, HOUSING POLICY AND THE NATIONAL ECONOMY

This brief, and necessarily much simplified, description of the housing system in the Soviet Union, Poland, and Yugoslavia shows that institutional solutions differ from one country to another. The models would be seen to differ even more if the description had not been limited to institutional aspects and the mechanism of operation, but had covered also the relative size of the various housing sectors, the relative amount of new construction under different auspices, and the relative weight of different sources of finance. Certain economic values are also essential for the description of the model, such as the relation between the real social cost of housing and the price paid by the consumer, the relation between rent and construction costs, rent and wages, and wages and construction costs.[1]

It is only in this fuller context that the models can really be understood. Some readers may be surprised at the relatively large extent of individual house ownership and construction. This is due mainly to the high — though rapidly diminishing — proportion of the population residing in rural areas and engaged in agriculture. The socialized sector (State and co-operative housing, which are interchangeable up to a point) is growing dynamically in all the three countries and is closely linked to the economic and social objectives of housing policy.

The common features of the three housing models described derive from their common property order and from the related objectives and forms of activity. Some of these common features are listed below :

(*a*) The profit motive is eliminated as an incentive and purpose of activity in housing, where the only objective is the satisfaction

---

[1] As few indications of this kind will be found in the annotations.

of social needs (State sector) and individual needs (individual sector). Co-operative housing is an intermediary form.

(b) Housing is incorporated into the system by which the economy as a whole is planned and run, and is subordinated to the general purposes of social and economic development. This fact finds expression in the planned determination of the proportions and size of financial and other resource expenditure, as well as in the policy of housing standards.

(c) The State enters, in various forms and to various extents, into the economic activities concerned both with new housing construction and with the management of existing housing.

(d) The State intervenes through economic or administrative measures in the shaping of the housing system in non-public sectors.

The combination of all these elements creates an overall setting in which it is usually quite possible to achieve the general objectives of housing policy in line with the socialist countries' programmes for social and economic change. Apart from certain targets concerning the improvement of housing conditions, these programmes ultimately aim also at changes in the system of satisfaction of housing needs. These latter objectives may summarily be described as social, or State, preferences as distinguished from individual preferences. The two types of preferences, of course, exercise mutual influences upon one another.

From this point of view, housing may, in theory, be understood as a social service rendered to the individual by the State (society), either against payment or free. Alternatively, housing may be understood as a sort of public-utility good which, for social reasons, may have to be subsidized to some extent. In the latter case, the market mechanism may be utilized for the distribution and, up to a point, for the production of this good. At present, the housing model of the Soviet Union is closest to the first solution, and that of Yugoslavia closest to the second.

Both these concepts are characterized also by other economic aspects. In the first case, the State and its agents, whatever their form (central organizations or local authorities such as People's Councils or municipalities) are responsible for the accumulation and use of the funds needed for housing construction and management, and most of these funds originate in sectors other than housing. In the second case, it is up to the individual citizen (the consumer) to accumulate the resources and to choose among different ways of consumption. This system makes room for the accumulation of supplementary housing funds. Housing here is a paying part of the national economy and may increasingly become an equilibrating factor on the consumption market.

It is surely not by accident that the tendency to raise the share of the population's private resources in housing finance is more marked in Poland and Yugoslavia than in the Soviet Union : their economic potential is smaller and their housing construction not nearly as intensive as in the Soviet Union, which has for some years now occupied first place in Europe in this respect.

Chapter 13

THE PLACE OF HOUSING EXPENDITURE
IN THE TOTAL CONSUMPTION OF
A POPULATION

BY

TADEUSZ PRZECISZEWSKI
The Institute of Housing, Warsaw

I. PRELIMINARY COMMENTS

THIS study is a statistical approach to the question of the place and rôle of housing in social consumption in the light of the experience gained by People's Poland as a socialist country. What is particularly important in the analysis of consumption is to examine the proportion of housing expenditure in the total expenses of the population.

In view of the limited amount of statistical material and monographs on the subject in socialist countries, the problem will be analysed on the basis of Polish statistics and compared with results of similar studies carried out in capitalist countries of the West.

The results of numerous studies, conducted for approximately the last hundred years in all the economically developed countries of the West, have led to the formulation of a number of relationships which in the literature on the subject are considered to be fairly certain. These are chiefly such values as the degree to which quantitative housing needs are satisfied (in persons per room or in rooms per person ratio), the propensity to house ownership, the magnitude of income elasticity and the proportion of expenditure on housing in the expenses of the population as a whole. However, in principle this refers only to micro-economic research based on studies of family budgets.

A new problem arose when contradictions were discovered in income elasticity of housing expenditure, regarded respectively in the light of micro- and macro-economic data.[1] An increasing amount of statistical material points to the growing proportion of housing expenditure in the macro-economic scale. This refers both to the analysis of the historical trend in various countries on a national scale and in selected areas, as well as to inter-regional and international comparisons.

The considerable conformity of views in the West as to trends of changes in housing expenditure on a macro-economic scale is accompanied by a lack of agreement as to the sources and reasons for such contradictory trends in the macro-economic aspect as compared with micro-economic studies (in which the proportion of housing expenditure diminishes with the rise of family income).

II. HOUSING EXPENDITURE IN RELATION TO OTHER PERSONAL EXPENDITURE

The average proportion of housing expenditure in the expenses of the Polish family budget as a whole is very low. To evaluate it, we have at our disposal two types of data : (*a*) annual studies carried out since 1957 by the Central Statistical Office ; (*b*) the results of an Inquiry sent to 100 thousand families in April 1960 (on the living conditions of the non-agricultural population in September, October, and November 1959).

In 1957, studies of family budgets only covered families of workers and officials employed in four selected branches of industry ; in 1958–62 they referred to families employed in all State industries under central management. In 1963, studies were further enlarged to cover families employed in all sectors of the socialized economy (agriculture and forestry excepted). The number of family budgets under examination increased from over one thousand in 1957 to some 2·5 thousand in 1958–62 and about four thousand after 1963.

Owing to the fact that : (*a*) the one hundred thousand families Inquiry provides data for 1959 ; (*b*) no essential changes took place after 1960 in the level and proportion of expenses in the annual studies

[1] These contradictions have been discussed at an earlier date while analysing the question of private saving. The tendency was stressed then that the percentage of private accumulation in the total expenditure of population increases in the micro-economic profile and is rather stabilized in the macro-economic scale (see M. Friedman, *A Theory of the Consumption Function*, Princeton, 1957, Princ. Univ. Press, NBER and other authors writing on the subject, as S. Kuznets).

of family budgets — the analysis of housing expenditure will be effected basically in terms of 1959–60.

The proportion of housing expenditure in the expenses of family budgets examined by the Central Statistical Office, amounted to 1·1 per cent of total expenditure in 1959–60,[1] against 1·6 per cent in the 1959 Inquiry. The proportion of housing expenditure in an average non-farm family can be estimated at some 1·4 per cent respectively (constituting an intermediate figure between the results of both enquiries).

The reason for low housing expenditure is rent control, fixing in principle the amount of rent after 1945 at the pre-war level. Strictly speaking, the rent in rented houses consists of two parts : (a) rent in the exact meaning of the word, fixed at a very low level and in principle held constant ; (b) services, such as water, sewage, removal of garbage, chimney-sweeping, and other services granted by enterprises from outside. The cost of these services have not increased significantly during the period under review.

The fact that the proprietors of individually owned houses have declared extremely low housing expenses is due to the fact that they quoted expenses for services (water, sewage, removal of garbage) only, without including outlays for repairs, the equivalent of their own work for maintenance of the house and the rate of amortization.

Another stage of the analysis is the relationship between housing expenditure and changes of the main variables examined in the analysis of family budgets.

Generally speaking, this analysis — as well as the analysis undertaken below of the quantitative indices of satisfying housing needs — does not provide much information about the individual preferences of the population. The relationships in this sphere are dependent in a very high degree upon such important factors as the initial situation inherited from before the war, the influences of the social principles of dwelling allowances after the war, the interrelation of manifold features, characteristics of various regions of the country, etc.

Nevertheless, this analysis should be carried out because it is linked with other parts of these considerations (especially with the dependence of expenditure upon the different forms of ownership and administration of dwellings).

---

[1] This proportion increased slightly in the years 1961–63. According to incomplete estimates of family budgets for 1963, it attained 1·3 per cent.

The differentiation of the proportion of housing expenditure between families of workers and families of white-collar workers employed in industry is very small ; the percentage of housing expenditure amounted to 1·0–1·1 per cent of total expenses in the first case and 1·2 per cent in the second. This proportion results from the fact that while the housing expenses of white-collar workers' families are some 40 per cent higher than the workers' families, the incomes of white-collar workers are about 25 per cent higher.

In Polish statistics, the incomes which are recorded are *per capita* incomes and not, as in the West, the total incomes of the entire household. In addition, each income group has been divided into two sub-categories : (*a*) 'S'-families living alone in the apartment ; (*b*) 'NS'-families sharing a dwelling with other people (see Table 1).

The average income of families under (*a*) was somewhat lower than under (*b*) (754 and 875 zlotys respectively). The average incomes ranged from 315 zlotys (332 in households under (*b*) in income group I) to 2,432 zlotys (2,374 zlotys in income group VII).

The proportion of housing expenditure initially diminished with the increase of income and later on grew (in the highest income groups). The deviation from the general rule, noted in the studies of family budgets in the West,[1] was stronger in households sharing a dwelling with other families (*b*) than in families which were the only occupier of their dwelling (*a*).

When the number of family members increases, the percentage of rent decreases regularly (both in all families as a whole and in the various income groups taken separately).

The fact that the more affluent households are households with a smaller number of family members is the first reason for the increase in the proportion of housing expenditure in the highest income groups. Thus, for example, according to the annual study into family budgets conducted by the Central Statistical Office in 1960, the size of the average household was 3·37 people. However, this figure was 6·47 in the lowest income group and 1·31 in the highest.

The decreasing size of families leads to diseconomies caused by decreasing consumption scale, a phenomnon well known in the literature of the subject. According to Polish standards of designing apartments, dwelling space per person in a single-person flat is of

---

[1] These general rules are expressed (in the literature on housing) by the steadily decreasing proportion of housing expenditure in the total expenditure when the family income increases.

some 183 per cent of the average space in the largest type of apartments (for 6–7 people).

The greater increase in rent expenditure (parallel with income growth) in families sharing dwellings with other people than in families living alone is linked with the second reason for this phenomenon : the fact that families of the first type live in more expensive forms of dwelling than families of the second type.

III. HOUSING CONDITIONS AND RENTS

The relationships between dwelling space *per capita*, the income bracket and size of the household are based on the 1960 yearly questionnaire of the Central Statistical Office, concerning families of industrial workers. The data are similar to those of the Inquiry sent to the one hundred thousand families.

The number of square metres of dwelling space *per capita* grows regularly with increases in income level. The difference between the highest and lowest income groups is of 3·88 for industrial families as a whole, and 3·58 for workers' families.

In order to be able to evaluate the real range of differences between the housing conditions of families belonging to different income groups, it is necessary to eliminate the impact of diseconomies caused by the decreasing consumption scale (more affluent households being less numerous). For that, the nominal dwelling space *per capita* has been divided by coefficients of dwelling space per person resulting from the standards of apartment design. After that operation, the range of differences between *per capita* dwelling space indices dropped in families of industrial workers as a whole to 2·32 (from 3·88) and in workers' families to 2·1 (from 3·58).

The amount of dwelling space *per capita* as compared with the size of the household strongly decreases parallel with the increase in family members. The factual range of differences in the *per capita* utility surface, between 1 and 6 or multi-member families, which was nominally about 3·3, decreased, after corrections required by diseconomies of scale, to about 1·8. The similarity of housing conditions in both aspects of the analysis — according to income bracket and numerical size of the household — results, as already stated, from the correlation between the decrease in the numerical size of households and growth of their *per capita* income bracket.

Dwelling space *per capita*, according to social and professional groups of industrial families is as follows :

TABLE 1

DWELLING SPACE PER HEAD

	Sq. Metres Dwelling Space *	%
Workers' families	10·2	100
Families of administrative workers and employees	13·0	127
Technical staff	13·2	129

* Dwelling space comprises in principle the surface of rooms and kitchen without the rest of utility space (bathroom, corridors, etc.).

The next problem is the analysis of changes in rents (or other forms of charges) per unit (per square metre of dwelling space) in relation to incomes. This is shown in the following table : [1]

TABLE 2

RELATIVE RENTS OF DIFFERENT INCOME GROUPS

	Average of all	Income Groups	
		Lowest	Highest
Rent (or other charges) per unit in industrial families (zlotys)	11·79	8·42	20·04
Index	140	100	238
Of these : workers' families	11·67	8·42	20·78
Index	138	100	247

In intermediate income groups the rent (other charges) per unit gradually increases. In Polish conditions, this increase of rent is tied up with the following causes :

(*a*) to some extent — with the improvement in quality of dwelling equipment ;

(*b*) above all — with more expensive forms of dwelling (linked with the type of ownership and administration of the building), left to the disposition of families with higher incomes.

The amount of rent (or other forms of charges) per unit according to the level of equipment of the dwelling is illustrated by the

[1] See author's work, *Expenses and Housing Preferences of the Population as related with the Trends of the Economic Policy of the State.* Warsaw, 1963, *Arkady.* Publications of Housing Institute, No. 40, p. 85.

following table based on the one hundred thousand families Inquiry : [1]

TABLE 3

VARIATIONS OF RENT WITH LEVEL OF EQUIPMENT

Type of Equipment	Rent (or other Charges) per Month per sq. m. of usable space	%
Electricity	1·01	100
Electricity and water	1·03	102
Electricity, water and w.c.	1·09	108
Electricity, gas, water, w.c., bathroom	1·33	132
Electricity, gas, water, w.c., bathroom and central heating	1·90	188
Average	1·15	144

As can be seen, mainly taking into account the average figures, the degree of differentiation of per unit rents (or other charges) per one square metre of dwelling space depends to a relatively small extent upon the equipment of the flat (house).

IV. HOUSING EXPENDITURE AND FORMS OF DWELLING OWNERSHIP AND ADMINISTRATION

Dwelling stock in Western countries is most often classified into two groups according to the legal form of dwelling ownership : rented buildings and one-family houses. To these are gradually added buildings owned by a local authority or the State. Due to historical circumstances this division is much more complex in People's Poland.

Generally speaking, there are four forms of dwelling stock ownership :

(a) State buildings, which are buildings nationalized after 1945 and new buildings erected after 1945 ;

(b) privately rented buildings constructed before 1945 and not nationalized ;

(c) co-operative buildings ;

(d) individual (in principle one-family) houses.

[1] According to W. Litterer-Marwege, *Housing Conditions of Non-Farm Population in the Light of Enquiry of C.S.O. on Living Conditions* (1960). Warsaw, 1963, *Arkady*. Works of the Institute of Housing, No. 38, p. 48.

State property can be divided into two groups : buildings administered by people's councils (local government) and buildings administered by various State enterprises and institutions. There is a parallel organization of the co-operatives which are of two types : the renting co-operatives where flats are the common property of all members, and building co-operatives where flats belong to the various shareholders. Thus, we obtain in total six forms of ownership and administration of dwellings. The seventh form is the *subletting* of rooms (existing to some extent in our conditions).

As stated above, in the first post-war years, rents were fixed at a very low level. To this were added real charges for services (water, sewerage, removal of garbage, etc.). In the new State-built houses, the amount of rent plus services was gradually standardized. As rents do not suffice to cover the costs of maintenance, the State grants subsidies to the administrations of both State and private multi-family rented blocks.

For a long time, the highest subsidies were granted for buildings administered by enterprises. Next came subsidies for buildings under people's councils administration, followed by the administration of private blocks of flats.[1] The remaining groups, co-operative and individual buildings are self-financing. The charges for subletting are fixed by virtue of individual agreements.

In connection with the above principles of fixing rents (and other charges) for different types of dwellings, per unit rates in the main dwelling stock groups, according to the hundred thousand families Inquiry, were as shown in Table 4.[2]

The co-operative dwelling stock was not subject to detailed analysis when studying the answers to the one hundred thousand Inquiry. However, the real expenses borne by co-operators are, as discussed below, many times higher than rents in State administered or private rented flats.[3]

The rather rapid increase of per unit rates parallel to the income

---

[1] In 1960, on average, the inhabitants of rented flats only paid about 25 per cent of the real maintenance costs of buildings (excluding amortization) ; of the remaining 75 per cent about 28 per cent was covered by rents paid by other space users (mainly State and co-operative enterprises) and about 47 per cent was met by direct subsidy from the State budget. These subsidies were not evenly distributed, the inhabitants of dwellings owned by work enterprises only paid about 10 per cent of the real maintenance costs ; those living in dwellings owned by people's councils paid about 22 per cent and those in private rented flats about 48 per cent.

[2] According to W. Litterer-Marwege, *op. cit.*, p. 48.

[3] The reasons for the extremely low level of housing expenditure in individually owned one-family houses, revealed by the Inquiry, have been already discussed above.

TABLE 4

RENTS OR CHARGES FOR DIFFERENT TYPES OF DWELLINGS

	Zlotys per sq. m. of usable space	%
Average of all	1·15	100
Charges to owners of individual houses	0·20	17
Rents for tenants in buildings of work enterprises	1·01	88
Rents for tenants in buildings of people's councils	1·19	103
Rents of tenants in private rented flats	1·66	144
Fees for subtenants	1·72	150

growth, recorded in studies of family budgets, can be explained — to a large extent — by a wider use by more affluent households of forms of dwelling, that are not rent-controlled, such as co-operative housing or individual sub-letting. It should be added that the fees for sublet apartments are considered, on the basis of other sources, to be much higher than shown by the one hundred thousand Inquiry.[1]

V. COST OF HOUSING IN RELATION TO AN AVERAGE NON-FARM FAMILY BUDGET

This study is based on calculations made by the author and referring to the year 1960. The results of these calculations are given in Table 6. In the table the author compares the situation of co-operative member families with families living in blocks of rented flats (State and private). This comparison was undertaken, because in Poland there has been a change in the structure of housing supply; the change has resulted in a rapid increase in the share of co-operative building.

A basis for comparative estimates of housing expenditure borne by tenants in blocks of rented flats and members of housing co-operatives was provided by the number of square metres of utility space *per capita* and the maintenance costs of the building. The

[1] See article by the author : 'Costs of one-family houses and fees for sublet rooms in the turnover between population', Bulletin of the Institute of Housing, addition to the monthly *The Town*, No. 1/1961.

data is not easy to compare since the number of square metres of u.s. *per capita* was somewhat higher in co-operative buildings than in blocks of flats under State and private administration (it was estimated at 11·5 square metres u.s. in blocks of flats under State and private administration, 14·8 square metres u.s. in renting co-operatives and 17·2 square metres u.s. in building co-operatives). If the data were to be strictly comparable, an equal number of *per capita* square metres should be adopted in all three types, for example the figure relative to blocks of flats under State and private adminis-tration (11·5 square metres u.s.). The percentage of expenditure in total family expenses would amount then to 2·4 per cent in both renting and building co-operatives. The corresponding data has been given in Table 6 in brackets under figures illustrating the actual dwelling area *per capita* in 1960. In later years, as measures were adopted which limited the standard of dwelling space (including the co-operative flats), expenditure and its share in co-operative mem-bers' families budgets became to some extent closer to the above-mentioned lower limits (based on the amount of utility space in the rented, State and privately owned, multi-storey flats).

Lines 3–5 of Table 6 give the amount of State subsidies for the current maintenance of flats under State and local administration, as well as the total amount of expenditure (State and population), amounting to 4·3 per cent of total family expenses (State subsidies included). In relation to family expenditure, without considering State subsidies, the proportion of real expenditure would amount to 4·4 per cent (see figures in brackets).

So, despite lower fees paid by tenants, the total expenditure — State and private — for the maintenance of rented flats under State and private administration is considerably higher than in co-operative buildings (line 2).

In line 7, the amortization rate has been added to current expendi-ture and in line 6 it has been added in turn to the total expenses of families living in rented blocks of flats under State and private administration. Comparable proportions of expenditure are given in brackets, line 7 (7·6 per cent, 4·5 per cent and 5·2 per cent).

An evaluation of a hypothetical proportion of housing expenditure if it was to cover the full expenses required for a proper maintenance of the dwellings (these outlays have been insufficient so far) is given at the end in line 9. Under such conditions, the proportion of expenditure in housing co-operatives would be higher. These pro-portions would be close to each other in case of an equal number of square metres u.s. *per capita* and equal total expenses of families (figures in brackets).

The above comparative study of the relationship between housing expenditure and the average budget of families living in rented flats (under State and private administration) or co-operative flats, reflects a long-term situation and does not take into account the real charges borne by families living in co-operative flats during the period of bank credits repayment.

In practice, the existing differences in current expenses (distributed over the whole duration of the amortization period) are increased by differences in introductory charges (paid by tenants getting a new flat).

When getting a new flat in the housing stock of people's councils the family has to pay a deposit and a sum for bathroom installations to the amount of some 4 per cent of the apartment's value (according to investigations conducted by the Institute of Housing). When getting a flat from the stock of work enterprises the corresponding sum will amount to 10 per cent (at least 5 per cent if getting a repayable allowance from the work enterprise of the tenant).

For co-operative flats, the tenant has to pay an introductory share (15 per cent in renting co-operatives with the possibility of obtaining a returnable allowance from the work enterprise, up to some 50 per cent in building co-operatives) as well as to repay bank credits. In this case, the real expenditure of co-operative members' families will be higher by the difference between the amortization rate and the amount of bank credit instalments. Instead of a charge of about 3 per cent (in relation to total family budget expenditure) for the amortization rate in families living in renting co-operatives and about 4 per cent for those living in building co-operatives, the percentage of instalments (credit repayment) in total family expenditure would be of some 7 per cent in the first case and about 13 per cent in the second.

VI. SHARE OF HOUSING EXPENDITURE IN THE NATIONAL INCOME

The study of the full cost of housing carried out in the previous paragraph is an extension of information provided by research into family budgets of industrial workers and officials, so as to cover all non-farm families living in rented blocks of flats or co-operative apartments. Inhabitants of one-family houses in towns and in the country have been excluded. In connection with the conventional character of a number of outlays for the maintenance of dwellings in this group of buildings, no separate calculations were made, thus proceeding at once to the rôle played by the problem in the national income as a whole.

It is worth stating that these calculations present corrected data in relation to the statistics of the Central Statistical Office related to the scope and structure of the consumption fund in the national income.

The methods of calculating national income in socialist countries do not take into account labour spent for non-productive services. It is regarded as a factor that does not create national income (national product). The group of non-productive services, including housing services, appears only in the division of national income as the result of its redistribution.

So, in the final division of national income into consumption and accumulation :

(a) amortization and material outlays linked with non-productive services are included in consumption ;

(b) the value of net investment outlays (gross outlays plus real outlays for capital repairs and minus total amortization sum, consisting in our conditions of the part for amortization and the part for capital repairs) is included in accumulation.

The equivalent of housing services value in consumption, calculated in this way, is reflected only by the item of deterioration of dwellings. It amounted in 1955 to 1·9 per cent of total individual consumption (consumption out of the private incomes of the population) and dropped to 1·6 per cent in 1960. The low figures provided by this item result from approximative method of calculating amortization, according to which it exceeds to a small extent only the value of real outlays for capital repairs of dwellings (with a very small sum left for the second part of amortization, determined for the restitution of the existing buildings).

The work performed by the present author [1] in another place, aimed at giving a more realistic view of the amortization and calcu-

---

[1] In his article 'Methods of Calculating the Equivalent of Housing Services in the Consumed Part of the National Income and the Estimation of his numerical extent', *Ekonomista*, No. 2/1964, pp. 288-303.

lation of total outlays for all types of repairs, have led to an increase of the equivalent of the housing services value in 1960 up to 4–5 per cent of total individual consumption in the national income.

This calculation is taken in the limits of the existing methodology of calculating national income and it again omits the amount of personal outlays for current maintenance and administration of dwellings. According to the author, this amount would constitute about 1 per cent of total individual consumption in the national income.

VII. CONCLUSIONS

The system of an excessively low levels of rents (which makes it difficult and sometimes even impossible to formulate any rules as to the income elasticity and proportion of rent expenditure in family budgets) is now changed by way of increasing the proportion of co-operative housing (in which inhabitants bear the full costs of dwelling) — in the aggregate construction of dwellings in Poland.

The fact that the very low rents (and other housing charges) are being remedied only at the beginning of the third decade of People's Poland and not earlier is by no means accidental either. It was first of all necessary to liquidate the extremely acute social problems connected, among other things, with an advanced differentiation of housing conditions in workers' and white-collar families, dating back to the inter-war period. For instance, according to the 1931 General Census, housing conditions (in terms of persons per room and rooms per dwelling) of white-collar families were about twice as good as those of workers' families ; the corresponding figures based on the annual CSO questionnaire from 1960 record a reduction of this differentiation to some 25 per cent.

Since a start has recently been made to settle the question of the excessively low rents, one of the main theoretical problems which is now to be coped with is : what will be, in our conditions, the dynamic coefficients of macro-economic elasticity of housing expenditure. Having to reckon with a slower rate of labour productivity increase in building than in industry, we have to take into consideration, also in our conditions, the growing cost of dwelling construction (in relation to other consumption components). On the basis of available fragmentary data it is possible to envisage that the scale of relative changes with regard to industrial products will however be considerably smaller than in the capitalist economy.[1]

[1] This is due to the absence of building rent in cities and rapid progress in the industrialization of the building industry.

TABLE 5

PROPORTION OF HOUSING EXPENDITURE IN INCOMES ACCORDING TO INCOME GROUPS AND SIZE OF THE HOUSEHOLD

Size of the Household		Aver-age	Income Groups						
			I	II	III	IV	V	VI	VII
Average	S†	1·6	2·4	1·9	1·6	1·5	1·4	1·5	1·5
	NS†	1·5	1·9	1·5	1·4	1·2	1·5	1·7	1·9
Single person households	S	2·7	9·5	5·9	4·5	3·9	3·0	2·4	1·9
	NS	3·5	14·9*	8·4	6·0	4·1	4·1	3·2	2·8
Two-person	S	1·8	4·6	3·3	2·3	2·0	1·7	1·3	1·4
	NS	1·7	4·6	2·4	2·3	1·6	1·7	1·4	1·3
Three-person	S	1·6	3·5	2·3	1·9	1·5	1·3	1·3	1·2
	NS	1·2	3·3	1·6	1·4	1·2	1·0	1·0	0·8*
Four-person	S	1·6	2·8	2·0	1·6	1·4	1·2	1·1	1·1
	NS	1·0	1·6	1·3	1·0	1·0	0·8	0·7*	..‡
Five-person	S	1·5	2·2	1·7	1·4	1·3	1·1	1·1	..
	NS	1·0	1·4	1·1	1·1	0·9	0·6	..	..
Six-person	S	1·4	2·0	1·5	1·3	1·0	0·9	0·9	..
	NS	0·8	1·2	0·9	0·9	0·6	0·3	..	..

* 15 to 50 cases.
† S—households living alone in their flat.
   NS—households living with other people in the same flat.
‡ Less than 15 answers.

Source: W. Litterer-Marwege, *Housing Conditions of Non-Farm Population According to the C.S.O. Enquiry on Living Conditions* (1960). Warsaw, 1963, *Arkady*, p. 61, Works of the Institute of Housing, No. 38.

TABLE 6

FULL HOUSING EXPENDITURE PER CAPITA IN 1960
OF FAMILIES LIVING IN RENTED AND CO-OPERATIVE BUILDINGS

No.	Description	Rented Buildings*		Renting Co-operatives		Building Co-operatives	
		zl	%	zl	%	zl	%
1	2	3	4	5	6	7	8
1.	Estimated total expenditure in socialized non-farm economy as a whole (10 per cent lower than in annual family studies of CSO)	10,409	100·0	10,409	100·0	10,409	100·0
2.	Actual charges in rented or co-operative buildings	121	1·2	316 (245)	3·0 (2·4)	367 (245)	3·5 (2·4)
3.	Subsidies from the State	343	3·3	—	—	—	—
4.	Total expenditure (including state subsidies)	10,752	100·0	—	—	—	—
5.	Total expenditure by the State and individuals	464	4·3 (4·4)	—	—	—	—
6.	Total expenditure including amortization	11,080	100·0	—	—	—	—
7.	Expenditure with amortization	792	7·1 (7·6)	605 (470)	5·8 (4·5)	806 (539)	7·7 (5·2)
8.	Total expenditure (assuming proper maintenance of buildings)	11,272	100·0	—	—	—	—
9.	Expenditure assuming proper maintenance of buildings	984	8·7 (9·4)	1,133 (880)	10·9 (8·4)	1,419 (948)	13·6 (9·1)

* State and privately owned (non-nationalized multi-storey flats) together.

Chapter 14

THE HOUSING SITUATION AND PROBLEMS IN CZECHOSLOVAKIA

BY

JIRI MUSIL

Research Institute for Building and Architecture, Prague

I. DEVELOPMENT 1945 TO 1959

IN order to understand the present problems of housing in Czechoslovakia the development of the country after 1945 should be considered. In principle, three phases in housing policy should be distinguished. The first covers roughly the five years of post-war reconstruction ; the second the years from 1950 till 1959, when the first programme of house-building was published and co-operative building introduced ; the third phase, since 1960, is marked by a quick increase in the participation of the population in solving the housing problem.

Although the housing stock in Czechoslovakia did not incur such considerable losses owing to the war as was the case in the most stricken countries, it should, nevertheless, not be underestimated. During the war approximately 370,000 dwellings had been damaged or destroyed. Owing to the transfer of the German population from the border areas (on the basis of the Potsdam agreement in 1945) the post-war shortage was not quite as acute as in other European countries, yet it must be stressed that it was in the first post-war years that the number of new households quickly increased owing to the coming of age of the generation born in the twenties (a period of high birth rates). This considerably influenced the number of new marriages. The post-war increase in birth rate was a further factor demanding more dwelling space.

It was under these conditions that the post-war system was introduced ; the basic aspects of the system can be summed up by the following points :

(1) Key industries, later also the building industry, had been nationalized and houses with flats for rent were gradually taken over by the local authorities.

(2) Immediately after the war investment was concentrated on the industrial sector and the reconstruction of the economy, whilst investment in housing was comparatively small.

(3) Housebuilding was closely connected with the establishment of new industrial enterprises.

(4) The construction of private houses with flats for rent disappeared completely ; the building of private family houses was negligible.

(5) A system of allocation based on special regulations was introduced ; the local authorities allocated the dwellings.

(6) In order to prevent the increase of rents, rent control was introduced.

(7) Housing became part of a comprehensive social policy and was partly a social service.

(8) The fact that most of the land ceased to be privately owned reduced town planning problems and thus house-building problems.

(9) The first steps were taken towards the construction of dwellings according to 'type designs'.

In the second phase of the development of the housing system in Czechoslovakia, which started around 1950, it became obvious that the rate of building was too slow. Since 1955 the yearly production of dwellings has increased rapidly. It must be pointed out that only 40,000 dwellings had been built per year between 1950–55, which was quite insufficient for stabilizing the housing situation. In 1956, however, twice as many were built as in 1951 (see Table 1). Private house-building also began to gain importance at that time. At the beginning of the fifties 9,000 houses were built privately per year ; in 1956 the number was already 30,000. The reason for the increase of private house-building was the rising income of the population and the increase in State credit for private building.

At the end of this period co-operative house-building was introduced and an important document on housing problems was published ; the programme of house-building to 1970 forms an important part of it. According to this programme there should be built between 1959 and 1970 1,200,000 dwellings, thus on the whole solving the housing problem. Since 1959 investment in housing has increased and by 1960 the number of dwellings built annually had already reached 70,000.

II. THE PRESENT SITUATION AND PROBLEMS

When we consider housing in Czechoslovakia we must always differentiate between the Czech and Slovak regions. In the Czech regions, which represent the economically more developed part of the country and with a considerably lower natural increase of population than Slovakia, the housing situation is much better. The dwellings are more spacious, less occupied, but of older date.[1]

When comparing the standard of housing in Czechoslovakia with other countries it must be remembered that in the Czechoslovak census in 1961 a new and very strict definition of 'household' was introduced. The basis of the 'census household' was the family in the biological and not in the 'declaratory' sense. Also the definition of rooms is different from the majority of other European countries (see the notes to Table 2).

If we use the international definition, an average dwelling in Czechoslovakia contains 2·7 rooms and not 1·77 as stated in Table 2 by Czechoslovak definition. Likewise the number of persons per room is 1·30 and not 2·03. However, even after these changes it is obvious that the main problem lies in the fact that there are too many census households living together, and that the number of rooms per dwelling is too low. On the basis of calculations which assumed that the housing needs would be saturated when only 4–5 per cent of census households [2] would be left without dwellings of their own, the housing shortage in 1961 amounted to 284,000 dwellings. The equipment of dwellings in Czechoslovakia is more favourable than its space standard and is basically up to average European standards.

An interesting feature of Czechoslovak housing is the comparatively large number of houses with one or two dwellings only. This is due to the specific structure of Czechoslovak settlements. The relatively high degree of industrialization of the country was not accompanied by the concomitant concentration of the population into towns. Up to 1961, out of a population of 13,750,000 there were 5,840,000 living in communities with less than 2,000 inhabitants. Practically all of these inhabitants are living in family houses or farm houses. In medium and small towns the number of small houses is also considerable.

[1] The difference between the housing level in Czech and Slovak regions is clearly apparent from the fact that the Czech regions themselves have roughly the same housing standard as France or Italy.

[2] This concerns mainly some single persons who in the census were classified under 'individual households'.

From this fact it is furthermore apparent that in Czechoslovakia there is a considerable proportion (roughly half) of the dwellings in private hands. It is interesting that in Czechoslovakia more dwellings are privately owned than in such countries as for example Great Britain.

The Czechoslovak housing stock is on the whole not too old in comparison with some countries of Central and Western Europe. About 45 per cent of the dwellings were built before 1920 ; however 33 per cent were built between 1920 and 1945 and 20 per cent after 1945 ; for 2 per cent of dwellings the age is not known. There are only 12 per cent of the dwellings more than one hundred years old.

A very important fact is that until 1964, when a new Rent Act was introduced, the revenue from publicly owned houses did not cover even half the expenditure and the treasury had to subsidize the public housing stock by 57 per cent. In 1963 the expenses of the public sector of housing amounted to 2,859 million Kcs, the rent revenue to 1,227 million. The State subsidy to housing has been and is an intentional social policy which should mainly decrease the living expenses of the population in the lower income groups. According to expenditure statistics of working-class families, the proportion of the net rent formed only 1·5 per cent of the expenses of such families. The rents of other groups in the population having been higher, we estimate that on average the rent amounted to 2–2·5 per cent of the total expenses of Czechoslovak households. Such low rent could neither cover the repair, maintenance, and management of dwellings, nor raise means for building new dwellings. That is why the government decided in 1964 to increase rents, the aim was not the abolition of rent control, but only to decrease the State subsidy. The new Rent Act should also increase the exchange of dwellings, thus improving the utilization of the housing stock.

The main principles of the new Rent Act are as follows :

(1) All rented dwellings are divided according to their quality of equipment into four categories.

(2) The rent is calculated according to the living space and facilities, the rate per square metre being differentiated according to the category of the dwelling.

(3) There are three kinds of rent reduction. The first is a reduction made because of drawbacks in the dwelling and its equipment (cellar flats, damp flats, etc.) ; the second is the reduction in certain communities (small agricultural villages, etc.). It

is interesting, however, that the same rent is charged in the suburbs and in central parts of large cities. There is further-more no difference in rent between large cities and small towns. It was precisely the aim of the new Rent Act to unify the rents in the different parts of the country. The third reduction concerns the social situation of those using the flats, for example invalids, the blind, etc., and mainly families with children. Irrespective of the category, the rent for families with one child is reduced by 5 per cent, with two children by 15 per cent, with three by 30 per cent and with four by 50 per cent.

(4) The rent is increased if the living space is larger than the stated standard. The standard is 12 sq. m. of living space per person plus 6 sq. m. per family. If the dwelling has more living space than the 'standard', the rent is proportionally increased. However, there are many exceptions for dwellings in old houses, in certain communities, etc.

The local authorities entrust special housing organizations with the management of the housing stock. These managers, however, do not allocate the dwellings, this being the responsibility of the local authorities. In every community homeless persons or persons living in hygienically deficient dwellings must be registered with the local authorities. In communities with more than 5,000 inhabitants permanent work in the same community is the condition for entry on the waiting list. Anybody can check this waiting list. Every applicant obtains a certain number of points according to the impor-tance of his work, number of members of his family, present living conditions, etc. And from this the order of the applicants is decided.

The last phase of the housing system in Czechoslovakia, although somewhat simplifying the structure of the investors, also caused a greater differentiation in other respects. Out of the number of in-vestors which had existed so far (State, industrial enterprises, agri-cultural co-operatives, building co-operatives, and private persons) the industrial enterprises and agricultural co-operatives failed as investors.

Experience also proved that the conditions for co-operative house-building must be differentiated. Up to 1963 the following unified conditions were valid ; the member of the co-operative paid a membership fee of 40 per cent of the price of the flat, the govern-ment contributed 30 per cent and credited a further 30 per cent at 3 per cent interest. The loan had to be repaid within 30 years. As there was not the same interest in co-operative building in all parts of the country, there was introduced another, more advantageous arrangement, where the State loan was increased up to 50 per cent of the price of the flat, the membership fee was reduced to only 20 per cent and the interest to 1 per cent. If the price of an average flat amounts to 60,000 Kcs the member of the co-operative only deposits 12,000 Kcs, this representing — at an average monthly income of 1,400 Kcs — his income for eight and a half months. This made co-operative house-building more accessible to a wider public ; at the same time it can be presumed that the financial participation of the population on housing investments will be increased and this will in some degree divert the potential buyer to acquire housing instead of other kinds of goods. The original conditions with the 40 per cent membership fee have only remained valid in Prague, Brno, and Bratislava, where there is the largest interest in co-operative flats.

From long-term experience with State house-building and with the allocation of State dwellings there resulted a further differentiation in the co-operative house-building. Up to 1964 State house-building had to provide for the housing of—

(1) workers in the main branches of industry ;
(2) workers in medical service, education, shops, transport, and other essential services ;
(3) families with low income, numerous children, and families living in hygienically deficient dwellings ;
(4) families from houses which had to be demolished for various reasons.

The majority of dwellings built by the State were built for employees in industry, especially in mines and metallurgy. The allocation of dwellings from the State housing stock was one of the incentives given to employees in these industries. However, employees of 'preferred' industrial branches moved to other jobs after a few years but remained in their allocated flats. Thus the original aim of the State housing scheme did not help to induce workers to work in the 'preferred' industrial branches (*i.e.* mines, metallurgy, etc.). A new form of housing scheme was therefore desired in order to strengthen the link between employees and enterprises. This link was found in enterprise — co-operative house-building which will entirely replace the State housing scheme which had been intended to induce the worker to remain with the enterprise. The employee obtains from the enterprise a loan without interest equal to the full membership fee. If he remains in the enterprise for a certain period (10–15 years), the enterprise forgoes 90 per cent of the loan. Should the employee change employment earlier without any serious reasons (*i.e.* disease, etc.) he must repay the loan.

The increase in co-operative house-building and its advantages also affected the extent of private house-building. Its share was stabilized around 1960 at 30 per cent of the total house-building in Czechoslovakia. Later on, many families decided to give preference to co-operatives and therefore in recent years interest in private building has decreased. The government, in order to increase interest in private house-building, has lately introduced several new advantages : credit will be more advantageous in comparison to the past, interest was reduced from 4 per cent to 2·7 per cent, and in certain regions and to certain employees such as miners, agricultural workers, workers in metallurgy, interest-free loans from 15,000–25,000 Kcs are granted by the enterprise for the building of family houses. If the employee remains in the enterprise for ten years, the loan is forgone. A further condition states that the house must be built at such a distance from the place of work that daily commuting is possible.

The search for solutions to the present Czechoslovakian housing problems has resulted in the formation of new ideas on several matters. It has been found first of all that the housing needs are greater than was supposed in the programme of 1959. The census of 1961 disclosed that contrary to the assumptions of this programme there are less dwellings in the housing stock and on the other hand more households. This was due on one hand to the new definition of dwellings and households and on the other hand to so-called 'non-registered' losses of dwellings due to the fact that, especially in family houses, many families make one dwelling out of two (for example after the death of a member of the household). Closer analysis of the housing needs led also to the conclusion that after reaching a certain level of housing conditions, new previously unforeseen needs came up. Persons who previously did not want to live alone started to demand dwellings for themselves and the increasing difference between living in new and old dwellings causes new pressure for slum clearance. Therefore in Czechoslovakia, too, the solution of the housing problem is beginning to be looked upon as a continuous process and not as a single and definite action.

In this connection it is necessary to mention that the endeavour of the local authorities to replace old dwellings by new ones was already so great several years ago that the government had to issue special directives regulating the number of demolitions. Up to 1960 for every 100 new flats built 17 dwellings were demolished. In 1963 this proportion decreased to 10 per cent which town planners regard as too low a proportion, preventing radical urban renewal. However, a significant increase in demolitions cannot be accomplished owing to the necessity to keep every dwelling habitable as long as possible. The prolongation of the life of houses forces an improvement in the maintenance of the housing stock to which less attention had been paid than to problems of building new houses. The determination of the optimal proportion of demolition and new house-building is one of the most serious problems of present housing policy.

In recent years the size and number of rooms in new dwellings also started to increase whilst at the same time the price of an average flat (owing to the industrialization of the building industry, the decrease of the weight of construction elements and typification) became considerably lower. During the past five years the share of new flats consisting of three and more rooms has increased from 20 per cent to 40 per cent and the living space of an average flat from 35·9 sq. m. to 37·8 sq. m. In the new dwellings built since 1964 the average living space is 40 sq. m. Although the living space and the number of rooms is not yet quite satisfactory, it can be said that at present the equipment of the flats is quite good. In 77 per cent of the flats gas is laid on, 93 per cent of the flats have running hot water, 90 per cent are centrally heated and have built-in furniture.

Roughly 80 per cent of the flats are in houses built according to type designs, this being a further significant feature of the Czechoslovakian housing system. Approximately every five years a new series of type designs will be worked out on the basis of new technical, economic, and sociological analysis. The economic analysis determines their standards, and the share of flats of various sizes is being decided with the help of population projections regarding the probable number of members of the households that will move into new flats. The layout and equipment of the new flats, houses and house groupings is being decided on the basis of sociological investigations into family life, spending of free time, the living standard, etc. For the same purpose the inhabitants of previous types of flats are currently being interviewed. The purpose of all these studies is to design cheap flats which would comply with the basic requirements of the inhabitants, and which could be built by modern industrial methods and would be suitable under various local conditions. Even when most of the houses were built by the State, this task was very difficult and is all the more so now, when building is beginning to be mainly undertaken by co-operatives.

III. FUTURE TRENDS

At the end of the fifties it became obvious that State house-building would be unable to cover all housing needs. Co-operative house-building was therefore introduced and private house-building was stimulated. At present the main tendency is to try to decrease the extent of State house-building and to substitute co-operative house-building. At the beginning of the fifties the State built 75 per cent of the flats ; in the period between 1966–1970 it is assumed that its share will amount to roughly 20 per cent. A new system is therefore arising in which it is not only the government but also increasingly the user who decides the number, the placing, and partly also the size of the flats. This tendency is in accordance with the changes in the Czechoslovak economy, where the importance of supply and demand is to be increased and the market elements within the socialist economy are to be strengthened. The new Rent Act forms a logical part of this trend.

The greater participation of the inhabitants in financing house-building, and the support given towards the building of dwellings by so called self-aid will also influence the changes in the technology of house-building in which up till now chiefly heavy prefabrication was stressed, as well as the concentration of production and the production of construction elements in large series. The new system includes the tendency to disperse building sites and to decrease the average size of new housing estates and consequently will lead to new forms of prefabrication to complement those already in use.

An important aspect of the present development is the rapid differentiation of co-operative house-building caused by the great demand for dwellings in various parts of the country and the necessity to strengthen the relations between the employee and some enterprises. It remains to be seen whether or not there will be a greater differentiation in the level of the membership fees and the interest rates, and especially whether the differentiation of co-operative house-building will not affect the Rent Act according to which the level of rent is solely determined by the 'objective' properties of the flat.

As the inhabitants will increase their share by privately participating in housing investments, this will also change the methods of estimating the housing needs and the planning of house-building. It will be necessary to improve and specify the methods for the determination of the correct share of the three main types of house-building : co-operative, private, and State. It will be especially important to determine correctly the minimum extent of State house-building for social purposes, demolition and other. The determination of the share of co-operative and private house-building will also constitute a problem. In certain cases the household chooses to participate in the co-operative, in others they will decide upon the building of houses of their own. It will become the essential presumption of rational planning of house-building to know the conditions of this decision, *i.e.* the knowledge of the financial and social conditions of the families which join co-operatives and of the living traditions and so called preferences of the inhabitants.

The method of estimating the housing needs will have in consequence to be completed by the analysis of the effective demand for co-operative and private housing. This means of course that the planning of house-building will be a more complicated process including the analysis of households, income, and expenditure.

It can be said in conclusion that the new housing system will be a mixed system retaining in the old dwellings a halfway character of social service, whereas in the new house-building direct participation by the State will decrease. Considering that the share of new dwellings in the housing stock will increase it will be the co-operatives which will gradually become decisive in housing.

TABLE 1

DWELLING CONSTRUCTION AND INVESTMENT IN
HOUSING IN CZECHOSLOVAKIA

Year	Number of Dwellings Completed — in thousands	Number of Dwellings Completed — per 1,000 inhabitants	The Share of State Dwellings (in %)	The Proportion of Dwellings with Three and more Rooms *	Investment Outlays in Housing — In Millions Kcs	Investment Outlays in Housing — As a Percentage of Total Investment Outlays
1950	38·2	3·1	76·2	—	2,206	—
1951	30·9	2·5	72·2	—	—	—
1952	39·3	3·1	77·4	—	—	15·4
1953	39·0	3·0	75·5	—	—	17·1
1954	38·2	2·9	72·7	—	—	22·2
1955	48·8	3·9	70·4	—	4,970	22·4
1956	62·2	4·8	52·3	18·9	4,918	19·6
1957	60·3	4·8	51·5	23·4	4,933	18·1
1958	50·9	4·0	68·5	23·4	4,817	15·7
1959	66·9	5·0	65·4	19·2	5,361	14·7
1960	73·8	5·6	58·6	19·9	5,914	14·5
1961	86·0	6·3	42·3	21·7	5,906	13·6
1962	85·2	6·2	42·2	30·1	6,001	13·6
1963	82·2	5·9	26·5	38·1	5,795	14·7

* *Note* : By rooms is meant only living-rooms and bedrooms.

Source : *The Statistical Yearbook of CSSR*, 1963, SNTL, Prague, 1963.
Annual Bulletin of Housing and Building Statistics for Europe, UN, Geneva, 1963.

TABLE 2

HOUSING IN CZECHOSLOVAKIA, 1961

Territory	Living-Rooms and Bedrooms	Number of		Sq.m. of Living Space*		Sq.m. of Living Space	Households per 100 Dwellings
		Sq.m. of Living Space Per Dwelling	Persons	Per Room†	Persons†	Per Person	
Czech regions	1·80	35·4	3·36	19·6	1·86	10.6	112·9
Slovak regions	1·68	33·4	4·19	19·9	2·49	7·9	119·9
Czechoslovakia	1·77	34·9	3·59	19·7	2·03	9·8	114·7

* According to the Czechoslovak Census the living space is the area of living-rooms and bedrooms and that part of area of big kitchens which exceeds 12 m².
† According to the Czechoslovak Census the kitchen is counted as a room only when the size of the kitchen permits it to be used as a living-room. In other cases only living-rooms and bedrooms were counted as separate rooms.

Source : *The Statistical Yearbook of CSSR*, 1963, SNTL, Prague, 1963.

The Economic Problems of Housing

TABLE 3

DWELLINGS ACCORDING TO TYPE OF TENURE

(Data in Percentages)

| Territory | Type of Tenure | | | Total |
	Owner-occupied	Rented	Other	
Czech regions	43·7	47·9	8·4	100·0
Slovak regions	69·9	25·2	4·9	100·0
Czechoslovakia	50·5	42·1	7·4	100·0

Source : *The Statistical Yearbook of CSSR*, 1963, SNTL, Prague, 1963.

Chapter 15

HOUSING PROBLEMS IN DEVELOPING COUNTRIES

BY

LJUBINKA PJANIC

I. INTRODUCTORY

DWELLING conditions are one of the basic elements of social development. That is why through the concept of social development and the concept of balancing the economic and social development a principled concept has been given about the place of the housing economy and dwelling conditions in the socio-economic system. The definition of social development and of factors of its promotion is the starting point and to a certain extent also the theoretical basis, for the formulation of a principled attitude about housing policy.

If one departs from a broader concept of social development, from the fact that social development signifies also the promotion of the living standard, then this means that social development encompasses all the spheres of the living standard and all the activities upon which the standard of living depends. A consistent reasoning leads to the conclusion that social development encompasses three spheres : the living, working, and social conditions.

The following elements constitute the living conditions : employment and the social structure of the population, food, clothes, the supply of commodities, education, health conditions, social security, dwelling conditions and supply of communal services, communications, cultural conditions including leisure and recreation activities and cultural life. As a matter of fact living conditions encompass personal and collective consumption. Personal consumption is realized through the individual consumption of material goods whereby the existence of people is secured, while collective consumption is realized through the joint use of services offered by numerous institutions ; it includes all services ranging from dwellings to sports which cannot be organized individually and the characteristic of which is the collective use of funds and services.

The second sphere of the living standard is working conditions. They include the number of working hours, the length of the workday, the length of the working week, the number of holidays, the working and living period of man. Working conditions show the work behind the living conditions. That is why they above all represent the material cause of the level of the living standard formed.

The third sphere of the living standard is social conditions. The reasons for the inclusion of social conditions into the problems of social development are the following : it is not sufficient to create the general material frameworks favourable for the formation of a living standard at a certain level. It is equally important for man to be able to influence the social development, to decide about the factors upon which the living standard is conditional. This possibility can be created solely by a definite quality of social relationships, of the social position of man. In our system three essential elements determine man's social position : workers' self-management, social self-management and the fact that self-management bodies dispose of part of the national income. Incidentally, the workers' and social self-management are the institutional component parts of our economic and social system through which is achieved man's democratic right to decide about all the factors which are of importance for the living standard. The material basis of the realization of this democratic right is secured through participation in the distribution of the national income.

II. A BALANCED ECONOMIC AND SOCIAL DEVELOPMENT

Social development depends upon three basic factors : the degree of economic development, the socio-economic system, and methods of social development.

The degree of economic development is the basic factor upon which the basis of social development depends. Monetary and material funds needed for the social development are created through production. Ranging from personal consumption through housing construction, up to sports, cultural, and health activities, each of them requires above all material funds for its function and promotion. This is the basic influence of the degree of economic development upon the social development. In addition, there is another one of approximate importance. The economic development is the factor which causes and develops the needs in the sphere of social development, too. The more dynamic the economic development is, the more rapid is this influence and the more apparent it is. The influence is based upon the well-known law on the relationship between production and needs. The need to include new products in consumption, whether it is a question of personal consumption, flats, or any other sphere of collective consumption, are always initiated by production and their increase is caused by increased production. Economic development more directly influences the formation of new needs in the sphere of social development during the course of the process of urbanization. Economic development marks the process of industrialization, development and use of new technology in the production of material goods. Every industrialization process spells changes in the economic-social structure of the population and in the ratio between the urban and rural population. The number of inhabitants living on non-agricultural activities is growing with urbanization, and the number of urban settlements and of persons living in them is also growing. The more intensive industrialization is, the more intensive is urbanization, and the structural changes of the population are more rapidly taking place. These processes cause further changes in the manner of life and habits. in the structure and level of requirements. As a rule they cause qualitative changes in the structure of personal consumption, form the demand for better dwelling conditions, for a higher degree of education, culture, health protection.

This influence accounts for the fact that in economically developed countries the average level of social development is higher than in countries of medium economic development or in insufficiently developed countries. This influence also accounts for the fact that the structure of needs within the living standard greatly differs in countries which mutually differ by the degree of economic development.

The other factor upon which social development depends is the socio-economic system. For one thing, upon it depends the general ratio between the economic and social development, the attitude towards their proportionment, or rather, balancing. For another, upon it depends the place and rôle of the individual, of man, his influence upon the activities of social development.

The general ratio between the economic and social development comes down to the question of the proportions between them, to the question of the need and activity for their balancing. The socio-economic system determined the basic aim of development and methods of development. If the basic aim of the socio-economic system is a constant improvement of living, working, and social conditions of man's life and work then this aim gives also the ratio between economic and social development. For in order to achieve the basic aim it is necessary to secure through production the material conditions of social development. The steadier is the economic progress and the greater is the rate of economic growth, the objective possibilities for a continuous and more rapid promotion of man's living conditions are also greater. In this sense economic development has priority because it is the necessary and basic condition for every other development. However, economic development is not a goal in itself. Its purpose is social welfare because man is the pillar of the socio-economic system, the system exists for him and for his economic and social affirmation. In addition, the economic development cannot develop alone. One of the basic conditions for securing economic development is social development. All the components of social development directly or indirectly influence and facilitate economic development. Social development secures a more favourable qualification structure of the population, a better health condition of the population ; social development influences man's reproduction as a producer through dwelling conditions, the diet, recreational conditions, and thus secures the function of this basic factor of production. In this sense, economic, and social development represent an entirety of relationships, a uniform sphere.

On account of this correlation the problem of a balanced economic and social development is extremely important. This problem is expressed through the question as to whether the ratio between the economic and social development is a constant ratio, equal for every degree of economic development. The question is particularly important for developing countries and there are certain specific features in them. According to the experiences so far constant proportions between the economic and social development do not exist. They depend upon the policy of economic development and are specifically formed in definite stages of development. In certain stages economic development will be more rapid than social development while in other stages the ratios will be balanced. A higher degree of economic development facilitates not only a bringing together of the dynamic of social development and the rate of economic development, but is also an important priority of investments in social development. For there are two basic factors which define the policy of socio-economic development. Firstly, the creation of a material basis for social development must precede the desired social development. Secondly, possibilities for the further strengthening of economic forces of society are being created through the promotion of socialism.

This is the general ratio caused by the content of economic and social development. However, the manner and degree to which this ratio will be realized depends upon the socio-economic system. Hence, the fact that countries exist in which the degree of economic development is high, but in which social development lags behind the objective possibilities of that development. Hence, also the fact that an extremely varying ratio between the level of economic development and the level of the living standard exists in numerous countries.

The socio-economic system influences the social development also through the place and rôle which man has in that system. An active attitude of man towards all events in social development and towards all questions of balancing the economic and social development is undoubtedly extremely important and it can contribute to social development. However, the conditions for the realization of an active attitude are not the same in all socio-economic systems. They are well developed in some places so that the influence of men is fully expressed. In others they are only partially developed whereby the individual can mainly influence his own living conditions. It is considered sometimes that the process of industrialization and activation of man in this sphere need not always be positive and result in a positive influence upon the economic-social development. The importance of man's social position and of man's influence upon the legitimate economic and social development is absolutely denied sometimes. As self-management is one of the basic methods through which the activation of man and of his influence upon economic and social development is carried out, the question of man's social position is connected with the question of the inclusion of self-management into the socio-economic system.

The third factor upon which social development depends is the method of social development. The basic methods of social development are social planning and social policy. Social planning is a process consisting of the systematic adoption and implementation of decisions on the realization of definite aims. Thereby this is a lasting and complex process preceded by numerous and intricate quantitative analyses. Social policy represents a process in which a certain measure, or system of measures, is implemented in a certain area. It would be logical to achieve social development both through social planning and through social policy, or rather that social policy should be one of the basic links for the realization of plans for social development. In countries characterized by integral planning this proportion between social planning and social policy exists. However, in numerous countries social development is realized mostly on the basis of the social policy for individual spheres of social development. Incidentally, in these cases social policy is not the component part of a lasting, long-term, encompassing process based upon the system of adoption of decisions on the future aim and measures for the realization of that aim. Social policy then emerges as a periodical, relatively short, partial activation aimed at the elimination of negative manifestations occurring in a certain area.

Integral planning is not uniform by the manner in which it is being realized. Practice has demonstrated two methods : centralized and decentralized planning. Centralized planning exists when all the decisions and measures concerning social development are passed in a central state institution. This plan is of absolutely directive nature whereby local communities appear solely as one of the performers of the prescribed directives on their territory. The characteristic feature of decentralized planning is the existence of a whole series of participants in the process of planning social development. The place of local communities in adopting decisions on the aim and the implementation of measures for the realization of that aim is particularly characteristic in this method.

Emphasis should be particularly laid upon the fact that a difference in the possibility of centralizing the planning of economic development and of centralizing the planning of social development exists. The possibilities and even the tendencies for centralizing the planning of economic development are far greater. Social development is quite definitely territorialized and its function cannot be alternatively posed by any central decision. Social development is conditional upon the needs of the population living in a certain area, while economic development is conditional upon a series of factors of varied importance and location, which continuously change under the influence of technological development. For this reason a certain independence of local communities in the promotion of social development exists even in highly centralized planning systems.

III. THE PLANNING OF SOCIAL DEVELOPMENT

The effectiveness of social planning depends mostly upon how much it is connected with the planning of economic development. The mutual relationship between economic and social development which is of causal-consequential nature, determines also the ratio between economic and social planning. This ratio has several basic characteristics.

Social development cannot be successfully planned without planning the economic development. The planning of economic development promotes the material factor and the planning of social development promotes the human factor. As a matter of fact, were we to adopt the conditional division into physical and human investments, their connection would become more evident. Just as physical investments represent 'dead' capital without human investment, human investments may also emerge and develop solely on the basis of material ones. The co-ordination of these two factors, of production and producers, the material and human factor, physical and human investments, is possible through the parallel planning of economic and social development. Concurrence demands the same period, the same timing, both for economic and social development.

The inter-dependence of the economic and social development imposes the need to determine priority within both these spheres. This particularly relates to periods of dynamic development. The comparative lack of capital demands a different approach to roads of economic development. If the method of speedier industrialization is selected it entails the priority of production of means of production. A comparative lack of capital also does not permit the same treatment of all branches of social development. The priority policy will be pursued on the basis of factors influencing priority. The most general indicator for the distribution of funds intended for social development are the needs, their intensity and the urgency of their gratification. The intensity and urgency of the needs show which branch of social development demands greatest funds for securing a definite level of consumption. However, a situation may take place in which a whole series of services or at least some of them show a similar or approximate degree of intensity and urgency. The problem will then emerge of the classification of services by priority and of the distribution of funds on the basis of the priority adopted. Several factors influence the classification by priority : the economic significance of the branch, the general social importance of the branch, and the speed of activation of the funds invested.

Certain branches of social development are especially important for the economic development, or rather, they can be particularly important during certain stages of development. For instance, in countries the characteristic of which is the method of speedy industrialization, the process of urbanization is also dynamic. It causes, among other things, also the need for a speedier securing of housing space for the new urban population. Dwelling conditions thereby become one of the factors upon which depends the existence of the new producers and thereby also the very process of production. Thus housing construction obtains a certain priority in relation to other activities of social development. Education may be treated in a similar fashion. In the process of speedier industrialization or in the period of replacement of the old technology with new production technology, the accompanying process is the change of the qualification structure of the population which is achieved either through the retraining of the existing productive population or through the additional training of the new productive population or in both ways. In this case the needs for new school space, for greater investments aimed at making extensive education possible, are rapidly growing. In such a situation investments in education have an economic significance and therefore obtain priority.

The general social importance of individual branches of social development may also influence the formation of the priority list. The general social importance of a certain branch of social development very often appears on account of the need for the affirmation of the socio-political system, *i.e.* because the lagging of certain branches causes undesired political problems. The introduction of an expanded system of social insurance or the expansion of the system of social insurance has often been initiated by the desire to establish the new State administration, or by the desire to prevent the emergence of undesirable political consequences. If certain branches have been granted priority solely for this reason, their place of priority is often of provisional nature and, as a rule, permanence in the solution of such problems is not secured.

Sometimes the priority of individual branches in the distribution of funds for social development is affected by the speed of activation and degree of effectiveness of the investment of funds. If analyses prove, for instance, that investments in the building of bachelors' hotels may be speedily activated, then these investments may also be granted priority as doubly useful : economically, because this settles the question of accommodation of bachelors' households which are most frequently productive, or have been productive, and, politically, because the possibility of the emergence of political problems is thus eliminated.

All these problems can be settled through the concurrent planning of economic and social development. That is why the planning of economic and social development is a uniform process which may produce the desired results solely in its integrity.

IV. HOUSING AND SOCIAL DEVELOPMENT

Dwelling conditions in Yugoslavia do not correspond to the level attained in economic development. Their characteristic feature is, on the one hand, the lack of flats in the housing economy as a whole, and inadequate quality, on the other. These housing conditions are the consequence, above all, of the inherited level of dwelling from pre-war Yugoslavia, great destruction during the course of World War II and inadequate construction in the post-war period.

The unfavourable housing conditions have been tolerated so far because the industrialization of the country had priority in the policy of the economic and social development. The policy of the priority of economic development which contained the priority of the fund of accumulation over the fund of consumption and the priority of productive over non-productive investments, resulted in the aim from which one had departed while defining this policy. The low level of economic development has been overcome; conditions have been created for a further economic, but also more intensive social development. This policy had its justification in the concept of economic development, but this policy cannot find its justification in the concept of economic development if it exceeds the period of the tolerance of the disregard of social development on account of the economic one. When it is a question of personal consumption and dwelling conditions, as elementary component parts of the social development, the attention paid to the period of permitted tolerance is particularly important. The neglect of investments in these spheres for a prolonged period of time would not mean solely a relative demeaning of social development but also the weakening of the factor of economic development.

The change of the structure of distribution of the social product in the direction of the intensification of personal consumption, and the change of the structure of investments in the direction of the participation of housing investments, has become the direct task of the policy of economic-social development, *i.e.* of the housing policy as well.

Two solutions of two problems will therefore be of fundamental importance. The first problem is in what manner to activate through the housing policy all the possible sources of funds for housing construction, in order that housing investments obtain a favourable place in the distribution of the social product. The need to re-examine the source relates above all to the re-examination of rents as sources of funds for simple reproduction in the housing economy; and also to the discovery of the most adequate instruments for using part of the national income which must be intended for expanded reproduction in the housing economy. So far we had a housing contribution through which were formed funds of local funds for housing construction. The volume of the housing contribution depended upon the amount of the payment funds of employed persons, and appeared as the function of the employment of the population and productivity.

However, the solution of the first problem is closely conditional upon the solution of the second problem, the problem of the creation of the material basis for absorbing the formed quantity of housing investments. Moreover, the experience in the elapsed period stresses the need of the preliminary solution of the second problem. The substance of the mutual inter-connection of the volume of housing investments and the material basis formed through the productive ability of the building industry, by the degree of supply with basic elements of production and its organizational potential, is not capable of absorbing more effectively even the existing quantity of housing investments. The high price indices in the building industry are the synthetic indicators of this allegation. In this situation the increase of the part of the national income intended for housing construction would not be advisable. The increase of monetary funds without securing the material basis which would be able effectively to absorb the given quantity of funds, may have solely inflationary consequences in this sphere.

That is why a preliminary process should consist in the accumulative fitness of the building industry as the industrial flat producer. The pre-condition of industrial mass production of flats which presupposes the integration of capacities and funds, is to enable the building industry to become the exclusive pillar of the process in housing construction.

How will the building industry, under conditions of inadequate economic development, be trained for the function of industrial producer, is the matter of the current housing policy. Thereby it is still vital that the mass housing construction cannot be secured at the expense of the quality of the new housing fund. For the housing fund, in view of its lasting character, must serve for the needs not only of the present, but also the future generations.

My opinion is that no lasting solution of the housing problem in socialism exists. Just as there does not exist an absolute need or definite aim, there is also no absolute housing need. Although the logic of this reasoning seems so strong to me that it needs no argumentation, I would rather quote in the end Engels' thought from his polemics with Proudhon when he said : 'The housing question represents a long-term process which can be settled only when society will be transformed to such an extent that it may approach the abolition of differences between the town and the countryside. The solution of the social problem is not concurrently the solution of the housing problem, but the solution of the social question only facilitates the solution of the housing problem.'

Chapter 16

HOUSING IN AFRICA: SOME PROBLEMS AND MAJOR POLICY ISSUES

BY

D. A. TURIN [1]

Economic Commission for Africa

I. PREFATORY NOTE

THE present note attempts to provide a cursory review of some of the main housing problems facing the African continent and of the major policy issues involved. Within the limits of brevity imposed by the organizers of the conference, it will not be possible to substantiate any of the statements of this paper with statistical evidence or with bibliographical references. However, the note is based on the numerous studies carried out by the secretariat of the United Nations Economic Commission for Africa, to whose documents the interested reader might refer for further details.

Unless otherwise specified, the description of the 'present' situation will apply to the early sixties, *i.e.* the date for which statistical information is gradually becoming available for a majority of African countries.

II. THE SETTING OF THE PROBLEM

The total population of Africa in 1960 was 270 millions approximately. It was distributed roughly between the main subregions of the continent as shown on page 201.

Few African countries have taken more than one national census of population; it is therefore difficult to estimate the rate of growth of population over any reasonable period of time. Furthermore, when censuses had been taken in the past, their coverage was seldom comparable to that of the more elaborate censuses taken in the late fifties or early sixties.

[1] Mr. Turin is a member of the secretariat of the United Nations Economic Commission for Africa. The views expressed here are his own and do not necessarily reflect the policy of the organization.

	Millions	Percentage of the Total
North Africa	66	24
West Africa	86	31
Central Africa	29	11
East Africa	60	22
South Africa	32	12
	273	100

It has been estimated, however, that the annual rate of population growth for Africa as a whole was in the range of 2·2 per cent in the last decade, as compared with 1·6 per cent in the forties. This average covers in fact wide national differences, from a minimum of 0·8 per cent for Bechuanaland, Cameroun, and Somalia to a maximum of over 3 per cent for Ghana, Congo (Brazzaville), Kenya, Rhodesia, and Swaziland.

Data on the breakdown of rural and urban populations are even less reliable than those referring to total of population. An attempt has been made to estimate, for the main subregions of the continent and for Africa as a whole, the percentage of population living in centres of more than 20,000 and 100,000 inhabitants respectively. It would appear that the population living in large urban centres (more than 100,000 inhabitants) represents approximately 7 to 8 per cent of the total, and that population living in medium urban centres (between 20,000 and 100,000 inhabitants) would amount to 4 per cent of the total.

It is felt, however, that in many African countries settlements of less than 20,000 inhabitants have a definite urban character. Although accurate statistics are not available, it can be estimated that the urban population of the continent accounts for approximately one-sixth of the total.

The available evidence seems to indicate that the natural rate of growth of the urban and rural populations is of the same order of magnitude. However, Africa like all other developing areas of the world, is undergoing a rapid process of urbanization and the migration from rural areas to urban centres, especially the capital cities or the main coastal settlements, has gathered momentum in the last decade. Rates of growth of 5, 6, and even 10 per cent have been observed in the main urban centres throughout the African continent and there are no indications of a slowing down of this trend.

For the purpose of estimating the order of magnitude of the urbanization rate, two sets of assumptions can be adopted as a first approximation :

(a) that the population of the major urban centres doubles every ten years, which amounts to an annual rate of growth of approximately 7 per cent ;
(b) that 1/3 of the natural growth of the rural population migrates to urban centres, both medium and large.

The impact of such massive movements of population on housing requirements will be considered later in this note.

Demographic trends should be set against the economic background of the continent. The average *per capita* GDP of Africa [1] was about U.S. $100 in the early sixties. Again, this figure covered wide differences between individual countries, the lowest *per capita* income being that of Burundi, Chad, Ethiopia, Malawi, Niger, Rwanda, Somalia, Tanzania and Upper Volta (below U.S. $60) and the highest range being represented by countries above U.S. $200 (Gabon, Rhodesia, and Algeria) and by a number of countries in the U.S. $150–200 bracket (Ghana, Senegal, and Ivory Coast in West Africa ; Zambia in East Africa ; Libya, Morocco, Tunisia, and UAR in North Africa).

The industrial origin of the gross domestic product clearly indicates the main characteristics of under development with agriculture contributing 35 per cent, mining 7 per cent, and manufacturing 14 per cent only to a total which was estimated at some U.S. $32 billion for 1960. If the Republic of South Africa is excluded, the total GDP of the continent, amounting to over U.S. $24 billion in 1961, was broken down into 44 per cent from agriculture, 5 per cent from mining, 11 per cent from manufacturing, and 40 per cent from other sectors.

Total gross domestic capital formation in the early sixties was estimated at U.S. $5·0–5·5 billion, of which approximately 0·7 billion was contributed by South Africa ; this represented some 16–18 per cent of GDP. The high rate of capital formation of countries such as Algeria, Congo (Leopoldville), Ghana, or the former Federation of Rhodesia, was compensated by the extremely low rate prevailing in other countries, especially in land-locked territories of the West African subregion.

Aggregate figures on the share of gross domestic capital formation going into housing, building, and other construction and works are

[1] Excluding dependent territories and the Republic of South Africa.

not available for the continent as a whole. However, it is possible to extrapolate the information available from selected African countries which contribute about three-fifths of the total estimated capital formation of the continent.

It would appear from these figures that approximately three-fifths of total capital formation has been devoted to construction work in general, and approximately one-quarter to housing and related community facilities. If these orders of magnitude are provisionally accepted, investment in housing and related facilities would represent approximately one-sixth of total gross domestic capital formation or some 2·5 to 3·0 per cent of GDP.

Percentage wise, this proportion is not considerably lower than that of industrialized countries in Europe and America; however, in absolute value it amounts to a *per capita* expenditure in housing of the order of U.S. $2–3 per annum as against U.S. $30 to 40 for a typical industrialized country. If it is appreciated that building costs, for reasons that will be explained later, are not appreciably lower in a majority of African countries than they are in industrialized countries, although space and quality standards are, and that demographic pressure is several times greater than in industrialized countries, the size of the housing problems in Africa will be viewed in its true perspective.

III. THE RESOURCES AND THEIR UTILIZATION

An overall picture of the situation prevailing in the sixties as far as building materials and building components are concerned can be obtained from the table on page 204.[1]

The value of quarry materials (stone, aggregates, sand), asphalt, bitumen, of traditional materials used in the subsistence sector of the economy and of a number of miscellaneous building components which cannot be isolated from industrial and trade statistics, has not been computed in the table below. It can be estimated that these materials would account for a further U.S. $0·3 billion, of which approximately one-fourth is imported.

It will be seen that out of a total expenditure of approximately U.S. $1·3 billion, over $0·7 billion was spent on imported materials. Africa is almost totally dependent on imports for iron and steel products and for electrical fittings and fixtures. It imports more than

[1] Excluding the Republic of South Africa.

Building Materials	Domestic Production consumed Locally	Imports	Total Domestic Consumption	Billion U.S. $ Imports as a Percentage of Total Domestic Consumption
Cement	0·12	0·06	0·18	33
Cement products	0·06	0·01	0·07	14
Iron and steel products	0·04	0·30	0·34	88
Ceramic products, including glass and other non-metallic mineral products	0·04	0·06	0·10	60
Wood products	0·11	0·06	0·17	35
Paints and varnishes	0·02	0·02	0·04	50
Electrical fittings and fixtures	—	0·10	0·10	100
Totals	0·39	0·61	1·00	61

half its consumption of ceramic products, paints, and varnishes ; it exports large quantities of hardwoods, but imports the equivalent value in softwood used for construction purposes ; and one-third of its consumption of cement is covered by imports.

By far the greatest share of imports is from outside the African continent ; the massive import of building materials and components, which accounts for over 6 per cent of total African imports, represents therefore a substantial drain on valuable hard currency. The present situation, which is a consequence of past colonial policies, is all the more regrettable since African resources in raw materials, if suitably exploited, could cover entirely the present and future needs of the continent.

Energy is of course a major problem in Africa. Natural gas and oil are available north of the Sahara and, in smaller quantities, in West and Central Africa. Coal is a comparatively scarce commodity ; but by far the biggest untapped potential is hydraulic power. It has been estimated that not more than 1 per cent of the hydraulic power potential has so far been utilized.

Human resources present quite a different problem. While unskilled labour is abundant as in all developing areas, Africa is critically short of skills at all levels, and the construction industries are no exception. Employment statistics for African countries are very meagre. School enrolment statistics, which have a better coverage, indicate the following orders of magnitude for Africa as a whole in the early sixties : 18 per cent for primary education (first level), and 1·5 per cent for secondary education (second level), and 0·2 per cent for higher education (third level).[1]

The shortage of skills in the building and construction trades is particularly acute at intermediate level (site supervisors, clerks of works, foremen, etc.) and in the professional categories (architects, engineers, town planners, physical planners, etc.). There are only three schools of architecture and one of physical planning in Africa south of the Sahara (excluding South Africa). Vocational training schools exist in most countries, but their output is limited and their curricula are mostly unrelated to African conditions.

As far as the construction industry is concerned, the continent is characterized by the absence of African firms of any significant size, except in North Africa and in a few West African coastal countries. The largest building and civil engineering firms are expatriate and their managerial and technical staff is so far non-African. The emerging African contractor, often an artisan or a foreman who has set up business on his own, is comparatively inexperienced, lacks financial means, is not used to modern cost keeping methods and has not adapted himself to the use of machinery and equipment on the building site.

In the field of housing finance, a determinant rôle is played in most African countries either by the State itself or by public organizations set up with the assistance of the central government. The institutional set-up varies considerably from country to country ; it is possible however to distinguish characteristic patterns in French- and English-speaking countries south of the Sahara and in most countries of North Africa.

In French-speaking countries, the largest single investors in urban housing have been the 'sociétés immobilières', which have received capital aid from the metropolitan power. In English-speaking countries, two types of institutions have co-existed in the past : housing boards or corporations, on the one hand, and building societies on the other. Whereas housing boards have in the main limited their contribution to the financing of housing without intervening in design or the supervision of construction work, housing corporations have acted as real clients in the wider sense of the term.

Building societies, run on a profit basis, operate effectively in only one or two West African countries where from the very beginning

[1] These percentages are expressed in relation to the corresponding age groups.

they addressed themselves to the African clientele. But even in this case experience has shown that the basis of their operation has been such that the savings of the lower income population were used to finance the dwellings of the medium income sector. In the North African countries, the direct intervention of the State has been much greater and houses built directly by public authorities or with their financial assistance represents a predominant share of the total.

The period of amortization and the annual interest charged for housing loans varies considerably between the public and private sectors, for different types of houses and from country to country. By and large the periods of amortization are considerably shorter and the interest rates higher than in the industrialized countries. In countries receiving French aid, housing loans are usually reimbursable over 10 to 15 years, at interest varying between 2·5 and 5·0 per cent according to the category of dwelling ; in those countries receiving substantial financial assistance from the Commonwealth Development Corporation, loans to building societies and public housing authorities are usually reimbursable over 20 years or more, at an interest rate of 6 to 8 per cent. In North African countries public financing by the central government is often carried out at very low interest or at no interest at all.

Data on the present level of house-building costs have not been collected on a comparative basis nor is there a sufficiently wide statistical sample. The scattered information available points to a wide discrepancy both in standards and in cost per square metre. The lowest figures so far obtained correspond to a unit cost of approximately U.S. $20 per m.², *i.e.* a total cost of approximately U.S. $1,000 for a minimum of 50 m.². These figures apply to countries which have launched large house-building programmes over long periods of time. The highest figures, observed in land-locked countries of West Africa, amount to U.S. $80–100 per m.², *i.e.* U.S. $5,000–6,000 per dwelling.

These wide differences cannot be accounted for only by differences in the prices of building materials, since building materials represent not more than three-fifths of the total cost. A comparison between the cost of labour and overheads and a composite index of hourly wages (1 hour of skilled labour plus 2 hours of unskilled labour) shows a range of 1 : 2·5 between the lowest and the highest cost, thus clearly indicating that differences in the productivity of building labour are very great from country to country.

A breakdown of the cost of house-building by elements of building shows that the substructure accounts for approximately 10 per cent of the total cost, superstructure 40 to 55 per cent and finishes and equipment for the rest. By far the largest share of the total building cost is represented by the roof and external walls, including joinery.

Information collected from some twenty African countries on the use of space in new residential units shows that, in spite of the wide scatter of results, it is possible to indicate a range of minimum acceptable standards from the point of view of the most economic utilization of space.

Densities from 350 to 450 inhabitants per hectare can be achieved with one- or two-storey dwellings, corresponding to a ratio of built-up area to total area of about 15 to 20 per cent. Plots of 65–100 m.^{2} are compatible with such densities, and it is possible to provide an adequate network of primary and secondary roads without taking more than 20 per cent of the total site area. An average of 10 m.^{2} of floor area per person (including external covered space, which is of great use in tropical climates) could be accepted as a minimum while an equal amount should be devoted to private and public open spaces.

The evidence available indicates that, in many African countries, present planning standards are still far from these targets, and that consequently useful urban and peri-urban space is wasted, while the cost of providing and operating basic community facilities and services is disproportionately high.

It should be mentioned in this connection that only a handful of African countries possess a proper physical planning organization either at national, regional, or local level and that not more than two or three of these are adequately staffed. Most African capitals and some of the major urban centres have, at one stage or another, been covered by studies leading to a master plan or at least a zoning plan ; however, the implementation of such plans has never been very effective and hardly anywhere in Africa has an attempt been made to establish an overall physical planning policy on a national or even on a regional basis.

IV. SOME PROBLEMS AND MAJOR POLICY ISSUES

It has been established that very few countries in Africa have so far defined a comprehensive housing policy or elaborated short- or long-term housing programmes.

One of the essential requirements of this process is, of course, the assessment of housing needs. Few countries have indeed attempted to estimate present and future needs in the field of housing and related facilities, and those which have done so have had to face the fact that quantitative and qualitative needs considerably exceed available material, financial or technical resources.

It is not possible to provide an estimate of the total number of dwelling units required for the continent as a whole, in view of the wide differences in local situations and in the absence of reliable statistics on the main demographic, economic, and social indicators. But attempts have been made to define the order of magnitude of quantitative needs on the basis of a theoretical model corresponding to conditions characteristic of a number of African countries.

Thus, for instance, if it is assumed that urban population accounts for approximately one-sixth of the total, that it increases at a rate of approximaely 5 per cent a year (which means that it grows by 2·5 times every 20 years), that the average household size is in the range of 5 persons, and that overcrowding begins when more than 2 persons share a habitable room, it is possible to estimate that between 8 and 9 dwellings would be required per year per thousand inhabitants of urban population in order to meet net migratory demographic growth and to eliminate overcrowding over a period of, say, 20 years.

If the number of dwellings necessary to replace obsolete or insanitary dwellings were to be added to these requirements, the figure would be increased by anything from 2 to 5 dwellings per year per thousand inhabitants, depending on the conditions of the present urban dwelling stock and on the locally accepted standards for declaring dwellings unsuitable for human occupation.

As already pointed out above, statistics on the total number of dwellings built in any given country are non-existent in Africa ; for only a few countries can one estimate with a reasonable degree of accuracy the number of dwellings completed over a period of time in urban areas, or at least the number of those requiring a building licence.

The evidence available shows that the most advanced countries in this field have seldom built more than 4–5 dwellings per year per thousand inhabitants of urban population. In other words, in no African country so far has the number of dwellings built been sufficient even to prevent the deterioration of the urban housing situation.

No reference is made here to the problem of rural housing, which, with a few exceptions in North Africa, falls outside the monetary sector of the economy and on which overall statistical data do not exist.

The increasing gap between housing needs and housing programmes is still aggravated by the disproportion between the cost of the dwellings currently built by conventional methods in urban areas and the income of large parts of the population.

If the cost of a so-called 'low-cost' dwelling is expressed in terms of the annual income of the prospective occupant, it will be seen that in a majority of African countries this ratio amounts to 2·5–4 for a skilled worker and 5–8 for a non-skilled worker ; but there are cases where the ratio is as high as 10 to 12.

Taking into account the present level of house-building costs and the monthly rents, which, considering current amortization and interest rates, amount in a majority of countries to approximately 1 per cent of the initial cost of the dwelling, it will be seen that only a small fraction of the population can afford to pay for the dwellings currently built in urban areas, without devoting an exaggerated proportion of their incomes to rent.

For the sake of simplicity, the economic problem of housing in Africa could be stated in terms of the relationship between three independent variables :
—the income of the occupants, and more precisely, the part of that income that they are able or willing to devote to housing ;
—the recurrent expenditure on housing, the annual or monthly amount that should be paid to reimburse the capital, to pay interest on it and to cover management, maintenance and repairs ;
—the initial cost of housing and its related facilities, including land.

It has been shown above that, under present circumstances, the relationship between these variables is such that only a small portion of the African population can afford to pay for an urban dwelling of an acceptable standard. One must accept the fact that the cost of house-building is too high, or that the recurrent expenditure is too great, or that incomes are too low. Perhaps the three statements are valid at the same time ; what then can be done to improve the terms of the equation?

It may be appropriate to start from the income if only to stress once more that housing cannot be dissociated from overall development. So long as a large part of the population is excluded from the market economy and even that part of the population which belongs to such economy has an income inferior to a minimum living standard, it would be unrealistic to hope that an adequate solution could be found to the housing problem in developing African countries. Slums, shanty towns, 'bidonvilles', 'unauthorized compounds', and other picturesque labels are but an indicator of the apparently unbridgeable gap between needs and means.

In a majority of African countries, so-called low-cost housing programmes have in fact catered mainly — if not exclusively — for a comparatively small section of the urban population, *i.e.* clerks and civil servants. It is understandable that, in the early stages of nationhood, public authorities should have given priority to the needs of their employees ; it is perhaps regrettable that in so many countries such a policy should have led to the creation of a privileged class which not only enjoys security of employment and comparatively higher incomes, but also occupies better housing with a considerable element of subsidy from the rest of the community.

Elsewhere priority was given to housing those who work. In many African countries, a legal obligation was imposed on the employer to provide housing for his employees or to contribute to it in the form of a housing allowance. Company towns have thus sprung up throughout the continent, with the regrettable social and political consequences that are well known to countries which went through the industrial revolution : social and professional segregation, ties between housing and employment, lack of mobility of labour, etc.

It is possible to conceive a more flexible approach whereby existing employers, and especially the promoters of new sources of employment (industry, transport, trade, etc.), would be induced to contribute to the financing of housing for their own employees, but would entrust the actual execution of housing programmes and their subsequent management to public authorities or corporations.

The problem of course remains with regard to the large masses of urban population which cannot count on a regular income or whose income is below the vital minimum. Until such time as development bears fruit, interim solutions will have to be found, some of which are briefly referred to below.

If one considers now the recurrent cost of housing, it will be noticed that it is composed of two main elements. The first is the cost of the money, *i.e.* the amortization of the capital cost of the dwelling and its related facilities over a given period of time and the interest to be paid on this capital ; the second comprises the expenditure on the management of the house itself and its related services, the cost of its maintenance over a reasonable period of time and the cost of repairs necessary to keep it in adequate habitable condition.

In African countries desperately short of capital resources, it is inevitable that interest rates should be high and that amortization periods should be much shorter than those currently found in developed countries. Whatever means public authorities may devise to reduce the financial cost of housing, it would result in some sort of indirect subsidy to a particular sector of the economy, a policy which many countries are reluctant to adopt for obvious and usually sound economic reasons.

The alternative is to try to bring into the housing market new and so far untapped financial resources. Among these one could mention the growing deposits in national social security schemes, the capital accumulated by insurance companies or the special contributions levied on the employers. Examples of each of these approaches and of many others could be quoted from many African countries.

In spite of its superficial appeal, international financial assistance can make only a marginal contribution to this problem, since its limited resources — when compared with the enormous needs of the countries — have rightly been directed to sectors which contribute more effectively to the overall development of the country. But a well-oriented policy of external financial aid could, in many cases, provide the example and the seed capital for fruitful local initiative.

The conditions of success for the latter approach are of course that the receiving country should have a clearly formulated housing policy, a short- and preferably also a long-term housing programme and the administrative and technical machinery necessary to implement them. The era of massive foreign aid frozen in medium and high standard housing for civil servants is over throughout the continent.

As far as the second component of recurrent housing costs is concerned, it is evident that public authorities can do little to reduce the expenditure on management, although there is scope for improving some of the present arrangements for rent collection.

With regard to maintenance and repairs, it must be noted that the close relationship between the initial capital cost of a house and the future cost of maintenance and repairs is not fully realized by public and private housing investors. Because of the relatively young age of the urban dwelling stock in most African countries south of the Sahara, maintenance and repairs do not represent as large a share of total building activity as in developed countries.

But taking a long-term view, it is important to realize that low quality standards, especially in finishes, will inevitably lead to high maintenance expenditure in the future, which will divert essential resources from the construction of new dwellings. Also, the adoption of low standards in terms of floor space or equipment shortens the useful life of dwellings, with the result that dwellings built only ten or fifteen years ago are already obsolete by present standards and have to be replaced at an accelerated rate, as indeed is happening in many rapidly developing African countries.

Turning now to the cost of building itself, one might distinguish between its different components, before exploring the possibility of reducing the aggregate without impairing the quality of the product.

A large part of the building cost proper — up to 60 per cent — is represented by the cost of building materials, many of which are imported. An analysis of trends in the consumption of building materials, the summary examination of the available natural resources and a broad assessment of the capital investment required for the local production of building materials and components show that the total investment necessary to bring the capacity of the building materials industry up to the level of the estimated demand around 1970 would be of the order of U.S. $2·5–3 billion, of which 25 per cent would be needed for cement and roughly 45 per cent for iron and steel products.

An investment of this magnitude should be viewed against the perspectives of the economic development of the continent as a whole. If it is assumed that the GDP of Africa will grow at an annual rate of 5·5 per cent and that gross domestic capital formation will by 1970 account for at least one-fifth of the GDP, the latter will be in the range of U.S. $8–9 billion at the end of the current decade.

Over the same period, the cumulated investment in construction would amount to some U.S. $40 billion, of which approximately U.S. $20 billion would be accounted for by building materials. The total investment required to make Africa self-supporting in terms of building materials and components by 1970, would therefore represent not more than one-eighth of the total expenditure on building materials cumulated over the period and only two-fifths of the savings in foreign currency which could be obtained if locally produced materials replaced imported ones.

By 1970 the annual expenditure on imported building materials, if the present situation was allowed to continue, would be of the same order of magnitude as the total investment required to make Africa practically self-sufficient.

The local production of building materials and components, apart from its multiplying effects on the economy as a whole, would inevitably reduce the materials component of building costs. But a parallel effort should be devoted to reducing the labour component, characterized by an extremely low productivity which more than offsets the low level of wages as compared with developed countries.

The building industry in Africa is embryonic, badly organized, under-equipped and short of skills at all levels, especially in the managerial field. There is enormous scope for improving the quality-to-cost relationship of buildings of all kinds in Africa, and especially housing.

The above discussion on costs assumes that the building itself would remain unchanged; but there is considerable evidence that some of the present housing standards — both with regard to the structure itself and to the use of land and essential services — are unrelated to local conditions and often extravagant.

The variety of individual situations is too great to justify broad generalization, but it can be assumed that in many African countries a satisfactory human environment in urban areas could be obtained at half the present capital cost.

This could not be done overnight and considerable research would be required in many fields : functional requirements, quality standards, better designs, more economic services, better layouts, higher densities, etc., but such a target would constitute a real challenge to all those concerned with housing problems in the developing countries.

In the short run, some temporary solutions will have to be adopted, which, without jeopardizing the future, will enable the community to accommodate that large part of the population which is below an economic threshold. Several of these have been tried with different measures of success.

Aided self-help is one of them, and the experience of other continents is now being applied in a number of pilot schemes throughout the continent. 'Core houses' or 'nuclear houses' have also been tried out, together with simple schemes for the provision of basic materials or incomplete structures, as for instance the roof loan schemes which have operated successfully in Ghana over the last ten years.

Another successful approach has been the one adopted in Morocco and other North and West African countries, where the community has provided a bare minimum of sanitary facilities ('trames sanitaires')

on which the occupants were encouraged to erect their own structures, in some cases with the technical and financial assistance of the
public authorities. Unsatisfactory as these dwellings may be, they
have at least the advantage of safeguarding the future by providing
an infrastructure which can be developed when the economic
conditions of the country allow it.

The above brief discussion has concentrated almost exclusively
on the urban housing problem, it being admitted that the rural
housing problem is of a qualitative nature and, in any case, beyond
the present economic and technical capacity of most African countries.

It is of course tempting to speculate on the possibility of slowing
down or limiting the abnormal growth of urban centres in the continent, but the experience of the rest of the world is there to indicate
that such an approach is unrealistic. Furthermore it is open to
question whether the continent with the lowest rate of urbanization
of all should aim at further limiting the growth of its urban centres,
which are by and large the main poles of progress.

The concentration of population around the capital cities or the
main harbours, which is a reflection of the recent colonial past, does,
of course, constitute a serious problem. Only a comprehensive
physical policy at national and regional level could ensure that the
population of the main urban centres did not grow faster than their
economic potential and that secondary poles of attraction were
created outside what are already becoming unmanageable urban
complexes. For many years to come, the trend will continue ; it
can only be hoped that the implementation of forward-looking
policies in the field of physical planning will provide a framework
for a balanced development and create suitable conditions for preserving the future.

Chapter 17

HOUSING IN ISRAEL[1]

BY

NADAV HALEVI

The Kaplan School of Economics and Social Science
in the Hebrew University

I. THE BACKGROUND[2]

THE relevance of Israel's experience in housing for comparison with
other developing countries can be evaluated only on the basis of
some knowledge of Israel's general economic development, problems,
and achievements. Consequently, some general background material
on the Israel economy is presented first. This is followed by a
discussion of developments in housing, divided into goals and
developments, the rôles of public and private housing and quantitative
aspects. Finally, some current and future problems and prospects
are considered.

The outstanding feature of the Israel economy is the tremendous
growth in population, primarily the result of immigration. In May
1948, when independence was declared, the population was 800,000 ;
at the end of 1964 it was a bit over 2·5 million. But this growth was
not even. During the first three and a half years, mass immigration
doubled the country's population. Since then, immigration has
fluctuated, ranging from 20,000 to 80,000 per annum, but never
approaching the relative or even absolute level of the 1948–51 period.
However, even during years when immigration was relatively low,
it was a sufficient addition to the natural increase to make Israel a
country of rapid population growth, ranging from 2·6 to 5·5 per cent
per annum.

Israel's basic problem has been, therefore, the absorption of mass

[1] The author is indebted to Zvi Lubetzky and David Pines for commenting on a
preliminary draft of this paper. He must also acknowledge the benefit he has
received from close association with a current List Institute Israel Project study
being carried out by Zvi Lubetzky.

[2] For a general survey of the growth of the Israel economy, see Don Patinkin,
The Israel Economy: The First Decade, Falk Project for Economic Research in
Israel, 1960. The general comments and the figures in this section are based on a
forthcoming List Institute Israel Project study by N. Halevi and Klinov-Malul,
The Development of the Israel Economy.

immigration, a task requiring extensive economic development. Responsibility for development has been accepted by the government, aided by National Institutions such as the Jewish Agency. Development has been facilitated by large-scale capital inflow, amounting since 1949 to more than $5 billion. More than 70 per cent of the capital inflow was in the form of unilateral transfers, and the major share of it went to the public sector.[1]

The inflow of capital financed extensive capital formation, amounting generally to close to 25 per cent of total resources, combined with the rapid growth of labour inputs to increase national product. GNP grew between 1950 and 1964 at an average annual rate of 11 per cent, and despite the very rapid increase in population, GNP *per capita* has grown at an average annual rate of more than 5 per cent. The growth of the Israel economy has not been without great difficulties and periods of crisis. In the early years, the tremendous immigration was too large to be rapidly absorbed, and unemployment was a basic problem. But after 1954 unemployment gradually declined, and since 1960 has ceased to be a general problem.

It is against this general background that the development of housing must be examined.

II. THE DEVELOPMENT OF HOUSING

(1) *Goals and Development*

The concept of housing needs relates to the provision of housing services. The major concern of housing policy has been to ensure that housing services are provided. But the provision of these consumer services has had far-reaching effects, frequently serving other general economic objectives, but on occasion impeding their attainment.

Provision of Housing Services. The tremendous immigration of the first few years created a physical demand for housing, which became an effective economic demand because the need to provide shelter to the immigrants was accepted as a public responsibility. This public responsibility concerned both organizing the housing of new immigrants, and financing the housing for the vast majority that were without financial means. At first, the existence of a stock of abandoned property, some 50,000 housing units, gave a breathing period of several months. But despite tremendous efforts to build

---

[1] One source — German Restitutions, amounting in recent years to some $140 million annually — go to private recipients and directly affect the demand for housing.

permanent housing, demand far outran supply during the 1949–51 period, and various kinds of transition camps were hastily erected. No one was without shelter — a considerable achievement — but close to one-fifth of the population at the end of 1951 was housed in wooden, tin, or canvas huts — temporary, sub-standard, degrading, and in the long-run uneconomic accommodations.

After the cessation of mass immigration in 1952, and with better organization of housing activities, much progress was made to provide more permanent homes for the immigrants. At the same time, greater public attention was directed towards providing better accommodation for the veteran community.[1] In addition to veteran housing projects, comparatively limited in scope, organized by the Histadrut (*The General Federation of Labour*), the Government undertook several extensive projects. The private housing market was mainly oriented to the veteran community, although people moving to higher-standard housing sold their previous homes, to a great extent, to immigrants and newly married couples. In recent years, with the relative decline in the need for immigrants' housing, public efforts have increasingly turned to improving the housing standards, particularly of immigrants originally provided with sub-standard homes, and some thought is being given to the question of slum clearance. Thus, building activity consists of two parts, providing homes for the growing population, and raising the standard of housing. Whereas immigration primarily affects public housing, the general rise in personal incomes has affected both public and private housing. A third factor of great importance in recent years has been the receipt of restitution payments from Germany.[2]

Employment. Investment in housing served a second major economic objective, the provision of employment. Despite initial problems — shortage of materials and skilled labour — the construction industry was ideally suited for rapid absorption of immigrants in employment. The low capital-labour ratio in housing,[3] the high labour input (50–60 per cent) and the relative ease with which the

---

[1] The housing situation was one of relative congestion even before the impact of mass immigration. H. Darin-Drabkin, 'Economic and Social Aspects', in *Public Housing in Israel*, Tel Aviv, 1959, p. 18, cites a census of January 1949 which showed that average density per room was 2·18.

[2] The tendency to invest a sizeable part of lump-sum restitution payments in real estate is discussed in *Survey of Family Savings*, 1957/58 and 1958/59, Falk Project for Economic Research in Israel, Research Paper 8, Jerusalem, 1960.

[3] Michael Bruno in *Independence, Resource Use and Structural Change in Israel*, Bank of Israel, Jerusalem, 1962, pp. 52-57, presents estimates showing that the capital-worker ratio in housing was in 1958 only about 40 per cent of the all-industries average, and much lower than any ratio found in agriculture and manufacturing.

local building supplies industries could be expanded,[1] made housing an ideal employment generating branch, given the restraints of capital and foreign exchange shortage. In other words, given an influx of workers, relative to the existing capital stock, an effective demand for housing services could generate more employment than a similar effective demand for other consumer goods.

So much for considering alternative investment projects from the point of view of effective demand and a given capital stock ; *i.e.* where employment in *production* of investment goods is important. Comparison of housing with other investment from the point of view of *capital formation* leads to opposite conclusion as regards long-term employment effects : here emphasis is placed on whether the increase in capital stock is complementary to labour, providing more employment opportunities on the assumption of continued adequate effective demand. Once a house is built, it provides hardly any additional employment.

The contradiction between long-term and short-term employment aspects of housing were not very important in the early years, where short-run considerations prevailed. Housing was an immediate need of mass immigration, and provided considerable — though not sufficient — employment until these immigrants were housed. By then other investments had matured, in agriculture and industry, to absorb in more permanent employment building workers unemployed as a result of a temporary cut-back in housing activity due to a sharply decreased rate of population increase.

Dispersion of Population. The Jewish population of Palestine was concentrated in the coastal plain. For a number of reasons — defence considerations, long-term economic prospects — it was considered desirable to direct part of the increase of population to the Galil in the north and the Negev in the south. The dispersion was both geographic and occupational, to agricultural settlements and new urban centres, some based on exploitation of natural resources. During the immediate hectic years, this policy was impractical, but gradually a system developed whereby immigrants were sent directly from their port of arrival to agricultural settlements and urban centres where both housing, and ideally, employment, were waiting for them. Similarly, newly married couples and others of the veteran

---

[1] At first there were shortages of building materials, and necessary imports were a severe drain on foreign exchange sources, but by the end of 1953 Israel was a net exporter of cement, sheet glass, and plywood, although it has remained an importer of iron and wood. Cf. H. Darin-Drabkin, *Housing in Israel*, Tel Aviv, 1957, pp. 158-62.

population found it easier to solve their housing needs by moving to less central areas. Unfortunately, the provision of employment to immigrants frequently lagged behind the provision of housing in the 'development areas'. The contribution of housing to employment in these new areas is higher than the national average, reaching some 30 per cent of total employment, presenting a parallel in space to the development over-time discussed above.

Some Disadvantages. Investment in housing has not been without undesirable side effects. In a prolonged period of inflation, housing both influenced and was influenced by inflationary pressure. Cost of construction rose more than other investment prices until the devaluation of 1962, after which investment prices caught up, and both rose much more than consumer prices.[1] Land prices rose even faster, leading to widespread land speculation (which may be advantageous from the point of view of dispersal of population).[2] The profitability of land speculation diverted investment from industry and agriculture. The main long-term implication of this is discussed below in the concluding section.

(2) *Public and Private Housing*

Public Housing. The influx of one million immigrants, most without financial means to pay for housing on a commercial basis, forced the public sector, Government and the Jewish Agency, to participate directly in the supply of housing. The public sector's rôle was twofold : to provide the financial resources, and to see to it that the supply of housing on a less than commercial basis was forthcoming and distributed according to a scale of publicly determined priorities. Thus, there were aspects of finance, initiation of activities and control. The financial means were made available through the Government Development Budget, utilizing foreign grants and loans, participation of the Jewish Agency which also receives foreign unilateral transfers, and domestic loans. The decision as to allocation of funds between housing and other uses is part and parcel of the budgeting process.

The organization of public housing has been as follows : the Housing Ministry (formerly the Housing Division of the Ministry of Labour) takes responsibility for most urban public housing, and the Jewish Agency deals with agricultural settlements. The public

---

[1] With 1950=100, in 1963 the cost-of-living index was about 413, investment prices 686, and building costs 661. (CBS, and Bank of Israel data.)

[2] Although 93 per cent of the land area of Israel is public, the percentage of unoccupied land in public ownership in the main urban area is very much lower.

sector plans and co-ordinates housing projects, determining the number, type, and location of housing units, the way they will be financed, and for whom they are destined. In some cases, much more common in the early years, the Housing Division actually undertook the construction and allocation of housing. Gradually greater reliance has been vested in various subsidiary, public and semi-public companies. Public and semi-public housing companies are important and interesting Israeli institutions. They both carry out Government initiated activities, and undertake their own. Some of them deal with both housing and actual construction, and others are responsible for housing, but delegate the actual construction to contractors. The Ministry of Housing does not now carry out actual construction. Similarly, public funds are allocated to housing to an increasing extent through financial intermediaries, generally mortgage banks. Thus, whereas, at first the Government had ownership of physical assets, it has transferred control of most of these assets to Amidar, a public housing company, receiving financial assets in return. For particular projects, such as slum-clearance, special companies have been set up, jointly owned by the Government and the Municipalities. Thus, the general trend is towards setting up separate companies and agencies to specialize in organization of housing, construction, finance, and maintenance.

Originally, most public housing for immigrants was wholly financed from public sources, and rented to immigrants at a fee which at best covered only maintenance costs. In later years, accent has been shifted to outright sale of homes to immigrants, although the initial investment by the tenant is generally only 10–20 per cent of the cost of the house (in some urban areas more), and extremely favourable mortgage terms are granted for the remainder. Attempts are being made to encourage tenants to purchase homes which they have previously rented. For most other recipients of public housing, a sizeable fraction of the cost must be provided by the tenant, from savings, loans, or sale of his previous home. The new tenants' contribution has been increased, in older urban areas, to about two-thirds, with the remainder consisting of long-term loans from a mortgage bank (whose financial sources are generally subject to Government control) and medium-term loans from the housing companies. Thus, the term public housing is applicable in its widest sense to all housing initiated and partly financed by public sources.

Of particular interest to many developing countries is Israel's experience in town and regional planning. This is a major function of public housing, but one which cannot be dwelt upon here.

Private Housing. During the pre-State, Mandatory period (1919–1948), housing was primarily private investment. Private capital inflow found housing for rental in urban areas a relatively profitable and secure investment. The establishment of the General Mortgage Bank in 1921, which issued bonds to local and foreign investors, marks the beginning of a domestic securities market in Palestine. Throughout the 1930's bonds issued by this bank constituted an important part of all domestic securities.[1]

Physical controls on housing, rent control, and general inflation, sharply curtailed housing activities during World War II. Rent control has been maintained to date, and adjustments of the law have been sporadic, late, and inadequate to encourage a return to construction of dwellings for rental. Equally damping on this type of private housing was the persistent inflation which effectively eliminated the sale of non-linked bonds to the public by mortgage banks in 1955, a major switch-over had already been made from rental of homes to home-ownership. This trend has persisted: whereas in 1957 about 50 per cent of dwellings were tenant-owned, by 1963 this percentage has risen to 60,[2] and of the remaining 40 per cent at least half consist of immigrant housing far removed from rental on a commercial basis.

Thus, private housing was primarily for sale. In terms of financial costs — as opposed to real economic costs — private housing is more expensive than public housing. Public housing receives public land cheaply. It also receives much more generous terms of finance, as compared with private housing which must borrow in the tight money market. As a consequence, private housing is destined primarily for those who are unwilling to wait their turn for public housing, or who are willing to pay the higher prices for better quality apartments or better locations than are offered by public housing. Private housing is therefore mostly urban and of higher quality.

The Relationship between the Two Sectors. Although public and private housing are actually two different sectors, they are far from unrelated. One connection has already been mentioned: people moving to better apartments first sell, or transfer for key-money rented apartments, their previous abode. The upward movement depends on people moving in at the bottom — very little of Israel's

---

[1] Cf. M. Sarnat, *The Development of the Organised Securities Market in Israel*, forthcoming study of the List Institute Israel Project.

[2] *Statistical Abstract of Israel*, Central Bureau of Statistics, Jerusalem, 1964, p. 178.

sub-standard housing has as yet been demolished. Thus, a substantial number of potential recipients of public housing move into
the vacated property, in fact, if there is little immigration the demand
for private housing must decline.[1]

A second connection is in the market for building materials and
manpower; in the recent years of full-employment and inflationary
pressures, private housing has helped bid up prices of factors,
particularly of skilled workers, much to the concern of public housing. Thirdly, private housing sets the tone for size and quality,
forcing public housing to raise its own standards. Thus, it is clear
why, despite the easing of the public housing's burden implicit in the
first point mentioned, the latter two (particularly the competition in
the factor markets) have brought forth proposals for curbing private,
and particularly luxury, building. The fact that certain types of
non-dwelling construction, particularly public buildings, motion-
picture theatres, and the like, are viewed as more wasteful than even
private housing does not vitiate the desire to limit the rate of growth
of private housing.

(3) *Quantitative Aspects*

Though our subject is housing, it must be kept in mind that
housing is part of the construction industry; not only is there
great mobility of factors of production between various branches
of this industry, but some important statistical series cannot be
sub-divided. In 1963, of areas of building completed only some
70 per cent was for housing, the rest was for public institutions,
commercial, agricultural, and industrial buildings.[2] Similarly,
of gross fixed capital formation in construction, 50·2 per cent was
for housing, 23·4 per cent for non-residential buildings, and the
remaining 26·4 per cent for other construction works.[3]

On page 226 is a table giving a number of statistical series
relevant to housing. A general warning must be issued: many of
the figures, particularly for the early years, are not entirely reliable,
and minor changes must not be given too much importance. For
example, complete coverage of private housing commenced only in
1960. Despite this general qualification, the data available warrants
some quantitative conclusions, supporting qualitative statements
made earlier, regarding the rôle of housing and its development.

[1] An extended discussion of the important relationship between immigration
and private housing through filtering is contained in Z. Lubetzky, *op. cit.*
[2] *Statistical Abstract of Israel, 1964*, Central Bureau of Statistics, Jerusalem,
1964, p. 390.   [3] *Ibid.*, p. 149.

(1) In comparison with most Western European countries, the percentage of total investment (and total resources) devoted to housing is quite high. This is true not only for the peak period of 1950–52, but even in recent years when the per cent of investment in housing has been much lower, ranging from 30 to 34 per cent.

(2) The per cent of employment in construction is quite high, though not outstanding in international comparison : from only 6 per cent in 1948, it rose to over 10 per cent in 1951, plummeted during the 1952–53 recession, and rose thereafter to between 9 and 10 per cent. In recent years, there has been a shortage of workers in housing, which lent support to the trend towards increased mechanization strongly noticeable in the last four years.

(3) Housing units completed per thousand of average population, 16 in 1963, is very high in any international comparison.

(4) Building activity has been closely linked to immigration ; this is particularly true of public housing, and especially of temporary housing. Private housing fluctuated greatly in the early years, but since 1955 public housing has shown greater fluctuation. The main reasons for this are the fairly steady growth in incomes since 1955 and the preference for real estate assets as hedges against inflation and devaluation, facts of greater influence on private than on public housing, and that public housing fluctuates not only in response to changes in immigration but also due to unsteady expectations of immigration.

(5) There is a clear trend towards larger and better units both in public and in private housing, although the units in private housing are on the whole considerably larger than all but a few publicly built units. Whereas average density of the Jewish population per room was 2·3 in 1955,[1] higher than at the beginning of the period, by 1961 it had decreased to 2·1.[2] It should be mentioned that on the European basis of measurement — counting kitchens as rooms — the housing density per room in 1964 has been estimated at no more than 1·42.[3] The improvement in quality of housing services can be indicated by the fact that by 1963 over 93 per cent of families lived in homes with electricity (compared with 83 per cent in 1957), only 12 per cent had no fixed bath or shower, less than 4 per

[1] H. Darin-Drabkin, *Housing in Israel*, p. 211.
[2] *Statistical Abstract of Housing and Construction*, Ministry of Housing, 1964.
[3] Estimates of Planning Authority.

cent had no toilet facilities, and only 3 per cent had no piped water.[1] An additional indicator of the improvement in housing standards is that real capital stock of houses *per capita* has increased at an average annual rate of 5 per cent between 1953 and 1963.[2]

III. PROBLEMS AND PROSPECTS

Some of the adverse effects of excessive investment in housing, such as rising prices, land speculation, inflationary pressures bidding up factor costs and thus competing with higher priority projects, have already been mentioned. They are of considerable concern at the moment, but are not the most crucial problem facing policy-makers. The very success in achieving two major objectives — basic housing needs and employment — has diverted attention to a third problem, which looms as the major economic problem facing Israel in the next decade : how to improve Israel's adverse balance of payments. Since housing is not an exportable service, the alloca-tion of such a large share of total resources to housing is considered a 'waste of resources'. In particular, the diversion of private capital to housing, in response to higher rates of return, rather than to investment in industry has led to consideration of means to restrict 'inessential' housing and other construction. As regards the im-mediate balance of payments, a point frequently overlooked is that investment in 'luxury' housing is a substitute not only for other investment but also for consumption of 'luxury goods', such as cars and trips abroad. The import-component of housing including in-direct inputs, is only about 16 per cent, whereas it is much higher in most luxury consumer goods and in other investment ; thus inflation-ary demand diverted to housing actually decreases immediate imports.

To attain the long-run balance of payments objective, it is necessary to curtail current consumption in order to increase investment in potential export industries, and to curtail future consumption in order to divert resources to exports. Since housing is an investment which does not add to the economy's export potential, and commits the economy to long-term consumption of housing services, it is easily seen why policy-makers give it low priority. It is to be expected therefore that Government policy will try to be more restrictive in the future — though whether attempts at such restrictive policy will

[1] *Statistical Abstract of Israel, 1964*, p. 180.
[2] Bank of Israel and Planning Authority Data.

be primarily through monetary and fiscal policy, or substantially supplemented by more direct controls is not yet clear.

Another question which is gaining popularity, is what the rôle of public housing should be in the future. We have seen that the problems raised by mass immigration called for active public housing activity, which was facilitated by capital inflow going primarily to the public sector. Four years of mass immigration induces housing problems which it took some six additional years to solve. In recent years, Israel's situation is more normal in this respect. Population growth is, and will continue to be, more rapid than in other countries, but it is doubtful if the housing burden involved is really very different from that faced by other developing countries where internal migration is important.

Since it is reasonable to assume that substantial immigration will continue, that it will include a large proportion of people with very limited financial means and the ideology prevails that their right to adequate housing is a national responsibility, and finally, that public action will continue to be directed to dispersal of the increments to the population throughout the country, it follows that a sizeable public housing sector will remain for the foreseeable future.

The continuance of recent trends to decentralize public housing, by setting up special companies and removing the financing from the budget of Government, while perhaps desirable in many respects, does not alter the basic *raison d'être* of public housing in Israel, which is the provision of housing at less than full-economic cost. But a growing share of public housing is not really for low-income groups. The point of contention is that this segment of the population can obtain its housing needs from private suppliers. To the extent that it is thought desirable to give them a Government subsidy — cheaper land and credit — these can be provided through private housing. The rôle of direct Government activity in such cases is more a matter of ideological preference than of economic necessity.

Finally, is a return to provision of housing services on a commercial rental basis probable, or desirable? The present legal way of subverting rent control via large sums paid as 'key-money' is cumbersome and inefficient. It does not even provide a main advantage claimed for rented housing — greater labour mobility ; on the contrary, it impedes mobility. However, it does not appear likely that building for rental will become widespread in the foreseeable future even if rent control is abolished. Obviously, in non-subsidized housing, the occupant must pay the full economic cost whether on a rental or on a purchase basis. As a result of prolonged experience with inflation and rocketing land and apartment values, the population of Israel has a strong preference for home-ownership be it rational or not.

The purchase system widespread in Israel — co-operative apartment buildings of the condominium type, have one important advantage from the point of view of general economic policy : mortgage payments constitute a major part of private savings. Private savings in Israel average about 5 per cent of disposable income. Most of this is contractual savings, with real estate being the largest single item of asset accumulation of the population as a whole.[1] It is unlikely that the same amount of private savings would be forthcoming if homes were rented. Thus, the more investment in housing is financed out of occupants' savings, the larger will be total savings, and the larger will be non-housing investment in the near future and exports at a later period. It is therefore unlikely that policy measures will be taken to induce a significant shift back to housing for rental.

[1] Cf. E. A. Lisle, 'Household Savings in Israel, 1954 to 1957/8', *Bank of Israel Bulletin 21*, April 1964.

STATISTICAL APPENDIX

Year	Percentage Increase in Population over Preceding Year	Gross Capital Formation in Housing				Per cent of (Current Price) Investment		Employment in Construction	
		In L Millions (at Current Prices)	In L Millions (at Constant 1955 Prices)	As per cent of Total Resources	As per cent of Gross Fixed Capital Formation	Public	Private	In '000	As per cent of Total Employed
	(1)	(2)	(3)	(4)	(5)	(6)	(7)	(8)	(9)
1949	28·3							31	
1950	16·7	62·7	246·4	10·8	45·1			40	10·0
1951	15·2	105·2	287·2	12·4	46·6			51	10·2
1952	3·3	127·3	208·7	9·4	39·0			41	7·5
1953	2·6	133·4	166·0	7·9	35·6				
1954	2·9	179·4	212·1	8·3	37·5			50·8	9·0
1955	4·2	241·1	241·1	8·9	37·9	41·6	58·4	54·3	9·3
1956	4·7	235·0	209·5	7·1	33·6	40·3	59·7	49·8	8·4
1957	5·5	299·4	256·2	8·1	34·4	53·1	46·9	62·6	9·8
1958	2·8	300·2	252·2	7·2	31·9	47·5	52·5	64·3	9·8
1959	2·8	337·1	280·2	7·3	32·5	45·2	54·8	65·3	9·6
1960	3·0	346·9	273·8	6·6	30·9	40·4	59·6	65·3	9·3
1961	4·0	472·1	332·9	7·6	32·2	44·4	55·6	68·4	9·3
1962	4·4	662·7	411·4	8·4	33·6	48·4	51·6	75·2	9·7
1963	4·4	664·8	390·8	7·4	31·3	40·9	59·1	79·7	9·8

STATISTICAL APPENDIX—*contd.*

Year	Per cent of Net Domestic Product originating in Construction	Area of Permanent Housing Completed, in '000 Square Meters			Housing Units Completed			
		Public Housing	Private Housing	Total	Public Housing, Permanent	Public Housing, Temporary	Private Housing	Total
	(10)	(11)	(12)	(13)	(14)	(15)	(16)	(17)
1949		518	231	749	13,333	5,217	5,347	23,897
1950		833	364	1,197	16,492	13,751	7,000	37,243
1951		1,463	712	2,175	28,573	25,341	10,953	64,867
1952	9·0	869	1,168	2,037	22,366	3,305	15,142	40,813
1953	7·6	808	201	1,009	20,929	4,386	2,584	27,899
1954	7·6	816	578	1,394	18,274	—	7,506	25,780
1955	8·1	917	929	1,846	19,028	579	12,386	31,993
1956	7·3	914	921	1,835	18,439	2,275	11,962	32,676
1957	7·7	923	695	1,618	21,444	1,496	9,144	32,084
1958	7·8	1,101	827	1,928	23,162	—	10,960	34,122
1959	7·3	1,090	939	2,029	20,228	—	12,430	32,658
1960	6·9	1,047	894	1,941	17,627	—	11,070	28,697
1961	7·3	692	1,277	1,969	12,938	—	12,950	25,888
1962	7·9	1,284	1,395	2,679	23,707	—	14,030	37,737
1963	7·9	1,390	1,386	2,776	24,292	—	13,900	38,192

Sources : Column 1 computed from *Statistical Abstract of Israel 1964*, Central Bureau of Statistics (CBS), page 2. Columns 2, 3, 4, and 5 computed from *Statistical Abstract of Israel 1964*, pp. 146-7, and pp. 138-9. Total resources are defined as GNP *plus* import surplus. Columns 6 and 7 computed from *Israel's National Income and Expenditure*, CBS, Special Series No. 153, pp. 100-1. Data for 1963 computed from *Bank of Israel Annual Report 1964*, p. 248. Columns 8 and 9, 1950–52, Z. Lubetzky, forthcoming Study on Housing in the Israel Economy. 1954–63, *Bank of Israel Annual Reports*. An estimate for 1948, based on the census of population, is 6·1 per cent (G. Ofer, *Services in the Israel Economy*, forthcoming study of the List Institute Israel Project). Column 10 : 1952–59 *Israel's National Income and Expenditure*, CBS, Special Services, No. 153, pp. 104-5. 1960–63 : *Adjusted Estimates*, CBS, May 1964 (in Hebrew). Columns 11-17 : 1949–60, Lubetzky, *p. cit.*, based on CBS and Ministry of Housing Data. 1961–63 : Ministry of Housing Data.

Chapter 18

CHANGES IN THE OUTPUT OF THE BUILDING INDUSTRY AS A FACTOR IN THE DEVELOPMENT OF HOME-BUILDING

BY

EDWARD KUMINEK

Warsaw

I. THE SHORTAGE OF HOUSES

POLAND is faced with a difficult housing situation, the principal features of which are the shortage of homes compared with the number of families, a high density of occupants in the existing living space and the unsatisfactory standard of a large proportion of this accommodation.

The housing shortage is particularly marked in the towns, where in 1960 there were 122 households to every 100 homes. According to the estimated demand for independent accommodation for people living alone, the total deficit amounts to some 0·4–0·6 million homes. Most of the existing accommodation consists of units that are too small, which accounts for the high average concentration of 1·66 persons per room. The quality and fittings of much of the accommodation are unsatisfactory, particularly in rural areas.

Furthermore, there is an increasing demand for housing, owing to the total population growth and changes in its structure, combined with an intensification of the process of urbanization and a greater insistence on the quality of homes.

This situation calls for a considerable increase in housing construction.

II. THE BUILDING INDUSTRY

The Polish building industry is highly developed. In 1962, 841 thousand people were employed in socialized construction, representing 11 per cent of the total number of workers in the socialized sector. However, housing construction plays a relatively small

228

part in the building industry as a whole, and amounts to less than 30 per cent. The programme of industrialization now being implemented and the need to channel investments to other fields have had a decisive influence in this sector. It should be stressed that the industrialization programme provides for the expansion and modernization of existing industrial concerns on only a limited scale, but its main aim is to set up new undertakings, which consequently account for a large proportion of the building being done.

The building industry is known to have developed more slowly than industrial output. Although, when the socialized building industry in Poland was formed, the aim was to create a network of large State construction undertakings — and this is shown by the fact that the average number of workers per socialized housing construction concern is 570, while undertakings responsible for industrial construction each employ about 1,500 workers on the average — nevertheless the 'social' output in construction falls far below that of other industries. The value of the annual output of a building worker is 50 per cent lower than that of an industrial worker, and the national revenue produced by building, in relation to the number of employees, represents about 60 per cent of the income from industry. This difference can be explained to some extent by the very marked difference in the amounts of capital invested per employee, which is four times less in building than in industry.

More important is the fact that, despite the growth in productivity in the building industry which has been particularly pronounced in recent years, the rate of increase has been much slower than in industry as a whole, as can be seen from comparing the figures for the growth in the value of production (based on comparable prices) and for the growth in employment :

	1955	1962
Building		
Value of production	100	161
Employment	100	115
Industry		
Value of production	100	191
Employment	100	121

The relatively low yield from construction work and its slower growth rate can be largely attributed to the inherent nature of building output, namely the individual character of the product, the constant shifting of the site of production and the dependence on the weather, all of which call for the continual reorganization of the production process.

III. PRODUCTIVITY IN HOUSE BUILDING

For a long time, the level of productivity in the Polish housing industry was very low and it was even lower in the early fifties than before the war. This can be explained to some extent by the higher standard of homes built after the war compared with those built previously.

The figures given below, based on surveys conducted by the Warsaw Institute of Housing, illustrate the changes that have taken place in the productivity of home-building and show the amount of site work needed to build a residential block by conventional methods.

Man-hours	1950/51	1953/54	1956/57	1960/63
Per square metre of living space	60–65	50–55	40–50	25–35
Per cubic metre of the building	11–11·5	10–10·5	8·5–9	6–7

A typical feature is the low level of productivity at the beginning of the period in question which, as already stated, was lower than that of the pre-war period. This phenomenon arose despite the improvements made in the structure of the building industry (the organization of large, socialized undertakings) and despite the concentration of construction programmes, the mechanization of certain types of work (earth-moving, concrete mixing) and vertical means of conveyance on the sites. The main reason for this situation was the shortage of skilled building workers owing to the extremely swift expansion of building firms and above all the influx of workers from the over-populated countryside. This is borne out by the following figures : in 1949, 307,000 people were employed in socialized construction ; in 1950, 503,000 ; in 1951, 648,000 ; and in 1952, 720,000.

The comparison between the amount of work done per square

metre of usable living space and per cubic metre of the building is significant. The amount of work performed has decreased much more in relation to the area of living space than per cubic metre of the building as a whole. This proves that the changes in the design of residential buildings have produced favourable results, by planning the different levels of the building to acquire more profitable living space, by introducing new materials and better construction methods (such as allowing for the use of thinner walls) as well as by reducing the height of the storeys.

Although the possibilities of rationalizing building techniques are far from exhausted, this does not necessarily mean that building is radically transformed into an 'industry'. The transformation is bound up with industrialization of the building operations and thus with the introduction of technological methods appropriate to production on an industrial scale. Changes in technical methods should enable building to be freed from certain consequences which are inherent in the nature of the building product itself, *i.e.* its immobility and its individual character. In practice, the industrialization of the building industry and particularly home-building more often than not involves transferring the production of the main structural elements to factories, conveying them to the site and erecting the buildings by a highly mechanized process.

IV. INDUSTRIALIZATION OF HOUSE-BUILDING

The industrialization of house-building in Poland began in 1954 with the use of large structural elements for residential buildings. The first buildings, made up of large, room-sized prefabricated panels, were built in 1956. It is not the aim of this report to describe the technical solutions adopted, nor certain mistakes which have since been corrected. However, it is perhaps relevant to define the part played by industrialized construction in home-building generally. The living accommodation in rural areas is produced by individual builders of scattered single-family houses who still employ traditional methods that have been gradually rationalized. In contrast, in urban building, which accounts for almost three-quarters of all accommodation and, in particular, provides housing in communal buildings, the contribution of industrialized construction can be summarized as follows (on the basis of the volume of buildings on which work was started in the given year):

Construction Methods	Percentage of Buildings		
	1958	1960	1963
1—traditional	65·9	64	44
2—large elements	12·5	22	39
—in large blocks	12·4	19	28
—in large panels	0·1	3	11

The erection of buildings in large panels is a truly industrialized construction method ; the extent to which production is transferred to the factory, the degree of completion of the elements supplied, the reduced weight of the building and the predominantly industrial organization of the manufacture and erection of the elements, all confirm this.

The economic effects of industrialized construction are most frequently gauged by comparing the cost of the buildings erected by industrialized methods with that of traditional buildings. However, calculations of this type do not allow comparisons to be made on an international basis and, in view of the fluctuations in price levels and relationships produced by different price policies, do not even result in comparisons that are entirely valid on a national level. There also remains the inherent difficulty of analyzing construction costs owing to the features peculiar to each building and the local conditions under which they are built.

In spite of all these reservations, the buildings erected by industrial processes can be said to have proved more costly at the outset (by as much as 20–25 per cent) than traditional buildings. This difference decreased quite quickly as a result of the constant fall in the price of prefabricated elements and the rationalization of designs for residential blocks. At present, the cost of industrially constructed buildings has been brought down to the same level as that for traditional buildings and sometimes even to a lower level. It should be pointed out that, over the same period, the cost of traditional buildings has been substantially reduced by the introduction of more economical designs and the rationalization of building operations.

From the standpoint of the economic effects brought about by industrialization of building, the saving in social work is very significant. With industrialized construction, the site costs in terms of the labour expended are much lower than with traditional buildings. Recent analyses show that the labour required to construct a conventional building works out at an average of 6 to 7 man-hours per cubic metre of building, while only 3 to 4 man-hours are needed for buildings assembled in large panels. These figures are not strictly comparable, however, since part of the work on the large-panel building has, in effect, been transferred to the factories making the prefabricated elements. This makes it interesting to attempt to calculate the total amount of labour expended on two comparable residential buildings ; that expended on the site itself and so-called 'industrial' work undertaken throughout the entire act of building, from the extraction of the raw materials to the production of the final materials and manufacture of the elements. This calculation was made on the assumption that any elements not displaying differences in the two types of building (*e.g.* features regarding equipment) would be disregarded. The results obtained were as follows :

	Workers on Site	Industrial Workers	Total Labour Force
Traditional building	100	100	100
Large-panel building	52	149	70

It is noteworthy that 50 per cent of the labour expended on the large-panel buildings takes place on the site whereas this proportion reaches 80 per cent for traditional buildings.

Industrializing housing construction results not only in a reduction in the contribution made by the labour on the site and in the entire process of production, but also in a change in the professional structure of the workers. On the site, there is a particularly sharp reduction in the demand for certain traditional categories of craftsmen such as bricklayers, carpenters, plasterers, etc. This is extremely important since it takes a long time to acquire the necessary skills in these trades, whereas the new techniques needed in industrialized construction by machine operators, erectors, etc. are assimilated more rapidly. Over the production process as a whole, the number of workers employed in factories is much greater.

In transferring part of the building process to factories, substantial sums have to be invested in the plant required to make the construction materials and prefabricated elements. It has been calculated that the sums needed to increase output in the house-building sector are, per comparable living unit, 20 per cent higher for buildings constructed by industrial techniques than for conventional buildings.

Similarly, the influence of changes in the different production methods have been calculated, with particular reference to changes in the deployment of workers and in the use of power and the necessary investment funds. The calculations show that, owing to the present cost of labour, power, and machinery, a saving of 100 units in the cost of labour on a large-panel building site can be secured by spending the equivalent of 73 units to cover supplementary workers off the site and the necessary investments.

The reduction in labour costs stemming from the industrialization of housing construction offers a solution to the difficulties which arise when it becomes necessary to increase the number of workers in the building industry. These difficulties are particularly acute in industrial areas and large urban centres. They are due to the fact that labour is in short supply in these areas and that work on building sites is less attractive than in industry. The pattern according to which building workers go into industry on the completion of industrial buildings is well known.

The better working conditions in industrial undertakings, the greater stability of employment and the opportunities for achieving more worthwhile professional qualifications are the reasons behind this pattern. The industrialization of house-building offers a solution to these problems not only by employing fewer teams of workers, but also by the fact that the transfer of a large proportion of the production process to stable industrial concerns creates working conditions similar to those in industry.

House-building is concentrated in both industrial and large urban centres. The fact that it is concentrated in this way promotes the technical basis that is essential for industrializing the building sector and organizing large sites for this purpose.

In regions where there is a labour surplus and where house-building is seldom concentrated, there may be no cause for proceeding with industrialization. In such instances, small concerns manufacturing structural elements do not give the satisfactory results provided by mass production, and the creation of large concerns would entail increased distances between these and the building sites and thus an excessive increase in haulage costs.

Nor should the fact that industrialization requires an increase in investment be overlooked ; such investments are hard to come by in regions where accelerated development programmes are being implemented and considerable investment is called for in all sectors.

Under present economic conditions, the industrialization of house-building is somewhat restricted by technical factors, as well as being limited in scope.

During the past few years, industrialized home-building methods in Poland have made a significant contribution towards solving the difficult problem of the increase in the number of workers engaged on housing programmes. It also fulfils a less obvious and less appreciated function in that it encourages the rationalization of conventional building.

However, the industrialization of house-building cannot claim to be the only means of increasing the available accommodation to the extent that the difficult housing situation in Poland will be improved reasonably soon.

Chapter 19

SOME ECONOMIC PROBLEMS
OF HOUSING IN THE U.S.S.R.

BY

V. A. NAZAREVSKY

Association of Soviet Economic Scientific Institutions, Moscow

I. HOUSING CONSTRUCTION IN THE U.S.S.R.

TODAY, housing is one of the most burning problems in nearly all the countries of the world. It is a matter of great urgency in the U.S.S.R. as well. Since the very first years following the October Revolution the Soviet Government has been doing its utmost to ensure a rapid growth of housing construction. The successful development of the national economy enabled the Government to increase, from year to year, allocations for the expansion of the housing resources of the country.

HOUSING CONSTRUCTION IN THE SOVIET UNION
FROM 1918 TO 1960

Years	Completed Housing, Mil.Sq.M.
1918–28 (yearly average)	3·9
1929–40　　ditto	9·8
1941–45　　ditto	11·0
1946–50　　ditto	20·6
1951–55　　ditto	30·4
1957	52·0
1958	71·2
1959	80·7
1960	82·5

All in all, over one thousand million square metres of dwellings have been built during the existence of Soviet power. In recent years the Soviet Union has invariably led the world in the amount of housing construction. And this gigantic activity is easily explained. The rapid development of industry, agriculture, and other branches of the Socialist economy is not an end in itself. The principal objective is to meet the requirements of the working-people to the fullest possible extent. Therefore the rapid development of the national economy raises the standard of living and, along with it, the birth rate and the life span. This makes the expansion of housing construction an ever-increasing necessity.

The task facing the builders is complicated by a very important circumstance. For many years they were engaged in rehabilitating the industry, agriculture, and dwellings ravaged in the period of World War II. The German invasion resulted in the destruction of about 70 mil. sq. m. of housing in cities and towns, *i.e.* only a little less than what had been built between 1918 and 1940. 1,710 towns were demolished. 1,209,000 dwelling-houses were reduced to ruin. Hundreds of thousands of others were heavily damaged. No less destruction was suffered by rural areas. 3·5 mil. village houses were razed to the ground, 25 mil. people remained homeless, 32 thousand industrial enterprises were totally destroyed. All this, of course, put off the solution of the housing problem for many years and led to a serious aggravation of the housing shortage.

In the last few years housing construction has been carried out on a particularly grand scale. In the period from 1959 to 1965 more than 600 mil. sq. m. of housing, or about 15 mil. flats were built. In addition, many houses are built in the rural areas each year. Thus, in the last seven-year period as much housing was built as during the entire existence of Soviet power. Between 1959 and 1965 almost every other urban family received a new, larger, and more comfortable flat. In recent years the number of new flats per thousand inhabitants has been considerably greater than in any other country.

This vast amount of construction would have been entirely impossible without modern, highly developed industry, and, above all, its backbone, the manufacture of pre-cast reinforced concrete units. After 1954, a practically new modern building industry was set up. This made it possible to supply construction projects with new materials, thereby increasing labour efficiency, reducing the construction time and turning the building site into an assembly area. In the last decade about 280 mil. cu. m. of prefabricated reinforced structures have been erected in the U.S.S.R.

The further growth of housing construction in the U.S.S.R., and its technological progress are intimately connected with the development of large-panel house construction. As far back as 1963 each fifth house was assembled from large panels. At the same time, a new stage — pre-cast volume unit house assembly — has gained more and more ground. Experiments show that volume elements of houses completely fabricated and finished at factories reduce labour expenditure on site more than three-fold even if compared with the large-panel method. This is just what is needed for a complete industrialization of housing construction.

II. CO-OPERATIVE HOUSING CONSTRUCTION

The efforts to achieve the most rapid solution of the housing problem have led in recent years to the development of co-operative housing construction alongside State construction which continues to predominate. This opens up considerable possibilities for speeding up housing construction and raising its quality.

In 1962 the Soviet Government issued a special decree on the development of co-operative housing construction according to which the Construction Bank of the U.S.S.R. extended credits to co-operatives to cover 60 per cent of the estimated cost of the houses to be built. The remaining 40 per cent was paid by members of the co-operatives. The credit was extended for a term of 10 to 15 years and was repaid in equal annual instalments.

This decree was warmly welcomed by working-people. In 1962 as many as 847 co-operatives were organized. In that year co-operative-built housing in Moscow amounted to 54 thousand sq. m. ; in 1963 it grew to 200 thousand, reaching 400 thousand sq. m. in 1964. A similar situation took place all over the country. In 1964, co-operatives completed 4·7 mil. sq. m. of housing.

And yet, these were only the first steps. At the end of 1964 co-operatives received new privileges. As of January 1, 1965, the down payment was reduced to 30 per cent over the major part of the country's territory. The balance of 70 per cent is to be repaid in equal instalments over a longer period (up to 20 years instead of the former 10 to 15 years). The annual interest rate on the credit for co-operatives organized since January 1, 1965, has been reduced to 0·5 per cent. If the future owners of the flats should so desire, improvements are introduced into the finishing, planning, plumbing, and other equipment.

In addition the co-operatives no longer have to cover the expenses of pulling down old houses, structures, etc. Many building materials are now sold at reduced prices. All these privileges have brought about a new expansion in co-operative construction. At present, the number of such co-operatives is about four thousand, and the housing to be completed by them in 1965 has already reached 7·5 mil. sq. m.

In many localities, the development of co-operative construction is already resulting in a number of improvements in the housing resources of the country. A tremendous number of families who previously built individual houses with the aid of State credit [1] now prefer joining co-operatives. This ensures more advantageous terms of credit, an abrupt cut in the cost of the square metre and better-equipped flats, since individual construction often involves high expenditures on the water supply and sewerage systems. Building up an area with 5- to 8-storey co-operative houses instead of single-storey houses makes for a more convenient distribution of public utilities and better transportation arrangements. Taking into account these beneficial features of co-operative construction, planning agencies consider it necessary to lend every possible support in the next few years to this method along with a rapid increase in State housing resources.

The efforts towards a maximum growth of the planned Socialist economy and, consequently, towards raising the standard of living of the whole population have resulted in drawing up a far-reaching programme for the development of the entire country in the next two decades.

The task was set to 'solve the most acute problem of welfare of the Soviet people — the housing problem. Within the first decade of this programme the housing shortage in the country will be eliminated. Families living in overcrowded and poor-quality dwellings will receive new flats. Upon completion of the second decade each family, including newly married couples, will have a comfortable flat.' In order to tackle this tremendous task, the annual rate of construction will be increased several-fold and brought up to un-paralleled dimensions — 400 mil. sq. m. This great increase will completely cover all requirements for housing. Allowance has also being made for natural increase in population and the demolition of old houses.

It is also important to emphasize that these years will see not only the elimination of the housing shortage. The colossal achievements in the Soviet economy will lead in time to a rent free tenancy. Even

---

[1] The State provides all applicants with a credit for a term of 10 years amounting to 1,200 roubles for the construction of individual houses.

in the U.S.S.R., where the rent is already the lowest in the world, this fact can hardly be overrated.[1]

III. HOUSING POLICY

The housing policy in the Soviet Union is aimed not only at increasing the scope of construction work and the number of flats completed each year. Two closely related problems are being solved simultaneously, *i.e.* improvement in the quality of housing and a more rational development of urban areas. In fact, it is a matter of building a new type of town. In the next few years the new principle of area building will also bring about a complete change in the appearance of rural settlements. They will consist of multi-storey houses with all modern conveniences.

One of the most important tasks facing the builders is the improvement of the quality of the houses being built. Newly built houses will be altogether different from those built in the forties and early fifties. This development has occurred in various ways. Some idea of the improvement in the quality of the newly built houses can be obtained from the table given below.

Years	Percentage with Water Supply	New Communal Sewerage	Houses with Central Heating
15.7.1948—1.1.1950	49·2	42·2	44·6
1950–53	53·0	48·6	60·4
1953–54	67·6	63·6	69·5
1954–56	78·6	78·1	73·6

Since 1956–57 this process gained more momentum. Today, almost all the new houses are equipped with water supply, sewerage, and central heating. About 100 per cent of the new houses are supplied with electricity and the supply of gas to houses is developing at a tremendous rate. In 1945 only 18 urban areas were supplied with gas, and in these areas there was not a complete coverage. By 1956 the number of cities and towns completely supplied had grown to 73. In 1959 every fourth house built in the U.S.S.R. was provided with gas, and in 1965 every fourth house, including the old ones, had gas installed. Within only the last seven years 385 cities and towns and thousands of small populated centres have been supplied.

[1] The maximum rent is 3 to 5 per cent of the total family earnings.

The elimination of the acute housing shortage against the background of the undiminished gigantic amount of construction made it possible to abandon the emergency practice of the post-war years when several families had to be crowded into one flat. In 1958, a number of new house designs were urgently worked out providing for one-family flats. Within 2 to 3 years these types of houses which consisted as a rule of one-, two- and three-room flats, superseded all others. This was one of the most important changes in construction made during the past few years. All designs serving as a basis for construction, envisage well-equipped bathrooms and kitchens, built-in closets, mezzanines, etc.

The rapid improvement in housing results not only from the great scope of new construction, but also from the large-scale reconstruction of old houses. Reconstruction in old towns and villages is to cover all existing housing by 1980. Many old houses will be demolished and replaced by modern dwellings. All urban houses and the vast majority of rural ones will be connected to water supply and sewerage mains. Central heating will become universal. Nearly all flats will have bathrooms, showers, gas or electric ranges, and water heaters. Air conditioning will be widely installed, especially in Central Asian republics, in Transcaucasus, and in the southern regions of the Russian and Ukrainian republics.

It is noteworthy that further improvements in the types of flats and houses as a whole, strict standardization of building elements and parts, complete switch-over to modern fully prefabricated houses, by no means diminishes the importance of the beauty and external attractiveness of dwellings and whole districts. The struggle against the so-called architectural redundancies and for maximum economy should be combined with work aimed at creating a new style of twentieth century building, taking into account both the achievements of the past and the architectural and planning decisions arrived at during the last few years on the basis of utilizing more modern materials, and the new requirements of a modern town. The introduction of industrial methods should on no account mean monotony, bad taste. Attempts to design most comfortable, economical, and simultaneously attractive houses is one of the most important tasks facing all those who take part in the creation of a new dwelling.

The scale of the reconstruction of old towns can be judged by the example of Moscow where more than two thousand houses are being built at the same time. Between 1954 and 1963 more than 22 mil. sq. m. of houses were built there. About 3·3 mil. people received new dwellings. In 1965 another 3·5 mil. sq. m. will be completed. In the amount of construction, Moscow holds firmly the first place in the world, 18 flats per thousand inhabitants are built each year.

When building up residential areas, 16 different versions of the layout of flats and sections are used. About 50 per cent of the flats consist of two rooms with a total floor space of 30 sq. m., 25 per cent consist of one room. It is of interest to note that in future the percentage of one-room, and later of two-room flats will be reduced because of an increase in the floor space allocated to each member of the family. The percentage of three- and four-room flats will increase as will the floor space in two- and three-room flats. The layout of different flats differs in the arrangement of the kitchen, the bathroom, the toilet, and other accommodation. The semi-basements of many houses contain auxiliary enclosures for storage of bulky items, such as perambulators, bicycles, and so on. Each of them has built-in closets and mezzanines. The living space constitutes about 75 per cent of the total space. All new flats are provided with central heating, water supply, sewerage, bathrooms, showers, hot water. In the next few years the problem of telephone installation will be solved almost completely. In the next seven years alone 900 thousand new telephones will be put into operation.

IV. SOME CONCLUSIONS

In conclusion it will be useful to dwell briefly on some trends characteristic of construction in our time.

The rapid upsurge of the entire national economy in the U.S.S.R. is accompanied by a rapid growth of new towns. Representatives of widely differing professions in the U.S.S.R. have arrived at the conclusion that it is most expedient to build, not gigantic metropolises, but small and medium-sized towns which, as a rule, are most suited for the provision of maximum convenience in the organization of both the labour and the leisure of the whole population. Therefore the growth of large cities will be slowed down. To limit their growth, many satellite towns are being built. Moscow, Kiev, Leningrad, Kharkov and many other cities already have such satellites. Kharkov and Cheremushnaya present a brilliant example showing how the growth of large cities is being limited with the aid of satellite towns. The satellite Cheremushnaya is located 50 kilometres from Kharkov. According to the general project it is to accommodate 80 thousand inhabitants. The industrial enterprises of Cheremushnaya make up an industrial unit which, owing to its specific nature, is intimately bound to the industry of Kharkov. If the satellite had not been built, these enterprises would have to be set up in Kharkov, and this would inevitably hinder the proper organization of the city economy.

Satellite towns also absorb many old enterprises which cannot be reconstructed or expanded within the boundaries of the old city. The same is true of establishments causing contamination of the air, since the necessary protective zones can be readily created in the satellites.

Another example of the building of a new town is the small Lithuanian town Electrenai situated in the vicinity of the huge Lithuanian State Electric Power Plant. Its construction was begun in the summer of 1960. According to the general plan the total area of Electrenai is about 100 hectares. At the moment approximately 34 hectares have been built up.

Some data on the distribution of the built-up area is of interest. Dwelling-houses occupy 9 hectares, children's institutions and welfare buildings cover 15·2 hectares, the sports grounds comprise 3·9 hectares. A park of 10 hectares has been laid out. At present, the housing resources of the town amount to ten 48-flat, four 64-flat and one 120-flat blocks. In addition, there is a hotel for 36 guests, a school for 1,000 children, and two kindergartens for 135 children each, a polyclinic, a hospital, shops, and a number of utilities.

All the houses in the town are provided with central heating, hot water, gas, water supply, sewerage, and telephones. The houses and other structures are built of pre-cast reinforced concrete units. The building materials were delivered to the sites from the intertown base of the building industry located in Vilnius.

The estimated construction cost is 7·8 mil. roubles, including blocks of flats (3·7 mil. roubles) and public utilities (1·9 mil. roubles). The cost of living space was 108 roubles per 1 sq. m. The dwelling houses were built by the continuous production line method with the use of network planning. The construction time for a 48-flat block did not exceed 25 to 30 days. The labour expended on the construction of the town amounted to 15·7 thousand man-days.

When building new towns, as in reconstructing old ones, under the conditions of Socialist society with its planned system, elimination of private ownership of land and means of production, the town builders are, in fact, afforded unlimited possibilities for a reasonable, virtually scientific solution of the problem of settlement, based on a comprehensive consideration of the diverse factors of production, nature, economics, present state of transport and trends in its development.

The advantages afforded to the town builders by a planned economy can be fully utilized only provided all the work is carried out in accordance with a general plan. This refers equally to new building and the reconstruction of old towns. Without a scientifically substantiated general plan, no economical or rapid building is possible at present. A general plan permits the location of towns, workmen's settlements, State and collective farms in the most healthy area. The ground is paved for co-operation of engineering structures serving industrial enterprises and populated centres, avoidance of duplication, making them more perfect from the technological and economic standpoints. It is precisely the general plan of a town that makes it possible to co-ordinate progressive and economically efficient solutions of current problems with the long-range trends in economic development.

Ignoring or underestimating the importance of regional planning may lead to unjustified location of industrial enterprises and to building dwellings in insanitary areas, to duplicating uneconomical, low-power, technologically imperfect systems of water supply, sewerage, heating, to mass contamination of rivers, damage to forests. Therefore, at present, a general plan is one of the most vital conditions for starting the construction of any town.

Another significant factor which determines to a considerable extent the success of the builders of a new town is an early provision of a base for the building industry. Experience shows that in many cases it is advisable to set up a common base supplying several towns with building materials. This was done, for instance, when building a number of Siberian towns. The building base of the town of Angarsk simultaneously supplies pre-cast units to Baikalsk.

It should be emphasized that in building new towns particularly good results are produced by network planning based on the use of electronic computer techniques. The beginning of mass production of electronic computers designed to solve not only technological but also economic problems enable their wide application for construction control.

The results of the introduction of electronic computers are vividly demonstrated by the building of the new town of Angarsk. The use of new methods of control based on the application of electronic computers permitted the number of people employed to be greatly reduced with a simultaneous increase in the scope of the work. Whereas formerly 2,500 workers completed 80 to 90 thousand sq. m. of housing per year, now 600 workers complete over 120 thousand sq. m. per year. Considering the severe climatic conditions of Siberia, these results testify to the great achievements of the builders.

The information presented in the paper indicates that the development of housing construction in the U.S.S.R. has eliminated the serious housing shortage and within the next few years will enable the housing problem of the country to be solved completely.

REPORT ON THE PROCEEDINGS

SUMMARY RECORD OF THE DEBATE

BY

ADELA ADAM NEVITT

FIRST SESSION
THE DISCUSSIONS OF THE PAPERS
BY PROFESSOR DONNISON, PROFESSOR MUTH,
AND MR. CULLINGWORTH

Dr. Halevi, in opening the discussion, said that Professor Donnison's paper dealt with the important inter-relationship between economic institutions through which policies have to be implemented and the political realities which determine the policy goals of each country. The main object of Donnison's paper was to convince us that housing policy is extremely complex and that it cannot be fully understood without regard to all or most of the social science disciplines. In no other paper presented to the Conference were there so many provocative statements per page and Dr. Halevi had some difficulty in deciding which of the many topics raised to choose for discussion — a difficulty increased by a disconcerting habit Professor Donnison had of slipping in a qualifying statement just as one was poised to pounce on a generalization.

Halevi had intended to start the discussion by considering several points that are made concerning developing economies and poor economies, such as the allegedly more limited rôle of government in under-developed countries in the housing field and Professor Donnison's broad generalizations on stages of economic growth and their implications as regards the rôle which housing plays in these economies. He would, however, defer such comments because a special session would be devoted to developing economies and he thought that these points were not really in the main line of Professor Donnison's argument.

Professor Donnison listed the main functions to be performed in connection with the provision of housing (see page 2, points (*a*) to (*e*)). Dr. Halevi thought that the first was either too general, or in the more conventional meaning of the term 'planning', not necessarily essential. He would replace it by two others : (1) the determination of the extent of new construction, and (2) its financing. He would also single out 'selection of occupiers' from the rest of (*e*) and call it allocation of housing services. He agreed, however, with Professor Donnison that in principle such a list

247

was useful for analysis and international comparison of government housing policy.

He then turned to Professor Donnison's main discussion of the determination of the scope and limits of housing policy and he said that Professor Donnison's discussion of the concepts of 'needs', 'demand', 'requirements' for housing as perceived and interpreted by government were quite foreign to an economist who cannot define demand without regard to resources available, and he rephrased Professor Donnison's ideas in the following terms, which he thought more meaningful to an economist.

The publicly desired amount of new housing is a function of three things :

(1) some subjective concept of what is a desirable or a minimal standard of housing quantity, quality, and its allocation. This may differ from country to country, from régime to régime, and from one period to the next ;

(2) the resources available for housing. This depends on total resources and on alternative costs, and allows for cost saving via redistribution of the existing stock ;

(3) the expected effects of carrying out such construction on the economy ; *e.g.* employment, balance of payments, inflation.

One and part of three determine a public (or government) indifference map, whereas two and part of three determine a transformation curve. The desired amount of housing which is determined by the tangency of the transformation curve to an indifference curve may or may not differ by much from what it is believed a free market would provide. If it does, this may arise from :

(1) the pattern of income distribution ;

(2) market imperfections and institutional deficiencies ;

(3) divergence between social and private utility functions, as regards standards thought minimal, and the effects of housing or time preference.

The extent and nature of the divergence between the free market solution and the government desired solution will, in combination with the political and economic system, determine the extent and form of government intervention which may be in any or all of the functions listed.

Professor Donnison said many of the papers we would be discussing dealt with specific aspects of economic theory, or had presented case studies of the situation in particular countries. He had attempted to provide a common framework in which the analysis and empirical evidence of the other papers may be related and discussed. While case studies were often interesting for their own sake, it was in the inter-relationships between the theoretical and the empirical papers that the greatest interest lies. To understand these inter-relationships it is necessary to ask fruitful questions. The questions he poses are a political scientist's questions rather than an economist's and some of them may be the wrong ones — but the answers should at least be capable of examination. He was not concerned principally with questions of the type : 'Is a "free market" the most efficient system for the solution of housing problems ?' He asked instead, 'How do governments decide what the system should be efficient *for* ?' and 'What determines the character and scope of their own interventions and objectives ?'

Professor Lewis started the discussion on Professor Muth's paper by saying that as a Welshman, to whom both English and American were foreign tongues, he congratulated Professor Muth on his contribution to American, if not to English. If UREPOP increases according to forecast, and NEWORD keeps pace, then we shall shortly have a language of about two hundred million six-letter words, and the new translation of D. H. Lawrence will be 50 per cent longer than the original.

Professor Muth's thesis is that people on low incomes seek housing of minimum standards, and that because this is in short supply its price is high. This meant that its price per square foot is not much below that of superior accommodation, or may even be above it if the superior accommodation is not available in such small units as the slums. This is a phenomenon which is to be observed in a number of countries.

His difficulty in accepting Professor Muth's argument was the absence of a detailed analysis of the economics of slums. Professor Muth's statistical analysis has thrown up certain associations, but these are not necessarily causative. In common parlance, there are slums of two quite different kinds, which often overlap, but may have different causations. One kind is simply a dwelling which is so overcrowded that decent living becomes impossible. Another kind is a dwelling which is so primitive, or in such bad repair, that it is in some sense — other than overcrowding — below standard. In that the latter kind is often let at a low rent, this kind of slum may attract the poor in such numbers that the dwellings also become slums of the former kind. Slums could also be divided into two kinds in a different way : (1) dwellings which were built as slums, and (2) those which have become slums. He thought that in the U.K. the latter kind is more common. Buildings may become slums in three ways : first, rising standards may make the buildings obsolete. If standards change so that a house without a bath, or some other amenity is no longer acceptable to the mass of the people, then all such houses become slums. The second way in which an existing building may become a slum is through actual physical deterioration — such as when the timbers rot, the floors become damp or displaced and the whole house vibrates when the television is switched on. The third way is through becoming overcrowded.

A useful insight into the economics of slums is obtained if we begin by looking at dwellings which have become slums, in one of the first two ways. They have done so primarily because it has not been profitable for the landlord to keep them up to standard. In assessing the profitability the landlord has to take account of current maintenance costs and the expected differences in rent and final selling price which will arise from action, as opposed to inaction. It is for this reason that rent controls which do not take account of costs may breed slums. Here it is not a case of poverty creating slums but of low controlled rents doing so, and a statistical analysis should take account of this.

A similar effect arises when, for one reason or another, demand for the occupation of the site on which these slums stand is low. The buildings may be quite reasonable, but situated in an area which is not very popular. They can consequently only be let at rather low rents which are not high enough to cover repairs and decay sets in, and slums appear. Once started, the process spreads. This analysis related to slums of only one kind, and often a way of remedying the situation is to use physical planning measures, or sometimes local taxation measures, to boost the demand for these under-wanted sites, until it is more profitable for the landlord to repair or to redevelop than to let things stay as they are.

Professor Lewis next considered slums of the kind that arise from over-crowding, or which are built as such. In this case a large area of sub-standard housing may be very profitable, and it is undoubtedly true that it will be occupied by the poor. But he was not certain that the abolition of poverty would abolish the slums. Although such slums are costly on a square foot basis, they may still be cheaper than alternative accommodation, and there are some people whose preferences would induce them to stay in these overcrowded conditions. The provision of more houses of a better kind would probably cause some exodus from the overcrowded tenements, and to avoid having substantial vacancies the landlords would probably lower the rents. This would probably mean that a number of people would stay behind, in rather less crowded conditions. In that sense, the dwellings would be moving upwards out of the slum classifica-tion. But because the landlord would be having less rent, they would probably decay all the sooner, and so become slums of the second kind.

These remarks illustrated his main criticism of Professor Muth's paper, which is that while an association between slums and poverty had been shown, no causation had been established. This, Professor Lewis said, is not just the usual kind of criticism that can be made very easily of much statistical work. In the paper before the meeting variables relating to the history of the situation had been included but it did not appear to be an adequately dynamic analysis of the problem, and he could not agree that the tabulated results 'clearly imply that slums are mainly the result of poverty'.

Professor Muth, in replying, said that had it not been for the limit in length imposed upon him he would almost certainly have produced a much longer paper which would, in particular, have devoted more attention to a model of the relative demand and supply of poor quality housing and its spatial aspects. Clearly, however, such a model underlies his empirical analysis and he hoped soon to publish it along with more details of his empirical results.

Professor Lewis had stressed that many kinds of undesirable living conditions may be called slums. For purposes of analysis of housing problems, however, one must give specific content to such a term. Since governmental slum clearance policy typically aims at removing dwelling units of poor physical quality from the stock, it seems sensible to define slum housing as that below a certain physical standard. The important thing, however, is that his analysis is especially concerned with the determinants of poor quality housing. He had also studied the determinants of space as distinguished from quality of dwellings, and he believed their determinants were largely the same. Both space and physical quality vary primarily because of variation in income.

He would quite agree with Professor Lewis that rent control may lead to physical deterioration of dwellings. It was indeed striking that of the six cities examined by Duncan and Hauser in their study cited in his paper, only in New York where rent controls remained in effect did housing conditions fail to improve dramatically from 1950 to 1956. He also agreed that there were good reasons to believe that physical deterioration of certain units of the housing stock might result from a decline in the demand for their services. But he believed that his analysis demonstrated that this had seldom been the case in the U.S.A.

He strongly disagreed with Professor Lewis that overcrowding had, in fact, produced physical deterioration. It might be the case that increased density of occupancy in given dwellings would lead to greater costs of operation and depreciation. Where rents were controlled, of course, landlords may be prevented from raising rents to cover these increased costs, and maintenance of housing may suffer as a result. If rents are uncontrolled the landlord will increase rents to cover the increased costs of quality maintenance if it is profitable for him to do so. If the landlord fails to maintain his property, the question obviously becomes one of why it is not profitable for him to do so.

Finally, he objected to the issue of correlation and causation raised by Professor Lewis. He agreed that such a problem may always exist, and it was for this very reason that he made his inter-city comparisons and tested for least-squares bias. His income co-efficient in the equation explaining dwelling unit condition was quite similar in the inter-city and south Chicago comparisons. He submitted that this would not be the case if within cities lower income groups inhabit poorer quality housing because they had a smaller aversion to doing so in terms of effective demand. Likewise, if the latter were true, the effect of income should have vanished in the two-stage least-squares regression for south Chicago, but it became stronger if anything. This evidence strongly suggested to him that the association was indeed one of the effect of income on housing quality and not the reverse.

Mr. Turin said that we needed somehow to find a common thread to the problems which are referred to in each paper. These problems should be seen within a common conceptual framework. We might well ask why is a housing policy necessary ? We do not discuss the necessity for a policy on razor blades or television sets. Why then a policy on housing ? Is the housing problem new ? Does it arise because housing needs — normatively defined — are not at all the same as the effective demand for housing ? This is commonly accepted throughout the world. All countries today accept as a desirable objective the attainment of some minimum standard of housing for all families. This normative need is much greater than the effective demand in under-developed countries and somewhat greater in all countries, even in the U.S.A. A housing policy is required because the supply of the commodity is limited. These limits are imposed by the supply of building materials, the availability of skilled labour, and the shortage of land. The effective demand is limited because at the present level of housing costs many low income families cannot afford the rent of a standard house and a policy is required not only to increase the level of housing construction but also to ensure that families can afford to live in the houses.

Professor Netzer said that the idea that the building industry had inevitably a limited capacity to fulfil our wants was a notion as far from economics as one could possibly get. It is technically quite easy to expand the building industry. It is not like the aircraft industry which may be frustrated by a technical lack of inventiveness ; the building industry was technically very simple and it could technically be expanded quite easily. The difficulty arose when one remembered that the expansion of the building industry must be at the expense of some other industry. It was basically a question of resource allocation.

The reason for a social policy stems partly from income differences and all seem to be agreed that some redistribution of income may be necessary. Most people also seemed to be agreed that some minimum housing standards are necessary. We have to remember that most of the institutions which have an impact on housing have not been devised purely for this purpose — they have other goals. These institutions are regulated by governments and the regulations are normally imposed without any particular regard for their effect upon housing. Since governments intervene in all sorts of ways in an economy, we do not have anything remotely resembling the 'ideal' world of a free enterprise market economy. We have to accept the interventions of governments as a given parameter in our consideration of housing markets and one could justify further government intervention in the housing market to rectify any undesirable consequences of intervention made for other reasons.

Professor Muth said he did not think that a housing market was really so very complex. We should perhaps remember Milton Freidman's phrase, 'There is not such a thing as a free lunch'. Are housing needs so much more pressing than medical needs, food needs, clothing needs, etc.? We cannot have any of these goods or services free and he could not see why we should think that housing falls into some special category. It would be easier to accept that housing 'need' had some special characteristics if we knew (1) that there were market imperfections which restricted the allocation of resources to house-building although the returns on investment in housing exceeded alternative investments, or (2) if we could accept that some people, by failing to spend more of their income on housing, affect the preferences or opportunities of others. If we are going to say that people with low incomes must move to better housing than they would choose for themselves, then we must take into account the fact that we are curtailing their expenditure on other things.

Dr. Musil said it was extremely difficult to define needs in isolation from demand but none the less this had been done in Czechoslovakia. One could not order the social priorities of the country until one had some assessment of needs. The Czechoslovakian people could consider better housing as being a priority over having, for instance, a private motor car. Their priorities were first food, clothing, and shelter. When everybody had the minimum amount of these goods then other less essential goods could be considered.

Dr. Kuminek suggested that we needed to clarify our terms. A distinction should be made between needs which are defined in objective terms and needs which are defined subjectively. Subjective needs may be divided into (1) those determined as ambitions or wishes and (2) the ones generating demand. The latter stems from the wishes which are supported by the means indispensable for their satisfaction. Planning is based on objective needs which create the foundation for the planning of long-term government policy. Short-term planning should, however, also take into account the demand for dwellings. This is especially important when estimating the scope of co-operative and private building. The fulfilment of the short-term demands give some indication of the longer term needs and they can form one of the variables in drawing up the long-term plans.

We also needed to keep a clear distinction between (1) objectives of a housing policy, and (2) the means of achieving those objectives. The objectives were clearly social and aimed at improving housing conditions of the country. The reason why it was always necessary to have a policy specially designed for housing was that housing has a high capital cost and there are long supply lags which cannot be removed quickly. Minimum standards had to vary from country to country and from time to time. In Hong Kong, for instance, new minimum standards had been laid down. These standards implied that 20 square metres of space was acceptable for

7-8 persons, and that 2-3 thousand people could be housed on $2\frac{1}{2}$ acres. To us this may appear to be an extremely low standard, indeed perhaps no 'standard' at all. However, in Hong Kong this new standard is a substantial improvement on present conditions.

Dr. Holm, in introducing Mr. Cullingworth's paper, said that further clarification of the aims of housing policy was needed. If choices were to be made effective, there had, as a rule, to be as many means as there were stated objectives. But we should also discuss the interdependence and conflicts which would eventually arise between different objectives. In his paper Mr. Cullingworth had referred to a lot of different aims (goals ?) and mentioned some of the means that could be used to achieve them. It may be questioned if Cullingworth had made sufficient distinctions between objectives and means. Dr. Holm had tried to rearrange different aims for housing policy mentioned in the paper under the following headings—

Objectives which are intended to :

(1) increase the supply (consumption) of housing *per capita* ;
(2) increase the quality of the existing stock through (*a*) 'slum-clearance' (demolition), and (*b*) increased maintenance ;
(3) reallocate housing consumption within a given stock (for example, to meet the demand from large families, low income groups, etc.). Under special conditions we can add—
(4) to guarantee a general level of 'low rents'.

Dr. Holm then discussed different means for achieving the different objectives. He underlined that objective four is obviously of a special character as its primary purpose is not to add anything to housing consumption. It can only indirectly expand the demand and then possibly the supply. This objective must therefore be co-ordinated with means which fulfil the first objective. In order to attain this objective we had to use a general economic policy that stimulated investment in housing through favourable loans, etc. If we use 'low rent' as a means in housing policy, with an aim to expand housing consumption and at the same time have an economic policy with restrictions on investment in housing production we only cause stresses ; we get a 'goal-conflict'. In that sense rent regulation is one 'mean' among other means. He thought that the statements in Cullingworth's paper would have gained by a more distinct formulation of the objectives.

He also wondered whether Mr. Cullingworth had taken sufficient account of the increase in the quality of houses when he estimated that the rent income ratio was higher now than it had been at the beginning of the century.

Mr. Cullingworth said he had been aware of this difficulty and had qualified his statement by mentioning that the higher costs were partly due to the higher housing standards imposed by the State. The imposition of standards often had the undesirable consequence of pricing houses beyond the means of the poorer families. Nevertheless, it seemed to him that governments had a responsibility for setting a high enough standard to ensure that houses built today would not be out of date by 1980. The great durability of houses imposed this obligation. Some housing authorities in England were now imposing an obligation on all builders to supply sufficient space for a garage. This clearly imposes a burden on present-day families who neither have a car nor wish to acquire one.

There were many ways in which the problems which arose from such government policies could be mitigated. In the U.K. we had subsidies of various types ; family allowances, rent controls, direct housing subsidies, and (for the very poor) a system of financial aid which resulted in the State paying the whole of the rent.

Professor Maisel was worried by Mr. Cullingworth's formulation of the wages/cost of houses ratio. He seemed to be arguing that the capital output ratio is extremely high and that therefore a lot of capital was used and therefore no one could afford houses. The problem of housing could not be centred around the supply of new houses ; the old houses must also be taken into consideration. It was the problem of filtering which was of major importance and this might be analysed as a linear programming problem of the transportation type. Professor Gillies was editing some extremely interesting research into the way in which a housing market operated. It had been found that filtering could take place throughout the income scale if the building industry were building houses for the top half of the income distribution. The filtering process ensured that the poorer families were supplied with an adequate number of houses. Those who could not afford new houses received the units vacated by the people who had moved to newly constructed dwellings.

The ratio of rents to incomes had been mentioned and it would be interesting to know why Mr. Cullingworth had chosen 20 per cent. Why not 30 per cent or 40 per cent ? Incomes had risen very considerably and there was no reason why the ratio should remain constant with rising incomes. The present ratio was to some extent determined by the many distortions of the market which had been introduced by government interventions of one kind or another. Other studies had shown that houses now included more services, appliances, and other consumer durables. For example, people were now buying houses complete with electric washers, refrigerators, and so on because in this way they could buy the equipment on 5 per cent loans instead of the usual rates for this type of equipment of 10 per cent to 18 per cent. As a result, we would expect the percentage of income allocated to housing payments to be higher than in the past. It could not be held down to any arbitrary percentage.

Mr. Azcarate considered that the answer to Professor Maisel's question had to be broken down into its component parts. The amount of rent which a family should pay could only be answered at the political level and in France no clear political answer had been given to this question. A figure of 10 per cent or more of income was usually given, but this was not by any means a settled figure. One of the French housing subsidies is proportional to the income of the tenant, the number of children and the social category of the head of the household, and the level of rent or mortgage payments.

The question could more profitably be answered at a factual level. At present the proportion of income paid in housing costs (rent or mortgage payments) is about 8 per cent, but the dispersion is large for each income group examined. Extreme caution was needed in interpreting or using national average figures as there is very considerable dispersion about the averages quoted. There was also the problem of accommodation which was owned by occupiers who had repaid their mortgages or bought outright. Their current housing costs are extremely low.

As income increases for the individual family the proportion devoted to rent falls, but over time as all incomes rise the proportion has risen. In France this can be explained by the relaxation of rent controls and the impact of new construction.[1]

Professor Grigsby said the inadequacies of incomes had been discussed but it did not seem sufficient to say that we should raise the incomes of people defined as poor. It is sometimes thought that low income groups form a fairly homogeneous population and that they have middle-class values. This is far from the case in the U.S.A. Many low income families have problems other than low incomes, for instance mental and physical ill-health and lack of skills. So the question resolves itself into an examination of a range of different programmes such as social insurance, unemployment benefits, pensions, etc. It is necessary also to consider the impact of a housing subsidy policy not only upon the client population but also the non-client population. The welfare programmes which have been implemented in the U.S.A. have not had a wholly beneficial effect because of their undesirable psychological impact on both these groups.

Professor Gelting said that Mr. Cullingworth seemed to imply that the high capital output ratio in housing creates particular difficulties. But the durability of houses is an advantage, and in equilibrium high durability necessarily implies a high capital output ratio. What we are concerned with is, of course, economic rather than physical durability. And it may well be that in consequence of rising real incomes and more rapid changes in economic structure the durability of houses will decline.

Since much has been made of the difference between the so-called free play of market forces on the one hand, and government intervention on the other, it is probably not superfluous to point out that there is no such thing as a free housing market operating in a vacuum. The operation of the

[1] *Bulletin Statistique du Ministere de la Construction*, January–February–March–May (1965). Consommation. No. 3, July 1964. (Ed. Dunod.)

market is always conditioned by institutional arrangements and depends to a large extent upon government policies.

It would not be easy to state precisely what was meant by 'neutral' or 'non-discriminatory' policies. However, assuming such a definition to have been stated satisfactorily, we are confronted with two sets of questions.

First, a policy for housing may be motivated by the consideration that housing conditions affect a wider circle of persons than those immediately concerned. That is, the general maintenance of certain minimum housing standards may be considered a collective good justifying government intervention. The principal justification for more extensive intervention than this would appear to be a desire to improve housing standards as a matter of social policy, either because some members of the community are considered to be too poor to afford proper housing standards, in which case a more general effort to relieve poverty would appear the logical course of action. Or because the authorities take the view that a certain part of the population does not sufficiently appreciate or understand their own housing needs, and in this case the preferences of consumers are deliberately ignored.

Secondly, assuming intervention in a certain direction having been decided upon, a distinction may be made between interventions like taxes and subsidies, which conform with and act through the price mechanism, and interventions like rent control and rationing, which interfere with the operation of the price mechanism. It is primarily to the discussion of the various types of interventions in the housing market and their consequences that economists can contribute.

Professor Robinson said that if one was to justify the imposition by the State of a higher real expenditure on accommodation than individuals might wish voluntarily to make out of the same real income, the justification was to be found partly in the repercussions of family upon family. The effects of poverty were not confined within the limits of the house to the individual family. The poverty of the dockland district of Liverpool in the 1920's created an environment in which individual families with larger real incomes had great difficulty in raising their standard of living. Was it not necessary to take account of these external economies and of differences between individual interest and the interest of the community ?

Professor Gillies considered the question of whether it is better to have a policy specifically orientated to housing or one directed to evening out some of the fluctuations of income over the life span of a family and, more generally, the inequalities of income between one family and another. He said that there is a sector which cannot be met by the market and in the U.S.A. this sector is met by the public provision of housing. He did not think that a general income subsidy was necessarily the answer and would propose rent certificates as an alternative and rather better means.

Professor Muth was not convinced that individuals fail to spend enough of their incomes for housing. There are two factors by which one could justify a government policy of increasing housing consumption as such : (1) market imperfections which result in higher earnings of resources used to produce housing than the same resources used in other ways, or (2) external economies of the sort that imply that a dollar's expenditure on housing yields benefits to others that the individual does not take into account when making his expenditure. To his knowledge there had been little empirical demonstration that either of these conditions existed. The subsidization of interest rates has the undesirable effect of encouraging greater durability than is appropriate, and a straight income or rent subsidy is therefore to be preferred. Two examples of housing market imperfections in the U.S.A. were the federal income-tax subsidy to owner-occupied housing and federal mortgage programmes, and these were both the result of governmental programmes rather than the workings of the private market. He was convinced that government actions had already been far more important quantitatively than private ones in producing imperfections and inequalities in U.S. housing markets. The question of a desirable housing policy is partly a value judgment and partly a matter of empirical fact. He believed that in the U.S.A. the effects of larger incomes on the expenditure of the relatively poor had done far more than government action to improve housing quality. The average subsidy obtained by families living in public housing in the U.S.A. during the middle fifties was about $125 per month plus the value of utilities, or more than $1,500 per year. Thus it cost the government just slightly over $1,500 per year to eliminate one substandard dwelling through income subsidy. This subsidy was large in relation to the tenants' incomes, which were mostly less than $4,000 per year. A study of housing quality suggested that about 40 per cent of families with annual incomes of $2,000 in 1949 inhabited substandard housing. An increase in their incomes of 10 per cent or $200 would, according to his results, have reduced this proportion to about 27 per cent. From 1950–56 the consumption of housing in U.S. cities increased by about 2 per cent per year, while the consumption of substandard houses declined by about 6 per cent per year. Thus, in the City of Chicago alone, 12,000 dwelling units per year were brought up to standard largely through the improvement of existing units. This compares extremely well with the average annual rate of construction of public housing units of 35,000 for the whole country. In the U.S.A. it would certainly appear that the growth of income coupled with a free housing market had done far more to raise the housing standards of low income families than government action.

In reply to a question from Dr. Arndt, Professor Muth said that the average incomes of households living in the census tracts of Chicago which had been examined varied considerably from area to area. When 40 per cent of the houses within the census tract were classified as substandard, the average household income was around $2,000 a year. When, however, a very much smaller proportion of the houses, say 3 per cent or less, were classified as substandard, the average income was around $5,000 a year. These household incomes related to 1949 prices and they included earnings of people living in the households but unrelated to the head of the household. The probability of a family with an income of less than $2,000 a year living in one of the slums was about 1-2 in 1950, but by 1960 it may have been very much higher. This was because the cost of housing had risen rather more than the price of other goods and services. However, people with relatively low incomes in 1960 generally had real incomes considerably higher than $2,000 in 1949 prices.

Dr. Arndt stated that in Germany the 'right' to a good house was seen in terms of a moral judgment and the acceptance of the need for a housing policy arose because like so many other countries Germany was in the process of attempting to raise its standard of living very rapidly. The United States of America was very much richer than the other countries of the world, but the U.S.A. had not solved its housing problem. The average income of a household in a Chicago slum was $2,000, which is more than the average income of German workers in the mid-1950's, but the Germans have no slums of the U.S. type. They felt, therefore, that a solution to the housing problem could not be achieved by simply leaving the price system to allocate houses. Some people were willing to live in substandard housing and spend a high proportion of their income on other goods rather than good quality houses. It is therefore necessary to have not only a housing policy, but also an urban renewal policy which would remove the slums and force some increased expenditure on housing.

Professor Muth said that the definition of a slum was relevant to this discussion. It seemed common to define a slum with reference to the average quality of houses within a particular country. As the average standard of houses in the U.S.A. is very much higher than the standard in many other countries, houses may be called a slum in the U.S.A. which in other countries might well be regarded as standard houses. As the average quality of the nation's housing stock rises so does the definition of a slum. In exactly the same way the definition of housing 'need' rises with each successful attainment of a higher general standard of housing.

It might be correct to say that there is no solution to the housing problem through a free market system. No economist would argue that a free market necessarily produces a socially desirable income distribution, but it would be better to attack the distribution of income or wealth rather than to isolate the housing market as being in some way a special problem.

Professor Donnison sought to summarize the basic problems the Conference was confronting and the solutions proposed by different participants. These problems could best be grasped if the distribution of income over the whole life of a household was considered. In Western countries the middle classes tended to have an income which rose fairly smoothly to a peak in middle age (45-55) and then declined slowly after retirement. Superannuation schemes assisted by special tax treatment prevented a catastrophic decline even in old age. The picture for the working classes was quite different. Earnings began sooner and often rose to their maximum when workers were still in their twenties : they declined more sharply in late middle age and often fell to a very low level indeed after retirement. If the earnings of working wives and the dependents to be supported were added to the picture, then household income per head showed two pronounced peaks — at the point of marriage when the family typically consisted of two earners, and in the late forties, when there might be several earners and no dependents. These peaks, and the corresponding troughs in early parenthood and in old age, were more marked for working-class families because their children were more numerous and because their income in retirement was lower.

In most countries, people passing through this cycle are likely to seek larger and better housing (to shelter their growing families) just at the point when their income per head is falling. The ratio of rent or mortgage repayments to income may then be cripplingly high. Rising income (national and personal) and inflation (which reduces the real cost of servicing loans) may subsequently reduce the burden of housing costs as household income per head rises to its second peak. Rent/income ratios may then be far below the level that the household could bear, until they rise again to a higher level in old age. Institutional arrangements for the finance of housing — whether for rent or for owner occupation — and procedures for the decontrol of rents often exacerbate this imbalance, and hence compel a restriction of housing standards in order to ensure that shelter costs are kept within reach of families with relatively low income per head.

In fact, the market is extremely imperfect in most countries of the world. People of fifty, for example, often have difficulty in borrowing money (because their remaining working life is short) although they are capable of sustaining high rent/income ratios ; hence they are unable to buy a new house unless they have one to sell. Thus in many countries there is a scarcity of small, high quality dwellings which would be attractive to shrinking households with relatively high income per head. The immobility of the middle-aged is largely a function of the market and it has multiple effects throughout the whole market. If governments intervened at this point to make moves easier, secondary and tertiary moves could be made by young families who are at present made immobile or forced to accept unnecessarily low standards of housing by the inability of the middle-aged to vacate older and larger family houses.

The interventions of government so far discussed are largely designed to meet the needs of families entering the first trough in income per head. They include subsidies and housing allowances, more general redistributions of income (through family allowances and tax relief) and fiscal benefits for the house purchaser (most systematically deployed in Western Germany). In the Soviet Union the first Rent Law (1927) fixed a relatively high level of rents and employed special reductions for larger and poorer households. Since then, inflation and rent control have reduced many of the rents in the U.S.S.R. to very low levels. The recent rapid growth of co-operative housing schemes in many centrally planned economies poses the problem in a new form. In effect, the burden of redistribution between age groups appears often to be borne by the middle-aged relatives of co-operative members who assist their children to find the payments required, and by industrial enterprises who make grants to enable their employees to enter co-operatives.

Professor Maisel : An answer to Professor Donnison's problem might be some form of contract with the family so that it pays less than the current rate of interest and amortization in the low income periods, and a higher than market rate in later periods. This would be particularly beneficial to the individual family during a period of inflation when we had both the cycle of income and a general increase in incomes.

SECOND SESSION
THE DISCUSSION OF THE PAPER BY DR. HOLM

Dr. Przeciszewski said that Dr. Holm had used his analysis to estimate the importance of different factors which influence a household's choice between accommodation units of different size and quality. The author had used the system of Pareto's indifference curves and had treated standard and size of dwelling as two different commodities. By using straight line iso-rental curves it had been shown that the highest indifference curve was attained at the point of tangency between an iso-rental line and an indifference curve. In Fig. 10 (A to C) an example is given of the 'income consumption curves' or the Engels curves which result from increases of income. The material for these examples was taken from a Swedish town whose housing market was illustrated in Fig. 3. These statistics showed that, in general, large households have a higher preference for space than small households. However, when households of a certain size were compared it was shown that as low incomes were increased, the increased income was devoted to improving the standard of accommodation. As incomes reached the average level, the consumption of space increased markedly and the income consumption curves bent off to the right. The author explained the convexity of the curves by the structure of supply. When a family wanted to raise its standard of housing at a reasonable cost it was faced with little real choice.

At the end of Dr. Holm's paper he stresses the imperfections of the housing market ; imperfections which make it difficult to interpret the results of an analysis of this type. Dr. Przeciszewski stressed that this was important because the possibility of moving house depended upon the supply structure of the market. In Sweden it may be that mobility was much influenced by the fact that in the inter-war period many small dwellings were built with a relatively high standard of equipment. Mobility also depended upon the ratio of new buildings to the existing stock.

Dr. Przeciszewski then turned to consider the merits of the paper as a whole. He thought that it showed great merit in extending some of the analytical tools and diagramatic analyses that are used in the general theory of supply and demand. However, he felt that the analysis was too restricted in scope and had many features which were more appropriate to other commodity markets than specifically to the housing market. The housing market has certain specific features to which the author refers but he does not then take them sufficiently into account in his analysis. Dr. Holm had considered the fixed locality of the housing market and the durability of dwelling units, but had laid no stress on the high level of costs per dwelling. The author also totally neglected the rôle of public intervention in a housing market and this led to a very high degree of abstraction in the analysis. Neither did he take into account the different types of tenure groups — *i.e.* privately rented accommodation, owner-occupation, public housing, etc. The increase in the individual family ownership of a single house had spread in many countries, although it may not yet play a very significant rôle in the Swedish housing market.

While stressing the usefulness of the analysis we ought, none the less, to remember that it was micro-economic in character and it was bound up with local markets. It would be useful to compare the results obtained by this type of analysis with the results obtained from more general analysis. Mass inquiries into household expenditure on a national, inter-regional, and international scale were required, together with macro-economic analysis of a theoretical nature. It was necessary to know (*a*) the 'need' for shelter space as measured by persons per room, and (*b*) the desire for better housing equipment measured usually by rent per dwelling or rent per room or per square metre of space, and (*c*) a measure of the propensity to shift to the individual family ownership sector of the market.

Dr. Holm, in replying to Dr. Przeciszewski, said that in writing his paper he had tried to give an example of this type of analysis and not to develop a wide and generalized model of the housing market. In doing this he could not see any reason why he should have put into his model the results of various types of public intervention. The model made a suitable base for discussion of the consequences of government intervention and its effects. He cited the example of Professor Muth's examination of slum clearance in the U.S.A. If one wanted to clear slums one could either subsidize the clearance of the slums directly or produce such a large stock of modern houses at such rents that there would be a movement from the poor quality houses to the better ones through the mechanism of the market. The Swedes had tried this latter course in the fifties when the demolition of many houses, including slum clearance, had proceeded rapidly as production of new houses increased. However, the Swedes had gravely under-estimated the expansion of demand which stemmed from increasing incomes combined with a large supply of cheap houses through subsidies and rent controls. For this reason an insufficient number of vacant houses had appeared at the 'bottom end' of the market. Dr. Holm thought that he could make a model which involved various types of tenure — in particular individual house ownership — but he had not done it here because he wished to keep the model simple.

Professor Lindbeck (Chairman) suggested that the discussion might concentrate upon two aspects of Dr. Holm's paper. First, what was the purpose for which the model could be used? Could local authorities anticipate the demand for housing from this model and concentrate new building in certain sectors, thus helping the market to move in a direction of equilibrium in such a manner as to avoid the increase in rents which a completely unregulated market might have produced?

Secondly, how should Dr. Holm's analysis be evaluated from an analytical point of view? For instance, were the assumptions reasonable? Would the shape of the curves in Fig. 10 (A to c) have been different if the quality of houses had been measured in some different way? On the whole, the model seemed rather rigid on the supply side. It would be interesting to know what were the possibilities of conversions making the composition of the supply of dwellings much more flexible than was suggested by the model. Dr. Holm's assumption that housing preferences were a function of the existing stock of houses was an interesting one. He also asked if there were any empirical evidence in support of this hypothesis.

Dr. Holm thought that the possibility in Sweden of increasing the supply of accommodation by conversions was limited and this was why he had stressed this aspect in his analysis. In the U.S.A. there were many large houses which could be converted and thus in a time of housing shortage and a demand for small dwellings the supply could increase to meet the demand. While there were, of course, many differences in the structure of different housing markets there were also many similarities, and he gave as an example the relationship between persons per room and persons in households for the United States, England and Wales, and Sweden. While Sweden had a higher ratio of persons per room than either of the other two countries, the distribution of the available rooms over the different sizes of households was remarkably similar in the three countries.[1]

---

[1] *Statens Offentliga Utredninger*, 1963–65. *Konsumtionsmönster på bostadsmarknaden.* Stockholm, 1964, p. 105.

He agreed that the shape of the curve in Fig. 10 was in some degree dependent upon the chosen method of measuring the quality of accommodation. However, he was satisfied that within a given scale, comparisons of the spread of households between various standards of accommodation could be made, both between groups of households within one market and between different local markets.

Dr. Halevi pointed out that the standard classes had been based on quality differences, but other factors such as location should be included as separate things to be studied. Could these things be included in Dr. Holm's analysis? If his analysis was to be used for policy making purposes the standard classes used should be greatly simplified. He also wondered about the parallel lines which were used to show the effect of income increases. There were two questions about the iso-rental lines. (1) Should the lines be curved? (2) Would the iso-rental lines behave in the same way once the market moved to a position in which there was a high consumption of both space and quality? Furthermore, if the standard classes were not very narrowly defined the paradoxical result of crossing iso-rental lines might occur, thus making this analysis impossible.

Mr. Cullingworth said that the rate of residential mobility varied with the age of the household and was lowest for elderly people. The housing conditions of elderly households were determined to a large extent by the availability of housing and housing finance, costs and rents at the date when the household moved. Present conditions were not therefore a reliable basis for prediction.

Professor Maisel agreed with Mr. Cullingworth, but thought that the question was one which could be posed in terms of marginal and average elasticities. Which had Dr. Holm used in his diagrams? If it was the average elasticities, then any particularly high or low marginal rates would not apply. If the average was influenced by a very high immobility of the population, which meant that many people were not in an equilibrium position, the predictions made from the model would be wrong.

There was some difficulty in measuring a standard in terms of physical attribute and Professor Maisel suggested that Dr. Holm could have used rent per square foot of space as a measure of standard classes or as a measure of quality. He had done this with U.S. data and thought it would be satisfactory for the Swedish market. In examining the U.S. data Professor Maisel had found that about half the increased expenditure on housing consumption had been spent on getting a higher quality and half on a greater amount of space. The income demand for housing thus seemed to be divided between space and quality.

Professor Gelting : Dr. Holm's indifference chart assumes by implication that standard is measured in terms of money cost, since otherwise it would be purely accidental if the iso-rental curves were straight lines. If standard was measured in some kind of physical units, we might have transformation curves of almost any curvature.

Professor Lindbeck thought that the Conference was perhaps overlooking the fact that Dr. Holm's statistical analysis was based on a market in disequilibrium. The example was taken from Sweden where markets had been influenced over a long period by rent control. A difficulty in such a market was the identification of an ex-post situation with an ex-ante demand curve. As the curves which Dr. Holm had produced were heavily influenced by a long period of rent controls they could not perhaps be used for predicting the future.

There was, indeed, some difficulty in measuring the quality of houses by an ordinal index of their quality and the iso-budget curves given in Fig. 9 as straight lines would only arise by accident if the measurement was made by such an index instead of in terms of money. The lines seem, therefore, to imply a conversion into prices per square foot of space and by unit of quality. However, the budget lines in the figures are only examples of what they could look like. The principles of the analysis would not change if the budget lines were non-linear.

Professor Maisel thought that an important issue raised by Dr. Przeciszewski was home ownership versus rental. Sweden seemed to have more choice of housing with reference to standard of accommodation, rather than by choice of tenure. Most dwellings in Sweden were in large apartment blocks and not the small individual houses common in the U.S.A.

Dr. Holm said tenure would not appear to be such a problem in Sweden. There was very much less owner-occupation in that country than in the U.S.A., and he had found from his research that when four or more rooms were demanded, families with equal incomes seemed to be indifferent as between owner-occupation or renting. However, the statistical material upon which this was based was very weak, and Dr. Holm thought that one reason for this lack of clear preference for owner-occupation might be the effect of rent control and the control which the Swedish government exercises over the building of houses for sale.

Mr. Turin said that if we assume that rent bears a fixed relationship to the initial cost of building, the horizontal scale on Fig. 9 should be chosen to take into account the effect of this on the total cost of a dwelling. Therefore the rent and the size of dwellings should not be expressed so much by the number of rooms as by the floor area. The relationship between the cost of a dwelling and its area for each category of dwellings was a linear one and was also a function of the number of rooms in the dwelling. It is only if the horizontal scale of Fig. 9 is selected to take into account the marginal cost of floor area that the iso-rental lines could be assumed to be straight.

Professor Lewis said that Dr. Holm's curves were of all dwellings and when the rents of new and old dwellings were combined this would take care of Mr. Turin's objection. It was not only the cost of building which had to be considered but also the cost of land.

The Economic Problems of Housing

Professor Muth thought that one could reasonably expect a certain uniformity of rents if one only considered building costs but that one could find large variations if location was taken into account. The land costs would influence the space used and could make a large difference in rents per square foot of dwelling space.

Mr. Ståhl said that the problem confronting an economist who tried to formulate a model of the housing market was the construction of a model of N dimensions. This was an extremely complicated and difficult task, and we had therefore to decide what simplifications could be introduced into such a model so that while the model reflected the world we were examining, it was also sufficiently simple to be of some practical use. It was clear from the paper before us that we had two quite distinct problems. One was the problem of constructing a theoretical model and the second was the availability of statistical material which, in practice, tended to determine the use to which such models could be put and the number and type of variables which could be introduced into such a model.

Professor Donnison said that he thought that some of the difficulties of our discussion were due to the fact that in the back of our minds most of us had a 'model' of a housing market which we were not making explicit. He thought that it was often useful to think of demographic movements first, then in terms of supply and demand, since demographic movements operated in broadly similar ways in most countries. People had opportunities and incentives for moving when they were young but as they grew older the chances of their moving became more remote. The intervention of governments had generally tended to reinforce this pattern by favouring young householders, and this was shown in Dr. Holm's paper (Fig. 10) where age discriminated more clearly between housing standards than size of household. In many countries there were insufficient dwellings of high quality and small size. In England the demand for good small dwellings (particularly among elderly households) could not be satisfied; meanwhile the quality of their existing larger accommodation remained low. When one household vacates accommodation it increases the supply to other households wanting to move, but if it becomes increasingly difficult for a family to move after the head of the household has reached the age of 40-45 and they therefore continue to occupy the house at, say 70-75, the quality of their houses became so low — relative to the quality of newly built houses — that young people no longer wanted such accommodation. If, however, these people were to move as their own children left home, their houses might be only 25-30 years old and the quality would not therefore be so out-of-date and we could expect young newly married people to move into the vacated houses. If we had a more thorough knowledge of the demographic structure of households, carried out by some form of cohort analysis, we could then examine the economic factors which might render it easier for these households to move in the directions they wanted and in directions that might also make better use of the existing stock of houses.

Dr. Przeciszewski, in summing up the discussion, said that it had shown the general usefulness of such a method of analysis. However, the model did have some weaknesses and, in particular, it was desirable that one should be able to define more precisely the notions of size and quality on a housing market. There were, however, great possibilities in the model. It was very important to be able to predict demand, and such predictions were bound up with the disaggregation of the market. This model only applied to a small market and he wondered what would be the result of extending this analysis to the nation-wide basis ; there must exist very much more freedom of movement within the nation as a whole than within one small region or city. He thought the points that Professor Donnison had made could be incorporated into this model, improving its validity and usefulness for the analysis of the housing market.

Dr. Holm believed that the model could be used for prediction and in Sweden they have tried to use this type of model to calculate the demand for houses of various sizes. They first independently examined the demographic factors and the consumption patterns of households, then they studied the move upwards and to the right which is portrayed in the model. An example of the type of conclusions which came from the model is that a slow increase in population with a given income increase meant that in Sweden it was necessary to build more five- and six-bedroom houses than would be necessary with the same income increase but a larger population growth due to migration. They had also studied the income elasticity of demand for accommodation and space. There is some difficulty, however, in dividing the increased total expenditure on housing between that which was devoted to buying more space and that which was used for the purchase of higher standards of accommodation. So far only the demand for space had been examined with any degree of precision.

THIRD SESSION

THE DISCUSSION OF THE PAPERS
BY PROFESSOR LINDBECK, MR. STÅHL,
AND PROFESSOR GELTING

Professor Donnison, after complimenting Professor Lindbeck on the elegance and clarity of his exposition, said there were two major barriers to communication confronting the conference : the barrier of ignorance inherent in all international comparisons, and the problems of communicating between different disciplines, each of which tends to pose different questions about the same phenomenon, and to be at its most rigorous at points where other disciplines resort to lazy-minded assumptions. A great deal could be learnt if these international and inter-disciplinary barriers could be surmounted and it might therefore help the Conference get to grips with these problems if Professor Lindbeck's paper was discussed on both these fronts. There could be no doubt about the importance of the objectives stated in the first paragraph of his paper : but were the questions he was asking appropriate for the attainment of these objectives, and were the assumptions employed in his analysis applicable to countries to which it was intended to apply ?

In most of the countries to be considered, society — or its government — was prepared to tolerate big differences in income, but increasingly unprepared to tolerate equivalent differences in housing conditions. That is to say, opinion on housing was moving in the direction it had followed at least a generation earlier in dealing with education and medical care, and many governments were therefore confronted with the following problems:

(*a*) people had to be given some security of tenure : the opportunity *not* to move (except in predictable and tolerable circumstances) had to be assured ;

(*b*) it followed that *some* system for the regulation (not the freezing) of rents was required in areas of shortage ;

(*c*) but this could be disastrous unless steps were taken to ensure adequate repair and maintenance in property deemed suitable for further use ;

(*d*) a well-maintained stock of dwellings would not achieve its purpose unless it was distributed amongst households with reasonable equity, and appropriate minimum standards of occupation were achieved ;

(*e*) this could not be achieved unless opportunities for movement and the exercise of choice (both desirable for their own sake) were likewise preserved ;

(*f*) finally, an adequate stock of rented accommodation had to be kept in the market and must not be allowed to disappear through transfer to owner-occupation and non-dwelling uses, or unplanned demolition.

These problems (unlike those posed by Professor Lindbeck on page 57) are not independent, but are logically related one to another : they do not assume the existence of one form of general rent control and they are not an argument for rent control, but pose instead the kind of problems that may actually confront Ministers of Housing. They may therefore go further to clarify the general problem to be examined.

They may suggest, for example, that the price of new housing should be reduced while the price of older property should be increased, in order to encourage movement from one to the other and the opportunities for 'filtering' which this process provides ; meanwhile the price of the poorest housing may have to be reduced to render it sufficiently unprofitable to compel its replacement. Discriminatory rent regulation may be needed to promote the construction of selected types of dwelling in selected locations. Likewise, it may be asked whether appropriate investment in the repair and modernization of older property could best be achieved (*a*) by complete decontrol or (*b*) by taxes on tenants (the proceeds of which could be used either to encourage landlords to repair and modernize or to enable government to carry out this work) or (*c*) by encouraging tenants to acquire their own housing and invest their own money in improving it. A problem-oriented approach may prove more fruitful than a simple confrontation of arguments for and against rent control.

Turning to more specific questions concerning Professor Lindbeck's analysis, Professor Donnison asked :

(*a*) Why was it implied that the stock-supply (SS) curve (see diagram 1 on page 55) for dwellings would in time move to the *right* under the influence of price increases ? Where land uses and densities were tightly restricted, and taxation and the institutions providing capital operated to channel investment in certain directions, submarkets often developed which might lead to improvements in the quality of dwellings (through conversion and modernization) coupled with a reduction in their quantity.

(*b*) Why was the demand curve for dwellings assumed to have a uniform slope ? Demographic factors — particularly the relation between marriages and household formation — and the high economic and social costs of combining households once formed might produce a highly inelastic demand in face of price increases and a highly elastic demand in face of price reductions — an 'L'-shaped curve.

(*c*) Why assume that rent controls necessarily reduce the supply of housing ? In most countries employing rent restrictions new houses are subject to a minimum of control, or to none at all. Moreover, taxes on property, borne by the tenant, have in some countries been increased since the introduction of rent controls to a level that may actually have increased the relative price of shelter including tax — and the tax may be used (as in the U.K.) partly to finance new building.

(*d*) Why assume that landlords have a propensity to save that is higher than their tenants' ? In many parts of the U.K. it has been shown that landlords' incomes are lower than their tenants'. This, together with the substitution of taxes for rent may make rent decontrol inflationary.

These questions make it clear that the operation and potentialities of rent regulation cannot be understood unless this instrument of housing policy is related to the many other forms of government intervention that impinge on housing and unless the different sectors of the housing market are distinguished and the relationships between them clarified. A macro-economic model is needed for this purpose.

The Economic Problems of Housing

Professor Lindbeck first took up Professor Donnison's point about the relevance of his assumption on the behaviour of supply. He thought it was reasonable to assume a positive correlation between the level of rents and the construction of new houses by private builders, and also a positive correlation between rents and expenditures for maintenance and improvement. All this would tend to give the UU-curve a positive slope and thus shift the stock-supply curve to the right. He thought that this would be true whether the index of houses was one based upon number of dwellings or, as in his paper, on volume — *i.e.* space standards and quality as well as numbers.

The shape of the demand curve presented some problems due to possible irreversibility of demand, which as Professor Donnison had pointed out, might make it look kinked. His conclusions were not, however, in principle dependent on the particular shapes of the demand and supply curve, as long as the former had a negative and the latter a positive slope. The *quantitative* effects on rents of shifts in the curves were of course influenced by their elasticities. He did not, however, think that the elasticity of the demand or flow-supply curves were zero in many situations. Not even if the house index was based solely on number of dwellings was it likely that demand was completely inelastic. For instance, some young people may not set up a separate home but stay longer with their parents when rents are high. Rent levels can also influence the geographical distribution of households in the country. For instance, high rents in the capital city will reduce economic incentives for people to move there.

The six objectives of rent policy which had been given in his paper (page 57) were an attempt to list the main arguments in favour of rent controls which had been presented by Swedish supporters of such control. In looking at Professor Donnison's list of housing policy objectives he did not feel that they differed widely from his own list, though Professor Donnison's list seemed to be a mixture of goals of housing policy and specific problems arising in a rent-controlled market. He agreed, however, that the objective of giving security of tenure was one that he had not discussed and that this aspect may be important in certain situations. On the whole, however, he felt that this was a difficulty which arose mainly during a period of shortage — *i.e.* when rents for some reason were below the equilibrium levels. This means, of course, that the problem of security of tenure may be a very important one, not only during a period of control but also some time after decontrol of rents, as it may take a few years to restore a smoothly functioning market. This seemed to be an argument for *successively* removing rent control rather than abolishing it overnight, and also for having protection of tenure during this period of successive decontrol.

Professor Netzer, in opening the discussion of Mr. Ståhl's paper, said that it was directed to the underlying problem of the workings of nonmarket interventions in mixed or market economies. This problem was common to several other papers and Professor Netzer's reactions to the approaches which had been made were in many ways similar to those expressed by other discussants and participants. Mr. Ståhl had built his model by a simple two-sector classification of the Swedish market. One sector, the F-sector, consists of profit-maximizing private owners of housing. The other sector is one in which prices are determined by administrative rules related to historical and actual costs ; this includes rent-controlled properties.

There was an intriguing parallel between the market structure in Sweden and that in his own city of New York — the only place in America with rent control. Of the privately-owned tenant-occupied dwellings about 1·5 million are subject to rent control, and in New York the position was as follows :

F-sector	0·5 owner-occupied	
	0·4 uncontrolled rental	
	0·9	
C-sector	1·5 rent controlled	
	0·2 publicly aided — subsidized	
	1·7	

Rent control, as in Sweden, seems to affect housing policy of publicly assisted non-profit-making agencies via rent/income relationships which determine pricing goals used in considering a new project.

Mr. Ståhl discusses certain aspects of the four questions which are given on page 75 of his paper :

(1) What rules are used to determine rents in the C-sector ?
(2) How do these affect the distribution and allocation of the cost ?
(3) How is housing investment affected ?
(4) Are there possible rules for rent fixing in the C-sector — assuming its perpetual existence — that minimize the distortions from Pareto optimality ?

The essence of this discussion is Mr Ståhl's simplified and elegant model of this type of housing market. The most important implication of the analysis was that when a large part of the housing supply (and additions thereto) are operating outside a pricing system, great demands are made upon non-price planning methods.

Mr Stahl's model and analysis supports, as do several other papers submitted to this Conference, the general proposition that rents set without reference to any system of prices are not usually efficient and the houses are not allocated in a way which produces a consistent redistribution of real income. This would suggest two things. First, a clear separation of the two fundamental objectives : (1) resource allocation ; (2) income redistribution. Different instruments will usually have to be used for the attainment of these two quite separate and distinct goals. Secondly, if the income redistribution goal is handled, price determination in the *C*-sector of publicly assisted or controlled housing should follow market principles so as to optimize allocation. This calls for optimizing *F*-sector behaviour by the *C*-sector decision makers who are largely public and quasi-public agencies (a difficult enough prescription), combined with rent subsidies to deal with problems of the type raised by Professor Donnison. The policy prescription might be gradual elimination of rent controls plus optimizing the rents of publicly-owned housing, combined with large-scale rent subsidies and re-allocation subsidies, including sizeable cash moving allowances. The present approach to these problems is apt to result in the tenant remaining in unsuitable accommodation. This may be considered better than pure non-intervention but it is surely not a sufficient or happy resolution of the problem.

He could not, however, whole-heartedly accept the approach of some Scandinavian contributors and he raised one fundamental objection to their analysis. Optimizing behaviour on the part of all sectors, plus income redistribution devices, makes sense only on the assumption that the *F*-sector is in fact a rather well functioning optimizing free market régime. But, as noted in previous discussions, this is hardly the case. Tax devices, credit arrangements, land use controls, etc., etc., in addition to the traditional forms of market imperfections (such as the abysmal lack of knowledge on the part of market participants in some countries, collusive practices in others), make the *F*-sector far from a smoothly and comprehensively optimizing one. This is not to say that the very fact that the market produces more of one type of housing than of another is evidence of imperfection. Market solutions and institutions favouring, say, young married couples with incomes above average, may be no more than a reflection of (*a*) their incomes, and (*b*) their demand for housing *vis-à-vis* other goods. Some of the deliberate public policy interventions in the *F*-sector (like preferential credit arrangements) are insufficient for their averred purposes, just as the policy in the *C*-sector has often been inadequate. Probably we should urge a régime of optimization throughout the market with direct public interventions of a discreet and discriminating nature of many kinds. Short of that, we can urge that *all* interventions be avoided.

Dr. Halevi doubted whether Mr. Ståhl had been right to go back to a simple Pareto optimizing model. If the market had made some minor movement away from the optimum position, a simple intervention might be enough to bring the economy back to an optimum. But in most countries the housing markets were so far from being in equilibrium and there were so many imperfections — some caused by governments and some by the market structure — that it was necessary to make use of the theory of the second best developed for international trade theory by Meade, Lancaster, and Lipsey. Mr. Ståhl's model was of doubtful use in a dynamic market situation with multiple distortions.

Mr. Ståhl said there was little that he wished to add to his paper. The important thing now was to consider ways in which rent decontrol could be most painlessly introduced. He gave a method which had been discussed in Sweden from a theoretical point of view and has the merit of clearly distinguishing between the allocational aspects and the income-redistribution effects.[1] Let us assume that the aim of state policy is to maintain exactly the same distribution of wealth and income after decontrol as before. In principle this can be attained if the increase in wealth which the landlord obtains is given back to the tenant. One possibility is that the landlord gives each tenant a bond on the amount of money (possibly fixed in real terms) which is equal to the discounted value of all future payments due to an increase in rents. This bond must be given to the tenant, who has an option to remain in the rental unit he occupied at the time of decontrol.

By such a measure the distribution of income and wealth is unchanged. But the consumer is now in a market with equilibrium prices and no shortage. The possibilities of choice have increased and the tenant can optimize his consumption. A tenant can choose between the possibility of not moving (and paying the increased rent with the amortizations and interest payments of the bond issued by the landlord) or moving and thereby choosing a rental unit that by definition must be 'better' and still keep his old privilege of the old rent but now in the form of a bond. This system means that tenants are given the freedom of choice, while all privileges of the rent control system are turned into cash.

This proposal might seem a little ridiculous as nobody really wants to preserve the income distribution which resulted fortuitously from rent controls and inflation. The proposal does show, however, that there is not a necessary connection between the income and allocation effects of rent control.

Professor Muth said he was grateful for the opportunity to discuss Professor Gelting's very fine paper. He especially congratulated Gelting on giving empirical content to the economic effects of rent control. It had been Professor Muth's experience that empirical information is the best bridge to international and especially inter-disciplinary understanding, and he believed that good empirical evidence is especially needed in the housing field. For this reason he wanted to stress that Professor Gelting's contribution to our understanding of the quantitative effects of rent control was a very welcome and worth-while one indeed.

[1] R. Bentzel, A. Lindbeck, and I. Ståhl, *Bostadsbristen* (The Housing Shortage), Stockholm, 1962, pp. 105-7.

The Economic Problems of Housing

Professor Muth suspected that the failure of rents to adjust upward may be more apparent than real and he questioned Professor Gelting's reference to the 'stickiness' of rents. In the U.S.A. it would appear that even well maintained properties tend to depreciate at the rate of about 2 per cent per year and the rental value of given properties declines by a similar amount. If in this situation income were to grow by 3 per cent in a given year, an income elasticity of housing demand of +1 to +1·5 would imply an increase in demand of from 3 to 4·5 per cent. In response to such an increase Professor Muth estimated that the stock of housing would increase by about one-third of the increase in demand in a year's time. Thus, the excess demand for housing at the old rental level would be 2 to 3 per cent of the stock at the start of the year. The rise in rentals by the year's end depends, of course, on the relative price elasticity of housing demand. If the latter is in the range − 1 to − 1·5 as his studies led him to believe, the rise in rent by the end of the year for units of given quality would be from 0·5 to 3 per cent. But the change in the rental of any given unit, which is 2 per cent smaller, would be between − 1·5 to +1 per cent. Thus, it might seem that rental levels had not adjusted very much to the changed conditions, while, in fact, they had fully done so.

In his earlier study of housing demand in the U.S.A., Professor Muth had taken a regression of rent on *per capita* income and the housing stock. The period used, 1915–41 with war years omitted, was one of large changes in money rent levels. If rents were slow to adjust to changing market conditions he would expect to have found that actual rents were less than average rents for given disposable incomes and the housing stock, in years for which rents were increasing and vice versa for years in which rents were falling. In only 11 out of 25 cases did he find the pattern of residuals in rent implied by the sticky rent hypothesis.

Further evidence against this hypothesis could be found in C. Rapkin, L. Winnick, and D. M. Blank, *Housing Market Analysis: A Study of Theory and Methods,*[1] which presented data on rent levels in relation to occupancy rates for the U.S.A. for the years 1930–38. Their data indicate that occupancy rates were furthest below average when rents were falling most rapidly and vice versa when rising, as the sticky rent hypothesis would suggest. When the rent index is deflated by an index of the general price level the tendency becomes considerably weaker. Further adjusting the rent index for changes in disposable income and the housing stock using the regression equation described above yields a quite different pattern, namely one in which, except perhaps for 1930–32, rising rent levels were associated with rising occupancy rates throughout the period. The latter is to be expected in the general hypothesis that rising relative prices of retaining an asset is to be accompanied by increasing intensity

[1] C. Rapkin, L. Winnick, and D. M. Blank, *Housing Market Analysis, A Study of Theory and Methods*, U.S. Housing and Home Finance (Washington : U.S. Government Printing Office, 1953).

of use and definitely do not show the cyclical pattern implied by the hypothesis of sticky rents.

He then turned to a discussion of the quantitative impact of rent controls on rents in Denmark. He thought that, using elasticities of demand which he had previously estimated and Professor Gelting's estimates of the growth in the housing stock for Copenhagen, one could derive some rather reliable estimates of how far rental levels are currently below the free market equilibrium level. Assuming income and price elasticities of housing demand both equal to unity and the *per capita* increase in the adjusted housing stock in Copenhagen of 24 per cent implied by Professor Gelting's Table 3, for a 50 per cent increase in real income would give an expected increase in rentals of about 16 per cent since 1940. According to Professor Gelting, however, rents in Denmark have declined in real terms by about 40 per cent or are currently around 50 per cent below the free market equilibrium level.

The figures cited in the paragraph above and in Professor Gelting's Table 2 suggested to him that housing consumption has increased much less since 1940 than would have been the case in a free market. As the income elasticity of housing demand seemed to be approximately one, he would have expected an increase in the housing stock of about 50 per cent, or by 20 per cent more than the increase in adjusted stock of 24 per cent implied by Table 3. In Professor Muth's own study (of which his paper at this Conference reports a part) he estimated the income elasticity of the proportion of dwellings with more than one person per room to be between -0.6 and -0.2. With an increase of real income of about 50 per cent this would imply a reduction of from 30 to 60 per cent in the proportion of dwellings with more than one person per room. Yet, only for two-room apartments in Aarhus does it appear that the decline in the person per room ratio has approached this. It therefore seemed quite clear that during the period of rent control in Denmark the consumption of housing has increased much less on average than Professor Muth would have expected under free market conditions.

Finally he commented on Professor Gelting's interesting discussion on the effects which the removal of rent controls would have on consumer expenditures. Possible inflationary or deflationary effects are hardly good reasons for not eliminating a bad policy, as these aggregate effects could be eliminated by the use of other fiscal or monetary measures. Still, the strength of such effects might have to be determined as a practical matter in order to take the necessary off-setting action upon decontrol. He quite agreed with Professor Gelting that differences in the average income level of tenants and owners are not likely to be important. A study of the U.S. market by Professor Gale Johnson [1] had demonstrated that rental income is of greater than average importance for both the relatively high and the

[1] D. Gale Johnson, 'Rent Control and the Distribution of Income', *American Economic Review*, Vol. XLI (May 1951), pp. 569-83.

relatively low income groups, and important recent research [1] on the consumption function had suggested that a fairly constant fraction of disposable income is spent at all income levels. This same research suggests, however, that the fraction of income spent varies inversely with the variability of income receipts and directly with the level of government welfare programmes applicable to an income recipient. Both have obvious effects on the motives for savings by consumers. Thus, the transfer of income from tenants to owners might tend either to increase or decrease consumption expenditure, but the direction in which the effect would go is difficult to foresee.

Professor Gelting's regression estimates were consistent with the hypothesis that a rise in rents would increase consumption expenditure out of a given disposable income, but because of the large standard errors of the coefficients of rent the results were not very conclusive and may reflect something quite different. Professor Muth would have expected the rental expenditures of households to be closely related to the households' 'permanent' income. Thus at a given level of disposable income households with higher than average rental expenditures have permanent incomes which exceed their current incomes, and we could then expect them to save less than the average amount for their current income level. Data for the U.S. economy suggest that, except for the Great Depression and war years, a fairly constant fraction of income has been saved, despite great variations in relative rents. Thus, he doubted whether variations in rental expenditures have any appreciable effect on aggregate consumer expenditure.

Professor Gelting said he would first like to express his appreciation of Professor Muth's comments. At present he wished to make only two brief remarks. First, the extent of stickiness of rents, cannot unfortunately, be tested on recent Danish experience. Neither the pre-war nor the post-war period is suitable for such a test. It was impossible because of the impact of rent controls over the past twenty years and the period of the 1930's was also unsuitable because there were no movements in other prices or in incomes which called for a major adjustment in rent levels. This meant that it was necessary to go back to the years before 1914, when in some periods of high business activity the vacancy rate dropped to less than one per cent. However, it would be difficult to judge to what extent such shortages were due to a stickiness of rents and to what extent to a failure of demand to respond to rising rents.

Secondly, he would like to supplement the information in his paper on the regression of savings on income and rent. A linear regression of rent on income shows a marginal propensity to spend on rent of some to 4 to 5 per cent ; however, the regression accounts for only a quite minor share of the total rent variance, largely because of the co-existence of several

---

[1] See especially Milton Friedman, *A Theory of the Consumption Function* (Princeton, N.J.: Princeton University Press, 1957).

rent levels under a régime of rent control. Thus, rent control allows us to treat rent as an independent variable, largely unrelated to income.

Professor Lewis said that in the U.K. we had the paradox of fifty years of rising standards of living coinciding with a period in which a declining fraction of the population is paying the free market rent (or ownership costs) of its housing. We may agree that everybody has a right to a minimum standard of housing, and if he cannot afford the rents of such houses there is an argument for subsidy — which may take the form of rent control.

If rent control allows owners to keep property in good condition the 'fair controlled' rent must rise with maintenance costs. If it is also to encourage the provision of private housing for letting purposes then the 'fair' rent must also include an allocation for profit. Why do current free market rents differ from such 'fair rents'? The main cause is scarcity, and this is a function of location. It reflects, and is reflected in, land values. If profit from the ownership of location is adequately tackled, the idea of rent control may be unnecessary. He felt we must look at it in this way because a growing population and a fixed total supply of land result in land prices rising more rapidly than the general level of prices. A discussion of rent control which ignores land values is a partial, and perhaps a dangerously partial, form of analysis.

Professor Muth said that Professor Donnison's list of reasons for rent regulation seemed very much like a list of the disadvantages of rent control. Security of tenure is no problem in a free market. Because of the added cost of obtaining a new tenant, a landlord would almost always prefer to retain a present tenant. Where rentals are held below the free market level and when authorities permit increases with a change in tenant, it is clearly in the landlord's interest to obtain a new one whenever possible. To give another example, mobility of households among dwellings is much easier in the absence of rent regulation. It would appear that Negroes in the U.S.A. have had much greater opportunity to obtain better housing since the end of rent controls. Regulation typically works to the disadvantage of younger families with children and encourages shifts in housing from the tenant to the owner-occupied stock. In his opinion, rent controls are a very poor instrument for the attainment of virtually any social goal. The only set of policies he could think of which are worse in this respect is U.S. agricultural policy. At a later stage in the debate he added the assertion that the effects of rent control are bad, regardless of their institutional setting and tend to be more severe the further rents are below the free market equilibrium level.

Dr. Halevi drew the participants' attention back to the fact that Professor Lindbeck's paper gave an example of a particular tool which could be used to examine the effects and problems of rent control. He thought it advisable to centre the discussion around two basic questions. What are the objectives of housing policy, and is rent control the best means of achieving the given policy ? In dealing with any one particular housing situation it was first necessary to ask whether the position of the country was one of very acute shortage or was it one of a slight shortage. If the shortage was such that equilibrium could be fairly easily attained without resort to rent controls it might be appropriate for the government to take steps to achieve equilibrium within a free market setting. If, however, the shortage was very great the most appropriate immediate action might be the control of rents.

While he agreed with each of Professor Lindbeck's six conclusions and thought that most housing policies could be attained by ways other than rent controls, he was not satisfied that the construction of new dwellings could be sufficiently rapid to dispense with the need for some control of rents. If the housing market had a very small excess demand an increase in rents might induce a rapid increase in the completion of new houses. When, however, a severe shortage existed a very large increase in rents would not result in a large increase in the housing stock in the short run. Thus rent controls may be necessary temporarily — not as a desirable end in itself, but to prevent the other side effects not mentioned by Professor Lindbeck.

Professor Lindbeck said that the important question to ask the supporters of rent control was : is this an efficient method of securing the goals of housing policy ? He thought it was a rather inefficient method as compared with other techniques. For instance, if the authorities wanted to influence the distribution of income or housing consumption in favour of low-income families with young children, he thought a much more efficient means of attaining this was a direct transfer payment or housing subsidy to these particular families. In an equilibrium market such families, if given proper financial assistance, can always get an apartment, but when rents were held below equilibrium landlords tended to prefer families with no children.

Professor Gelting considered that the first two points made by Professor Donnison (security of tenure and rent regulation) were of crucial importance to Professor Donnison's argument and they reflected a distrust of the market mechanism. The last four points which he had given as objectives of social policy were simply consequences of the first two points.

Professor Maisel, in agreeing with Dr. Halevi, suggested that further research was required to calculate the inefficiencies of rent control and the costs of making the adjustments necessary to achieve an equilibrium level of rents in markets with varying degrees of housing shortage. He stressed the institutional differences between countries and gave as an example the greater mobility of American families who were unlikely to stay in a house for more than ten or twelve years.

Dr. Kuminek said that the discussion had been rather wide since housing policy had been taken as covering both economic and social policy at one and the same time. The opinions of the participants from the U.S.A.

were characteristic in that they placed emphasis upon economic policy. Professor Donnison had broadened the issues by considering housing policy from both an economic and a social point of view. He had not been concerned solely with rent control but with the control of the whole housing market; rent control was, of course, one means of controlling the market. In assessing the effects of rent control it is important to consider the housing situation in the country under consideration. The United States' experience, for example, was mainly based upon housing situations in which there had been a large stock of houses relative to the population. In Western Germany where rent control was introduced after the war the sphere of rent control was diminishing as the shortage of dwellings was being overcome. However, each member of the Conference was tending to argue from his knowledge of one or two countries and it was clear that the examples being given were not comparable with one another.

Mr. Cullingworth drew attention to the U.K. experience of rent control and said that three of the main criticisms of rent control did not appear to apply to this country without qualification. Statistical evidence showed that mobility was the same amongst families living in privately rented accommodation, owner-occupied dwellings and local authority subsidized houses and flats. Under-occupation of accommodation which was often thought to be caused by rent controls was most severe in the U.K. in owner-occupied houses. At the 1961 Census it was found that a smaller proportion of private landlords' tenants were 'under-occupying' their premises than were owner-occupiers. It was true that the standard of maintenance of controlled rent houses was very low, but this was due to several causes. The low level at which rents had been controlled, the age of the houses in the controlled sector, and the type of landlord — who was often an elderly woman who regarded the house as a self-perpetuating source of income.

Professor Robinson asked what income elasticities of demand American and other data suggested for house space. Recent British statistical inquiries showed that between 1913 and 1964 consumers' expenditure taken as a whole, at 1958 constant prices rose from 100 to 208; the gross capital stock in the form of dwellings at constant prices of 1958 had risen approximately from 100 to 225; over the period 1938 to 1964 consumers' expenditure rose from 100 to 153; the gross capital stock or dwellings rose from 100 to 149 — in both cases about *pari passu* with consumers' expenditure. If income elasticity was nearer 1·5 than 1·0 (as he had understood Professor Muth to believe) the British stock of dwellings would appear to be very far short of being an equilibrium stock, in the sense that the market value of a house would be close to its cost of production. If so, it would seem necessary to choose some method of handling the short period situation. Or should one allow the market to push rents to very high levels? Or should one control rents, at a level high enough to stimulate house building, but lower than the market level, and do all possible to facilitate house building? He believed that there was a stronger case for the latter policy than Professor Lindbeck admitted.

Professor Netzer said that since 1940 the percentage increase in housing expenditure had been similar to the overall increase in consumption. The U.S.A. now seemed to have an overall equilibrium in the housing market. The only area of continuing shortage was New York City which was also the only place in which rent control was still in operation. While he thought that the control of rents prevented the attainment of an equilibrium in New York, he did not think that rent control had led to a serious deterioration in the standards of maintenance as a minimum level of repair was enforced under the rent controlling regulation; while the property was not as well maintained under rent control it was not allowed to fall into a state of complete disrepair.

Dr. Holm mentioned some of the difficulties in estimating the demand for houses since this did not depend only upon the elasticity of demand generated by present households, but also the division of households into two or more small households and the secular movement of population from rural to urban areas. But he thought that in Sweden the income elasticity of demand would be about 1·0. The regulations controlling rents had been altered to allow higher rents for well-maintained houses, but this had been a rather late development in Sweden. One of the side-effects of rent controls had been an increased clearance of slum property. This could occur more cheaply when rents had been kept artificially low. However, this beneficial effect of rent controls had been somewhat offset in recent years when it was feared that low rents had led to the demolition of houses of better quality which should have been retained. He thought that some consideration should be given to the problem of setting rents under conditions of rent control during periods of rising incomes and prices. What policy should be pursued in setting a controlled rent? During the period 1950 to 1960 controlled rents in Sweden had risen roughly in line with other prices.

Professor Donnison said that in the U.K., after seven years in which half the stock of private rented housing had been decontrolled, there had been no increase in house-building to let, and no greater mobility in decontrolled property than elsewhere (if the special sector of furnished housing is excluded). The distribution of the decontrolled stock had not improved but had grown relatively worse than that found in other sectors of the market and the relationships between landlords and tenants had deteriorated. Thus in some countries the abandonment of rent controls is not a simple answer to the housing problems which confront governments. Other solutions should also be considered — for instance, the redistribution of incomes, or matching the distribution of employment and population with housing supply, or public acquisition and administration of much of the housing stock. Rent regulation (not control) must be considered in relation to these and other potential policies. It is not good enough for Professor Lindbeck to say that 'we have no generally accepted theory for the behaviour of co-operative and public enterprises in the housing market' (p. 60) and to complain that 'it is difficult to construct a theory which explains the behaviour of governments' (p. 62). If economists cannot apply their skills to these problems — showing, for example, the consequences that these and other policies may have for employment, productivity, savings, and inflation — they condemn themselves to an arid analysis of rigorous but irrelevant models or to naive advocacy for, or against, rent control.

Professor Lindbeck agreed that rent control should not be examined in isolation from other factors. Thus, a fruitful question to ask seemed to be : what are the effects of different pricing systems when combined with various economic and social policies? For instance, if the goals are (*a*) a high level of house construction, (*b*) a more equitable income distribution (*c*) a consumption of housing which is more evenly distributed than incomes, an appropriate policy-mix may include the following instruments : (1) subsidies or easy credit to house builders ; (2) taxation of capital gains derived from houses ; and (3) subsidies of housing consumption by low income groups. Rent control can, of course, be included in such a policy-mix, but it seemed to create more problems than it solved. He also pointed out, in reply to Professor Donnison, that the fact that there is no generally accepted theory to explain the behaviour of governments and co-operatives did not mean that economists had no theory to explain the effects of actions taken by governments and co-operatives.

Returning to the problem of rent control he said that if we start from a situation of controlled rents then it was important to consider the point at which decontrol should start. He thought that there are good reasons to start the decontrol in old dwellings in order to allow the rents which have been longest controlled to rise so that a rent structure more in accordance with consumer preferences could be created. He could not quite understand the tendency in many countries for the rents of new houses to be decontrolled first, whereby a considerable excess demand may be created for factors of production in the building sector. Such a policy would usually tend to make the time structure of rents deviate even further from a correspondence with consumer preferences.

Regional decontrol might also present some problems. Any increases in rents in moderate-sized towns unaccompanied by similar increases in rents in large cities would create additional incentives to move to large cities. Regional decontrol is also connected with problems of taxation and subsidies because these are most efficiently imposed or granted on a national level, and it would be difficult to undertake special fiscal and social policy actions in decontrolled areas.

The decontrol would, he pointed out, tend to increase the saving ratio of the economy as a whole, because approximately half of any increase in rents would be taxed from landlords. This factor rather than possible differences in the marginal propensity to consume of landlords and tenants was the important one in considering the effects of decontrol on the saving ratio of the economy.

The importance of the price system was very clear both in a centrally planned economy and in the less planned economies. The problems which arose in different countries were very similar when there was a deviation from an equilibrium price system. An equilibrium price system can be reached in many different ways, and it could theoretically be created by having a computer fed with equations of preference and production functions. From these an attempt might be made to find the optimal solution. Alternatively, the market mechanism can be used as the computer ; the market system had, of course, the great advantage that it did not have to be fed with preference and production functions which were for all practical purposes unknown.

When reliance is placed upon the market mechanism to achieve equilibrium prices this was not the same thing as *laissez-faire* because government actions can be taken in order to shift the demand and supply curves in whatever direction was desired. There are many methods by which these shifts in demand and supply can be achieved, for instance through taxes, subsidies, transfer payments, and direct regulations. It was, Professor Lindbeck thought, necessary to make a clear distinction between relying on the market and *laissez-faire*. An active government can achieve much by manipulating the supply and demand curves rather than by trying to fight against market forces. Government policy is simplified if prices are used as an integral part of a general policy rather than being opposed and fought against ; he felt that the inefficiency of housing policy in many countries showed this very clearly.

Another point which Professor Lindbeck said he felt must be made related to the mistaken belief that rent controls could not be removed until there was an equilibrium in the market. This was, he said, an extremely dangerous way of arguing, because as we all know control of prices produced a disequilibrium. In an expanding economy with rising prices and incomes it is very unlikely that an equilibrium would be reached if there were rigid rents. In theory it might be possible to fill the gap between the demand and supply of new dwellings by building a great many new houses and flats, however in many countries with rent control governments are not willing to devote the factors of production to housing which consumers 'demand' as a result of artificially low 'controlled' rents. New building cannot in any case produce an equilibrium in the market for houses which were produced at an earlier date. It is important that a housing policy shall be consistent in its operation on both the demand and supply sides. In many countries policy operating on the demand side of the equation has been based upon a higher evaluation of housing than has the policy operating upon the supply side. The decisions of policy which determine supply have been forced to take into consideration the general limits to the supply of resources to the economy as a whole.

Professor Gelting considered that a fairly complete catalogue of the ill effects of rent control had been discussed. However, one effect of rent control had not been mentioned during the discussion : the moral and intellectual corruption of the people who enjoy the arbitrarily distributed privilege of living in underpriced apartments.

FOURTH SESSION

THE DISCUSSION OF THE PAPERS
OF PROFESSOR HOFFMEYER AND K. MORDHORST
AND PROFESSOR GRIGSBY

Professor Gillies said that his comments on Professor Hoffmeyer's excellent paper were brief, some were general, some more specific. First, as Professor Muth pointed out earlier in the week, it is exceedingly encouraging to see empirical work. On the rather thin evidence of the crises in building in 1907–8 and the impact of Wicksell, it has long been assumed in Denmark that long-term interest rates have been important in determining the demand for housing. It is only by testing such assumptions with empirical evidence that progress is made.

Secondly, it is interesting to everyone at the Conference that economists in all countries have problems with data. In Denmark the problem — at least from the point of view of an American — is particularly severe since no data are available for house building outside Copenhagen prior to World War II ; figures for investment in housing are not available and there is poor information on real income. Rents have changed substantially and the traditional 'quality' problem of housing economics is as much a problem in Denmark as elsewhere. Professor Hoffmeyer is to be congratulated on overcoming these data problems so well.

The particularly interesting conclusion raised by Professor Hoffmeyer's paper is that although the long-term interest rate seemed to influence Danish house-building in the inter-war years, it had no definite influence before World War I. Whilst he was not competent to judge, he wondered — and Professor Hoffmeyer might wish to comment on this — whether the pre-World War I data are as accurate as the post-war and whether this could affect the conclusion.

Professor Hoffmeyer's paper raises a number of particular questions which are important. The first question relates to housing policy. In some countries, particularly the United States, policy has been very closely associated with interest rate manipulation — on the assumption, of course, that changes in interest rates do affect the volume of construction. Indeed, the majority of U.S. housing policies have been based on the assumption that the terms and conditions under which mortgage credit is made available are the most significant factors in the housing market. The FHA home loan insurance programme is based on the proposition that changes in the terms and conditions under which mortgage money is made available directly influence construction. There has been wide fluctuations in building in the post-war period in the U.S.A., and most of the decline in building occurred when the economy was booming and interest rates were rising. Increases in building occurred when the economy was in general decline and interest rates were falling. The general position adopted in view of these circumstances was that housing was basically anti-cyclical and this was associated with fixed interest rates on mortgages. In other words, during a rise in business activity when interest rates in general rose, the fixed rate on mortages became less attractive to investors — and so they went out of mortage lending and building declined. Thus it was generally conceded that interest rates were the major factor in housing starts at least over the short run.

This situation was true only when there was a basic backlog of demand created by family formation and income distribution. In 1965, despite a decline in interest rates on mortgages, total house-building has declined substantially. It thus appears that interest rates may only be a significant factor in causing changes in the volume of building under special circumstances. The evidence suggests that in the 1930's a drop in mortgage interest rates did not stimulate building when there was no effective demand — and the same is true in 1965. In short, in the U.S.A. interest rates have not in the long run been very effective in changing the pattern of building, except in very special situations.

This rather loose state of affairs was tightened up somewhat by the work done by Professor Maisel in which he had concluded, after extensive analysis, that movements in housing starts are a function of inventories and that the direction of causation appears to be through inventories rather than final demand or changes in interest rates. This conclusion was, and is, at great odds with the conventional one (*i.e.* change in mortgage rates) and if correct has a great impact for policy.

He turned then to some questions of methodology raised in the paper. Professor Hoffmeyer had basically constructed a model showing the operational significance of a relationship between the rate of interest and house-building. He is concerned, as are most model builders, primarily with demographic factors, changes in real income, in vacancies, and the long-term rate of interest. The demographic factors are allowed for by the assumption that changes in the number of married couples represent the major influence of demographic factors on house building. This assumption was made because the data showed a constant relationship between effective demand for housing as measured by number of housing units and the number of married couples, but Professor Gillies questioned whether or not this adequately handled the impact of demographic forces. Is there, for instance, no doubling up among young married couples and no relationship between levels of prosperity and the rate of family formation?

The most important issues posed for the Conference by the paper were, he believed : (1) is the inventory theory or the interest theory an explanation of fluctuations in house building? And (2) whichever of these two is correct will it be possible to derive a general theory of house-building fluctuations which would be applicable to all countries at all times? If we are unable to do this it must mean that we have failed in some measure at the theoretical level of our economics.

Before discussing the second issue he recalled Lionel Robbins' essay 'The Nature and Significance of Economic Science' and the importance of dividing social policy and objectives from their economic implications. Only after we are satisfied with our theory should we consider the implications for policy which are implied by the acceptance of one or other of these theories.

Mr. Ståhl said Professor Hoffmeyer's paper raised two points about the statistical methods used in this type of econometric model. The first was the problem of identification. Was it legitimate to use the singular equation approach to this kind of market? The second problem arose from an attempt to test fifty-four different relationships. If these relationships were uncorrelated and were being tested at the 5 per cent significance level, you would be bound to end with an average of two or three significant results. What criteria had Professor Hoffmeyer used in rejecting spurious correlations and retaining those which were valid and relevant?

Professor Muth did not think the fifty-four regressions led to any problems of random good results because they were largely variations of the functional relations between variables. There was, in fact, only one additional variable introduced into some of the equations. The problems which were involved here were very similar to those encountered by Henry L. Moore when he derived his dynamic demand curves for steel. Presumably the problem is holding enough factors which influence demand besides the rate of interest constant so that the effect of the interest rate can be discerned. He was surprised that the interest rate showed up so strongly in Professor Hoffmeyer's analysis because so many other variables had been neglected. In his own analysis he had only found the rate of interest to be a significant factor when he had introduced variables which described income, the price of houses, and the total stock of dwellings. If the effects of these variables were not eliminated the coefficient of the rate of interest was actually positive. He did not think that the demographic factors — apart from the effects of an increase in population — were very important. He had tried to find a family formation factor but had failed to do so.

Professor Maisel stressed that there were two different problems here.

The first related to the value per dwelling unit where one might expect the rate of interest to have an influence and the second was the more interesting problem of the response of the market to the demand for additional houses. How long does it take a particular market to produce additional houses? What types of lagged situation do we have and what are the variables which influence the lags? Professor Hoffmeyer's paper was useful because it brought out this concept of the lagged response. We could not assume that the lags in different countries would be of the same length, nor necessarily caused by the same factors. In the U.S.A. early research studies suggested that there were very long lags and that these were caused by the poor organization of the construction industry.

In his own work, Professor Maisel had regarded the availability of credit as an important factor in influencing inventory movements. He therefore took the short-run rate of interest as the best measure of funds available to builders. Statistics needed for an examination of the U.S. market were the fees paid by builders over and above the interest rate. Most builders had to use short-term financing to cover the period of building and they obtained loans which, on the average, were only outstanding about three months. Each loan involved the payment of fees and if these were added to the rates of interest charged, the true interest paid on the loans was at a minimum 12 per cent and could reach the high figure of 25 per cent. We tended to think of interest rates as lying between 4 and 8 per cent, but when you were dealing with the cost of money to a builder you had to take into account the true interest rate.

The demographic factor was, he thought, of some importance. Professor Lewis [1] had constructed a model upon which Professor Maisel had drawn; there was a factor of migration incorporated into this model.

Professor Lewis said he had looked at home-building in Great Britain since 1700 and his ideas lay between those of a purely demographic explanation and that in which the rate of interest is all important. There has been a long cycle in house-building from as far back as 1700, with a span of roughly twenty years. Basically this has been a demographic cycle, often shifted one way or the other by economic factors, but the basic demographic demand is never long thwarted.

The big upturns have come when such a demand has been accompanied by an abundance of credit and other conditions associated with low interest rates. As the boom has continued, the economy has also prospered. Other forms of investment have taken place. Imports have risen, and consumer expenditures have been high. To finance all this activity a great deal of credit has been necessary — not simply in terms of long loans, but also to provide working capital for the actual builder. In this way the activity

[1] J. P. Lewis, 'Building Cycles: A Regional Model and Its National Setting', *Economic Journal*, Vol. LXX, Sept. 1960.

associated with rising building has had an impact on interest rates, rather than the other way around. Eventually the high activity, and possibly weakened balance of payments, has led to a general credit strain. Some shock or other has caused a contraction of credit at a time when the strain is great. A crisis develops. Unemployment follows, and for a variety of reasons, building declines. This is only a very brief explanation of a theory he propounded in *Building Cycles and Britain's Growth*.[1] He had found that the link with the rate of interest works in both directions; it affects, and is affected by, the amount of house-building; the demographic factor was an important determinant of the overall amount of house-building.

He wanted to do an econometric analysis of British building, but was compelled to adopt a more historical analysis partly because the statistics did not exist at the right level of aggregation, and partly because he wanted to find an economic explanation. He felt that Professor Hoffmeyer's analysis did not provide this. There was no model here. One needed a system of equations explaining the demands for and supply of different kinds of houses (*e.g.* speculative houses, owner-occupied houses, etc.). In each of these equations one explanatory variable may be the rate of interest, and the total volume of building will be one factor explaining the rate of interest.

Professor Gelting recalled that shortly before World War II Professor Tinbergen studied the influence of the long-term rate of interest on residential construction in the United Kingdom and the United States.[2] Tinbergen's results could not be interpreted as showing any direct effect of the selected interest rates on residential construction. They responded rather as a movement in sympathy with the availability of credit for building. A similar mechanism may have been at play in Denmark.

Another factor which may affect Professor Hoffmeyer's analysis was that between the pre-World War I period and the 1930's the relationship between the long-term rate and the availability of bank credit changed profoundly. Before 1914 the long-term rate in Denmark depended closely upon the international capital market, whereas during the 1930's the Danish capital market was largely a closed market. It was also necessary to remember that whereas before 1914 rates of profit were generally high relative to the rate of interest both in building and in competing fields, the 1930's was a period of widespread depression. We should not, therefore, expect to find a similar pattern in the movement of the rate of interest and in building before 1914, and during the inter-war period.

Professor Robinson asked Professor Hoffmeyer whether he had made any

---

[1] J. P. Lewis, *Building Cycles and Britain's Growth*, Macmillan (London), 1965. See also: 'Growth and Inverse Cycles: A Two-Country Model', *Economic Journal*, March 1964.

[2] J. Tinbergen, *Statistical Testing of Business Cycle Theories*, I. *A Method and its Application to Investment Activity*. (League of Nations, Geneva, 1939.)

use of the Marshallian real rate of interest concept. We had now had twenty years of continuing inflation and the real rate of interest may have more relevance than the money rates of interest. The best hedge against inflation for young professional people was the purchase of a house, preferably a large old house. Since high rates of interest were associated with inflation it seemed important to take into consideration the effect of expectations of future inflation on the willingness of borrowers to pay these high rates of interest.

Professor Hoffmeyer said, in reply to Mr. Ståhl and Professor Lewis, that it was hardly fruitful to have a general discussion about model building and statistical investigation. At no time had he accepted statistical results without having sound theoretical reasons for doing so ; from a theoretical point of view the best statistical results were, of course, often 'unreasonable' and had to be rejected. Finally, on this point, he stressed that the work which he and K. Mordhorst had been doing was thought of as a short-term model, explaining short-term fluctuations in house-building. It was only in a long-term model that the difficult problem of quality was encountered.

The problem of availability of capital raised by Professor Maisel was probably not quite as important under Danish conditions, because there was and is free access to long-term (40-60 years) finance. Loans of up to 75-85 per cent or more of the assessed value of the property could be obtained by raising mortgages. Short-term building loans were so profitable for the commercial banks that they could generally be obtained quite easily.

In reply to Professor Robinson he said that the real rate of interest and inflation had only been of great significance in the post-war period and was not relevant to the period under review because inflation had not been widespread. Furthermore, most building in this period was apartment houses, built by companies or small groups of people. Owner-occupied houses had only increased in importance late in the period. The owners of apartment houses would have a greater possibility of investing in other types of real asset and they would have no special incentive to invest in houses to protect the real value of their savings.

Summing up, Professor Hoffmeyer commented that in the first version of the paper, which was sent to Professor Gillies, he had written that the analysis showed a connection between the rate of interest and house-building in the inter-war period. A more thorough study of the statistical computations had reduced his confidence in this conclusion. Professor Gillies' two crucial questions about the inventory theory and transfer-ability of the results to other countries had not been clarified in the discussion, which was disappointing but understandable.

Mr. Ståhl introduced Professor Grigsby's paper by presenting the following mathematical formulation, which generalized and identified the problems discussed by Professor Grigsby.

Equation [1]
$$K_t = \int_t^{T_k} [h(t) - c(t)]e^{-rt}\, dt.$$

Equation 2
$$L_t = \int_t^{T_1} a(t)e^{-rt}\, dt.$$

When amortization occurs more rapidly than the rate at which the asset depreciates, the purchaser is being forced to undertake involuntary saving. If it is the other way round the owner occupier is, in effect, dis-saving. An ideal amortization system is one which permits the value of the loan to follow identically the value of the capital. If there is a difference between T_k and T_1 this means there is some difference in the maturity of the loan and the expected life of the house. If K_0 is greater than L_0 the market is producing too high a down payment. If $\dfrac{dK_t}{dt}$ is not equal to $a(t) - rK$, it means that the amortization rate has not been balanced with the rate of depreciation.

This, Mr. Ståhl thought, was the basic model underlying the material which was presented by Professor Grigsby, who gave some examples of the inequalities which have been found in the U.S.A. We needed to ask ourselves whether these were due to an excessive risk aversion by the lenders of money or to some other cause. If, as seems likely, they were due to risk aversion, the introduction of insurance schemes and some change in the banking system should be sufficient to bring the market into balance.

Professor Grigsby said that the participants should see this paper in its proper context, because it was perhaps rather particularized for an international conference. The origin of the paper was a controversy which arose in Philadelphia and in which bankers were asked how they set the loan terms which they offered on various types of housing. The conclusion was reached that (1) the bankers perceived the risks of their loans incorrectly, and that (2) once they had acted on an assumption about the economic life of houses in a particular area, this assumption was likely to be made true by their own future actions.

If it became more difficult to obtain loans in older residential areas, ownership of houses shifted to landlords renting them for profit, and these

---

[1] Footnote to Equations 1 and 2:

K_t = capital value at time t
T_k = durability of capital
T_1 = durability of loans
$h(t)$ = rental value
$c(t)$ = operating costs, maintenance costs, etc.
r = interest rate (measured as an intensity)
$a(t)$ = loan payments.

landlords had lower levels of maintenance than owner-occupiers; the houses therefore deteriorated more quickly, thus confirming the bankers' expectation of a short period of life. Builders, meanwhile, felt confident that a liberal mortgage policy permitting borrowers to purchase the older stock of houses would lower the level of new building and thus if the policy was intended to increase the stock of dwellings it would, in the long run, be self-defeating.

Professor Muth said it had been suggested that the phenomenon observed in Philadelphia was due to an irrationality of the market, but it may have a very good explanation. It has often been suggested that the rate of return on capital is higher in one area of investment than another and that there are imperfections of the market which prevent a transfer. However, when an attempt was made to examine this assumption there was frequently no confirmatory evidence discovered. Lending risks in housing are associated with changes in the neighbourhoods. The neighbourhood may be in the path of an expansion of a low income group, and there will be considerable doubt about whether the expanding group will by-pass a neighbourhood or not. These doubts will tend to depress the prices of houses and increase the risks of lending in several neighbourhoods until the low income group moves into one or other of them.

It was not clear to him as to why it should be profitable for landlords to follow a policy of low expenditure on maintenance. If they skimped on maintenance when a lower income group moved into the area this might well be because the rent paying capacity of these groups was lower and it was not necessarily to the benefit of the tenants that very high maintenance standards should be maintained. He could not understand why, in a competitive market, it should be assumed that all lenders are incorrect in being willing to lend on the same terms. Is it not possible that the lenders have, in fact, correctly assessed the risks of the market and are all lending on about the same terms because of their correct assessment of the risks involved? There is always a danger in saying that 'I am right and all the rest of the world is wrong'. He did not feel that in this case it could simply be assumed that the lenders do not know what they are doing if it was not understood why they are doing it.

Professor Grigsby said they had had a number of interviews with lenders and tried to find out how they perceived and estimated their risks. No evidence was found of foreclosure experience which could justify their predictions. The lenders were mainly small institutions, however, and each might very well have suffered if it had accepted risks which the others had rejected. No new lender trying to expand in the market would be willing to do so by specializing in accepting the most risky properties as security for his loans. It is possible that this was a sector of the market which the government should step in to support. Such support need not necessarily last very long because once the market had obtained experience of the relatively small risks involved it would support itself. In considering why landlords might pursue a policy of skimping on maintenance it had to be remembered that the landlord was maximizing the money income from the property whereas the owner-occupier was not. Therefore, if property shifted from the owner-occupied sector to the private landlord sector the level of maintenance frequently fell.

Professor Maisel said it was worth examining some of the reasons for the divergences which seemed to exist between the mortgage loan and the expected length of life of the house. Three points were of special interest. The first was about the pooling of risks. Professor Muth had indicated that lending institutions do take risks but Professor Maisel thought it fair to say that they are biased against doing so. They are risk averters and this gives a bias to the situation. This seemed a possible area in which the government might intervene to increase the willingness of these lenders to carry certain risks. Secondly, in considering the owner-occupiers and their greater willingness to maintain their houses, they probably do have lower costs. They profit from the tax advantages which they enjoy. In addition, in the U.S.A., where labour time is extremely expensive, most owner-occupiers do small maintenance jobs themselves, but the landlord has to pay someone else for these and it is very much more expensive. The third question which arises relates to the logic of attaching a savings policy to a housing policy. If there is an excess demand in the economy and it is necessary to lower this demand, it is intelligent to impose mortgage terms which increase the level of owner-occupiers' savings. If, on the other hand, there is too little demand, savings should be divorced from housing. An interesting aspect of inflation is the division of the gains obtained on equity and the losses which are incurred on loans. Because of the risk aversion of lenders there is a reluctance to split the gains and the losses between borrowers and lenders. There is a very good reason for a loan system which carries high loan charges at one period of the life of the loan and a lower loan charge at another period. In the U.S.A. it was found in a study that the biggest risks of non-payment on mortgages occurred in the first two years of a loan on a new house. Finally, we might try to make use of the law of large numbers and arrange things so that the lender averts the 'expected' value of risks rather than their variance.

Professor Hoffmeyer agreed that many monetary institutions were risk averters but the reason was mainly the enacted rules regarding placement. Recent Danish experience showed, however, that a private insurance scheme made it possible for the savings banks to give mortgage loans on both new and old houses on the same conditions of up to 85 per cent of the assessed value. In a period of excess demand for funds it was hardly surprising that the best securities were chosen.

Professor Netzer said that, in America, lending institutions tend to vary all the terms of a loan when they consider the various risks of different assets. In housing, differences in down payments may well be the most important element in loan terms from the standpoint of purchasers' decisions, and interest rates the least important. However, lending institutions tend to vary down payments and maturities more than they vary interest rates, between new and old houses. In part, this is because usury laws place effective maximums on mortage interest rates. Also, the Federal Housing Administration's maximum interest rates for insured mortgages do not vary between old and new properties.

There are other factors which tend to discourage lending on older and riskier properties. In New York State, for example, savings banks which dominate the mortgage market may lend on properties which are more than 35 years old only on quite restrictive terms regarding down payments and maturities. If any mortgage market is dominated by particular types of well-established institutions, new lending institutions may have to lend on the more risky investments in order to break into the market. They are hardly likely to seek expansion in this sector of the market if they confront interest-rate ceilings.

It is interesting to contrast mortgage lending with the other principal form of lending to individual consumers, instalment lending or hire purchase. The latter is a high-volume operation, with high interest rates and not inconsiderable loan losses. Legislative restriction of mortgage interest rates partly explains the greater aversion to risks in housing finance ; finance companies expect some loan losses but mortgage lenders operate to avoid *all* losses. In part, this is due to the much greater cost and difficulty of foreclosure in connection with housing.

Professor Grigsby said they had investigated whether, in fact, the lender was looking at the borrower or the property when the risks of the mortgage were assessed. It seemed that some lenders turn down borrowers who would have been good risks, but it was impossible to say definitely whether it was the borrower or the house which received most attention when a lending institution was deciding whether or not to make a loan.

Mr. Ståhl agreed in his concluding statement that the time structure of mortgage terms and the assessed risks were extremely important. There were three problems which could be distinguished : (*a*) imperfections due to conservative and excessive risk aversion in the credit market ; (*b*) the possibility of getting better predictions of the rate of depreciation and the rate of inflation. If this was possible we could plan our amortization periods very much better. The last problem was (*c*) the construction of new types of amortization plans that are flexible and can be adjusted with changes which occur over the life of the loan. One example is the index loan which is made in money terms but for which the rate of amortization is dependent upon changes in the general price level or, more specifically, upon changes in building costs. On this important point he referred the Conference to his own discussion of this matter, and particularly to pages 80 and 81 and Fig. 3 of his paper.

FIFTH SESSION
THE DISCUSSION ON THE PAPERS BY
PROFESSOR NETZER AND PROFESSOR GILLIES

Professor Gelting opened the discussion of Professor Netzer's paper by saying that we must be very grateful to Professor Netzer that he has undertaken the important and difficult task of analysing the combined effects of tax policies on housing, and in particular the consistency of these policies with the measures taken in other fields more directly related to housing.

While Professor Gelting could not agree that the balanced budget multiplier theory implies that total private expenditure is increased by a parallel increase in public expenditures and taxes, he would suggest that a more important aspect of fiscal policies concerns the effects of the overall balance between income-absorbing revenues and income-creating expenditures. Thus, provided that total employment is to be maintained, an increase in revenues relative to expenditures must be balanced by a lower rate of interest, so that total output is kept up, larger private investment compensating reduced consumption. Being relatively sensitive to the rate of interest, residential construction may be expected to account for a large part of the investment increase.

Turning to the main subject of Professor Netzer's paper, the differential tax effects on housing, a distinction may be made between tax effects relating to housing as against other forms of production and consumption and tax effects which discriminate between different types of housing consumption, in particular rented versus owner-occupied accommodation.

These two different effects do, of course, interact on one another. It is pointed out that the income taxes of a number of countries provide preferential treatment for owner-occupiers by the complete or partial exclusion of the rental value in the tax base. The effect of this will normally be not only to change the structure of, but also to raise, the total level of housing consumption. The precondition for the latter effect which is given by Professor Netzer is that at given income levels owner-occupiers generally consume more housing than renters, but this is unnecessarily restrictive. It should not be viewed as an additional favour to owner-occupiers that under the United States' system house-owners are permitted to deduct mortgage interests and certain taxes in computing their income since these deductions would be entirely appropriate if the rental value was included in the tax base.

The preferential treatment of house-owners creates discrimination in two dimensions; between different types of consumption expenditures, and following from this, between different levels of income. The discrimination between types of housing consumption might be removed either by including the full rental value of owner-occupied houses in the income-tax base, or by allowing tenants to deduct their rent. The latter procedure would not, of course, remove discrimination between housing and other consumption, nor would it presumably be neutral in its effects on different income classes.

In conformity with traditional theory Professor Netzer distinguishes between building taxes which impose a real burden on housing investment and consumption, and land taxes which are likely to be capitalized into the value of land. If, however, Professor Netzer is right in stating that a significant share of the return from private investment in real estate takes the form of capital gains — and Professor Gelting thought he was right — land taxes may also be expected to act as disincentives.

Taxes on transfers of titles to real property pose a difficult theoretical problem. The fact that any newly constructed house may be expected to become subject to a tax on transfers several times during its lifetime will discourage new building. On the other hand, as Ricardo [1] pointed out, the tax on transfers will interfere with a re-allocation of resources, and thus decrease the effectiveness of the utilization of the existing stock. To that extent transfer taxes might, like rent control, call forth a larger volume of new building.

In so far as the net effect of any given tax system is to promote or discourage housing consumption as against other forms of consumption, it may be asked if this effect will not tend automatically to be neutralized through compensating changes in other parts of the economic system. If, for instance, the tax system on balance discourages housing, and if residential construction is particularly sensitive to interest rate changes then the incidence of the tax might ultimately be shifted back on to the rate of interest. The more sensitive other types of investment are to the rate of interest the smaller will be the decline in the interest rate, and the larger will be the change in investment structure. Thus, in an open economy where international capital movements are highly sensitive to interest rate differentials, the final net effect of a differential tax burden on housing might be a tendency towards increased investment abroad.

Professor Netzer's paper raises the difficult problem of the definition of neutrality as a standard with which actual policies may be compared. Since Professor Netzer is interested in the question whether tax policies are in harmony with policies pursued in other fields, the concept of neutrality needs to be broadened correspondingly. The problem is further complicated by the fact that housing investment and consumption are highly sensitive to changes in institutional arrangements, and that some interventions are motivated by a desire to remove market imperfections which may raise the kind of complications dealt with by the theory of second best. Finally, since the hypothetical construction of an economic system operating without a public sector is so remote from reality as to be irrelevant, its operation can hardly serve as our standard. The con-

[1] D. Ricardo, *Principles of Political Economy and Taxation.* Chapter xiv, 'Taxes on Houses'.

clusion seems inescapable that the concept of neutrality can only be given a vague and arbitrary interpretation.

Professor Netzer said it was perhaps rather presumptuous to write a paper of this kind sitting in New York ; systems of taxation changed so rapidly in their detail that it was difficult, or indeed impossible, to be completely up to date and accurate about all the countries examined. New data had become available since he wrote the paper. There was, for instance, the Report of the Allen Committee on the rating system in the U.K. Most of the points which Professor Gelting had made were ones which he would be willing to accept as corrections and changes. He is entirely right to say that the deduction of mortgage interest payments from gross income is not an additional source of unneutrality, in addition to the failure to tax the net rental value of owner-occupied housing. The point is that, in the U.S.A., mortgage interest is deductible despite the fact that net rental values are *not* subject to tax. In estimating the magnitude of the unneutrality, one must add mortgage interest back into the national income accounts data to avoid double-counting.

Turning to the question of neutrality, he explained that the concept of 'neutrality' was used as a starting point to weigh the efficiency of any policy to achieve its purported goal. It was, of course, entirely true that if a tax discouraged investment in housing and reduced expenditure, this will have an effect on the performance of the whole economy. As the housing sector absorbs a large proportion of the national savings, any significant reduction in this sector will have an effect on interest rates which may in turn encourage new housing construction. It was necessary to start by a concept of 'neutrality' and look at the effects of different policies rather than start by saying that there is no standard because everything is too closely inter-related to everything else.

Professor Muth said that it is especially important to consider the general equilibrium effects of property taxes on house prices. If property taxes were imposed at uniform rates on all classes of assets everywhere, then the effects of the tax depend critically upon the elasticity of the supply of capital to the whole economy. For the U.S.A., research suggested that there had been an almost constant rate of saving regardless of the rate of interest. If this is so, one would expect to find that the net effects of property taxes would be to lower the returns to real estate and to have no effect whatsoever on the price charged to consumers.

It is clear that when taxes differ, either between different areas or between different types of assets, there will be a shift of capital from one type of asset to another and the prices of the services yielded by the investments will be influenced by the taxes. It is, however, exceedingly difficult to determine (*a*) the impact of taxes in raising the price of capital to particular users because the price paid reflects many other factors — in particular the risks involved, and (*b*) to determine the effect of the taxes on the capital stock. If we knew the differential rates charged because of tax differences we could perhaps apply an analysis somewhat similar to that used by Harberger in his analysis of corporation income taxes. We could then determine the net effects of differential taxes.

Dr. Halevi, taking Professor Muth's point a little further, said that in trying to asses the net effects of the various kinds of taxes the aggregate table such as Table 2 in Professor Netzer's paper was helpful, but it was only a first step. In countries where we have a very high degree of differentiation between taxes imposed on houses, on materials used in house building and upon the incomes of people who use the houses, we needed a dis-aggregated approach. Just as in fiscal policy it was necessary to obtain the net effects of taxation on income by examining each income class, it was also necessary to dis-aggregate before reaching any firm conclusions about the effect of taxes on house-building or consumption.

He thought that Professor Netzer may have minimized the use of indirect taxes in the housing field. In Israel indirect taxes were important. There was, for example, a very high excise tax on cement and much higher taxes on the more expensive building materials used in high quality housing. These taxes considerably exaggerated the difference in cost between housing to various income groups.

Professor Lewis said that taxes may have unsuspected side effects — often long-run effects — which outweigh the more obvious short-run effects. For instance, what effect on house-building (in the long run) would the abolition of purchase taxes on motor cars have? To what extent will the capital gains tax turn investors from the attractions of capital appreciation in equities to the more solid security of building societies? Karl Marx [1] wrote graphically of how the speculative builder made his profit out of land values rather than the actual building operations, and this is still true in many cases today. How will a tax on land values affect this?

Professor Maisel raised the general point of whether tax policies had been (in all countries) an important variable in the housing policy field. In California, for example, there was an extremely important tax policy of exempting veterans from considerable property taxes on owned homes. This scheme was introduced in 1870 for the specific purpose of helping the veterans of that early period, but it has probably been one of the most significant variables during the last ten years in the Californian housing market. He wondered whether this field of research on exemptions and tax subsidies had been neglected. Professor Netzer had brought out the important point that there is a discrimination against the lowest income home-owners. The higher your income the greater the subsidy you receive to purchase a home. However, in the U.S.A. the individual home-owner could not deduct an amount for depreciation of his house, whereas the landlord could do so. It might be that if this was taken into

[1] K. Marx, *Capital*, Vol. II, pp. 233-4, in the edition published by the Foreign Languages Publishing House, Moscow, 1957. Book II, chap. xii in other texts.

account the difference between the owners and tenants might appear to be somewhat less than that suggested by the figures which had been given.

Professor Netzer agreed that if you allowed the home-owner to deduct depreciation allowance on the same basis as the investor (landlord) you would probably get a lower net tax revenue than the estimates he had given. He also made the point that under the new U.S. tax arrangement, buildings were less favoured than equipment through the system of depreciation allowances.

Professor Maisel said that if the financial arrangement was one in which the investor had a very small equity, with a very large fixed interest mortgage, the equity holder had all the advantages of investment credits and depreciation allowances and the returns to the equity could then become extremely high. In the U.S.A. the equity holder did not obtain investment credits which are given in some countries, but they obtain all the advantages of accelerated depreciation allowances and this raised the returns on property investment. These concessions and tax arrangements were the only way in which the U.S.A. managed to get investment in high risk housing. Whether the policy was introduced with this object in mind was not, however, clear.

This 'high' risk housing was being built upon central urban land which the government had cleared. The risks were high because there was no market information about the rental value of dwellings which could be built. The equity holder could obtain a 95 per cent guaranteed government loan, but the risks of financial failure were very great and past experience suggested that in two out of three cases the equity was lost and the government foreclosed on the property. It was a good example of the market concept of having a specialist to manage and use his skills, efficiency, and initiative. Although the returns on the entrepreneur's own investment could be very large when the development of the site was successful, the return was not large in relation to the total capital employed.

Professor Hoffmeyer said, in opening the discussion on the paper presented by Professor Gillies that this paper raised the question of evaluating the price mechanism as an instrument for attaining social goals. Five major points could be listed at which decisions have to be taken : (*a*) the amount of resources to be used in house-building and the efficiency with which the resources are used ; (*b*) the quality and type of housing ; (*c*) geographical location of housing. These three points involved production decisions. The last two decisions are : (*d*) who is to occupy the dwellings, and (*e*) how much are they going to pay ? So far, the Conference had concentrated discussion on the second, fourth, and fifth points, and in particular the most efficient combination of free market forces and government interference. Professor Gillies is concerned with three policy aims ; an increase in low income housing, an increase in owner-occupied houses in general, and thirdly a rational town development. The problem is to find ways of promoting these aims within a given institutional framework.

The Economic Problems of Housing

Professor Gillies maintains that experience has shown that in the U.S.A. it is necessary to formulate 'private oriented' programmes. The reason he gives for this is that if policy instruments are formulated as direct government interventions or in a way which will not intimately link any major private element to the programme, failure is certain. Professor Hoffmeyer agreed that the existing institutions of the economy have to be used, but he was not wholly in agreement with the manner in which Professor Gillies had formulated his conclusions.

It was probably true that favourable conditions for borrowing had influenced the rapid growth of owner-occupation after the Second World War in the U.S.A. Such housing has, however, also grown rapidly in other countries where the availability of funds for this purpose has not been easy. Professor Hoffmeyer's major point of objection stemmed from the widespread experiences of institutions which, although slow to change, did none the less adapt themselves to new demands made upon them if the incentive was strong enough and they could obtain higher profits. He gave two examples of the way Danish institutions had adapted to changed circumstances. The first was the example of the relation between non-profit and private profit house-building. The changes in the relationship had been enormous and they had occurred as a result of government regulations which were formulated in such a manner that private expectation of profit remained a strong force in the market. This operated from the entrepreneurial side where flexibility and capacity for adaptation was fairly high. The second example was of credit institutions which were often extremely slow to adjust to a new situation or to new demands. However, in 1958 when there was a major change in Danish housing policy and a shift from the government finance of house-building to private finance the lending institutions adapted themselves very quickly to this change. Denmark obtained an extremely rapid growth in the construction of one-family houses, the expansion was wholly financed by the private market and it coincided with a period of high interest rates.

This gave a rather different picture from Professor Gillies' general argument regarding the FHA system. His general conclusion had been that if low income housing was rented by official institutions at a very low price they would be successful, and that the same would be true if private house-builders could obtain more than normal profit by building and renting houses to low income groups at a low rent, plus a subsidy. In Denmark they had some experience of this type of scheme and the private market worked well in the house-building industry. Putting these thoughts into more general terms, Professor Hoffmeyer said that he could not accept offhand that the institutions could be treated as exogenous magnitudes.

The second problem raised by Professor Gillies was that of long-term town planning. He hoped that the exchange of views between the Eastern economies and the much less planned Western economies might be very fruitful. In the paper before the Conference the need for some sort of town planning was shown to be necessary and it was assumed that the market mechanism failed to bring about the necessary town planning or redevelopment. Professor Gillies stresses the need to find some system of incentives which will operate through the existing institutions to produce by indirect means social aims regarding the development and geographical location of towns. Professor Hoffmeyer fully agreed that the market mechanism seemed to have failed very badly in the U.S.A. with respect to town development, especially if we take as a standard of measure the European aim of establishing a comprehensive town plan. He was not, however, entirely convinced that it was necessary to pay so much attention to private building enterprises and capital market institutions. As with housing standards, so also in town planning, it should be possible to achieve much with qualitative rules and it was not necessary to use a policy of town planning to introduce any extreme changes in existing institutions. It was possible by legislative act to require every large community to make a town plan and it should also be possible to make regional plans for new towns. Whether this was politically possible is another question. They had some experience in Denmark of the system he suggested and they had not found it necessary for one large area of land to be owned by one decision-making unit. He very much doubted whether it was possible to amalgamate land holdings under the present institutional framework; in the planned economies of Eastern Europe the land could, of course, be controlled by one decision-making body. Given the ownership conditions of the mixed economies this was hardly possible.

In summarizing the two problems which he hoped the meeting would discuss he said : What incentives can call forth housing for low income groups ? Secondly, what regulating controls were most necessary for long-term planning and how would these rules affect and be affected by the institutional structure of different societies?

Professor Gillies said in reply that he had intended to prepare an appendix to this paper which would have given first a criteria for measuring the success or failure of U.S. government housing programmes and secondly the presentation of more empirical data. However, like so many good intentions, he had been unable to fulfil this one. His views on the low income housing programmes of the U.S.A. had to be seen against the background of U.S. policy. Basically this had been one in which the government constructed, owned, and subsidized houses for low income groups. He felt that this had not worked and he would like to see the development of some sort of incentive to private entrepreneurs to get them into this market.

On long-term planning, he said that it was a fact that legislation was now being introduced which was intended to lead to the construction of New Towns on the periphery of metropolitan areas. Regardless of whether this was a good or bad policy, he did not think that the current legislation would bring about the policy objective. There was not enough incentive for either the lending institutions or the builders. This brought up the whole infrastructure of an industry and the possibility of persuading an industry to carry out some government determined social aim or plan. At the present time in the U.S.A. they had perhaps reached a new stage in their housing policy ; 62 per cent of American families now owned their own homes and the mortgage markets were operating reasonably well. It was now time to turn to some of the unresolved social problems and, in particular, to the problem of low income housing. The infrastructure of the housing market was not organized to cope with this problem, and the question therefore arose as to how it might be adapted to meet his need.

The second point which he hoped would be discussed was the possibility of constructing a general economic theory which could be applied in all nations. Could economic analysis be undertaken in a vacuum or was it closely determined by the institutional background familiar to the economists of different countries ? Can a conclusion that interest rates allocate resources, which is drawn from U.S. studies, be applied directly to a country like Poland with its very different institutional background ?

Dr. Holm said that in considering town planning it was necessary to bear in mind the long- and short-term objectives and situations. In the short term it might be desirable to permit the building of a house and the taking of profit by the builder, but in the long run the position and architectural quality of the house might mean loss of amenity to the community. This possibility was, he thought, the reason why town planning had developed in many Western European countries where it was regarded rather differently than in America. In practice the differences between countries were accentuated by differences in institutions. For example, in Sweden the local authorities were powerful organs of planning and drew substantial tax revenues from income tax. They had a large official organization charged with responsibility for town planning. They had also divided the processes of planning very much more than the Americans. The town planners planned the urban areas but the construction and design of individual buildings was left to contractors, and one of the Swedish problems was to get a better liaison between the planners and the contractors.

There appeared to be two broad approaches to town planning. The American method in which the site to be cleared or developed was determined by town planners but the contractors drew up the plans for the internal development of the site ; or alternatively a detailed plan for the whole town could be drawn up and then private contractors could build each individual building in accordance with the detailed town plan. The two methods were independent of the institutions of any particular society and he asked Dr. Kuminek which of the systems were used in Poland.

Dr. Kuminek said, in reply, that the town-planning functions were carried out by city or town authorities. The plans were prepared by the officials and then approved by the city or town governments. There were two stages in the planning process. First, the long period development forecast. This covered a period of 20-25 years and was a very general plan giving both needs and resources. The second stage of the planning process was to develop what is called a 'general' plan. This is a phased plan covering shorter periods of the long-period forecast. These plans are co-ordinated with the general economic development plan for the region or the city as a whole. This plan is fairly detailed and takes into account the major investments which are to be made in each sector of the economy. The separate parts of the general plan had to be considered in relation to the builder. If the State housing agency intended to set up a major housing project, it was the State agency who drew up the plans for the particular project ; in doing this it would, of course, take full account of the general plan. When the site was to be financed and developed by co-operatives or by individuals, the municipal town planning department worked out a detailed programme and allocated to the various co-operatives or private builders the particular sites upon which they were to build.

Dr. Przeciszewski said that in the paper before the Conference there were two types of problem : (*a*) the evaluation of American housing policy, and (*b*) the efficiency of the new laws which were being introduced. As regards (*a*) Professor Gillies had done a very thorough piece of work, to which he would only add that the supply of new dwellings by the public agencies was limited to the replacement of demolished houses. There was, therefore, no net increase in the housing stock. As regards the second point, Dr. Przeciszewski said that it was not only in the sphere of housing that social objectives such as those involved in housing low income groups could not be attained. The American economic and social system was in general unable to redistribute income in a manner which permitted the attainment of this type of social aim.

Professor Gelting said that in connection with the question of the efficiency of the price mechanism as an instrument for locational allocation, he would like to call attention to a recent paper by O. A. Davis and A. S. Whinston[1] last year in Kyklos, where the process of allocation is studied by means of a model in which all building lots are auctioned simultaneously with subsequent 're-contracting'. The main difficulty which makes the achievement of equilibrium difficult is the existence of external economies, *i.e.* an important characteristic of any given site is the use to which surrounding sites are put. For this reason zoning may facilitate the marketing process, especially if the sale of building sites extends over a long period of time.

When discussing the allocation of housing space it has been said that the availability of some vacant dwellings is a precondition for the effective and orderly operation of the market. The situation is similar for the market in

[1] O. A. Davis and A. S. Whinston, *The Economics of Complex Systems — the Case of Municipal Zoning.* Kyklos, 1964, p. 419.

building sites, and recent Danish experience provides a good illustration of the unfortunate consequences of an excess demand in this market, which was due in general to a deficiency in public investments in infrastructure.

Mr. Azcarate asked Professor Gillies whether the American government action in attempting to solve the housing shortage of the early fifties had resulted in an increase in the price of houses. In France they had been worried about this consequence of extending easy credit terms to house purchasers and had imposed a maximum price for houses bought with the aid of government loans. If this had not been done he thought that the increased demand would have raised prices rather than increased the supply of new dwellings.

Professor Gillies said, in reply, that there had been considerable controversy in the U.S.A. as to whether the FHA did increase the supply or not. A study by Saulnier, Halcrow, and Jacoby [1] came to the general conclusion that the policy had had the effect of raising prices rather than increasing supply. More recent studies seemed to indicate that the programme had introduced economies which had led to a greater output than would have occurred without the programme. There had been some tendency for the higher prices to be met by easier credit terms which tended still further to put an upward pressure upon prices. However, this was a very unsettled question and he could not give any definite reply.

There had been a special programme for apartment buildings which permitted investors to borrow money. This was done in the hope that it would increase the supply of flats to let, but, in fact, the programme was not successful in increasing the supply of apartments in spite of the availability of interest rate subsidies. The great increase in apartment buildings started in about 1957 and Professor Gillies thought that it was the result of a basic change in the age population which led to a large increase in the demand for this type of accommodation to which the builders responded in classical style by increasing the supply. The FHA programme supported the builders of apartment blocks just as it supported the building of houses for individual families. This experience suggested that U.S. government programmes have not initiated changes in market supply, but that when these occur programmes like the FHA supported them.

SIXTH SESSION

THE DISCUSSION ON THE PAPERS OF
PROFESSOR ANDREJEWSKI AND DR. PRZECISZEWSKI

Mr. Turin said that there were several points raised in Professor Andrejewski's paper which he thought of general interest. The first was that

[1] R. J. Saulnier, Harold J. Halcrow, and Neil H. Jacoby, 'Federal Lending and Loan Insurance' (Princeton University Press for the National Bureau of Economic Research, 1958).

the very low rent policy in Socialist countries had been conceived in the first instance as a part of a more general policy of moving from a capitalist to a socialist state. Immediately after the war there also seemed to be an association between the low rent policy and the overall policy of directing investment away from housing to othter sectors of the economy. His second point followed directly from the first. Where did the necessary funds for housing investment originate ? Professor Andrejewski had made a distinction between the U.S.S.R. where the rent did not even cover maintenance costs of housing and where funds for housing were therefore accumulated outside the housing sector. The funds were allocated at central level and for all practical purposes may be said to come from the state budget. Yugoslavia was at the opposite extreme of socialist countries and there the housing funds were accumulated within the housing sector at the local government, Republican government, and Federal government levels. The revenue from a special tax imposed upon salaries was used for housing in a manner which was rather similar to the French system. Construction costs were financed by interest bearing bonds and the same principles applied equally to State, co-operative, and private construction. This was the unique feature of Yugoslavian housing and Professor Andrejewski had placed Poland between the two extremes of the U.S.S.R. and Yugoslavia.

Because rents were very low in the U.S.S.R. and Poland the allocation of houses was done through an administrative system which allocated dwellings according to need and social priorities. This did not apply so much to co-operative housing which was gradually being priced at an economic cost and where consumers' preferences could be expressed. In Yugoslavia the costs of all housing was being aligned to the true costs, so that consumers' preferences could express themselves throughout the market.

These differences had led Professor Andrejewski to consider the function of the State in the provision of houses. One could regard housing as a social service like education or health which is supplied either free or for a very small charge ; or alternatively housing could be regarded as a public utility for which the charge would be a reflection of the economic costs of supply, but for social reasons these costs may have to be subsidized. Mr. Turin thought that the suggestion that a public utility may be subsidized attenuated the division made between a social service and a public utility and a greater difference in attitudes to housing may be found in the methods used to accumulate the housing fund. If individuals contributed their personal savings to the housing fund then it seemed highly likely, if not inevitable, that private preferences would gradually come into the open. Professor Andrejewski goes so far as to suggest that in time it may become an equilibrating factor in the consumption market.

Dr. Halevi thought that Mr. Turin had been right to draw attention to

Professor Andrejewski's distinction between looking at housing as a social service or as a public utility. The distinction seemed to Dr. Halevi to be more quantitative than qualitative. It was, however, interesting to associate this distinction with the second one of (*a*) State responsibility for accumulation and (*b*) consumer responsibility. This was particularly interesting in the light of Professor Andrejewski's last sentence where a shift from one concept of housing as a social service with government responsibility for accumulating funds, to the second concept of a public utility with private responsibility for accumulating funds, is identified with the economic potential of the various countries.

Dr. Musil thought that the differences between the socialist countries could be explained by looking at the differences in the history and government of the various countries. Yugoslavia was a Federal Republic and each state retained some independence in its housing policy. On the other hand, in a Socialist planned economy it was necessary to have a close inter-relationship between each sector of the economy. Independence and inter-dependence could only be achieved in Yugoslavia by some decentralization which meant, amongst other things, that each region took some responsibility for accumulating the funds devoted to housing construction. He could not agree that the differences were associated with the extent of the shortage. Yugoslavia had a great housing shortage and thus it could hardly be correct to assume that the evolution of housing economics would necessarily move towards the Yugoslavian pattern as the shortage of housing declined.

Dr. Kuminek said that there is a difference between the number of houses built by various house-builders and the sources of the financial means allocated for the purpose. Thus, for example, in 1963 public building constituted 52 per cent of the total houses constructed in Poland, co-operative building 16 per cent and the private sector 32 per cent of the total. Two-thirds of the capital used to finance this building came from State sources and the remaining third from the resources of the population building co-operative flats and one-family houses. Thus public funds are used to finance both the construction of flats provided by the State and also for the grant of mortgage loans to co-operative and private builders. The housing fund is not derived entirely from the State budget; a significant source of capital for housing was the 'profit' income of industrial undertakings which allocated a part of their profits to the housing fund.

Mr. Turin said that he understood from the paper before the meeting that the size of the private housing sector was largely dependent upon the size of the rural population. As urbanization and industrialization continued it was thought that the private sector would shrink. On the other hand we had been told that private housing was developing, for instance in Czechoslovakia, for entirely different reasons, and that the attempt to draw upon private savings in several of these countries was enlarging the private sector regardless of whether the population was urban or rural.

Dr. Musil said that in Czechoslovakia they wanted to stimulate private house-building in some parts of the country and they also wanted the private house-builder to help them to solve the housing shortage. Once the shortage was overcome they would not necessarily continue with this policy. Most of the private houses being built were in small towns and villages and they were built mainly by manual workers who commute to the larger industrial towns.

Dr. Kuminek said it was difficult to reply for Professor Andrejewski, who was unhappily absent from this meeting, but Dr. Kuminek's own opinion was that in Poland the small one-family house was not the traditional form of housing construction ; he thought that as population moved to the towns more families would be housed in flats. Flats could very conveniently be in 'collective' ownership, and for this reason he thought that private house-building would decline with urbanization. The Polish tradition of building blocks of flats in towns was very old and he thought it unlikely that the small family house would suddenly become the popular form of city design.

Dr. Halevi asked Dr. Musil whether it would be correct to think that the total amount of housing was determined by the State and the division between the three types of house-ownership left to be determined by the amount of private savings.

Dr. Musil said that this interpretation was not entirely correct because the need to increase savings may stem from a need to decrease the general level of consumption. The State also wished to encourage the co-operatives because they had found that the people preferred them and maintained the flats to a higher standard.

Professor Lindbeck said it was important here to make a clear distinction between the government as a saver and the government acting as an intermediary in the capital market. In Sweden, for example, about 25 to 30 per cent of the capital for mortgage loans came from the government, but this was because the government usually issued bonds and financed mortgage loans from the funds raised. The government could withdraw from such a direct participation in the capital market and let private institutions raise the capital and give the mortgage loans. These loans could possibly carry a government guarantee, and if this was done a change of the type suggested would make little or no difference to the national allocation of resources. On the other hand, it is possible to have a system where the government financed housing out of budget surplus rather than by issuing bonds. Dr. Kuminek had told us that 52 per cent of the Polish housing fund for 1963 had been used to build State housing and Professor Lindbeck wondered how much of this was the result of government saving through budget surplus and how much was the result of government intervention in the capital market by issuing bonds.

Dr. Przeciszewski said that in Poland the government had credit institutions which collected the savings of individuals and co-operatives. These

savings were then disbursed amongst the various borrowers. Dr. Przeciszewski had carried out research on the credits granted to individuals and
co-operatives in the period up to 1960 and he had found that the amount of
credit granted to individuals was approximately equal to the amount which
individuals had accumulated in the special State Savings Bank.

Professor Grigsby said, in introducing Dr. Przeciszewski's paper, that it
was a little difficult for him to discuss this paper because he had little
knowledge of Polish conditions. However, the paper suggested several
issues of general policy and he wished to concentrate upon these. The
first of these general questions had occurred to him when he compared the
average size of Polish dwellings with those in the United States and
Western Europe. He found it interesting to speculate on the assumption
held in many Western countries that overcrowding is correlated with bad
health and special social problems. The Polish housing standards would
suggest that this assumption should be re-examined and perhaps questioned quite seriously.

In Poland it is felt that rents are much 'too low' and should be raised,
but in the U.S.A. many persons believe that rents are too high and that
because shelter is a 'merit' good, its market price should be lowered so
that families will consume more of it. What level of rents is 'best'?
Heavily subsidized rents certainly enable the poorest families to pay their
housing costs. On the other hand, they may tend to cause governments
to allocate fewer resources to housing than would otherwise be the case.
Then, over the long run the policy of reducing rents to improve housing
conditions may be self-defeating.

Professor Grigsby wished to know what had been the redistributive
aspects of the Polish housing policy on over-all welfare. As the rents paid
by families were lower than the costs of housing, the government was
clearly re-distributing income. The extent of this redistribution was very
difficult to measure since almost everyone appeared to be paying a very
low rent. Presumably this meant that everyone was making a contribution to housing costs through general taxation. There were two other
questions which arose from this thought. First, could Poland have
obtained more house production if there had not been this redistribution
of income but the market had been allowed to operate more freely?
Secondly, is the redistribution of income of more importance than increasing the aggregate investment in housing? The answer to this question is
not obvious, for it is theoretically possible for an increased investment in
housing to be associated with a general decrease in welfare. The welfare
effects depend upon the allocation of the newly built houses, and whether
the resources are used to build relatively few houses of a high standard or
more houses at a lower standard.

Dr. Przeciszewski had observed in his paper that the income elasticities
calculated for the U.S.A. might not hold in other countries. This raised
the question as to whether they can be influenced by government policy.

We need a much longer time horizon and there had been some tendency for the Conference to concentrate upon rather short-term analysis and policy recommendations. For instance, rent control had been discussed in relationship to the objective of better maintenance of houses, reflecting a short-term attitude. The effect of rent control in inhibiting or encouraging the improvement of dwellings is the long-term question which needs to be asked.

The discussion of equilibrium positions had also appeared to Professor Grigsby to be of a rather short-term nature. It would be more profitable to think of a dynamic long-term equilibrium and to consider the short term rather as a pathway towards equilibrium positions which might well be out of date by the time they were reached. Likewise the repeated references to efficiency indicate a preoccupation with the short-term allocation problem rather than the more serious problem of increasing production, preserving adaptability and flexibility in the urban structure, and encouraging innovation. Further, consideration of quality has largely been ignored and yet without taking into account the quality of dwellings being built, figures giving changes in investment levels over the long run are of little significance.

In conclusion, Professor Grigsby said that the paper raised the question of the allocation of resources between housing and other sectors. As Professor Robinson suggested earlier in the Conference, every society has many aims and it may well be impossible to allocate the amount of investment to housing over the time period in which we would like to achieve certain housing objectives. Furthermore, housing aims could possibly be achieved more quickly by first allocating resources to certain non-housing sectors of the economy.

Dr. Przeciszewski said, in reply to Professor Grigsby, that in Poland rents were regarded as 'too low' because they did not cover the current costs of maintenance. Most Polish economists thought that rents should be increased to what was called the 'economic level' but the definition of this rent level presented some difficulty. Sometimes it included, but at other times excluded, such things as the amortization of the capital and the cost of carrying out capital repairs over the total life span of the building.

The determination of the amount of resources which could be allocated to housing was, as Professor Grigsby had suggested, a difficult one. If investment was concentrated in the productive sectors of the economy it would produce a greater national income from which a larger investment in housing (and other non-productive sectors of the economy) could be made in future. In practice Poland had allocated varying proportions of the available investment funds to residential building at various stages in the growth of the economy. In the early fifties there had been a concentration on productive industrial investment; in the late fifties on house building. In 1961 there was a renewed effort to increase industrial investment and the proportion devoted to housing had to be limited.

Dr. Kuminek said that the low level of rents would not curb the construction of new buildings in Poland because there was no direct link between the level of building and rents. There was, however, an indirect influence of rents upon building which showed itself in the proportion of dwellings built by the different types of builders but not in the overall level of building. When the government invested in the construction of dwellings a subsidy was paid on these dwellings and continued for many years. As the government wished to reduce the level of the annual subsidy it was encouraging building by both co-operatives and private individuals. Houses built by the co-operatives were given an initial subsidy but not an annual one, thus the occupiers of these dwellings had to bear the annual costs of maintaining their accommodation.

SEVENTH SESSION

THE DISCUSSION ON THE PAPERS OF
DR. MUSIL AND MADAME PJANIC

Dr. Kuminek said that there were several points of particular interest in Dr. Musil's paper which he would like to stress. The first was the changes which had occurred in the Czechoslovakian building and housing policies. These were now aimed at getting an increase in State subsidized co-operative and private individual houses. These changes had also occurred in other Socialist countries and were accompanied by some changes in rental policy in both Yugoslavia and Czechoslovakia, where an attempt was being made to reduce the State subsidies which covered the maintenance costs of dwellings. Under the Rent Act 1964 the Czechoslovakian government had also introduced a rent differential based upon the quality of the dwelling. The higher rents which resulted from this policy were reduced for large families and the poorer households. An attempt had also been made to reduce 'under-occupation' by charging an additional rent which increased progressively for every square metre of dwelling space which exceeded the standards laid down. The Act had only been in operation for a short space of time and it was still rather early to assess the results of the increase in rents, but Dr. Kuminek hoped that we should learn something of the effect of this new policy on the maintenance of the housing stock and on the household budgets of various groups in the population.

One of the consequences of the shift in policy towards co-operative building and away from State building might be some change in the mass production of identical prefabricated dwellings. As the co-operatives built on a smaller scale and showed some preference for individual designs the building industry might have to develop so that it could meet this new type of demand.

The new method of estimating housing needs which the Czechs had introduced after the 1961 Census were of particular interest. The definition of a 'census household' was designed to show not only the existing number of separate household units but also the potential new household formation. This was done by grouping members of one household in accordance with their social and family needs and not simply with reference to the fact that during a time of housing shortage a group of people were living together and forming one household. This was an interesting departure from the normal practice ; it might, however, exaggerate the housing needs of the population by not taking into account the number of people who voluntarily join up and form one household although they are not related. It was also necessary to take into account the impact of the new housing policy in estimating housing 'need' because a new added emphasis was given to 'need' (the demand for different types of dwellings and the aggregate demand which could be met out of the private income of individual families). It was therefore very necessary for the government to estimate both types of needs — objective needs and demand.

Dr. Musil explained in reply to Dr. Kuminek that the Czechoslovakian housing situation was rather complicated by the fact that they still had some families living as tenants in privately owned family houses. These tenants made their own tenancy agreement with the owners of the houses. The rents which had been set by the Rent Act 1964 were the same all over the country and varied only according to the space and quality of the dwelling. This was regarded as reasonable since the price of all other things was the same throughout the country and so were the incomes of people in similar occupations. This made it difficult to persuade, for example, doctors or teachers to leave Prague and work in other parts of the country, but the overall housing policy was designed to make it easier for people to get a house in the less favoured areas of the country, and funds were allocated to those areas of the country to which it was hoped that people would move. Another way in which they differentiated between houses in various parts of the country was to set a higher 'down payment' (membership fee) for a co-operative flat in Prague than for the same flat in a smaller town. As there are no parallel arrangements made to differentiate the rents charged for State flats this created certain tensions and distortions in the policy of persuading people to leave the larger cities.

Dr. Musil stressed that in his country the 'housing problem' was now regarded as a continuing economic and social phenomena. They no longer believed that the shortage could simply be overcome by building a certain number of houses. Now that they were catching up with the quantitative shortage they were confronted with the qualitative needs and had started to pull down some of the older houses.

Mr. Turin asked Dr. Kuminek and Dr. Musil what were the underlying factors in this change of policy. Is the ultimate purpose of encouraging more co-operative housing and private building to draw resources into the housing market that would otherwise be untapped? How is it that in a centrally planned economy such an indirect means has to be resorted to rather than the more direct means of taxation? What has happened in the Czechoslovakian economy which has led them to adopt a kind of economy which is frequently known as a mixed or market economy?

Professor Maisel asked for clarification of the advantages and disadvantages of private home ownership, whether individual or co-operative. In Mr. Turin's, Dr. Kuminek's, and Dr. Musil's papers the same basic question had been raised and he had listed five points on this aspect of housing. (1) It gave the advantage of self-labour for construction, maintenance, and management so that costs are lowered. (2) There may be differences in the initial costs, due to difference in design when an individual or small group were allowed to determine their own choice of dwelling. (3) Individuals may lay more stress on housing consumption and away from other goods, thus private ownership, as opposed to public, may result in the consumption of more housing. Related to this is the fact that they will be helping to finance their housing by saving more. (4) Home-ownership is often a very good personal investment. (5) The traditional point of whether or not ownership had an adverse effect on the mobility rate.

Professor Lindbeck added a sixth point; in Czechoslovakia it was a politically convenient method of using the pricing system more effectively. While they were reluctant to raise rents in private and state-owned houses the Czechs had been willing to raise the price of housing by encouraging co-operative ownership.

Dr. Arndt thought that one of the great experiments of our time was the introduction into a socialist economy of allocation through the pricing mechanism. Could it be that the governments of these countries were running very short of funds for housing by the late fifties and they tackled this problem in two ways? First by raising rents, and secondly by bringing more private funds into house-building. Both policies are closely related and as more evidence becomes available of the amount which people are willing to pay for their own homes a knowledge will be gained of the amount of rent which people might be willing to pay for similar state flats. They could go still further by introducing a differential tax which took some account of the advantages of living in large cities.

Professor Gelting said that evidently there is still a strong excess demand in the Czech housing market. He presumed that in consequence the vacancy rate was extremely low and would like to have Dr. Musil's views on the effects of this on the geographical mobility of labour.

The undesirable effects of rent control in Western European countries had been reviewed. In so far as the continued operation of rent control is dictated by distributional considerations it would appear to be even more difficult to justify in the socialist countries than in Western Europe. Increased rents would normally accrue directly to public authorities and in any case the distribution of income is subject to rather closer government control than in the West.

Professor Hoffmeyer said that if he had understood the paper properly, he thought the Czechoslovakian government was starting by establishing a 'fair rent' and from this they were to move to a free market. He wondered if the way in which the housing of some workers was now being attached to their jobs might not have far-reaching policy implications. If a worker obtains a flat on more favourable terms if he takes a certain job, does it not mean that he must stay in that job, and if he leaves that he will lose his flat ? This must lower mobility and in a period of changing excess demands for labour in various industries, it must prevent the workers from moving to the sectors where they are most needed. The device of giving special housing to selected workers is used to increase mobility in the short run, but it will have adverse long term consequences.

Dr. Musil replied that the problem is mainly associated with two industries. The mining and the heavy steel industries. The work in these industries is difficult and unpleasant and, as wages do not differ much from one industry to another, it is difficult to get workers to stay in the least pleasant industrial occupations. Other incentives were therefore given and, in particular, State housing. However, the workers work for about two years in the selected industries and then find some method of staying in the State flat but moving to another job. They therefore introduced a scheme which is a combination of State and co-operative housing ; a mining concern will pay the membership fee for a miner to become a member of a co-operative. If he leaves the industry before a certain number of years he has to repay a proportion of this fee to the enterprise.

Professor Hoffmeyer said this was basically a concealed wage differential to miners which had to be paid when there was full employment in the country and an acute shortage of miners. He felt, however, that there was an element of economic compulsion in tying the wage differential to housing as it meant that someone without liquid resources was unable to repay the fee and leave the industry.

Professor Muth said that in a free enterprise economy the miners wages were not just a reflection of the demand for miners but also of the alternative occupations in the mining areas. By attaching the house to the mining industry you prevented the spread of high wages to the other industries.

Dr. Musil said his paper had been a report upon the present situation in Czechoslovakia and he reminded the Conference that these short term policies had to be seen in relation to the long term historical development of the country. He was certain that when the current housing shortage had been met and they moved to the next phase of their housing development many new policies would be evolved.

Dr. Arndt introduced Madame Pjanic's paper and said that from Professor Andrejewski's paper he understood that the extent of the housing shortage in Yugoslavia was very much the same as in Poland. In both countries the number of persons per room was about 1·7 or 1·6 compared with the average for many Western European countries of 0·9 to 0·7 The relatively low level of house-building in these two countries was a symptom of their desire to industrialize and direct their limited building resources away from housing and towards factory and other building. Madame Pjanic's paper dealt primarily with the inter-dependence of economic development and the standard of living. Her main conclusion is that you cannot develop the economy independently of social conditions.

In reading the paper Dr. Arndt had tried to consider it as an address made to a Yugoslavian Committee which was responsible for allocating funds to housing. Such a plea might start by trying to link the special interests of the various Ministers to housing. To persuade, for example, the Minister of Agriculture that output in his field could only be increased by improved standards of rural housing. The other approach, which is perhaps the one chosen in this paper, is to find a common denominator which could possibly impress all the Committee members. This would mean convincing the Committee that social conditions have to be better now and not only in the distant future.

However, Dr. Arndt had some doubts about considering the paper in this way, because at the end of her paper Madame Pjanic says that she is unable to offer any solution to the housing problem, which she identifies as a conflict between the quantity, and the quality of new building. The country may either move over to industrialized methods and sacrifice quality, or have a much lower output of higher standard traditional houses. No decision can be made about this on the criteria which she offers in her paper. Furthermore, she says that there can be no 'absolute' need for housing and if increasing incomes draw additional resources into house-building the overall national economy will suffer. It seems then to be implied in her paper that the only way in which additional housing could be obtained is by an increase in private savings with a consequent reduction in other forms of private consumption. This could not, however, be allowed to affect the immediate output of houses because the construction industry is already fully employed.

EIGHTH SESSION

THE DISCUSSION ON THE PAPERS OF
MR. TURIN AND DR. HALEVI

Mr. *Azcarate* said that like Professor Grigsby, who introduced the paper on Poland, he had some difficulty in discussing Mr. Turin's paper on 'Housing in Africa' because he knew little of the particular problems which the countries of this continent had to overcome. He hoped, however, that Mr. Turin's excellent paper would emerge intact in spite of this limitation. He thought it best to comment on the paper by making a separate consideration of (*a*) investment, (*b*) the methods used to finance house-building, and (*c*) the level of rents.

Turning first to investment, Mr. Azcarate said that Mr. Turin had given a global estimate of housing 'need' of eleven to fourteen dwellings per annum per 1,000 urban inhabitants. This rate of house-building would be sufficient to cover the 'needs' which would arise if the rate of urbanization continued at its present rate of about 5 per cent per annum, and would also alleviate a little of the existing overcrowding.

It was difficult to know what significance could be attached to such estimates. The first problem confronting African States was that of employment. Until this problem was tackled no estimate could be made of the income available to meet housing costs and it was thus difficult to forecast the demand for dwellings. There was a grave danger that houses might be built and remain vacant if men were frequently unemployed and therefore unable to make regular payments of rent.

The second aspect of investment which needed to be discussed was the organization of the building industry in Africa. Mr. Turin had stressed that the industry was badly organized, suffered from a very low labour productivity and, above all, depended upon imports for many of the building materials used. Mr. Turin had given a quantitative estimate of the investment required to develop the building materials industries so that the African states could be self-supporting. The total investment which Mr. Turin thought to be necessary was equal to the estimated value of imports of building materials in 1970. The two criteria which should be used to choose between making investments in the building materials industry rather than in some other field were first the amount of additional employment which will be generated by alternative investments, and second the value of imports which alternative investments would save.

Mr. Azcarate then turned to consider the saving potential and propensities of different African States. He wondered whether there would be an increase in owner-occupation and what was the return on investment in rental housing. Turning to the level of rents he suggested that it might be desirable to build cheap houses with a relatively short life and involving high maintenance costs, rather than more durable houses which the Africans could not afford and which would have to be subsidized. It might be better for the governments of these countries to concentrate investment on the infrastructure of the urban areas rather than on high quality houses which could be developed later.

Finally, in order to obtain some idea of the effective demand for housing in Africa, it would be interesting to know where housing stands in the scale of preferences of African households. We needed to know the share of income devoted to housing. If this was related to the economic rents of new houses it would be possible to make some estimate of the amount of

The Economic Problems of Housing

government aid required to fulfil a part of the new building programme. This part of the programme would cover houses which are built for civil servants and are of a standard similar to those found in European countries. It would, of course, meet only a small part of the needs of the population.

Mr. Turin said, in reply, that he had not given anything in the sense of an estimate of African 'needs'. It was quite impossible to do this but he had found that if no figure was given many irresponsible guesses were made about the number of houses needed. His figure should be regarded more as a production target than as any assessment of either need or demand. Having put into sixteen pages the final results of over 500 pages of statistical material and computations there was necessarily much simplification; perhaps in places some over-simplification.

The purpose of this simplified formulation of a housing market was to give the governments of African States some clear idea of the inter-relationship between a house-building programme and other sectors of the economy, particularly the import/export changes which were implied by the programme and the various investments which were required to sustain the building industry. Up to quite recently housing had not appeared in the public development plans of these countries. When it did appear it was often in the form of a question-mark over the non-monetary sector of the economy. Mr. Turin emphasized that the 500,000 figure given in his paper was purely hypothetical; at present the number of houses being built was probably only about 100,000.

Mr. Turin turned then to the financial aspects of African housing and said that it was difficult to get money for less than 8 to 10 per cent, even in the semi-subsidized sector, and mortgages were seldom for more than 15 years. In general, one can estimate that housing costs (including amortization, interest, maintenance, and management) will be 1 per cent per month of the capital costs of construction, and with the present income distribution in the urban areas of most African countries less than 10 per cent of the households can afford to pay the economic rents of new houses. If the loan terms could be reduced from the figure of 1 per cent of the capital cost per month to 0·75 per cent (a major economic operation which seems most unlikely to be achieved) it would still only mean that 20 to 25 per cent of the population could afford the houses which are now being built.

Mr. Cullingworth introduced Dr. Halevi's paper and said there were two points which particularly interested him and which he hoped would be discussed. The first was land prices and land policy. The value of land had been mentioned in earlier discussions but he thought the experi-ence of Israel was of particular interest as, Mr. Cullingworth understood, 93 per cent of all the land in Israel was publicly owned. This, however, had not prevented a rapid rise in land prices and he hoped that Dr. Halevi could explain this apparent paradox. In a paper delivered at a Land Seminar held recently in Paris, figures were given in a paper by Darin-

Drabkin [1] showing the extent to which land prices had risen between 1958 and 1963. In 1958 the cost of developed land represented 15 per cent of the total housing cost of private dwellings and 4 to 5 per cent of the total housing costs of public dwellings. By 1963 these percentages had risen to 35 per cent and to 6 to 12 per cent respectively. It was not entirely clear as to what these figures referred to and he hoped Dr. Halevi would say something about the present Israeli policy on land, and in particular the relationship between land and housing policies.

The second point which Mr. Cullingworth made was on the preference for home-ownership to which reference was made in the paper. It has been said that owner-occupation produces a high level of maintenance and that it is an important way of increasing the total level of savings. He wondered, however, whether the demand for owner-occupation was merely a function of the institutional and tax arrangements in many countries. A survey recently carried out in Britain suggested that about 16 per cent of households moving into the owner-occupied sector were involuntary owners and would have preferred to rent accommodation.

Dr. Halevi said that in a descriptive paper of this kind when one was trying to give some brief outline of all the aspects of housing policy for a foreign audience, many things of importance had to be omitted and land ownership and policy was one of these things. Neither was a brief paper a suitable vehicle for new ideas or theoretical discussion of intricate points of economic analysis, but he had tried to pick out certain problems of housing in Israel and some of the policies which are of general interest and arise in many developing countries. First there was the economic question of the means which developing countries might use to attain a minimum standard of housing. The problem was one of the 'best' use of resources and we could leave the definition of 'need' or 'standard' on one side ; because, however you defined these things, it was clear that for many developing countries not even the lowest standard could be achieved for many years.

It was also necessary to examine the rôle of housing within the whole framework of economic development. Particularly the use of housing policy to achieve other aims ; for example, what is the rôle of housing and housing policy in urbanization policy? What is the rôle of the housing industry in developing industrialization? Is it a rapidly developing industry, does it have forward and backward linkages which would be important forces in raising the aggregate level of production?

On the first point raised by Mr. Cullingworth, Dr. Halevi said that in the areas of land shortage such as Tel Aviv only 40 per cent of the land ready for development was publicly owned ; the great bulk of the publicly

[1] Economic Commission for Europe, Committee on Housing, Building, and Planning, Seminar on the Supply and Allocation of Land for Housing and Related Purposes, National Monograph for Israel prepared by H. Darin-Drabkin (unpublished but see forthcoming monograph by H. Darin-Drabkin to be published by the Department of Social and Economic Research, University of Glasgow).

owned land was outside the town and city areas. As regards land policy and housing policy, he could not see why economists should object to land speculation, although he admitted that most of us have a deeply ingrained dislike of the speculator. The overall government policy was to persuade people to move from the heavily populated central coastal area around Tel Aviv to the north of the country and to the south.

The fact that land prices were rising in Tel Aviv should help the government to fulfil this policy. Relative to most other countries the distribution of income in Israel is fairly even and they now had a capital gains tax on land which seemed to be working well. A more difficult problem than land speculation arose when rents were set by the government for land which it leased out for development or agricultural purposes. Recently an attempt had been made to raise rents to a level which fully reflected the economic value of the land, but this was politically very difficult ; rents had, however, risen substantially recently and leases were re-negotiated every five years.

Professor Lindbeck said that Dr. Halevi had introduced the conflict between the two main functions of a pricing system. (*a*) To allocate scarce resources in an efficient way, and (*b*) to distribute income. He agreed completely with Dr. Halevi that it would be very inefficient to introduce price control on land, thereby destroying the first function of the pricing mechanism. However, the problem was to find a system of flexible land prices compatible with a 'reasonable' income distribution. If we have a situation where the government owned all the land it might be possible to accept a situation in which the market demand determined land prices (*i.e.* land rents) ; in a country where land is privately owned the conflict between private interests can be rather severe but can be lessened by the taxation of capital gains and rent incomes.

Dr. Arndt said he was interested to see that in Israel housing consumption was given a low priority because of balance of payments difficulties. It was not clear to Dr. Arndt that this was a wise policy. Some incentives had to be given to the workers to increase their productivity and he thought that housing had an important rôle to play as a work incentive. It also seemed to him that housing consumption made less demands upon imports than other kinds of consumption. Dr. Halevi had quoted the import content of dwelling units as about 16 per cent which was rather low. The import content of maintaining dwellings would, he believed, be even less than 16 per cent.

Dr. Halevi said that the balance of payments problem in Israel was the main problem of the coming decade. Israel was still in receipt of unilateral transfer payments which meant that at present they had no major problem ; but when these ceased in ten years' time they would have severe balance of payments problems unless they prepared an export trade now. He thought that this balance of payments problem should take precedence over current housing needs, but the immigration policy of Israel made a large house-building programme a matter of considerable political importance and priority. Slum clearance was given a lower priority and in this field there was a tendency to consider the full economic costs and implications of a clearance programme.

Professor Maisel asked Mr. Turin what were the problems of retaining the traditional type of African housing during the next decade or so while other investment projects were being undertaken? In Mexico, for example, some 'luxury' hotels consisted of 'indigenous' huts and he wondered whether European type housing in Africa was a status symbol. Or were there underlying economic or health difficulties which prevented the use of traditional African building?

Mr. Turin said that a distinction had to be made between the rural and urban environment. No African country (except possibly one or two in North Africa) was trying to do anything about rural housing. Up to five-sixths of the African population lived in rural areas and the discussion in his paper should not be taken to imply any general use of European building techniques. As regards the urban areas, the rapid rate of growth is such that houses have to be crowded together because the towns could not afford to lay down the infrastructure necessary for a widely dispersed town area. The indigenous African materials for huts were not available in towns. It is, for instance, impossible to obtain thatch within fifty miles of many African capitals. Another difficulty is that men in full-time urban employment cannot afford to spend the enormous amount of time which is used in rural areas to maintain and improve their dwellings. After each rain a mud hut has to be replastered. There are also grave fire risks involved when mud and thatch huts are densely packed together.

One of the characteristic features of housing policy in Africa is the present paternalistic approach which places employers under an obligation to house their employees. This has long been the custom in many African countries in which European industrial or mining concerns have operated ; the present custom of government building for civil servants stems from this tradition. The alternative approach is to provide, for instance, 20 per cent of a house for everyone and persuade families to provide the remaining 80 per cent by their own initiative. This is being done in Morocco, where the government acquire land and develop it with a minimum of community services such as roads, sanitation, piped water, and occasionally electricity. When the shacks which the local inhabitants built as temporary accommodation were pulled down the planned skeleton of services would form the pattern around which the permanent houses would be built.

As economic resources increased, governments tended to give further assistance, as for instance in Ghana where there is a special 'roof loans scheme'. Under this scheme a loan is given to cover the cost of materials used to make a more permanent roof than the individual could afford to construct out of his own resources.

The Economic Problems of Housing

Professor Donnison asked Mr. Turin whether he thought that in Africa there may be a development of the most industrialized methods of building side by side with the least industrialized. Would there be a quite different pattern of technological evolution of the industry than that which we had seen in Western Europe? Could this mean that the traditions and the experience of Europe will be peculiarly unsuited to advising and assisting the development of the African industry?

Mr. Turin said that the ILO had recently held a conference in Africa on the problem of employment and productivity in civil engineering work, with particular reference to the major policy issues involved in choosing between the use of heavy and highly efficient plant on the one hand, and the use of large masses of unskilled labour, on the other. The results of a number of pilot schemes carried out in several developing countries showed that in most cases it was possible to raise the productivity of unskilled labour quite considerably by comparatively simple and inexpensive methods, thus raising the threshold at which labour became competitive with plant (for instance in earth-moving operations).

As for the question of more industrialized methods of building of the type currently used in several European countries, Mr. Turin thought their application to developing countries was limited by factors such as the shortage of foreign currency for the purchase of the essential production machinery, by the comparatively small scale of present building programmes and by the relative abundance of cheap unskilled and semi-skilled labour. The economic implications of adopting highly industrialized methods of house construction, inevitably limited to the large urban areas, would have to be examined seriously before embarking on programmes of a scale comparable to that of more developed countries.

NINTH SESSION
THE DISCUSSION ON THE PAPERS OF
DR. KUMINEK AND DR. NAZAREVSKY

Mlle Salembien opened the discussion on Dr. Kuminek's paper by saying that he examines the Polish construction industry within the context of the Polish economy and traces the increased output of the building industry. Much of the increase has been through the use of industrialized processes and in 1963, 40 per cent of all urban houses were built with the use of these new techniques. This represented about 20-25 per cent of total construction. The cost price of the individual units, which at the beginning of the era of industrialization was 20-25 per cent higher than the cost price of traditional construction was now down to a level roughly equal to the cost of traditional building.

The effects of industrial production are two-fold; those on labour

318

and those on investment. Labour is clearly used less intensively in the industrialized building method and leads to a saving of approximately 30 per cent of the labour costs involved. In addition to the cost saving there are additional benefits in that the labour force which is employed is less highly skilled and has lighter work to do than the workers employed in the traditional types of building. The basic investment needed to make the industrialized construction units is about 20 per cent higher than the investment needed for traditional methods. The government has therefore to weigh the advantages of labour saving on the one hand against increased capital expenditure on the other.

Dr. Kuminek said that he would like to stress the great importance to the developing countries of the volume of output. This depended not only on the amount of investment but also upon the productivity which could be achieved in both the construction industry and the other closely connected industries. It is, perhaps, paradoxical that in Poland there should be industrialization when they still had some surplus labour in the rural areas. However, the reserve pool of adult labour in the rural areas has now been almost exhausted, and the young people born during the post-war period when population was increasing fairly rapidly, would not enter the labour market for some years. Furthermore, Polish housing needs are greatest in the industrial areas where there is a shortage of labour. Industrialized housing could only be economic under certain conditions ; (a) an urban concentration of population, and (b) continuity of production. There are certain basic characteristics of the building industry which will remain unchanged, and the possibilities of industrial building should not be over-emphasized.

Dr. Stone introduced Dr. Nazarevsky's paper by saying that the author had covered a large field and given a general picture of housing problems and their solution in the U.S.S.R. Some tantalizing glimpses of various aspects of housing problems are provided and Dr. Nazarevsky must not be surprised if we ask for much more. Dr. Stone thought that the best way to deal with the paper was to concentrate on one or two aspects.

In the last 40-50 years the U.S.S.R. has built dwellings with an aggregate area of over 1,000 million square metres. Sixty per cent of this has been built since 1959. As the total stock appears to be about 1,200 million square metres (*Annual Bulletin* — UN) the average age of dwellings must be remarkably low. Taking the average size of dwelling as about 40 square metres (p. 236) it would appear that there are about 30 million dwellings in the U.S.S.R. — about twice the number as in Great Britain for about four times the population. The urgency of the housing problem is therefore clear.

The figures given by the author (p. 240) indicate not merely a rapid rise in the volume of output of dwellings, but a rapid rise in quality. The proportion of dwellings provided with a water supply, communal sewerage, and central heating has doubled since the late forties. As water

319

and sewerage are rather basic, this omission was probably because of the need to economize in public utility services rather than to save on the construction cost of the dwellings themselves. He noted that most dwellings will be provided with full services by 1980 (p. 241) and wondered how much would be spent on the improvement of existing dwellings as compared with their maintenance and as compared with new construction in the future. The standards of floor space and fitting appear to be very low, and unless new dwellings are built to considerably higher standards, large-scale rebuilding will be necessary in order to raise minimum standards in Russia to levels usual in wealthy countries.

One of the most notable and interesting features of building in the U.S.S.R. is the use of large-panel construction and the introduction of the precast volume unit house. The former accounted for 20 per cent of production in 1963 (p. 237) and, as the author points out, such methods save a very large percentage of site labour but he does not tell us whether and to what extent they produce savings in total resources.

The construction industries in many countries have been going through a rationalization process in recent years. This is taking two forms — development of systems of factory prefabrication, and the use of techniques of scientific management to improve site processes. Methods of prefabrication have been developed in Great Britain on and off for the last 40-50 years, but the best methods have never been fully competitive with the traditional building techniques. Labour tends to account for only about 30 per cent of building costs and materials 60 per cent; prefabrication tends to raise the material costs still further. The importance of industrialized building may be that it enables labour which would not be attracted to site work to be utilized for housing construction. It also provides a challenge to the more traditional forms of construction and has been instrumental in forcing some rationalization of the old methods.

The conditions in the U.S.S.R. seem ideal for factory prefabrication; only 16 different types of layout are used (p. 241) and the sites are apparently large. The need for long periods of training for a rapidly expanding labour force is avoided and the problems of building under difficult weather conditions are minimized. For this reason it would have been interesting to know the comparative resources which are used in the U.S.S.R. in the two forms of building. To what extent have the techniques for on-site building been rationalized in step with factory prefabrication? And to what extent does the supply of materials and their costs favour one form as compared with another? The comparison of construction costs in different countries is so full of pitfalls and so relatively little explored that it is quite impossible to make any useful comments on the cost figures given. Cost comparison for different forms of construction and for different sizes of dwelling would, however, be of considerable interest.

It was interesting to read that in the U.S.S.R. it is thought to be more expedient to build small and medium-sized towns rather than cities. (p. 243). In Britain we are still trying to evolve some way of measuring the relative economics of settlement sizes, formation, and shape, and Dr. Stone wondered whether the decisions to build small towns were based on capital costs only or are all costs and benefits included? The favoured size — 80,000 persons — is about the size of the British New Towns.

Finally, the author has told us something about the ownership of housing and rent policy (p. 238). Co-operative housing seems to be an alternative to private housing rather than to State housing. The co-operatives obtain loans amounting to 70 per cent of the cost, which are repayable over 20 years, but individual house purchasers can only obtain a 30 per cent loan over 10 years. The rate of interest is negligible at $\frac{1}{2}$ per cent. Even so, co-operative housing appears to account for less than 10 per cent of house construction, so presumably State housing is even more heavily subsidized.

Turning to Dr. Kuminek's paper, he said that the implication of his figures was that the costs of industrialized system building fall rapidly at first — during the learning period — but settle down at a level similar or a little above the costs of traditional site construction. Our experience is similar. Generally, the components for industrialized building are more expensive than those for traditional building, because the latter are based on very cheap materials. Since delivered materials cost twice as much as labour, these costs must rise less than half the proportion that labour costs fall if industrialized system building is to be cheaper than traditional, and this is difficult to achieve.

Whilst there has not been any revolution in building construction, there has been a considerable range of innovations both in the form and method of construction. He did not think that there is any one point at which a revolutionary change is likely to occur which would radically reduce construction costs. Rather it is a question of making advances over the entire field of construction. This is what has happened, and there is no great break between what is called traditional and industrialized building.

Traditional building is simply the form of construction usual in a country at a particular time. It is the result of gradual evolution and is the economic response to the materials, labour, and knowledge available. Revolutionary changes are hardly to be expected in an industry as old as building. The cross-section of traditional forms used in the world today is parallel to the cross-section in the history of an industrial country.

The construction of housing is at present in a very fluid condition. There is an abundance of ideas, many of which are more successful technically than economically. In the absence of any systematic studies of relative costs it is impossible to determine how the industry will finally evolve. Such information as there is does not point to any overwhelming superiority in any particular direction. It is usually said that there are large economies of scale for system building, although there is very little evidence to support this. It is probably more important that factories should operate at a high level of capacity regularly, than that they should be very large. Really large orders for similar dwellings are difficult to obtain in Western countries because of the demand for variety. It may, however, be that firms and contracts in the U.K. need to be larger than at present for the economic exploitation of both organizational techniques and systemized building.

Mr. Turin said that some of the parts of a building have a practically infinite life (foundations, concrete, etc.); walls could last for centuries, floors and joineries for fifty years, equipment for twenty and finishes for only a few years. What then was to be considered the life of a house? It was, of course, tempting to speculate on the possibility of finding technical processes whereby considerable savings in initial costs could be achieved by building more temporary structures; the fact remains that no such system existed in practice. Indeed, building of a temporary nature had not only higher maintenance costs but also involved higher initial costs; in most cases the structural parts of a house could be built in a most economic way with long-life materials.

Since there was a limit to the reduction in initial costs of the building, the problem was how to find ways of reducing the ultimate cost — *i.e.* the initial cost plus the discounted value of future maintenance costs over the expected lifetime of the house. Interesting work in this field had been carried out in several European countries and the results had been analysed in a number of international studies.[1] It was true that the results of the calculations of the discounted value of future maintenance cost was affected by the interest rate used; however, the general pattern was not considerably affected within the range of interest rates currently applied in Europe in the financing of low-cost housing (between 4 and 7 per cent). The problem of ensuring a greater economic or social durability of new dwellings could, in fact, be approached in a different way. Since buildings were inherently durable, efforts could be devoted to design them in such a way that future changes would be made possible. Unfortunately some of the recent technological trends in house-building, in particular the reliance on heavy load-bearing elements in reinforced concrete enclosing small living spaces, greatly reduced the flexibility of future layouts. An example of the disadvantages of some of the building techniques recently introduced in many European countries, including the U.S.S.R., was the heavy, prefabricated service cores or fully equipped bathroom or kitchen units. These units meant that the part of the dwelling which was most likely to become obsolete because of technological progress or social development was precisely that which could least easily be replaced in the future.

[1] See in particular *Cost Repetition and Maintenance, Related Aspects of Building Prices*, UN Economic Commission for Europe, Geneva, 1963.

Dr. Holm said that he was puzzled by what appears to be a fundamental conflict of policy aims and actions in the U.S.S.R. On the one hand they were now encouraging co-operatives in which the occupiers put up 40 per cent of the cost of construction and the government gave a loan of 60 per cent, but at the same time it was stated that the long-term objective was to have State housing which was rent free. Were these two things compatible? It seemed to Dr. Holm that the one policy would make it difficult to achieve the other. He also doubted whether the U.S.S.R. could be any more successful than other countries in 'solving' their housing problem. In each country which had been statistically examined the space standards of housing had risen. In Sweden, for example, the increase in space consumption between 1945 and 1960 had been at 2-3 per cent per annum. He felt certain that as the general level of consumption in the U.S.S.R. increased there would also be an increasing demand for more consumption of housing.

Professor Lindbeck asked whether any consideration had been given to alternative methods of distributing the stock of houses. If the Russians were planning to abandon the pricing mechanism completely some alternative method of allocating houses to families would be necessary.

Dr. Nazarevsky said that this problem had to be considered in an historical setting and that in 1945 after the great destruction of houses during the war most people in the U.S.S.R. were pleased to obtain 9 square metres of space. Now that the amount of dwelling space had increased threefold few people were content with the small dwellings they accepted after the war. The Russians did not, however, think that the demand for space would rise indefinitely; once the present programme was completed households would be more or less content with the planned amount of space, and the strict rationing of space which was now imposed would be removed.

Dr. Kuminek said, in reply to the discussion, that one of the main factors in keeping up the cost of industrialized methods of production was the high cost of transport. The materials had first to be transported to the plant and then the finished parts had to be transported to the building site. Dr. Kuminek thought that the rationalization of the traditional building industry could help to increase productivity, but a maximum output was soon reached and it was then necessary to turn to industrialized methods if the volume of production was to be further increased. Western Germany had done much towards the rationalization of traditional building but had reached this ceiling of productivity and was now turning to industrialization. The difficulty of training rural workers for the building industry was that such workers are usually migrant, first-generation town-dwellers, and they start in the building industry but leave it as soon as they can in order to get jobs in factories. There is, therefore, an extremely large turnover of unskilled labour in the traditional building industry.

INDEX

Page references in the Index in bold type under the names of
participants in the Conference indicate their Papers or Discussions
of their Papers. Page references in italics indicate contributions
by participants to the Discussions

325

Index

Index

PRINTED BY R. & R. CLARK, LTD., EDINBURGH